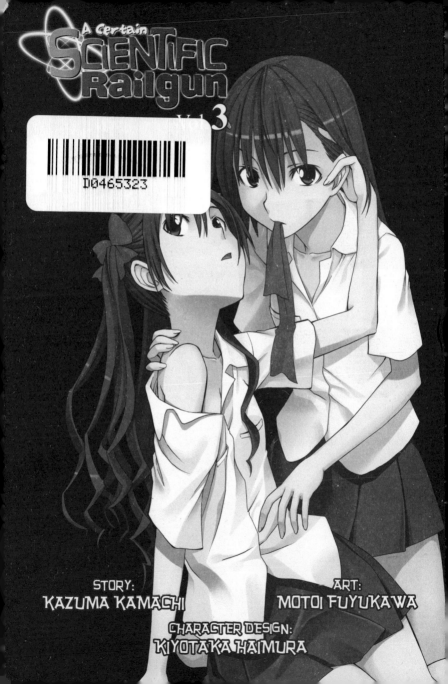

A Certain
SCIENTIFIC
Railgun

Vol.3

D0465323

STORY:
KAZUMA KAMACHI

ART:
MOTOI FUYUKAWA

CHARACTER DESIGN:
KIYOTAKA HAIMURA

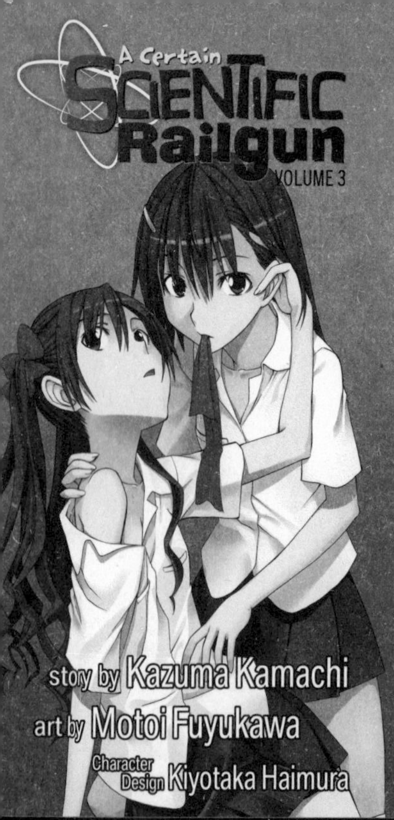
A Certain
SCIENTIFIC
Railgun
VOLUME 3
story by Kazuma Kamachi
art by Motoi Fuyukawa
Character Design Kiyotaka Haimura

STAFF CREDITS

translation Nan Rymer
adaptation Janet Houck
lettering Roland Amago
layout Bambi Eloriaga-Amago
cover design Nicky Lim
copy editor Shanti Whitesides
editor Adam Arnold

publisher Jason DeAngelis
Seven Seas Entertainment

A CERTAIN SCIENTIFIC RAILGUN VOL. 3

First published in 2009 by Media Works Inc., Tokyo, Japan.
English translation rights arranged with ASCII MEDIA WORKS.

ISBN: 978-1-935934-12-7

Printed in Canada

First Printing: February 2012

10 9 8 7 6 5 4 3 2

READING DIRECTIONS

This book reads from *right to left*, Japanese style. If this is your first time reading manga, you start reading from the top right panel on each page and take it from there. If you get lost, just follow the numbered diagram here. It may seem backwards at first, but you'll get the hang of it! Have fun!!

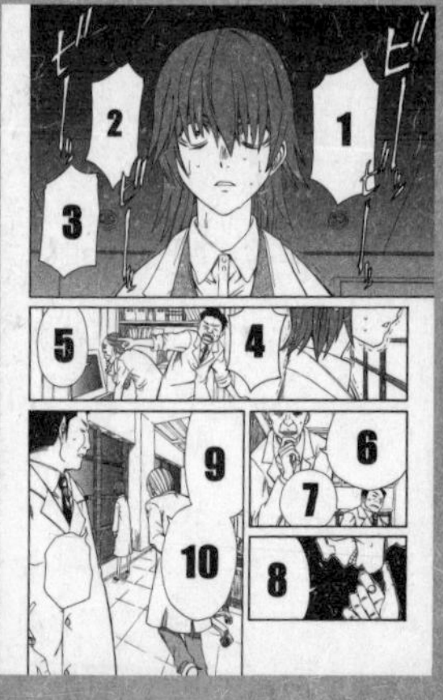
1
2
3
4
5
6
7
8
9
10

CONTENTS

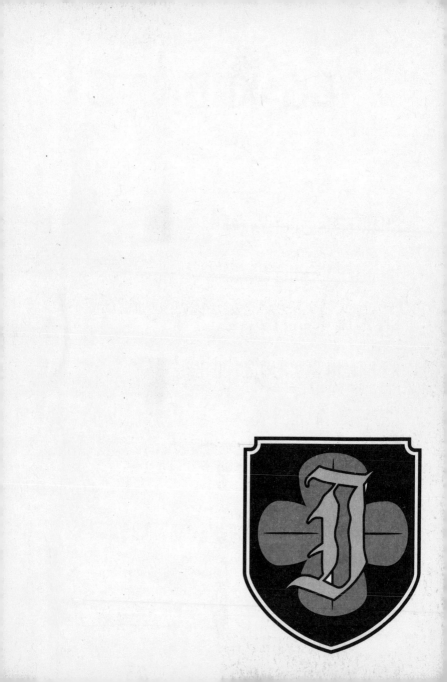

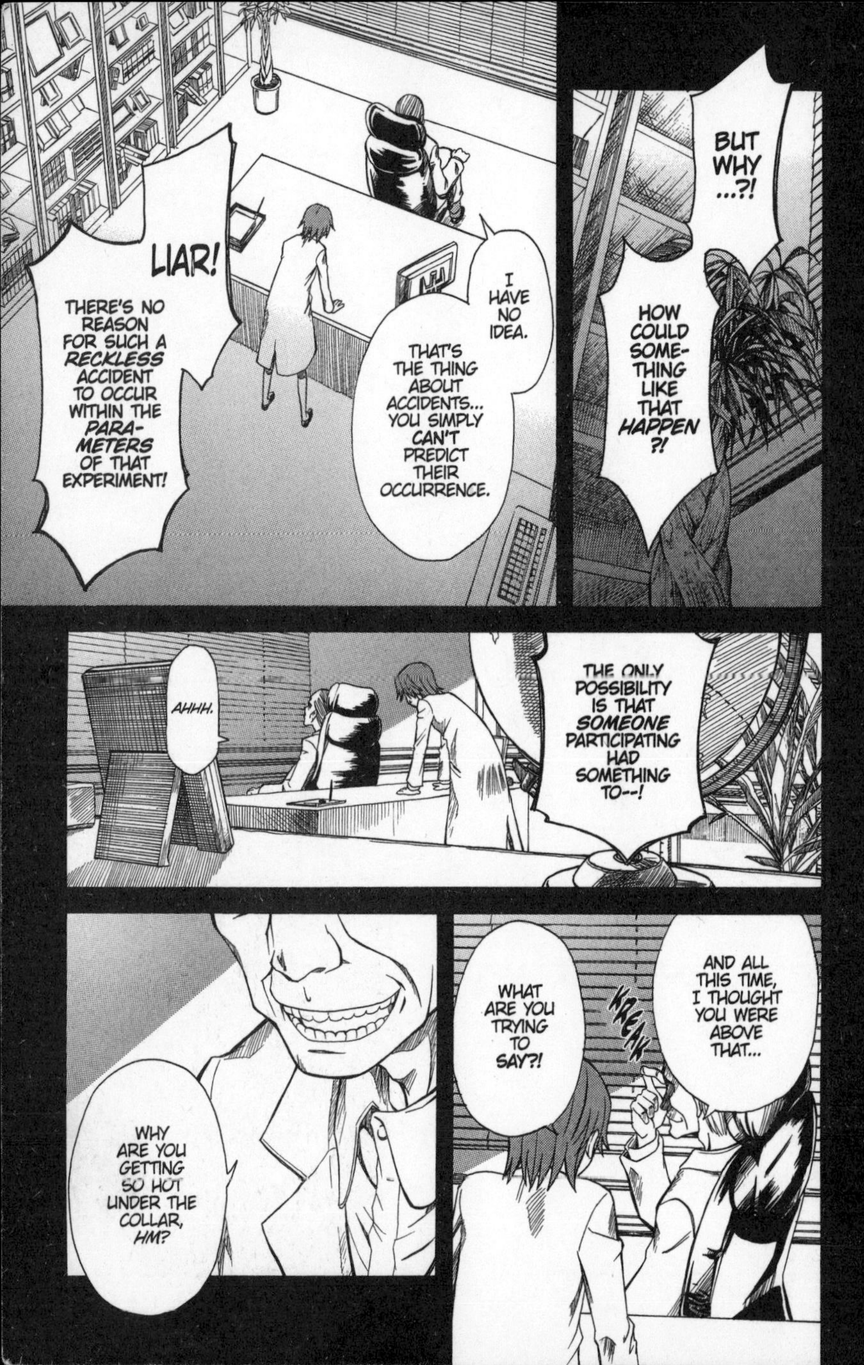
BUT WHY ...?!
HOW COULD SOMETHING LIKE THAT *HAPPEN* ?!
I HAVE NO IDEA.
THAT'S THE THING ABOUT ACCIDENTS... YOU SIMPLY **CAN'T** PREDICT THEIR OCCURRENCE.
LIAR!
THERE'S NO REASON FOR SUCH A *RECKLESS* ACCIDENT TO OCCUR WITHIN THE *PARAMETERS* OF THAT EXPERIMENT!
THE ONLY POSSIBILITY IS THAT *SOMEONE* PARTICIPATING HAD SOMETHING TO--!
AHHH.
AND ALL THIS TIME, I THOUGHT YOU WERE ABOVE THAT...
KREAK
WHAT ARE YOU TRYING TO SAY?!
WHY ARE YOU GETTING SO HOT UNDER THE COLLAR, *HM?*

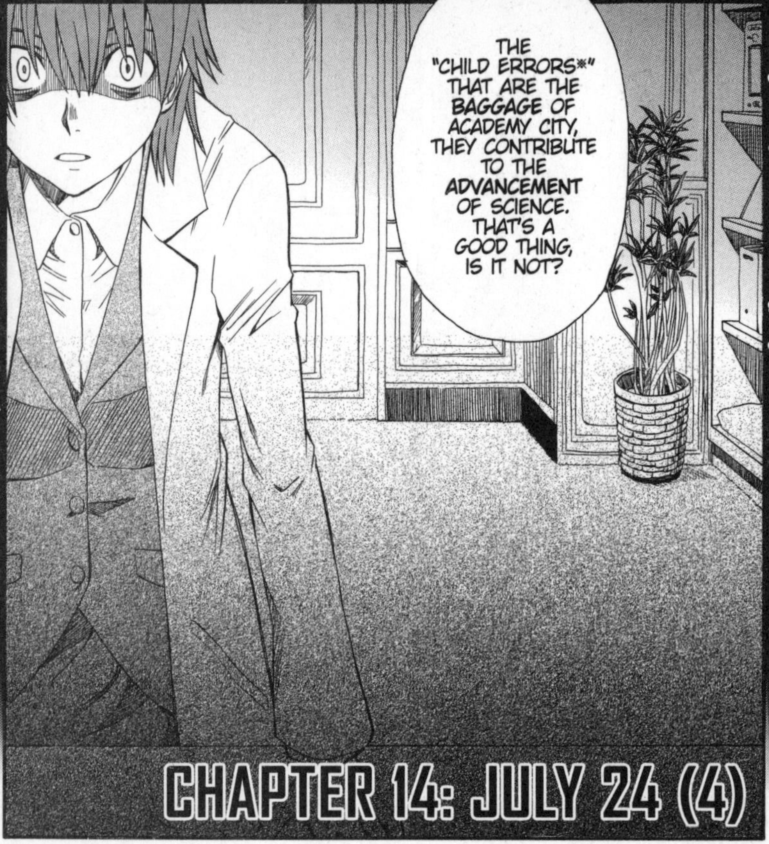
THE "CHILD ERRORS※" THAT ARE THE BAGGAGE OF ACADEMY CITY, THEY CONTRIBUTE TO THE ADVANCEMENT OF SCIENCE. THAT'S A GOOD THING, IS IT NOT?
CHAPTER 14: JULY 24 (4)

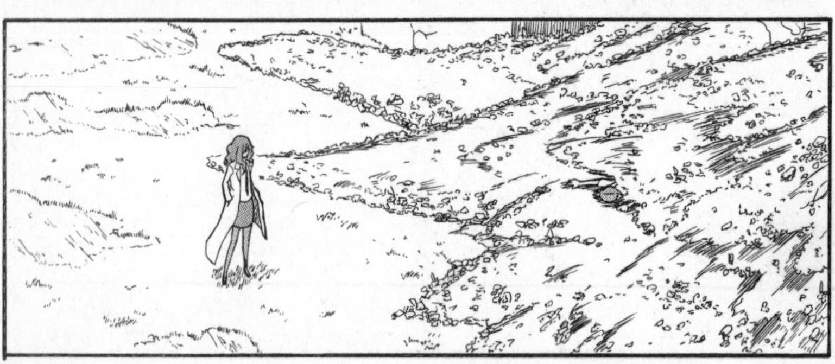

※Referring to the action performed by a parent in paying the cost of admitting their child to Academy City's dorms, but then disappearing immediately afterwards, without a trace. Additionally, it may also refer to the children who are left behind due to the result of such actions.

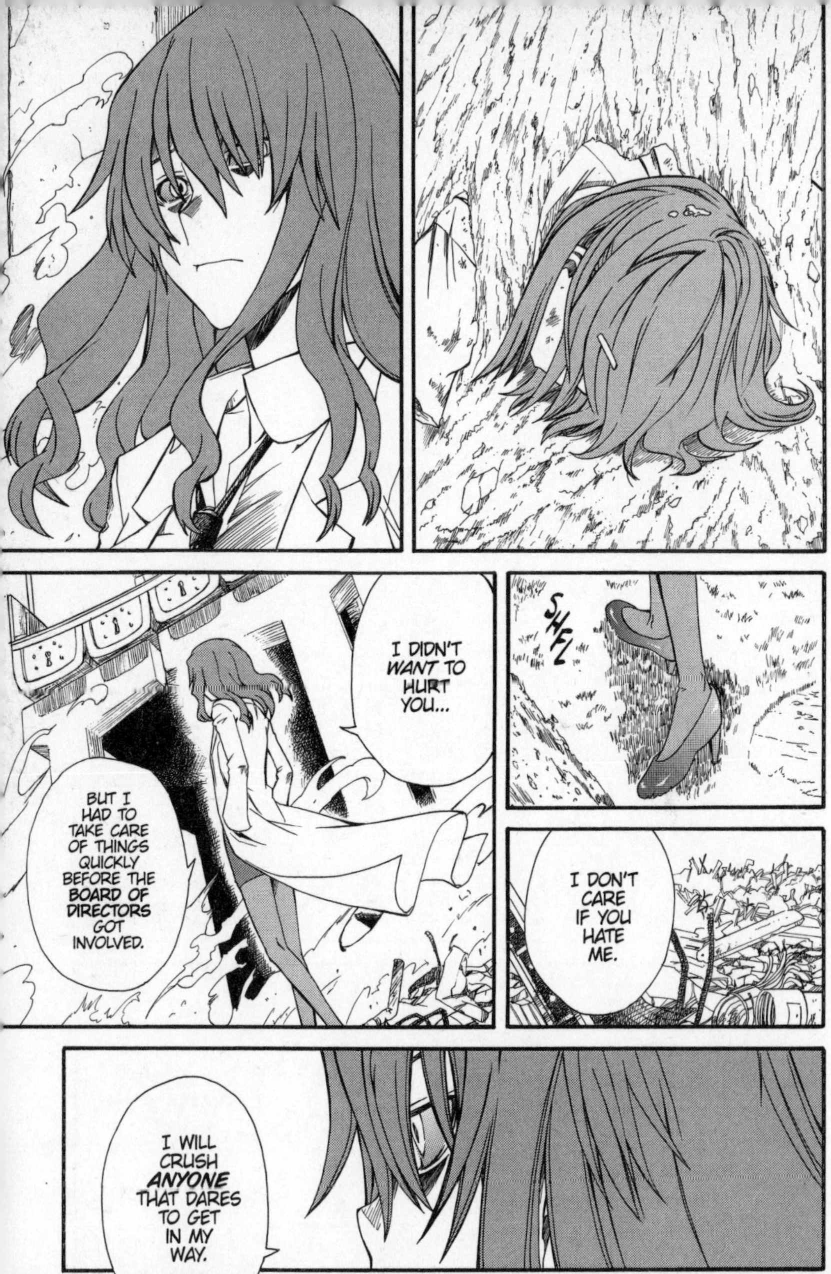
SHFL
I DON'T CARE IF YOU HATE ME.
I DIDN'T *WANT* TO HURT YOU...
BUT I HAD TO TAKE CARE OF THINGS QUICKLY BEFORE THE **BOARD OF DIRECTORS** GOT INVOLVED.
I WILL CRUSH ***ANYONE*** THAT DARES TO GET IN MY WAY.

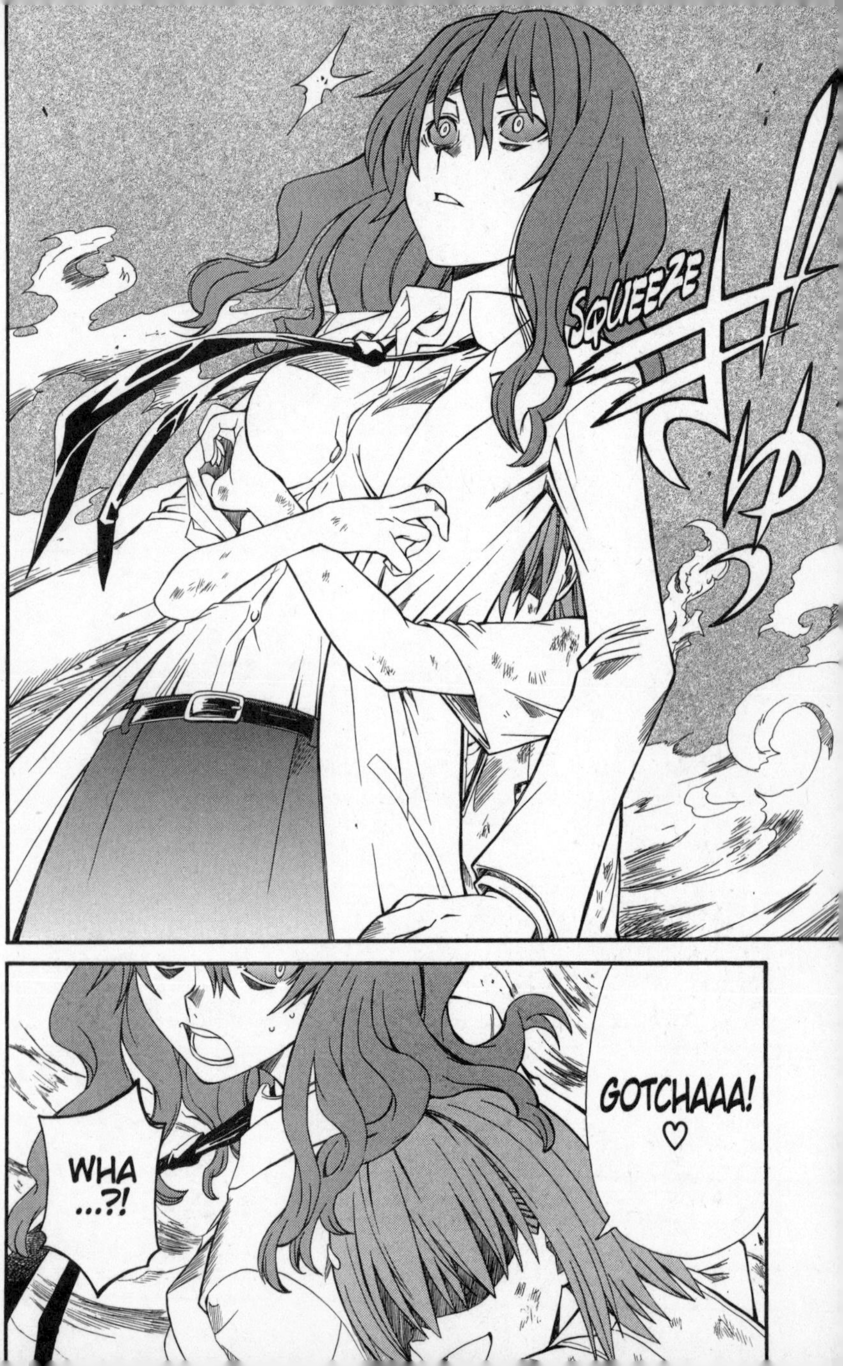
SQUEEZE
GOTCHAAA! ♡
WHA ...?!

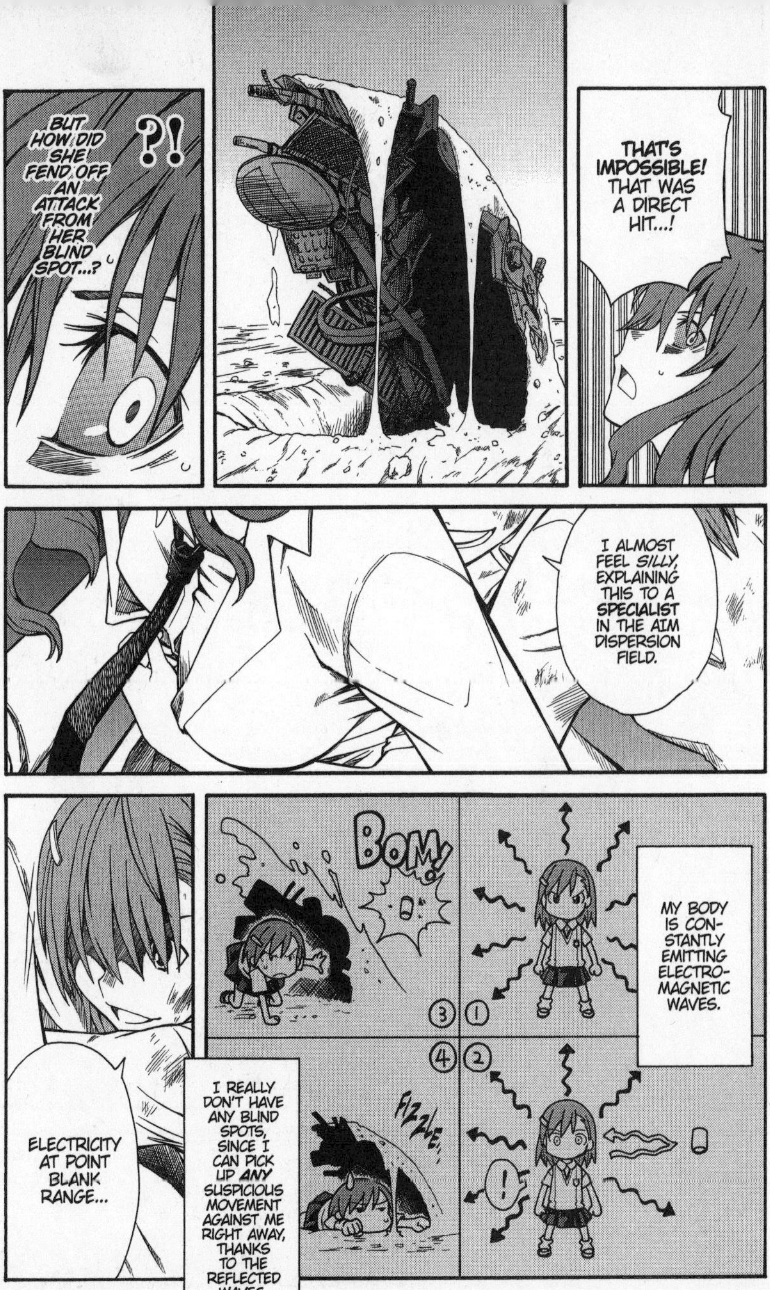
THAT'S IMPOSSIBLE! THAT WAS A DIRECT HIT...!
?!
BUT HOW DID SHE FEND OFF AN ATTACK FROM HER BLIND SPOT...?
I ALMOST FEEL SILLY, EXPLAINING THIS TO A SPECIALIST IN THE AIM DISPERSION FIELD.
MY BODY IS CONSTANTLY EMITTING ELECTRO-MAGNETIC WAVES.
①
②
③
BOM!
④
FIZZLE!
I REALLY DON'T HAVE ANY BLIND SPOTS, SINCE I CAN PICK UP ANY SUSPICIOUS MOVEMENT AGAINST ME RIGHT AWAY, THANKS TO THE REFLECTED WAVES.
ELECTRICITY AT POINT BLANK RANGE...

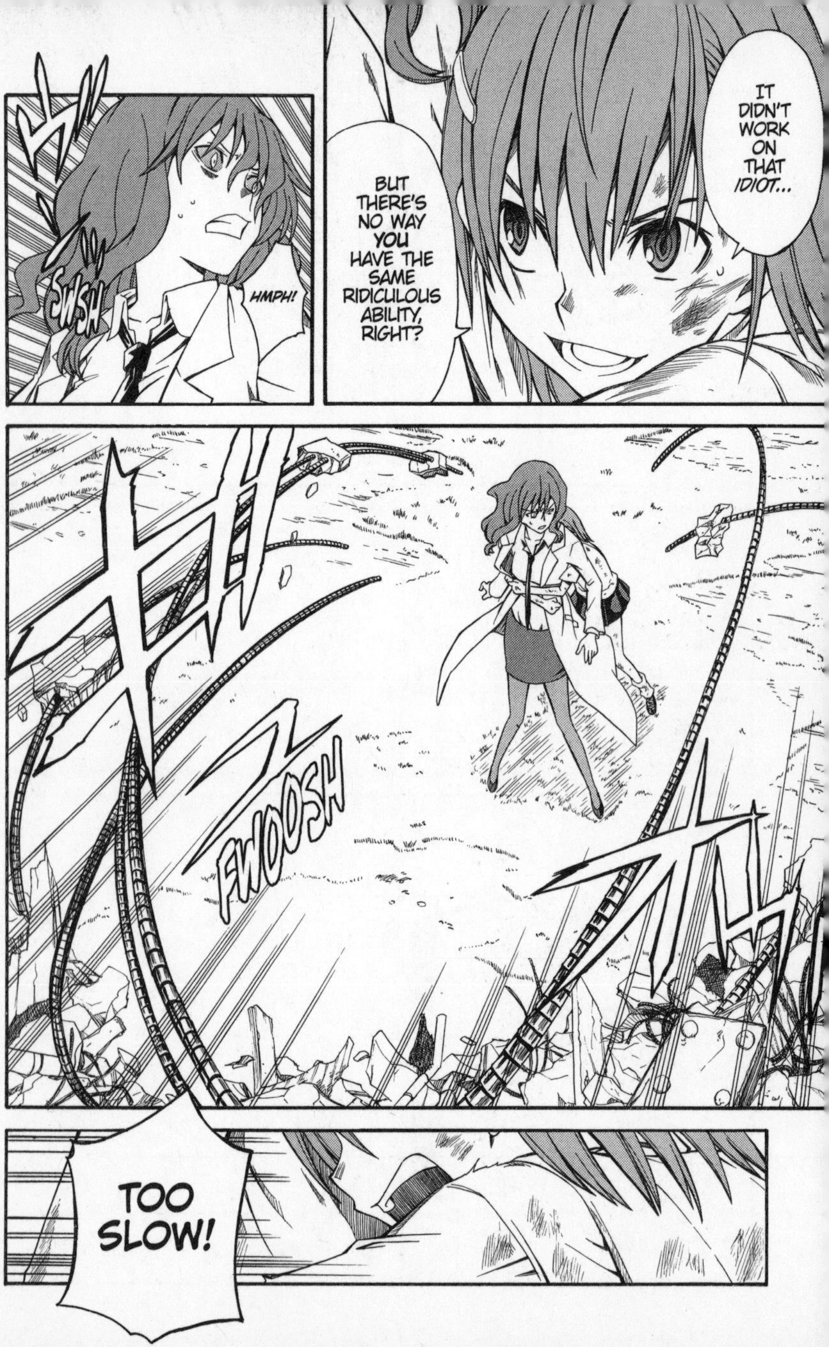
IT DIDN'T WORK ON THAT *IDIOT*...
BUT THERE'S NO WAY YOU HAVE THE SAME RIDICULOUS ABILITY, RIGHT?
HMPH!
SWSH
FWOOSH
TOO SLOW!

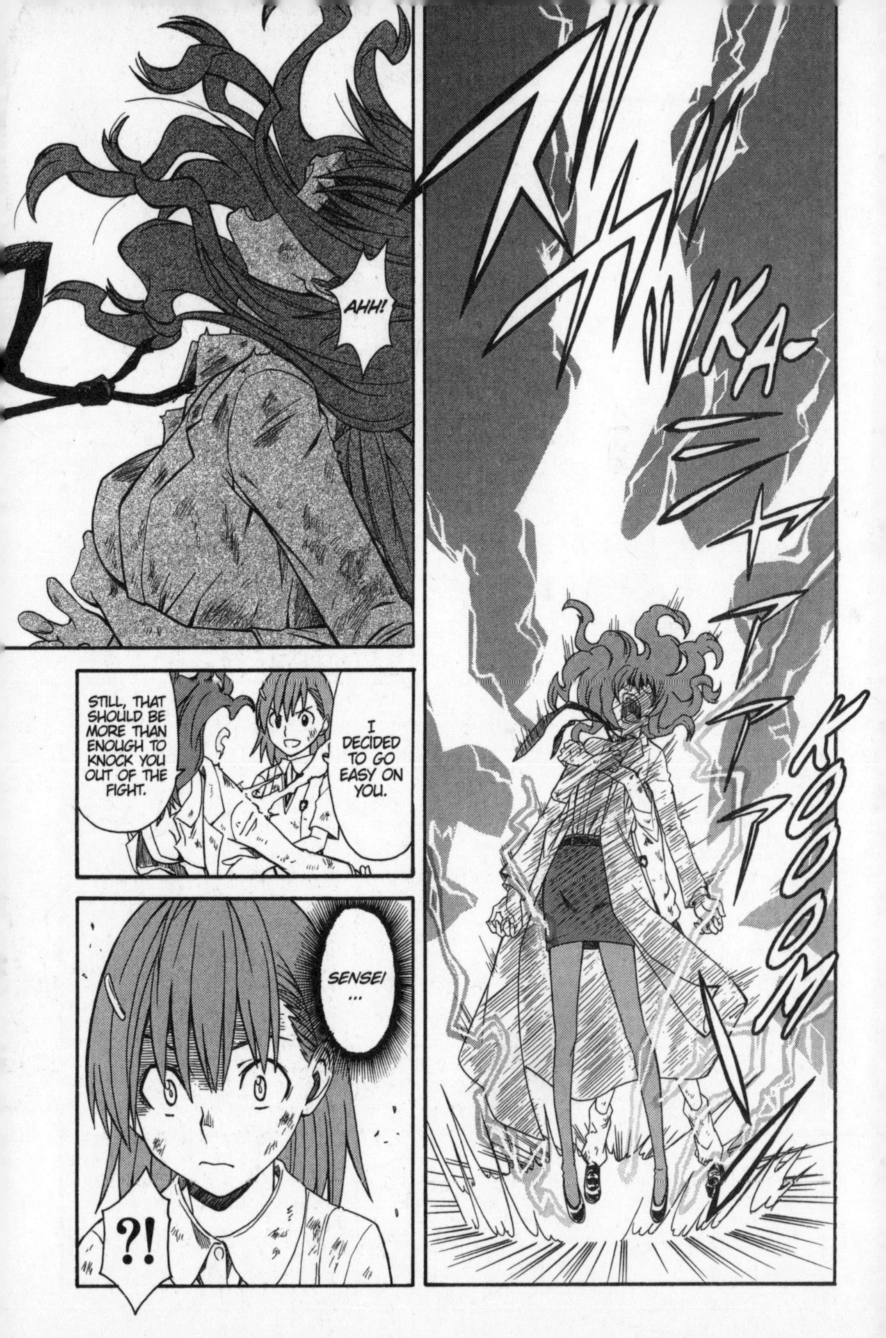
KA-
KOOOOM
AHH!
I DECIDED TO GO EASY ON YOU.
STILL, THAT SHOULD BE MORE THAN ENOUGH TO KNOCK YOU OUT OF THE FIGHT.
SENSEI ...
?!

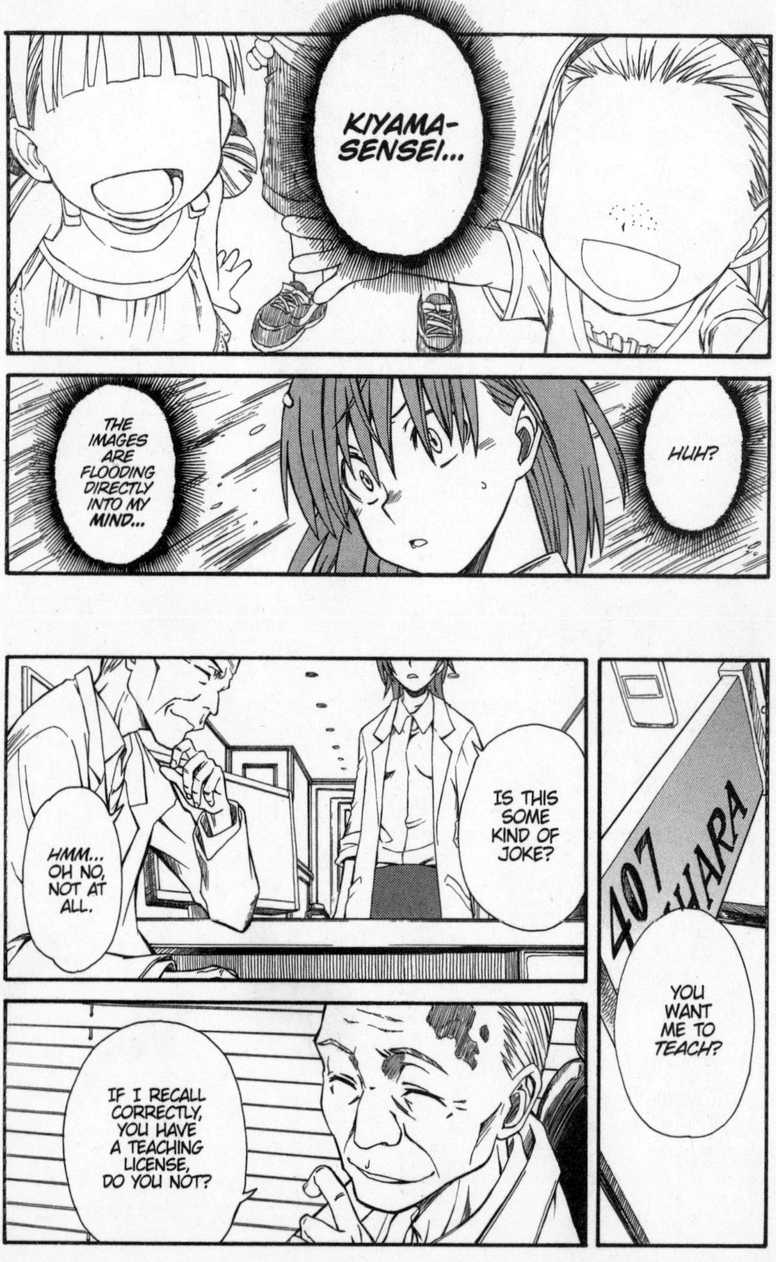
KIYAMA-SENSEI...
HUH?
THE IMAGES ARE FLOODING DIRECTLY INTO MY MIND...
407
HARA
YOU WANT ME TO TEACH?
IS THIS SOME KIND OF JOKE?
HMM... OH NO, NOT AT ALL.
IF I RECALL CORRECTLY, YOU HAVE A TEACHING LICENSE, DO YOU NOT?

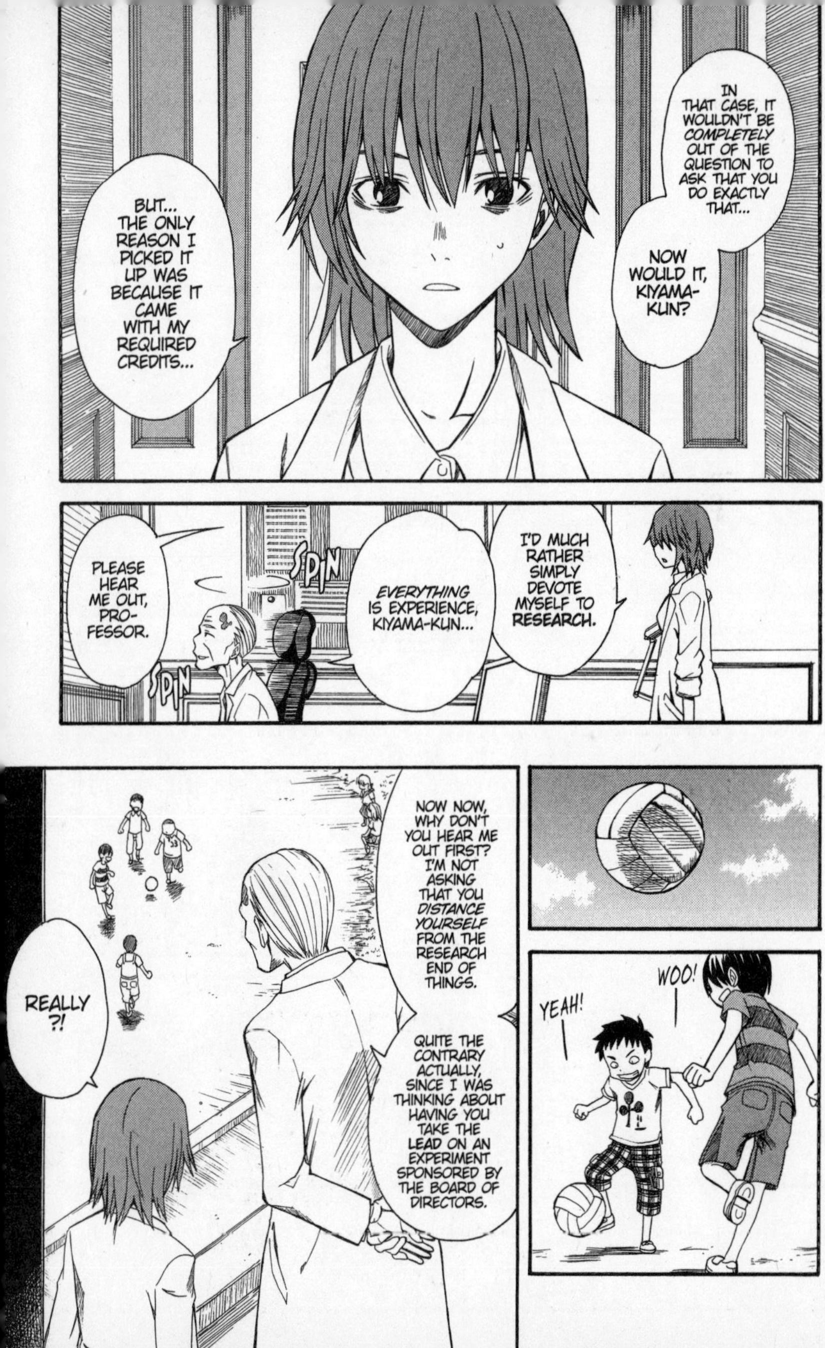
IN THAT CASE, IT WOULDN'T BE *COMPLETELY* OUT OF THE QUESTION TO ASK THAT YOU DO EXACTLY THAT...
NOW WOULD IT, KIYAMA-KUN?
BUT... THE ONLY REASON I PICKED IT UP WAS BECAUSE IT CAME WITH MY REQUIRED CREDITS...
I'D MUCH RATHER SIMPLY DEVOTE MYSELF TO **RESEARCH.**
EVERYTHING IS EXPERIENCE, KIYAMA-KUN...
SPIN
PLEASE HEAR ME OUT, PRO-FESSOR.
SPIN
WOO!
YEAH!
NOW NOW, WHY DON'T YOU HEAR ME OUT FIRST? I'M NOT ASKING THAT YOU *DISTANCE YOURSELF* FROM THE RESEARCH END OF THINGS.
QUITE THE CONTRARY ACTUALLY, SINCE I WAS THINKING ABOUT HAVING YOU TAKE THE LEAD ON AN EXPERIMENT SPONSORED BY THE BOARD OF DIRECTORS.
REALLY ?!

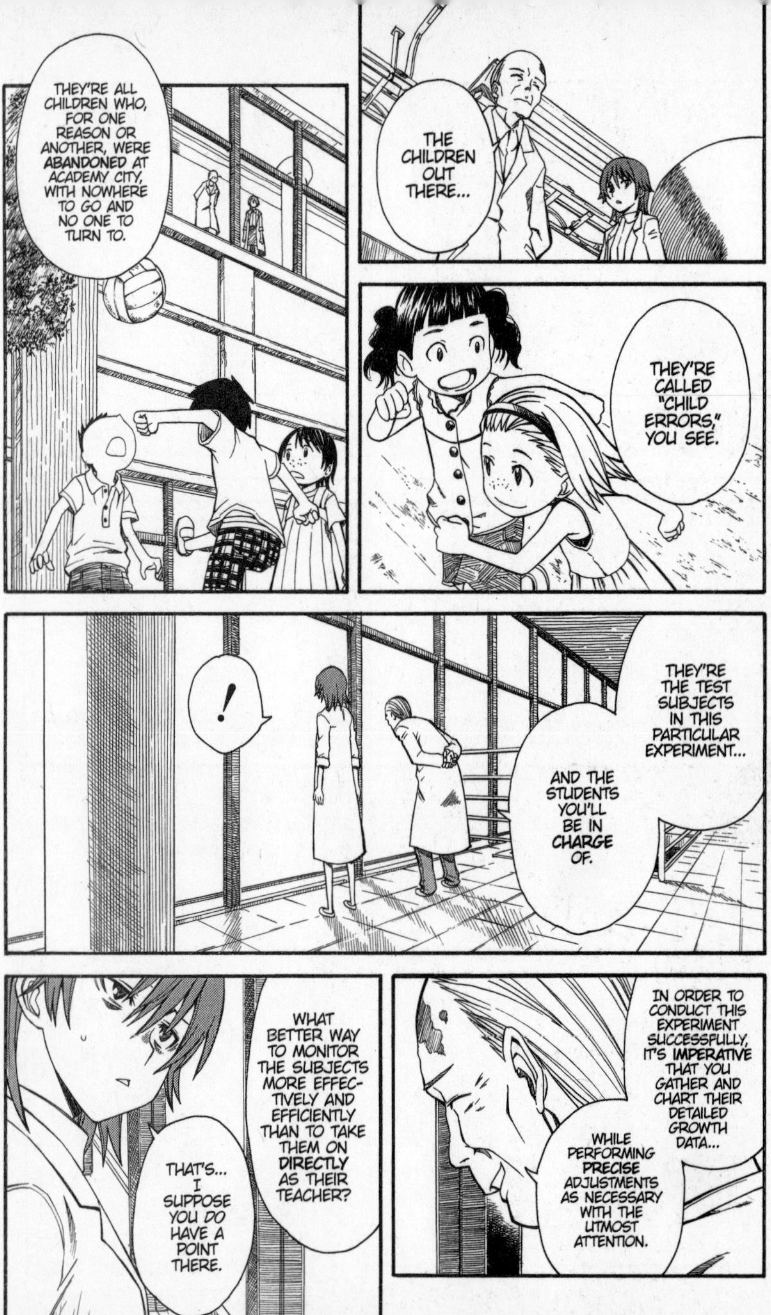
THE CHILDREN OUT THERE...
THEY'RE CALLED "CHILD ERRORS," YOU SEE.
THEY'RE ALL CHILDREN WHO, FOR ONE REASON OR ANOTHER, WERE **ABANDONED** AT ACADEMY CITY, WITH NOWHERE TO GO AND NO ONE TO TURN TO.
THEY'RE THE TEST SUBJECTS IN THIS PARTICULAR EXPERIMENT...
AND THE STUDENTS YOU'LL BE IN **CHARGE** OF.
!
IN ORDER TO CONDUCT THIS EXPERIMENT SUCCESSFULLY, IT'S **IMPERATIVE** THAT YOU GATHER AND CHART THEIR DETAILED GROWTH DATA...
WHILE PERFORMING **PRECISE** ADJUSTMENTS AS NECESSARY WITH THE UTMOST ATTENTION.
WHAT BETTER WAY TO MONITOR THE SUBJECTS MORE EFFECTIVELY AND EFFICIENTLY THAN TO TAKE THEM ON **DIRECTLY** AS THEIR TEACHER?
THAT'S... I SUPPOSE YOU *DO* HAVE A POINT THERE.

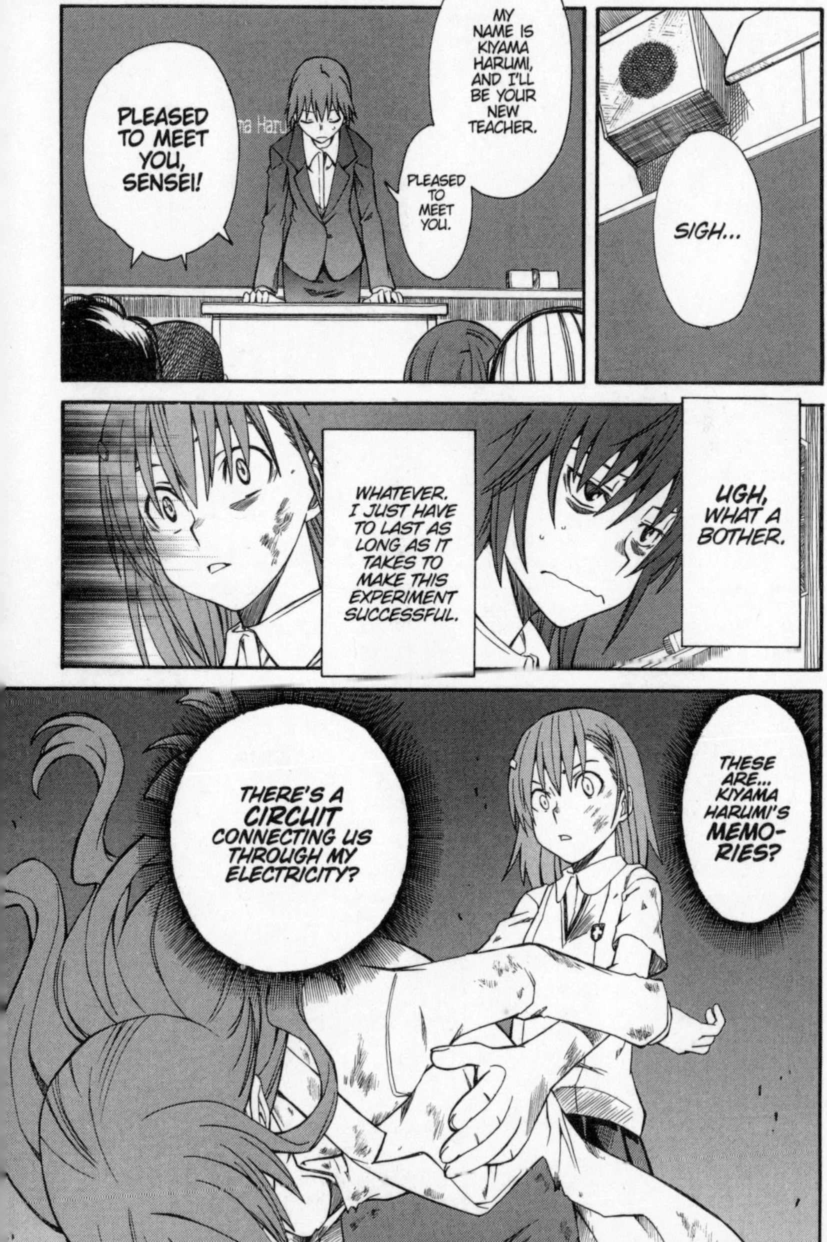
SIGH...
MY NAME IS KIYAMA HARUMI, AND I'LL BE YOUR NEW TEACHER.
PLEASED TO MEET YOU.
PLEASED TO MEET YOU, SENSEI!
UGH, WHAT A BOTHER.
WHATEVER. I JUST HAVE TO LAST AS LONG AS IT TAKES TO MAKE THIS EXPERIMENT SUCCESSFUL.
THESE ARE... KIYAMA HARUMI'S MEMO-RIES?
THERE'S A CIRCUIT CONNECTING US THROUGH MY ELECTRICITY?

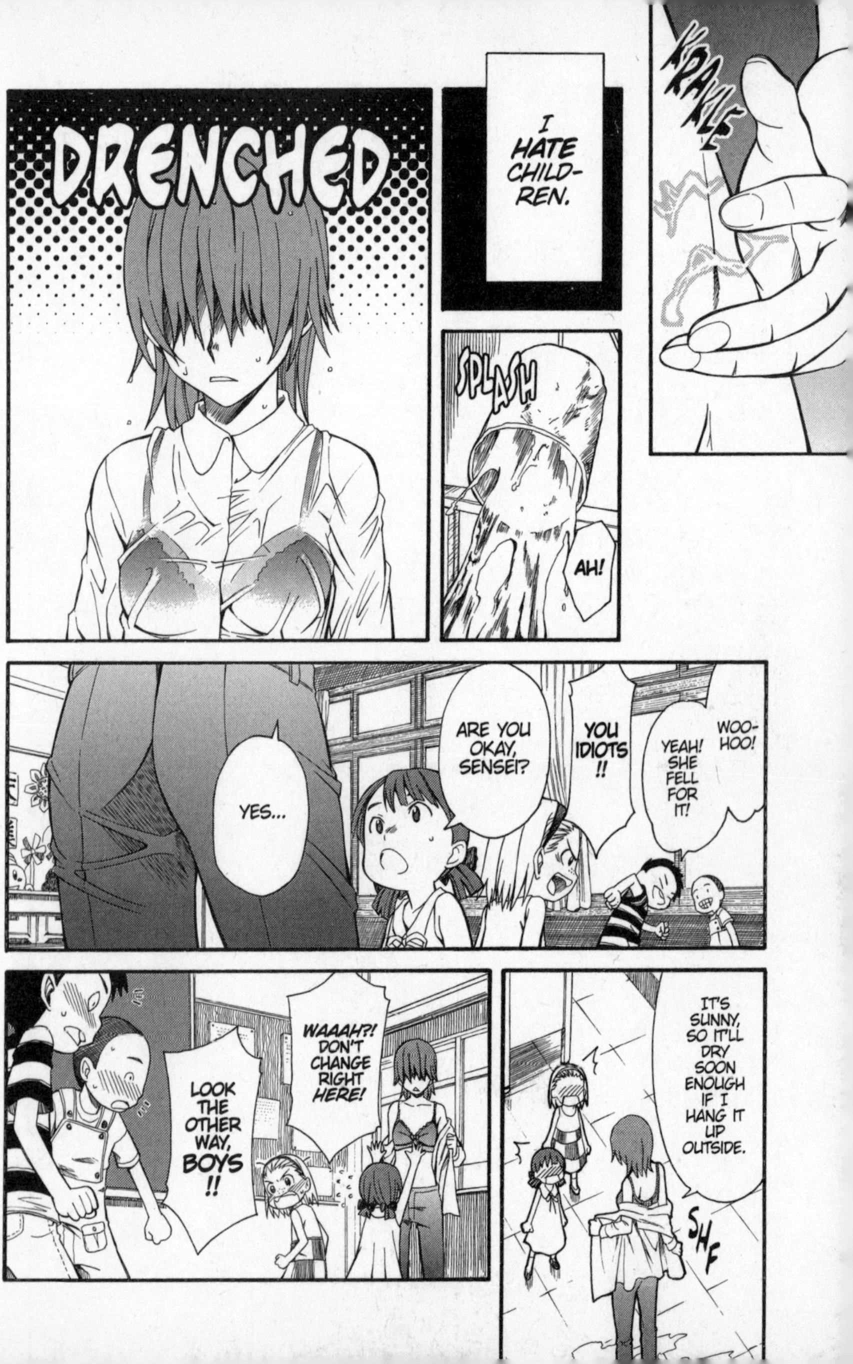
KRAKLE
I HATE CHILDREN.
SPLASH
AH!
DRENCHED
WOO-HOO!
YEAH! SHE FELL FOR IT!
YOU IDIOTS!!
ARE YOU OKAY, SENSEI?
YES...
IT'S SUNNY, SO IT'LL DRY SOON ENOUGH IF I HANG IT UP OUTSIDE.
SHF
WAAAH?! DON'T CHANGE RIGHT HERE!
LOOK THE OTHER WAY, BOYS!!

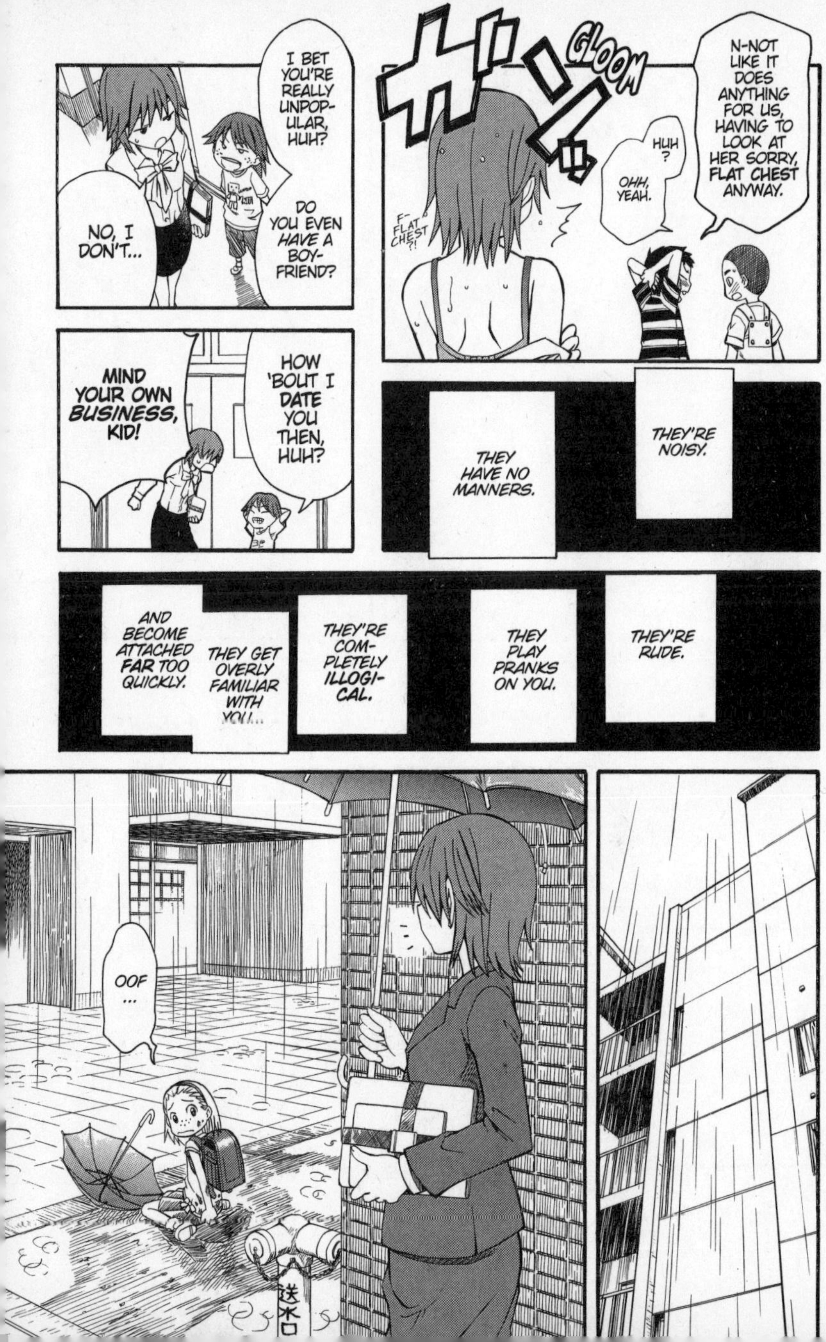
N-NOT LIKE IT DOES ANYTHING FOR US, HAVING TO LOOK AT HER SORRY, FLAT CHEST ANYWAY.
HUH?
OHH, YEAH.
GLOOM
F-FLAT CHEST?!
I BET YOU'RE REALLY UNPOPULAR, HUH?
DO YOU EVEN HAVE A BOYFRIEND?
NO, I DON'T...
THEY'RE NOISY.
THEY HAVE NO MANNERS.
HOW 'BOUT I DATE YOU THEN, HUH?
MIND YOUR OWN BUSINESS, KID!
THEY'RE RUDE.
THEY PLAY PRANKS ON YOU.
THEY'RE COMPLETELY ILLOGICAL.
THEY GET OVERLY FAMILIAR WITH YOU...
AND BECOME ATTACHED FAR TOO QUICKLY.
OOF...
送水口

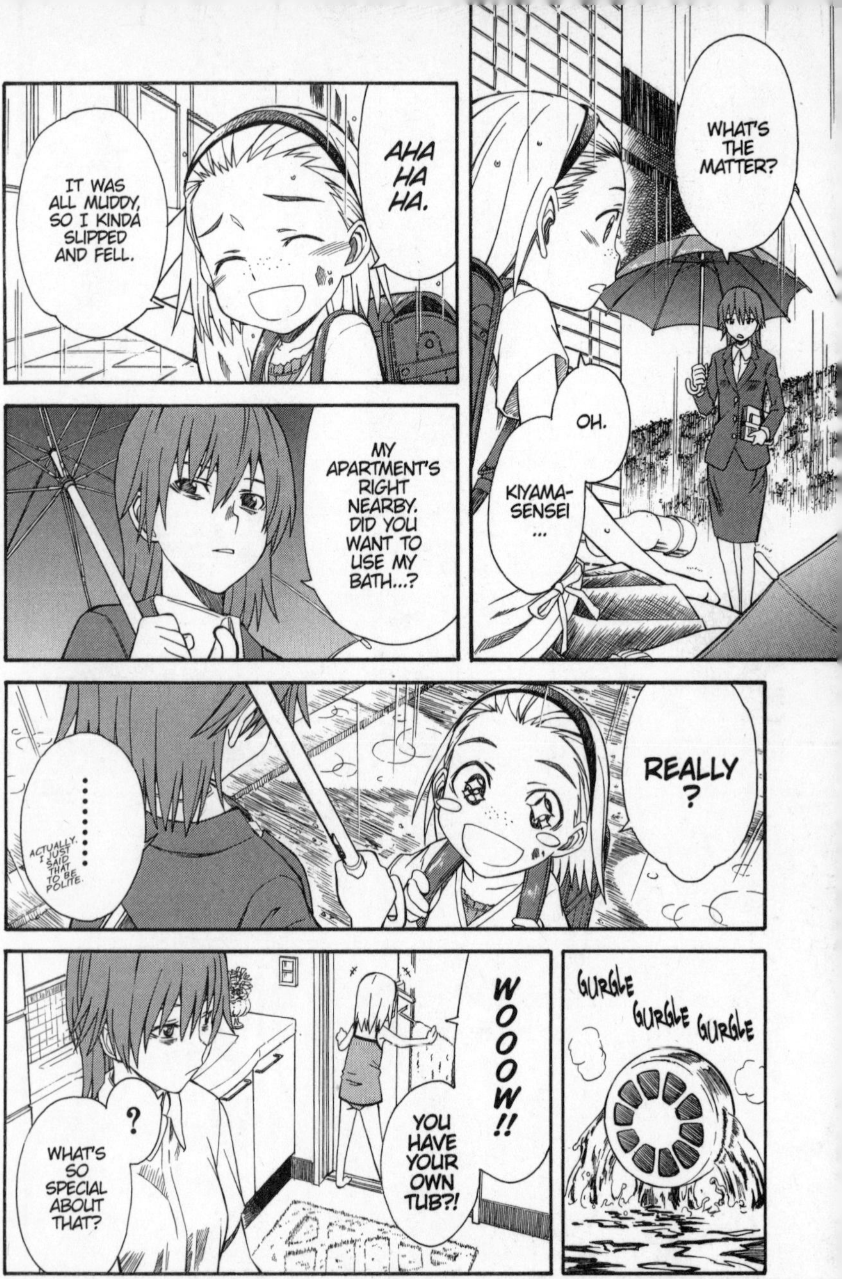
WHAT'S THE MATTER?
OH.
KIYAMA-SENSEI ...
AHA HA HA.
IT WAS ALL MUDDY, SO I KINDA SLIPPED AND FELL.
MY APARTMENT'S RIGHT NEARBY. DID YOU WANT TO USE MY BATH...?
REALLY?
......
ACTUALLY, I JUST SAID THAT TO BE POLITE.
GURGLE
GURGLE
GURGLE
WOOOOW!!
YOU HAVE YOUR OWN TUB?!
?
WHAT'S SO SPECIAL ABOUT THAT?

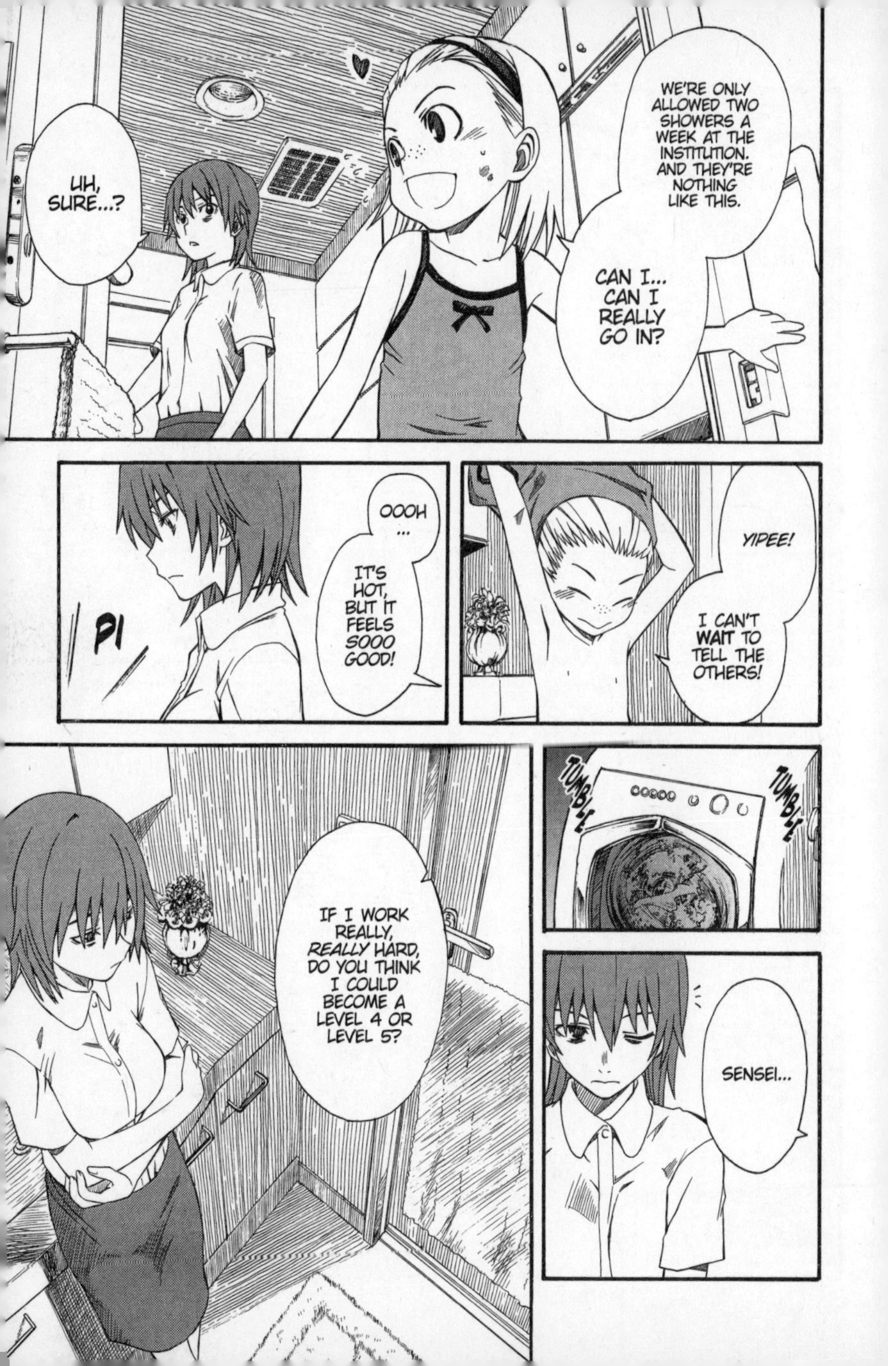
WE'RE ONLY ALLOWED TWO SHOWERS A WEEK AT THE INSTITUTION. AND THEY'RE NOTHING LIKE THIS.
CAN I... CAN I REALLY GO IN?
UH, SURE...?
YIPEE!
I CAN'T WAIT TO TELL THE OTHERS!
PI
OOOH ...
IT'S HOT, BUT IT FEELS SOOO GOOD!
TUMBLE
TUMBLE
SENSEI...
IF I WORK REALLY, REALLY HARD, DO YOU THINK I COULD BECOME A LEVEL 4 OR LEVEL 5?

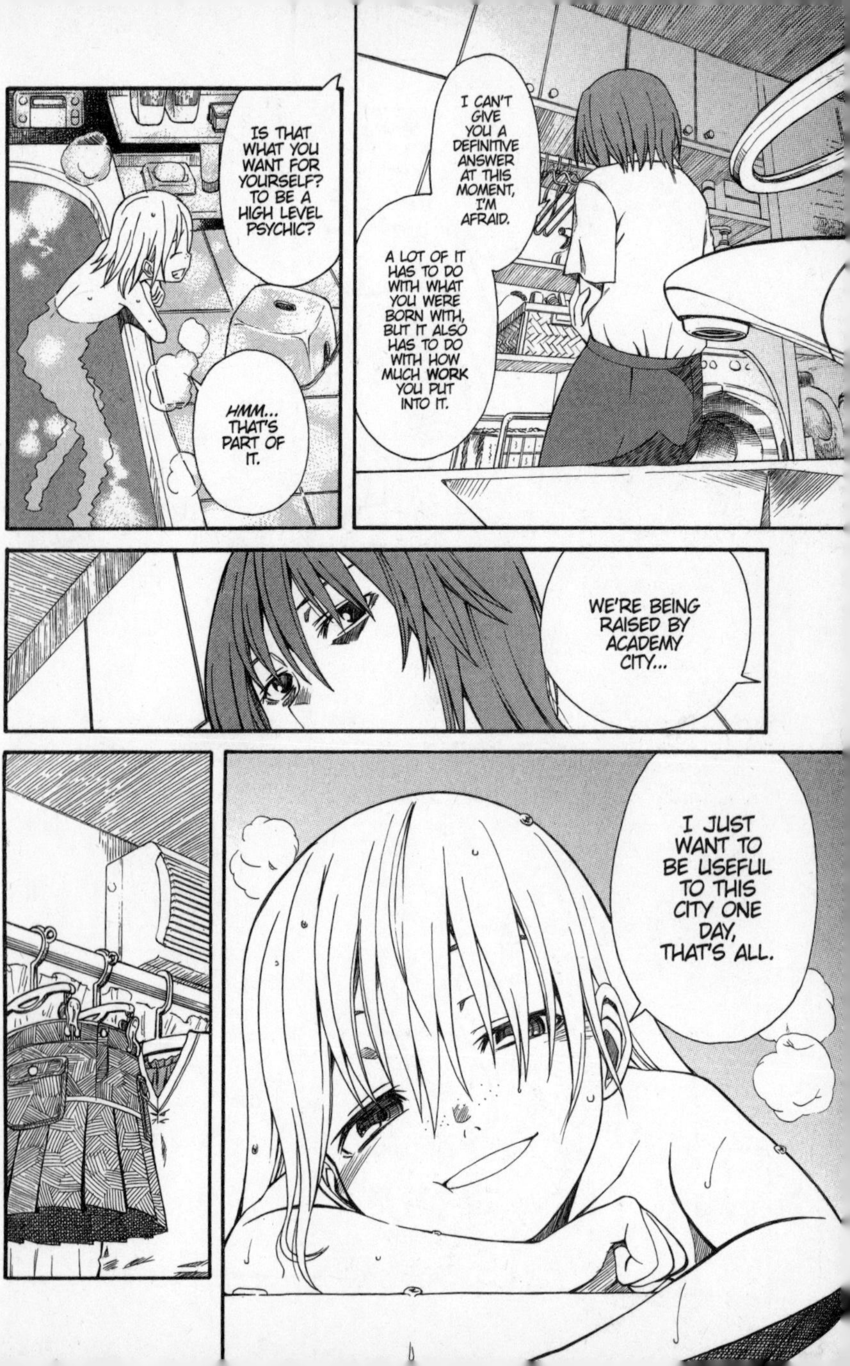
I CAN'T GIVE YOU A DEFINITIVE ANSWER AT THIS MOMENT, I'M AFRAID.
A LOT OF IT HAS TO DO WITH WHAT YOU WERE BORN WITH, BUT IT ALSO HAS TO DO WITH HOW MUCH WORK YOU PUT INTO IT.
IS THAT WHAT YOU WANT FOR YOURSELF? TO BE A HIGH LEVEL PSYCHIC?
HMM... THAT'S PART OF IT.
WE'RE BEING RAISED BY ACADEMY CITY...
I JUST WANT TO BE USEFUL TO THIS CITY ONE DAY, THAT'S ALL.

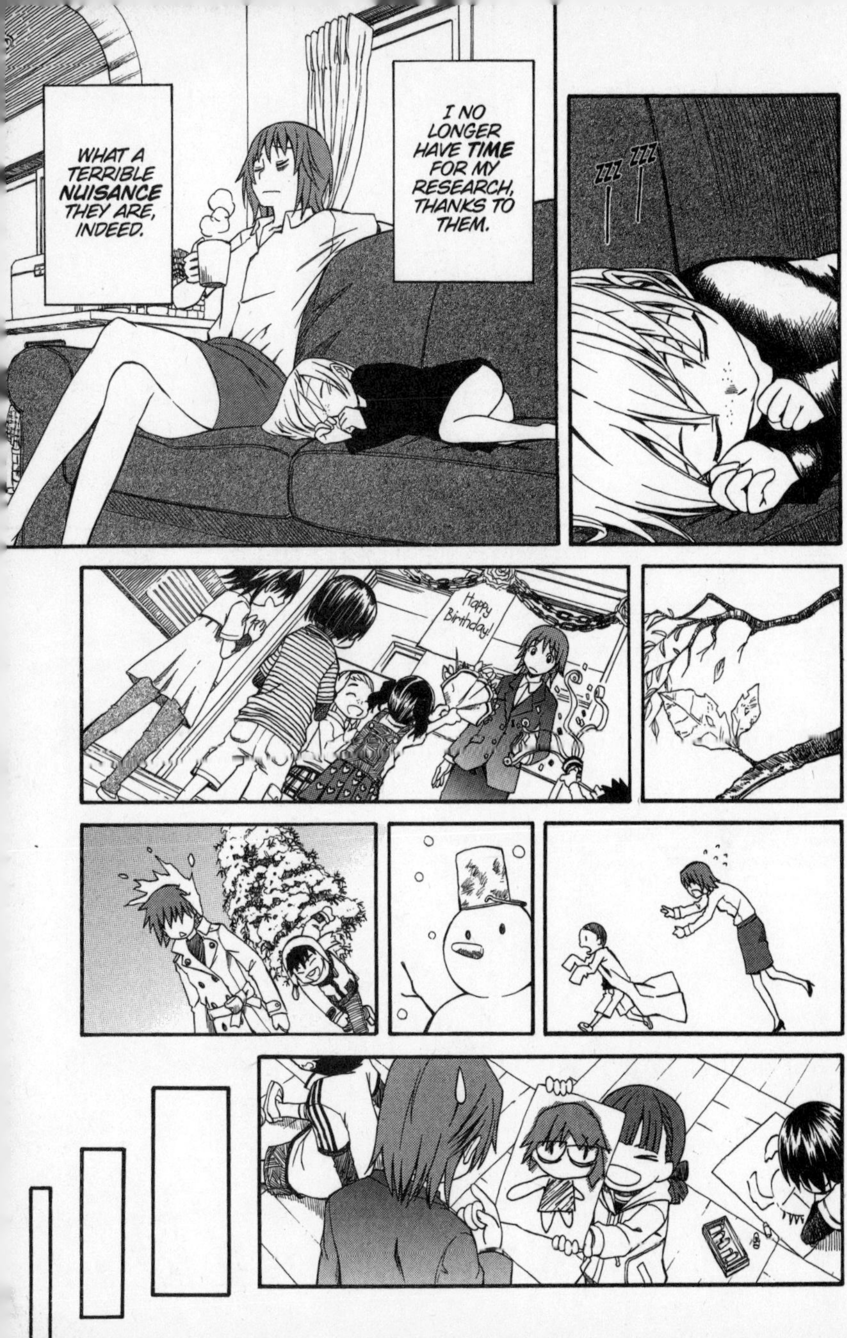
ZZZ ZZZ
I NO LONGER HAVE TIME FOR MY RESEARCH, THANKS TO THEM.
WHAT A TERRIBLE NUISANCE THEY ARE, INDEED.
Happy Birthday!

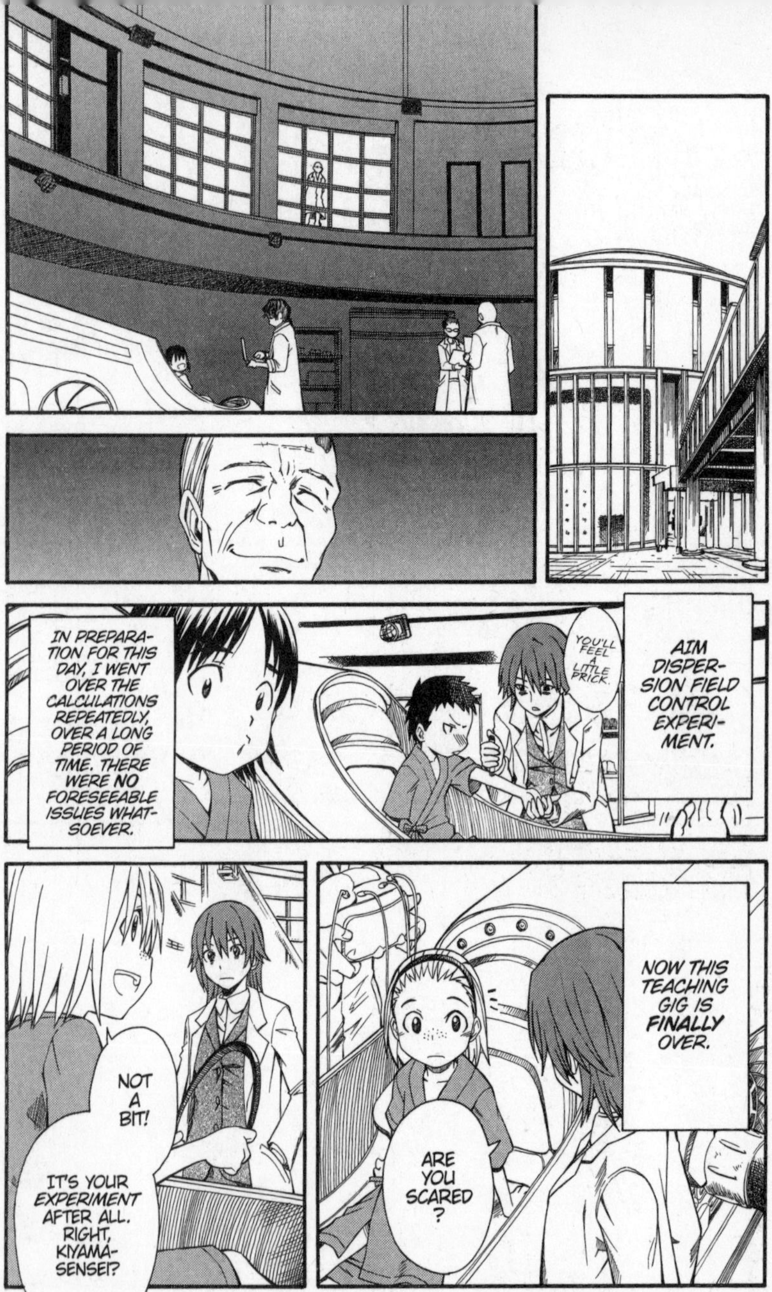
AIM DISPERSION FIELD CONTROL EXPERIMENT.
YOU'LL FEEL A LITTLE PRICK.
IN PREPARATION FOR THIS DAY, I WENT OVER THE CALCULATIONS REPEATEDLY, OVER A LONG PERIOD OF TIME. THERE WERE NO FORESEEABLE ISSUES WHATSOEVER.
NOW THIS TEACHING GIG IS FINALLY OVER.
ARE YOU SCARED?
NOT A BIT!
IT'S YOUR EXPERIMENT AFTER ALL. RIGHT, KIYAMA-SENSEI?

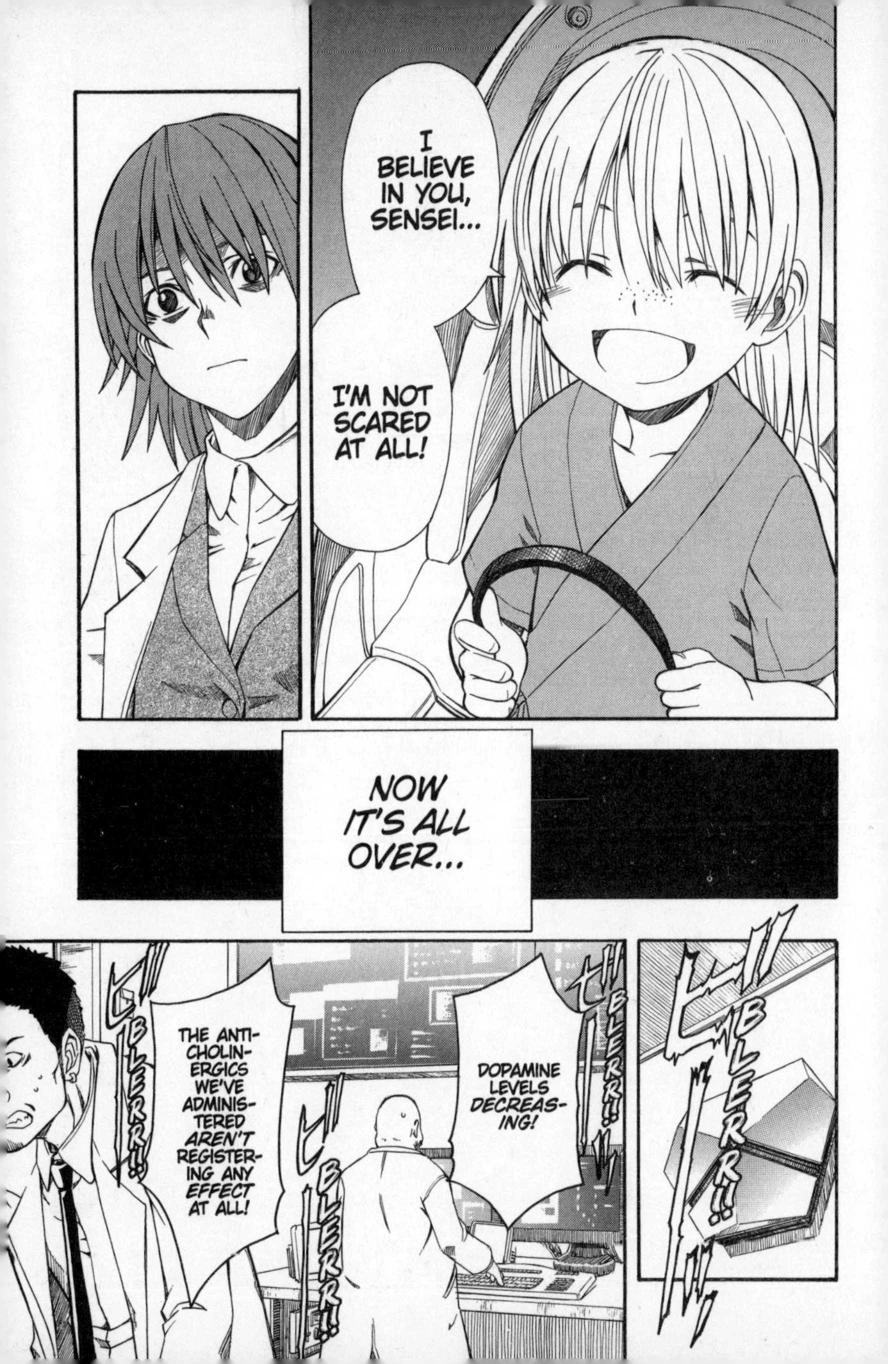
I BELIEVE IN YOU, SENSEI...
I'M NOT SCARED AT ALL!
NOW IT'S ALL OVER...
BLERR!!
BLERR!!
DOPAMINE LEVELS DECREAS-ING!
BLERR!!
THE ANTI-CHOLIN-ERGICS WE'VE ADMINIS-TERED AREN'T REGISTER-ING ANY EFFECT AT ALL!
BLERR!!

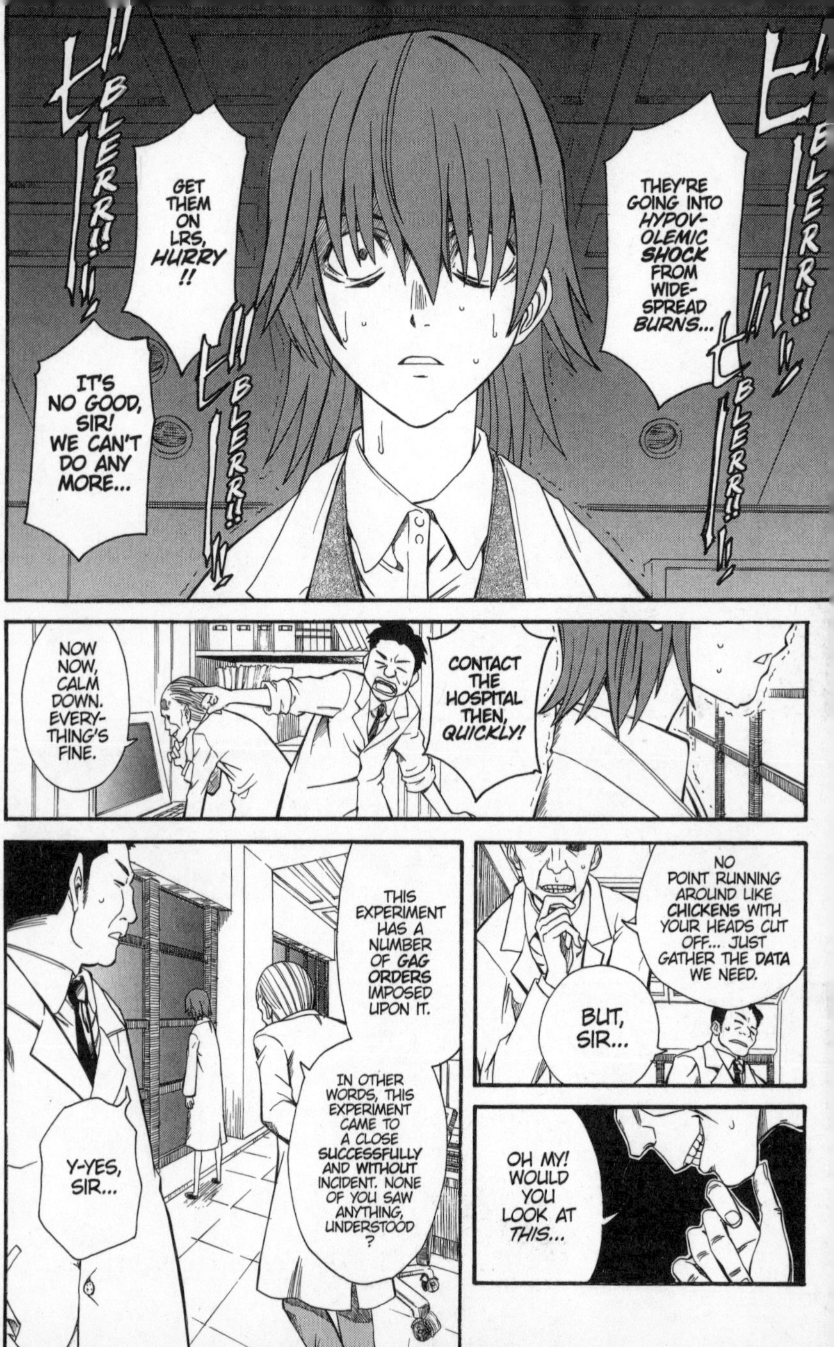
BLERR!!
THEY'RE GOING INTO HYPOVOLEMIC SHOCK FROM WIDESPREAD BURNS...
BLERR!!
GET THEM ON LRS, HURRY!!
BLERR!!
IT'S NO GOOD, SIR! WE CAN'T DO ANY MORE...
BLERR!!
CONTACT THE HOSPITAL THEN, QUICKLY!
NOW NOW, CALM DOWN. EVERYTHING'S FINE.
NO POINT RUNNING AROUND LIKE CHICKENS WITH YOUR HEADS CUT OFF... JUST GATHER THE DATA WE NEED.
BUT, SIR...
OH MY! WOULD YOU LOOK AT THIS...
THIS EXPERIMENT HAS A NUMBER OF GAG ORDERS IMPOSED UPON IT.
IN OTHER WORDS, THIS EXPERIMENT CAME TO A CLOSE SUCCESSFULLY AND WITHOUT INCIDENT. NONE OF YOU SAW ANYTHING, UNDERSTOOD?
Y-YES, SIR...

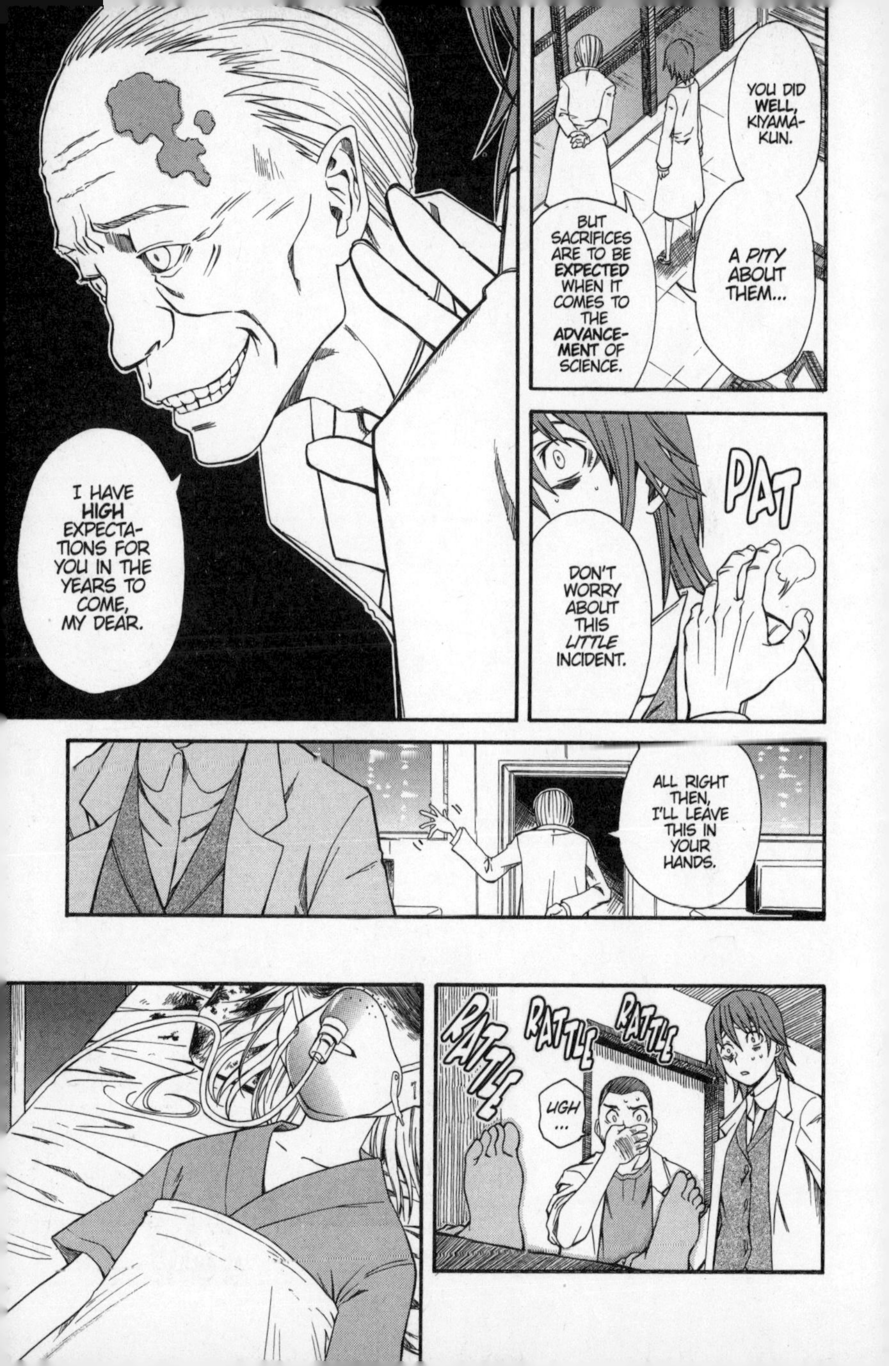
YOU DID WELL, KIYAMA-KUN.
A PITY ABOUT THEM...
BUT SACRIFICES ARE TO BE EXPECTED WHEN IT COMES TO THE ADVANCEMENT OF SCIENCE.
PAT
DON'T WORRY ABOUT THIS LITTLE INCIDENT.
I HAVE HIGH EXPECTATIONS FOR YOU IN THE YEARS TO COME, MY DEAR.
ALL RIGHT THEN, I'LL LEAVE THIS IN YOUR HANDS.
RATTLE
RATTLE
RATTLE
UGH ...

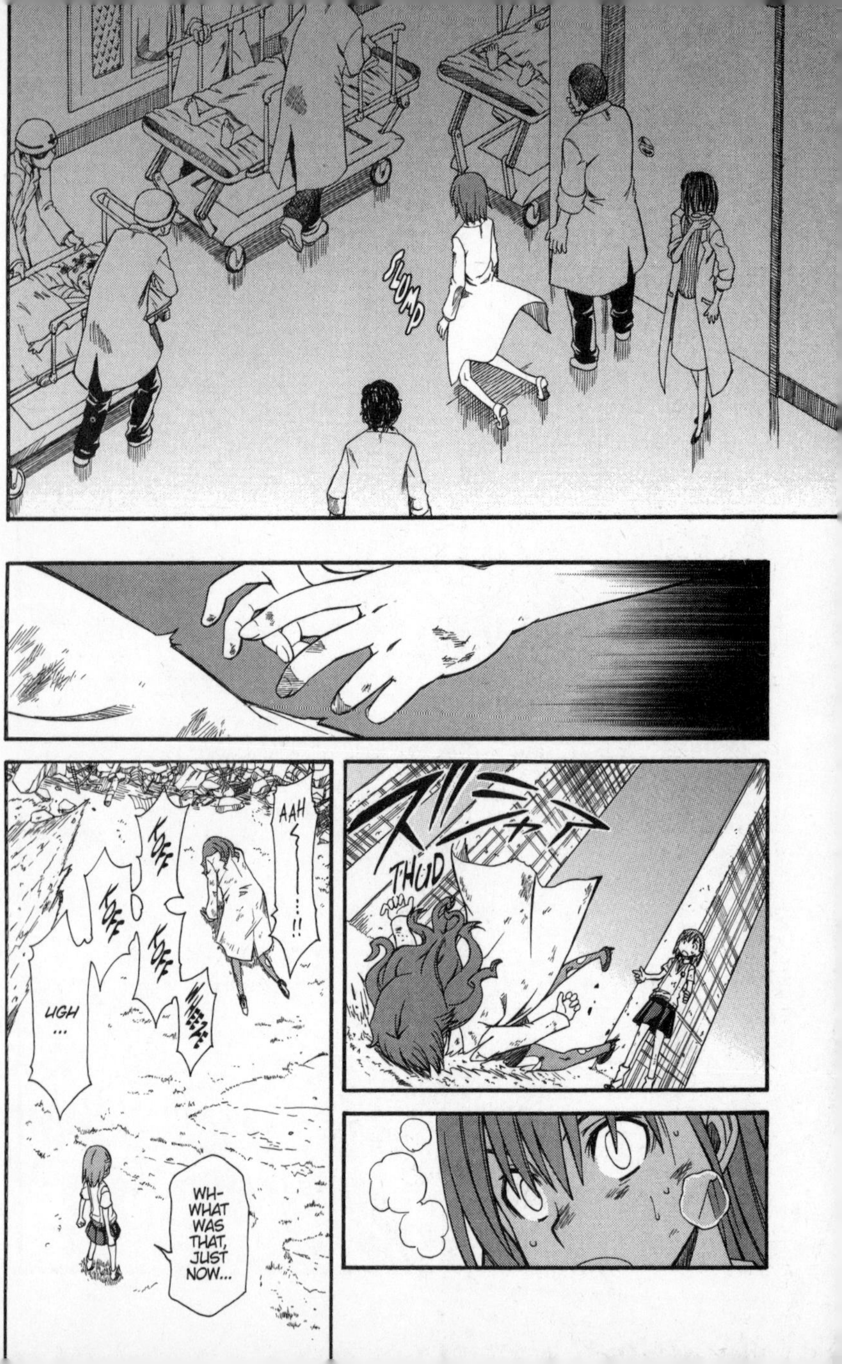
SLUMP
THUD
AAH~ ...!!
KOFF KOFF
KOFF KOFF
WHEEZE
UGH ...
WH-WHAT WAS THAT, JUST NOW...

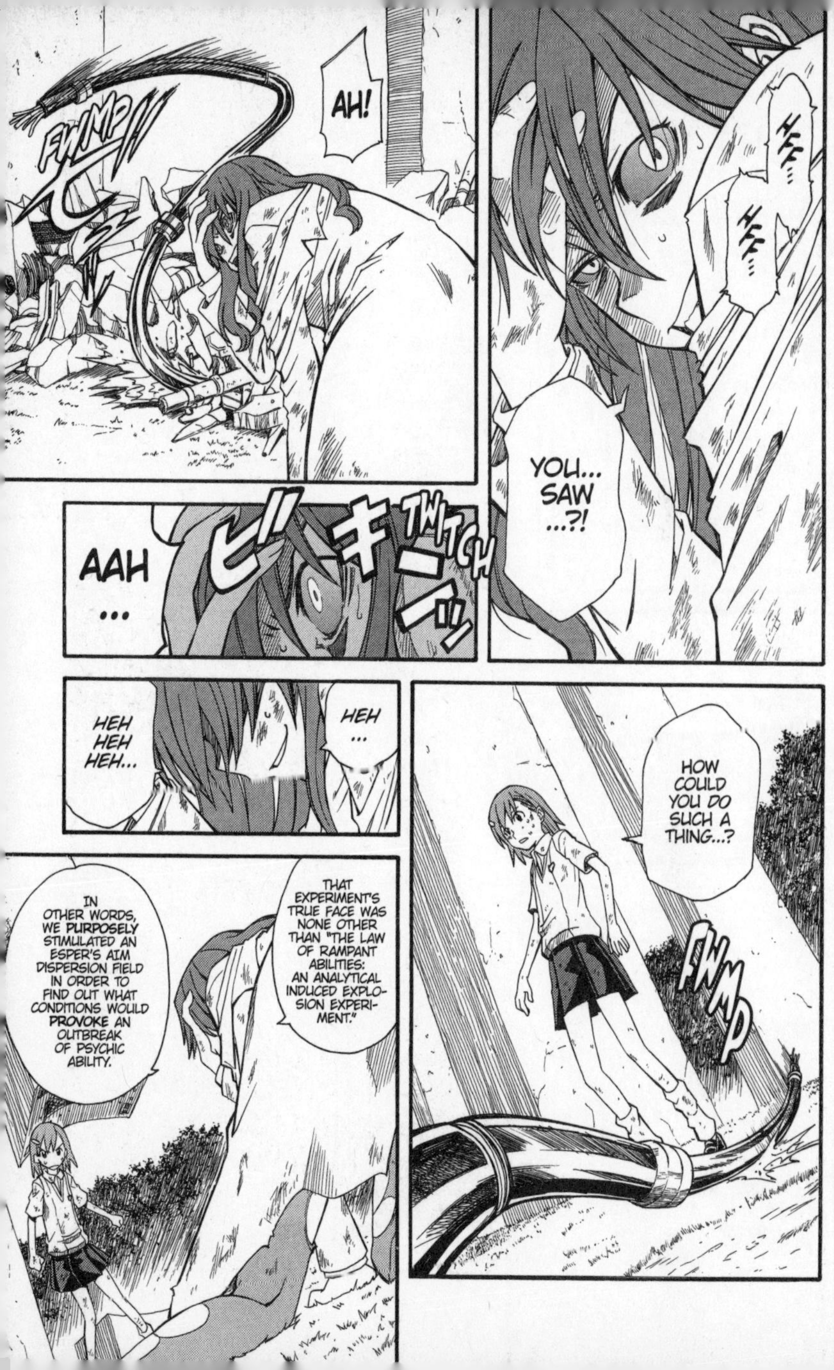
HFF...
HFF...
YOU... SAW ...?!
AH!
FWMP!!
TWITCH
AAH ...
HOW COULD YOU DO SUCH A THING...?
FWMP
HEH ...
HEH HEH HEH...
THAT EXPERIMENT'S TRUE FACE WAS NONE OTHER THAN "THE LAW OF RAMPANT ABILITIES: AN ANALYTICAL INDUCED EXPLOSION EXPERIMENT."
IN OTHER WORDS, WE PURPOSELY STIMULATED AN ESPER'S AIM DISPERSION FIELD IN ORDER TO FIND OUT WHAT CONDITIONS WOULD PROVOKE AN OUTBREAK OF PSYCHIC ABILITY.

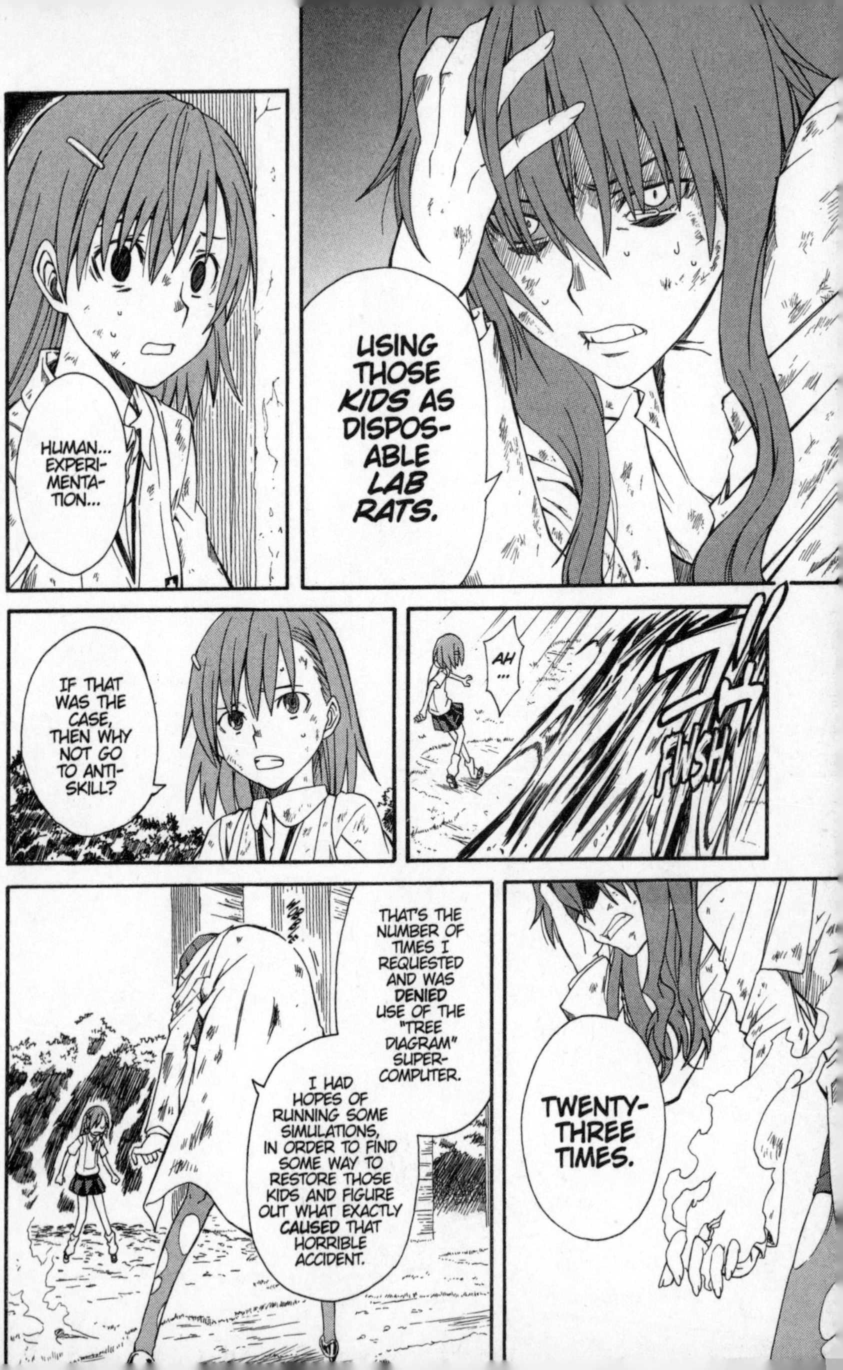
USING THOSE KIDS AS DISPOSABLE LAB RATS.
HUMAN... EXPERIMENTATION...
AH ...
FWSH!!
IF THAT WAS THE CASE, THEN WHY NOT GO TO ANTI-SKILL?
TWENTY-THREE TIMES.
THAT'S THE NUMBER OF TIMES I REQUESTED AND WAS DENIED USE OF THE "TREE DIAGRAM" SUPER-COMPUTER.
I HAD HOPES OF RUNNING SOME SIMULATIONS, IN ORDER TO FIND SOME WAY TO RESTORE THOSE KIDS AND FIGURE OUT WHAT EXACTLY CAUSED THAT HORRIBLE ACCIDENT.

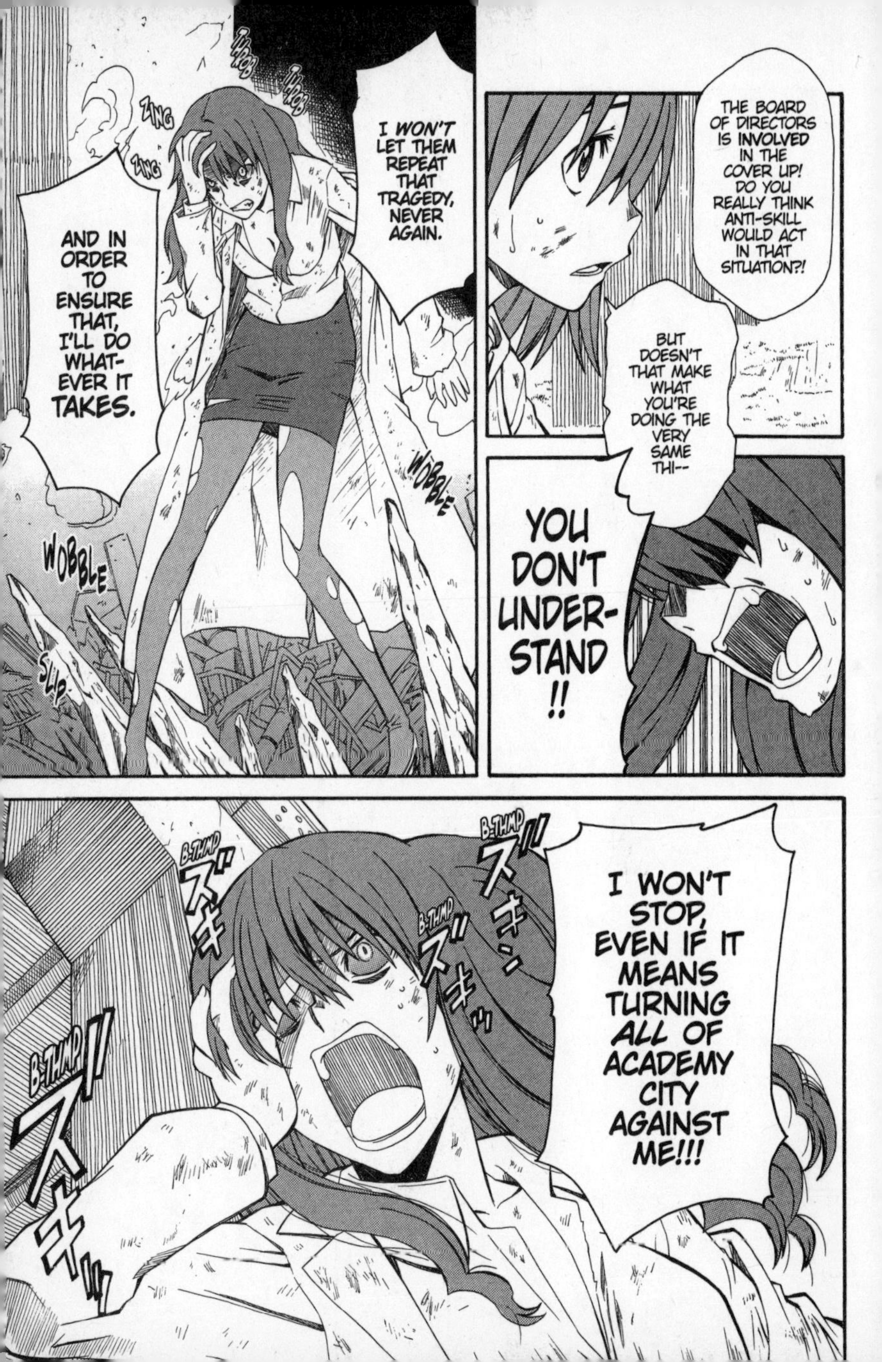

THE BOARD OF DIRECTORS IS INVOLVED IN THE COVER UP! DO YOU REALLY THINK ANTI-SKILL WOULD ACT IN THAT SITUATION?!
BUT DOESN'T THAT MAKE WHAT YOU'RE DOING THE VERY SAME THI--
YOU DON'T UNDER-STAND!!
THROB
THROB
I *WON'T* LET THEM REPEAT THAT TRAGEDY, NEVER AGAIN.
ZING
ZING
AND IN ORDER TO ENSURE THAT, I'LL DO WHAT-EVER IT TAKES.
WOBBLE
WOBBLE
SLIP
B-THMP
I WON'T STOP, EVEN IF IT MEANS TURNING *ALL* OF ACADEMY CITY AGAINST ME!!!
B-THMP
B-THMP
B-THMP

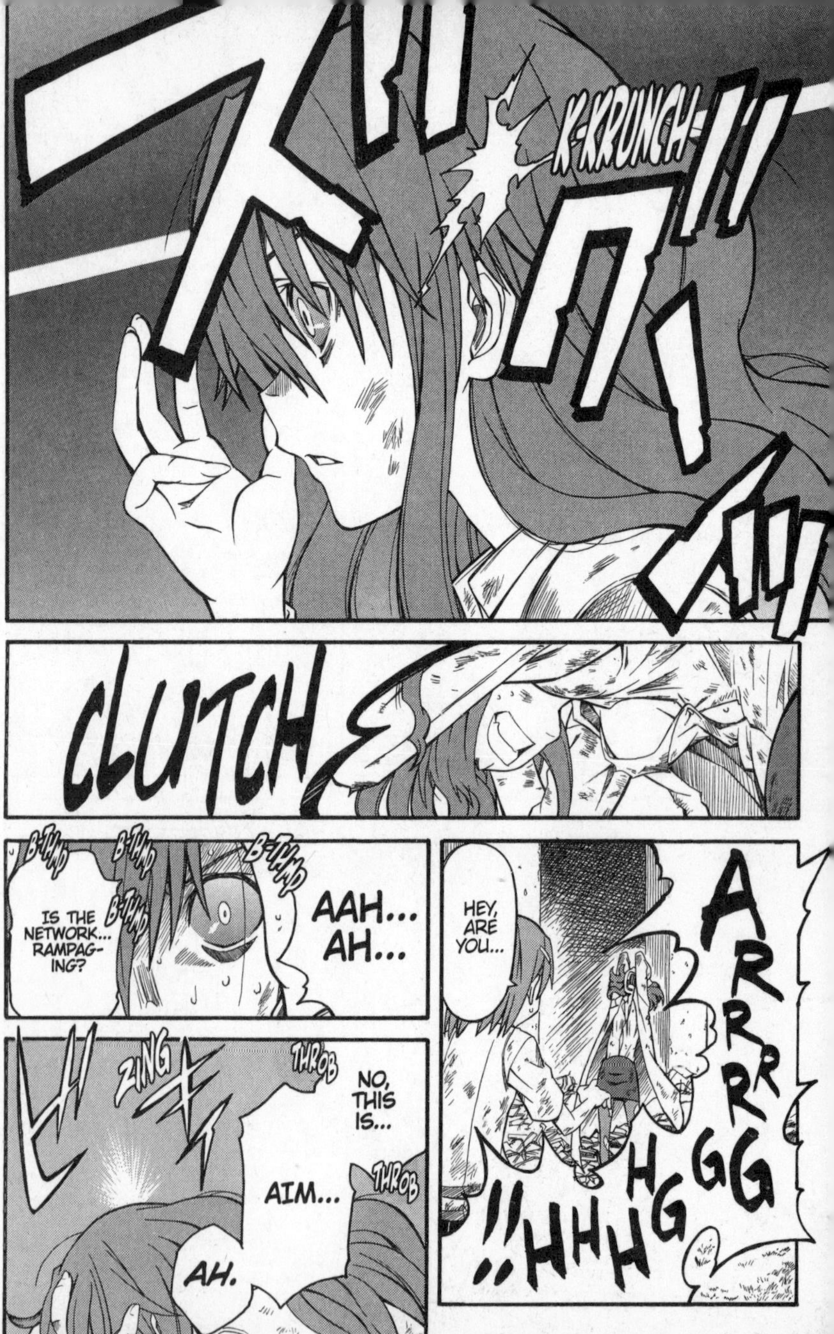
K-KRUNCH-
CLUTCH
HEY, ARE YOU...
ARRRRGGGHHHH!!
B-THMP
B-THMP
B-THMP
B-THMP
IS THE NETWORK... RAMPAG-ING?
AAH... AH...
ZING
THROB
NO, THIS IS...
THROB
AIM...
AH.

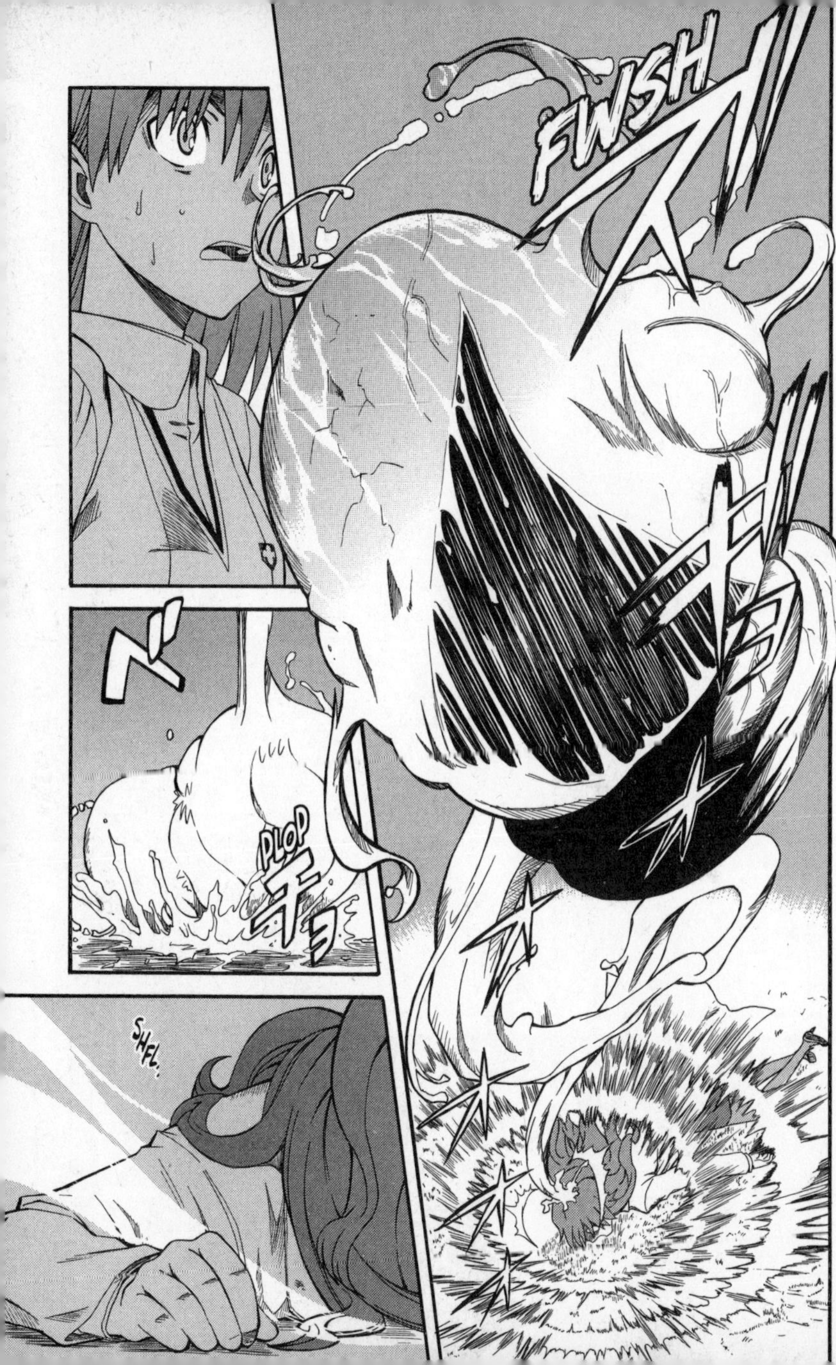
FWSH
PLOP
SHFL.

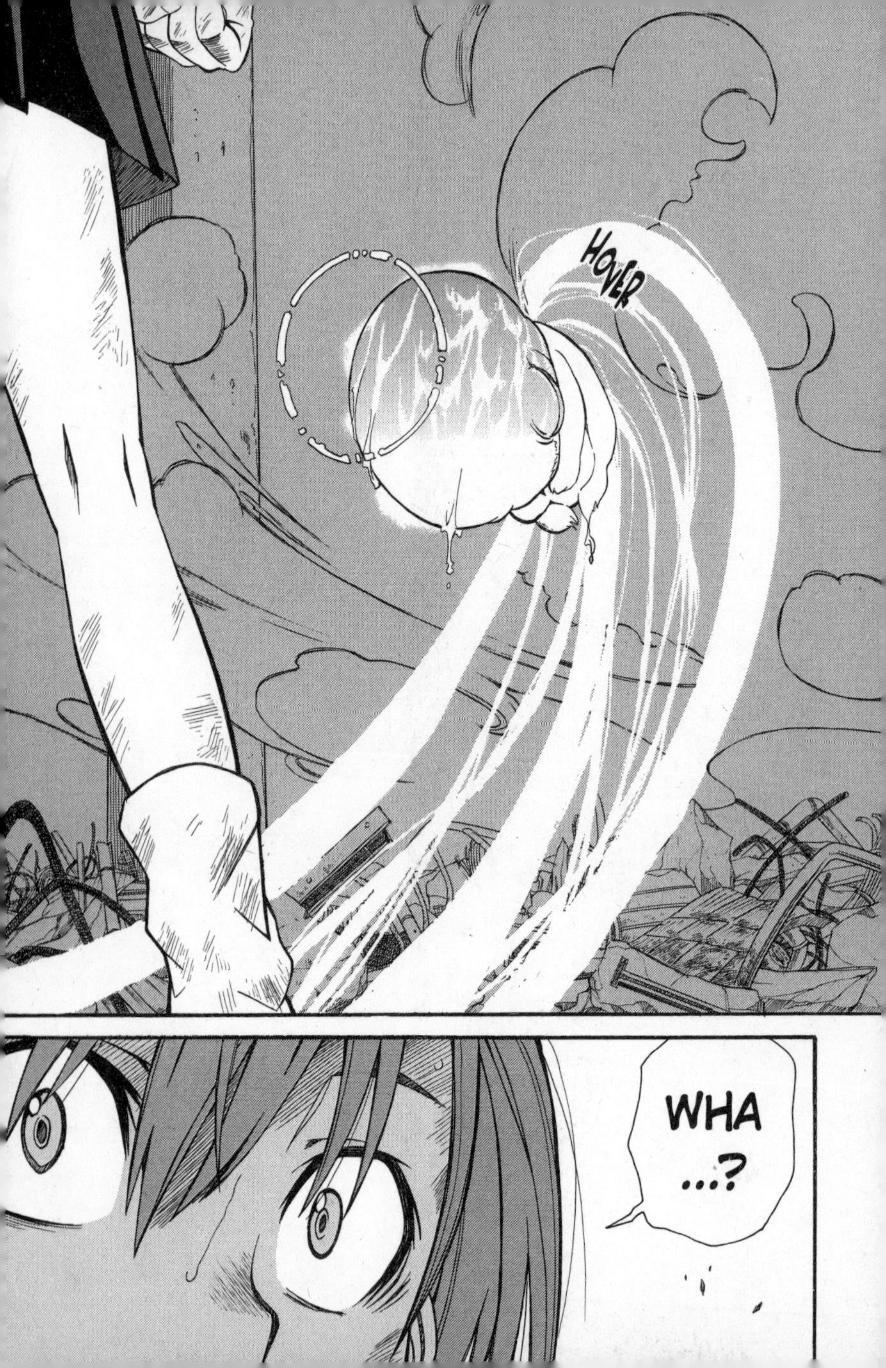
HOVER
WHA ...?

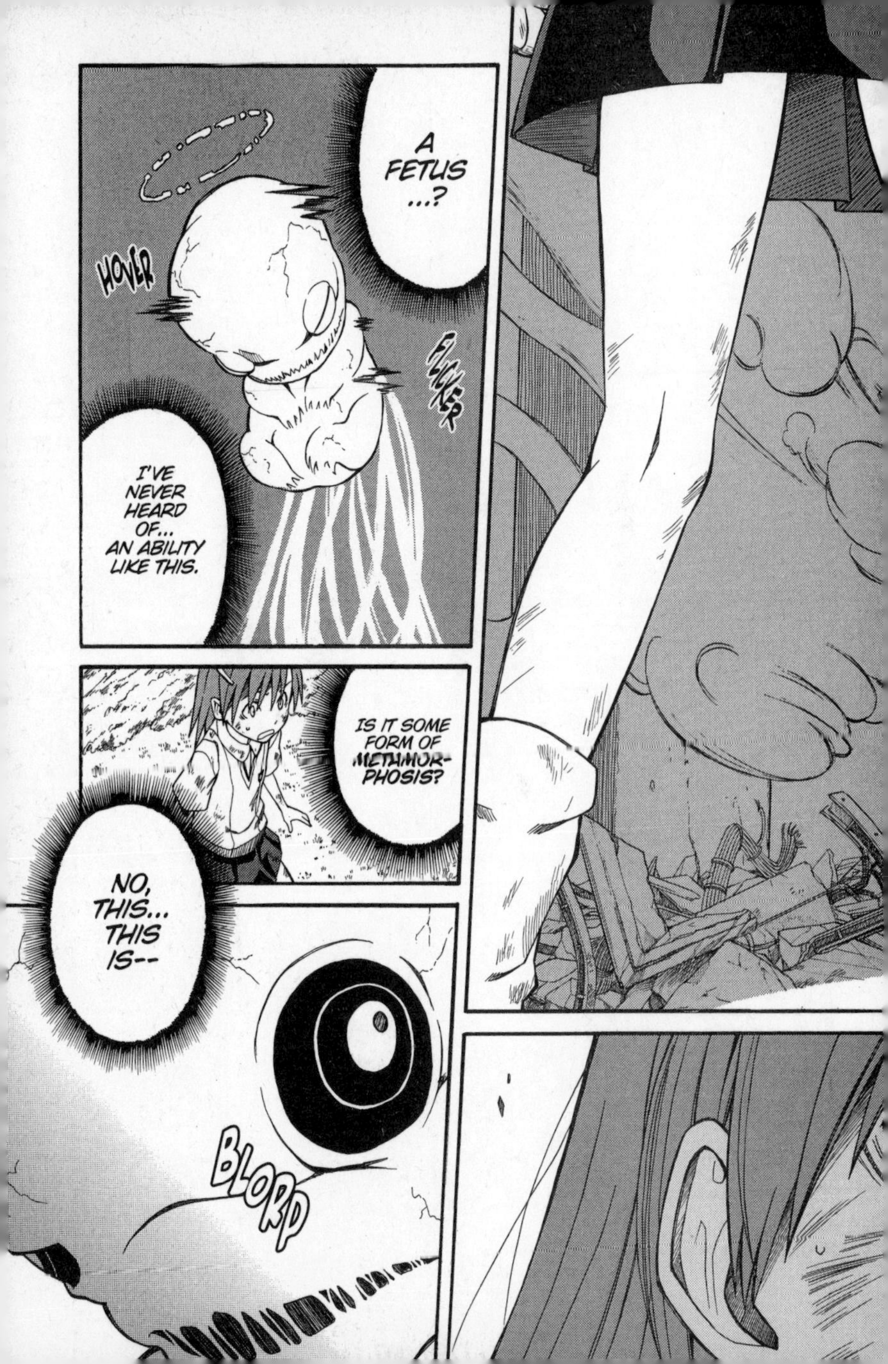
A FETUS ...?
FLICKER
HOVER
I'VE NEVER HEARD OF... AN ABILITY LIKE THIS.
IS IT SOME FORM OF METAMOR-PHOSIS?
NO, THIS... THIS IS--
BLORP

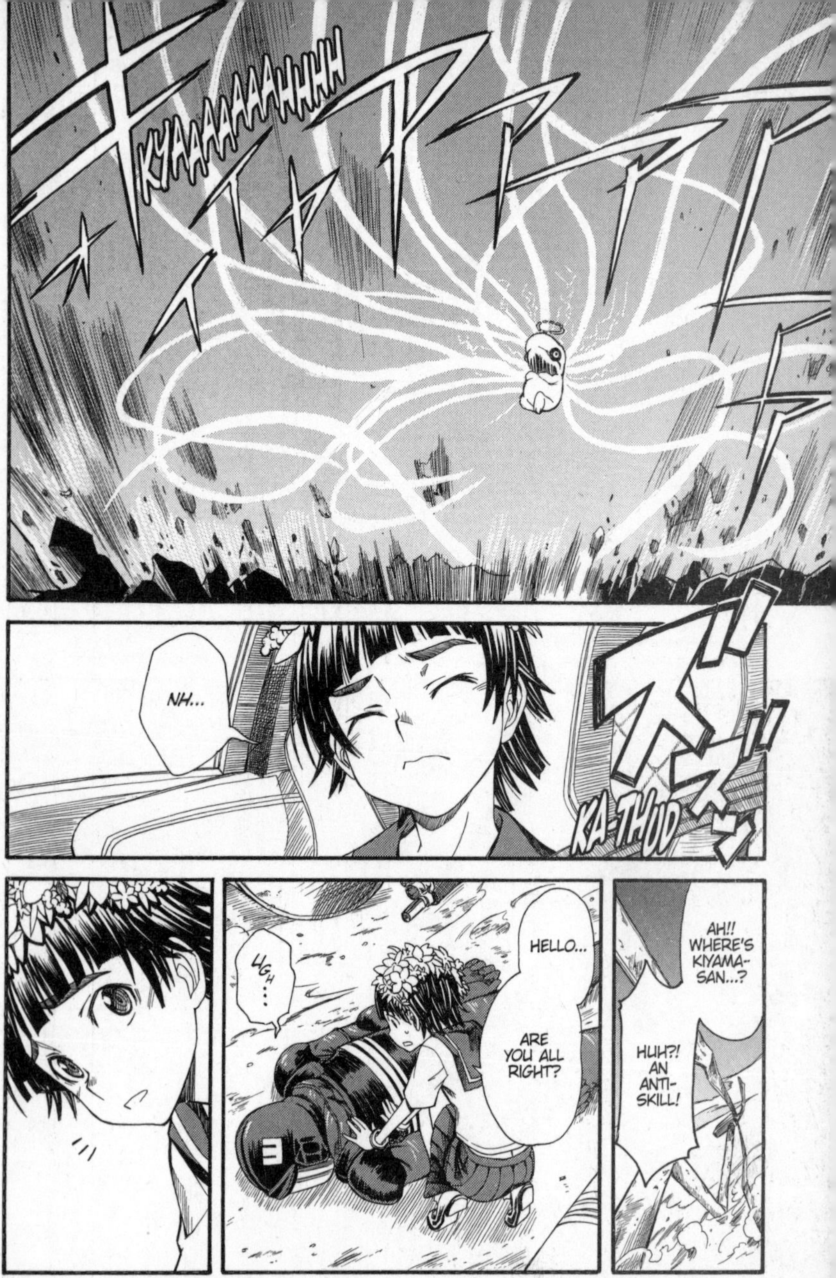
KYAAAAAAHHHH
KA-THUD
NH...
AH!! WHERE'S KIYAMA-SAN...?
HUH?! AN ANTI-SKILL!
HELLO...
ARE YOU ALL RIGHT?
UGH...

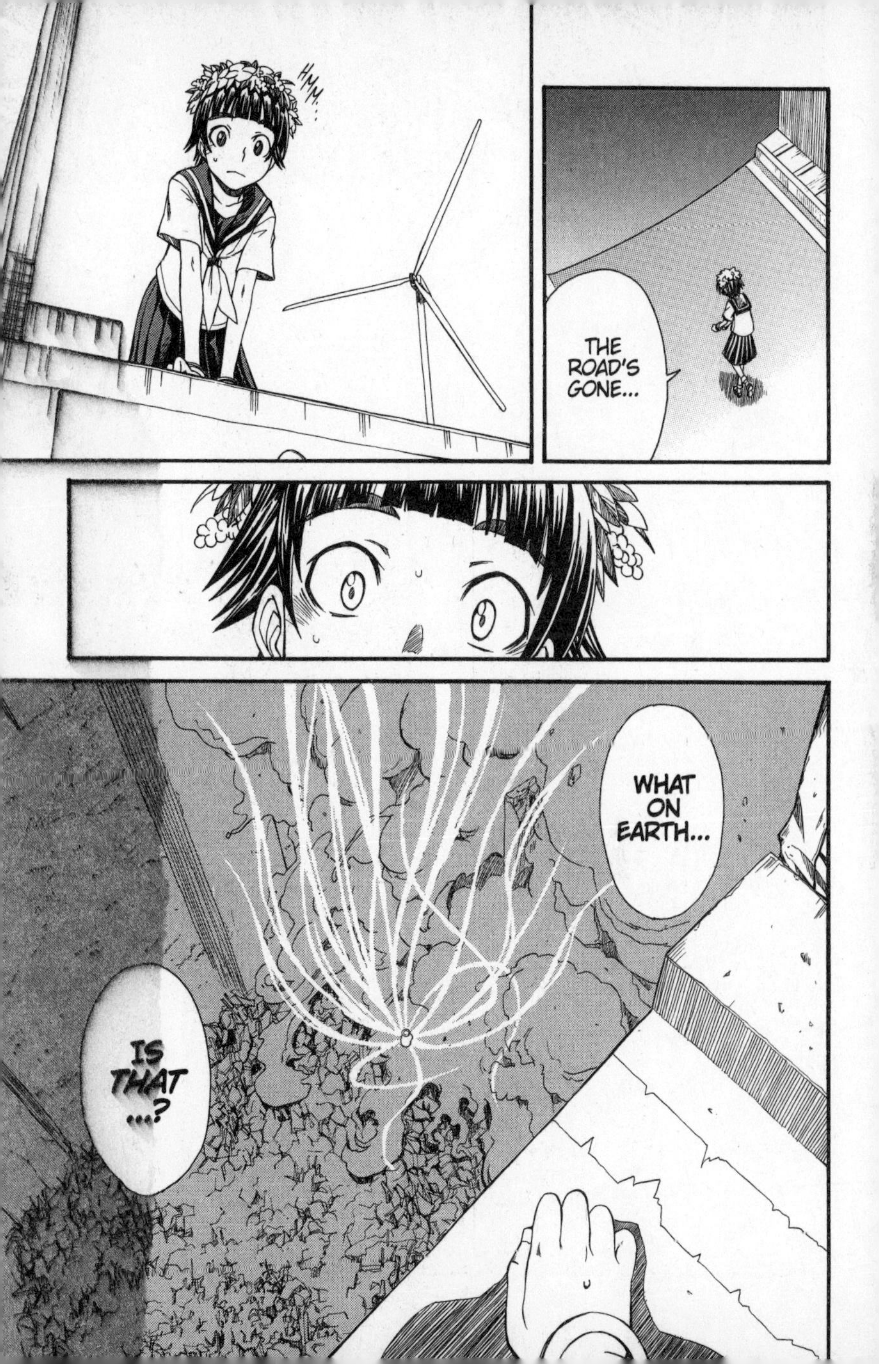
THE ROAD'S GONE...
HMM
WHAT ON EARTH...
IS THAT ...?

Kiyama: Rough Sketch

ⓔNormally looks quite sleepy.
 Her bottom lashes have quite a bit of
 fullness to them.

ⓔWhen she reveals her true nature,
 the hair she had held back shifts forward.

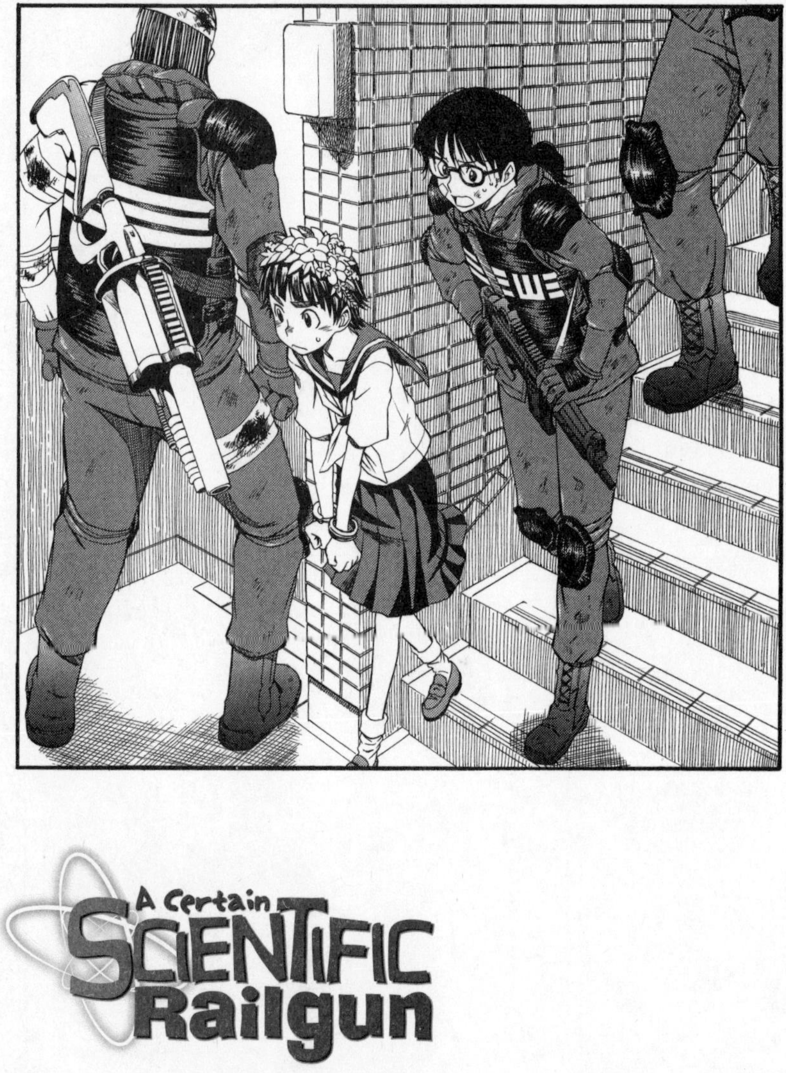

A Certain SCIENTIFIC Railgun

CHAPTER 15: JULY 24 (5)

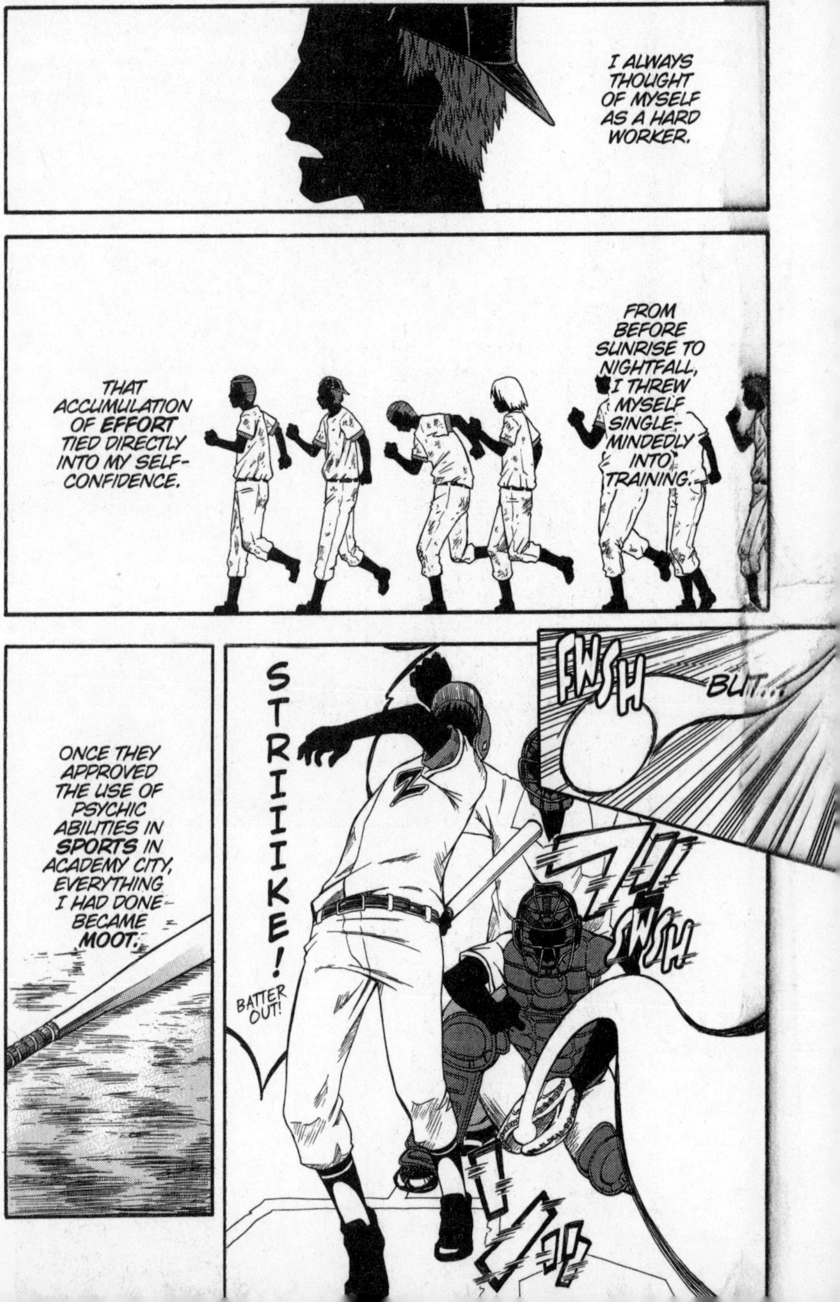

I ALWAYS THOUGHT OF MYSELF AS A HARD WORKER.
FROM BEFORE SUNRISE TO NIGHTFALL, I THREW MYSELF SINGLE-MINDEDLY INTO TRAINING.
THAT ACCUMULATION OF EFFORT TIED DIRECTLY INTO MY SELF-CONFIDENCE.
FWSH
BUT...
SWSH
STRIIIKE!
BATTER OUT!
ONCE THEY APPROVED THE USE OF PSYCHIC ABILITIES IN SPORTS IN ACADEMY CITY, EVERYTHING I HAD DONE BECAME MOOT.

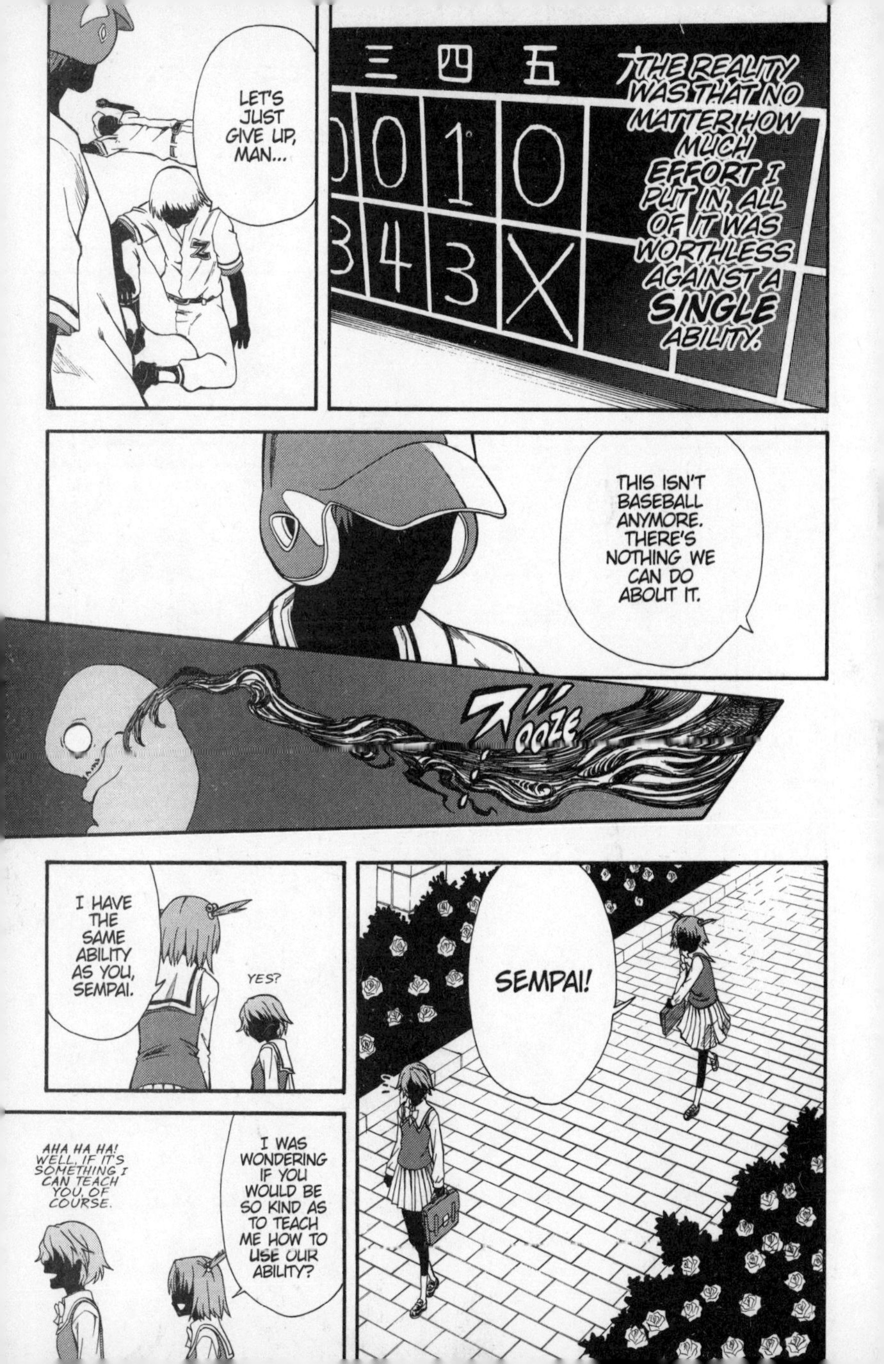
THE REALITY WAS THAT NO MATTER HOW MUCH EFFORT I PUT IN, ALL OF IT WAS WORTHLESS AGAINST A SINGLE ABILITY.
LET'S JUST GIVE UP, MAN...
THIS ISN'T BASEBALL ANYMORE. THERE'S NOTHING WE CAN DO ABOUT IT.
OOZE
SEMPAI!
YES?
I HAVE THE SAME ABILITY AS YOU, SEMPAI.
I WAS WONDERING IF YOU WOULD BE SO KIND AS TO TEACH ME HOW TO USE OUR ABILITY?
AHA HA HA! WELL, IF IT'S SOMETHING I CAN TEACH YOU, OF COURSE.

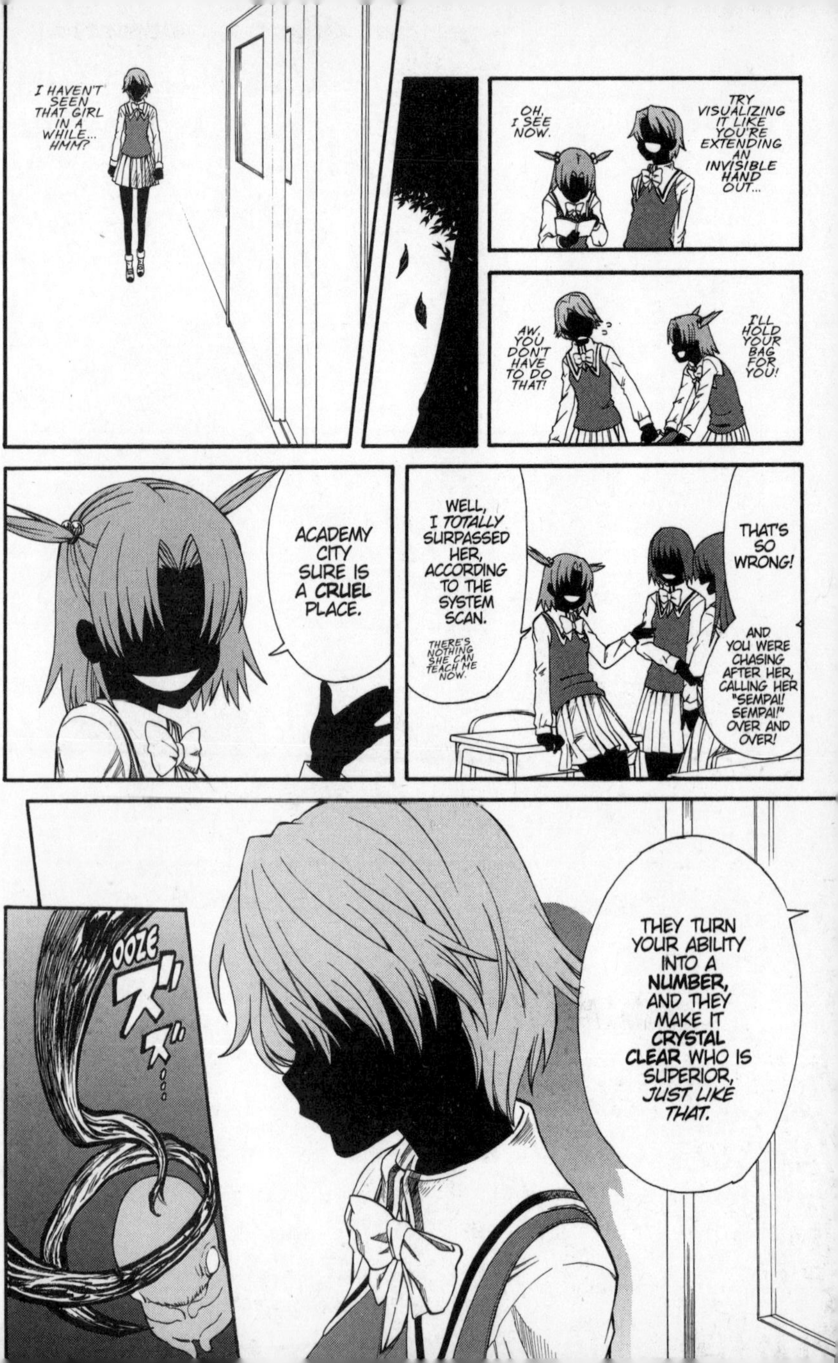
TRY VISUALIZING IT LIKE YOU'RE EXTENDING AN INVISIBLE HAND OUT...
OH, I SEE NOW.
I'LL HOLD YOUR BAG FOR YOU!
AW, YOU DON'T HAVE TO DO THAT!
I HAVEN'T SEEN THAT GIRL IN A WHILE... HMM?
THAT'S SO WRONG!
WELL, I *TOTALLY* SURPASSED HER, ACCORDING TO THE SYSTEM SCAN.
AND YOU WERE CHASING AFTER HER, CALLING HER "SEMPAI! SEMPAI!" OVER AND OVER!
THERE'S NOTHING SHE CAN TEACH ME NOW.
ACADEMY CITY SURE IS A **CRUEL** PLACE.
THEY TURN YOUR ABILITY INTO A **NUMBER**, AND THEY MAKE IT **CRYSTAL CLEAR** WHO IS SUPERIOR, *JUST LIKE THAT.*
OOZE

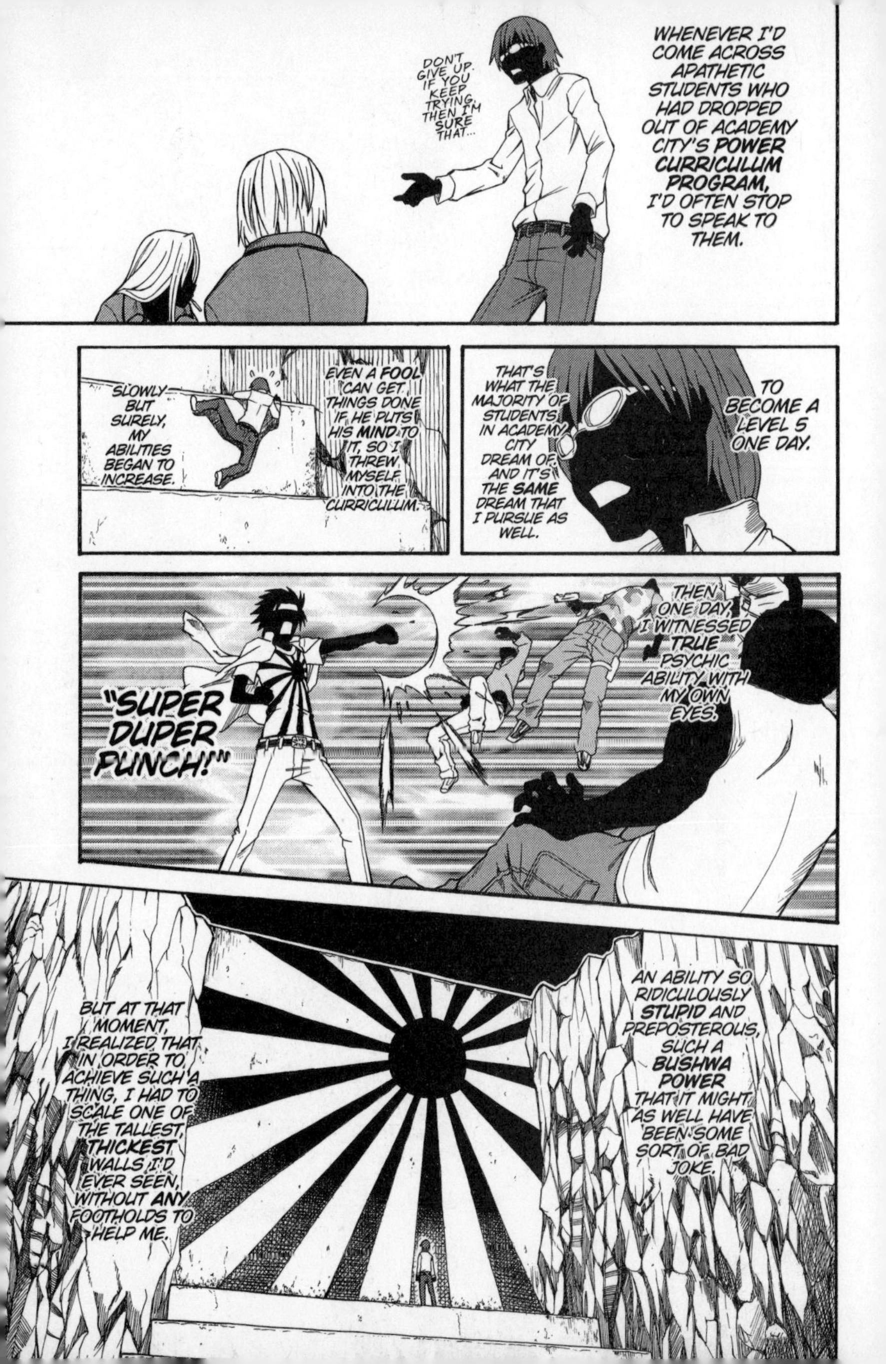
WHENEVER I'D COME ACROSS APATHETIC STUDENTS WHO HAD DROPPED OUT OF ACADEMY CITY'S **POWER CURRICULUM PROGRAM,** I'D OFTEN STOP TO SPEAK TO THEM.
DON'T GIVE UP. IF YOU KEEP TRYING, THEN I'M SURE THAT...
TO BECOME A LEVEL 5 ONE DAY.
THAT'S WHAT THE MAJORITY OF STUDENTS IN ACADEMY CITY DREAM OF. AND IT'S THE **SAME** DREAM THAT I PURSUE AS WELL.
EVEN A **FOOL** CAN GET THINGS DONE IF HE PUTS HIS **MIND** TO IT, SO I THREW MYSELF INTO THE CURRICULUM.
SLOWLY BUT SURELY, MY ABILITIES BEGAN TO INCREASE.
THEN ONE DAY, I WITNESSED **TRUE** PSYCHIC ABILITY WITH MY OWN EYES.
"SUPER DUPER PUNCH!"
AN ABILITY SO RIDICULOUSLY **STUPID** AND PREPOSTEROUS, SUCH A **BUSHWA POWER** THAT IT MIGHT AS WELL HAVE BEEN SOME SORT OF BAD JOKE.
BUT AT THAT MOMENT, I REALIZED THAT IN ORDER TO ACHIEVE SUCH A THING, I HAD TO SCALE ONE OF THE TALLEST, **THICKEST** WALLS I'D EVER SEEN, WITHOUT **ANY** FOOTHOLDS TO HELP ME.

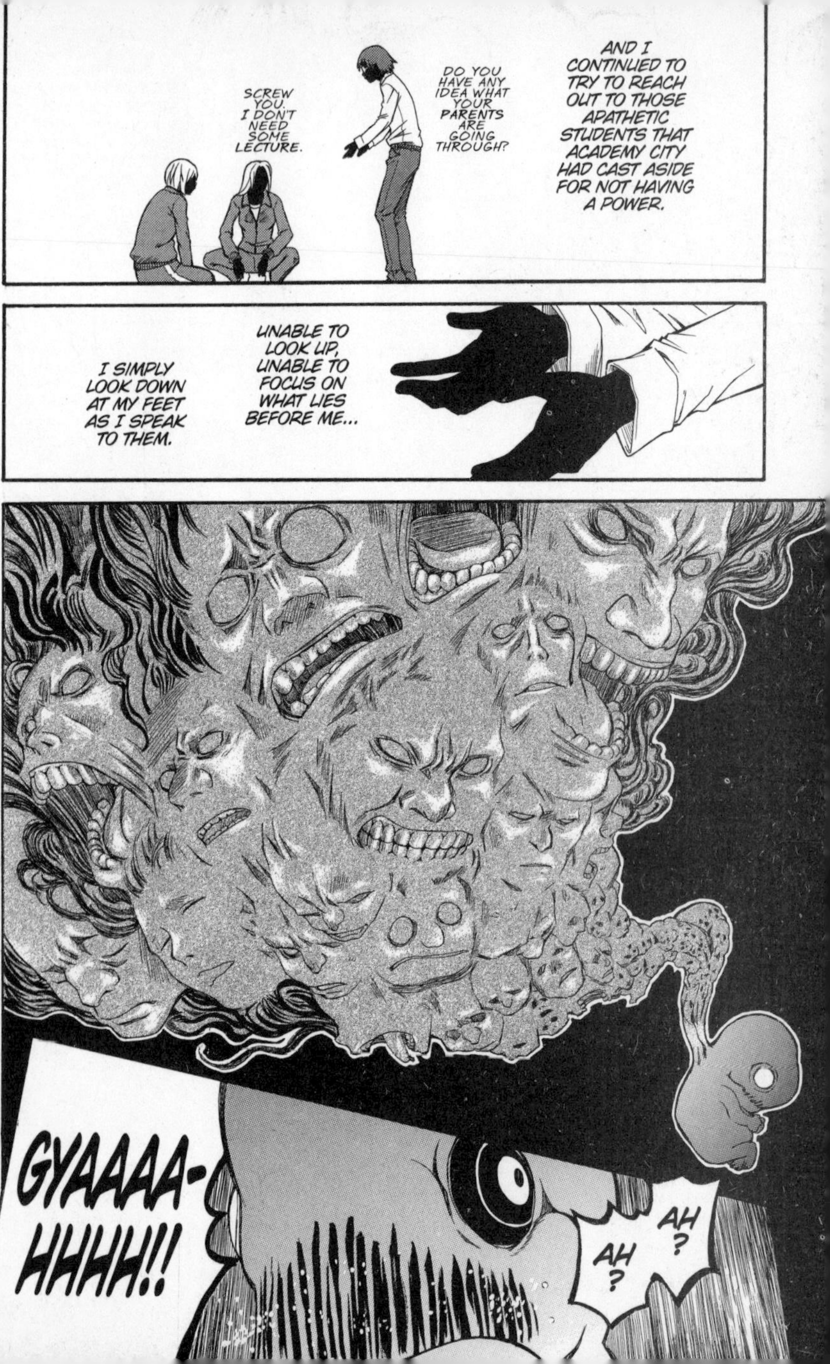
AND I CONTINUED TO TRY TO REACH OUT TO THOSE APATHETIC STUDENTS THAT ACADEMY CITY HAD CAST ASIDE FOR NOT HAVING A POWER.
DO YOU HAVE ANY IDEA WHAT YOUR PARENTS ARE GOING THROUGH?
SCREW YOU. I DON'T NEED SOME LECTURE.
UNABLE TO LOOK UP, UNABLE TO FOCUS ON WHAT LIES BEFORE ME...
I SIMPLY LOOK DOWN AT MY FEET AS I SPEAK TO THEM.
AH?
AH?
GYAAAA-HHHH!!

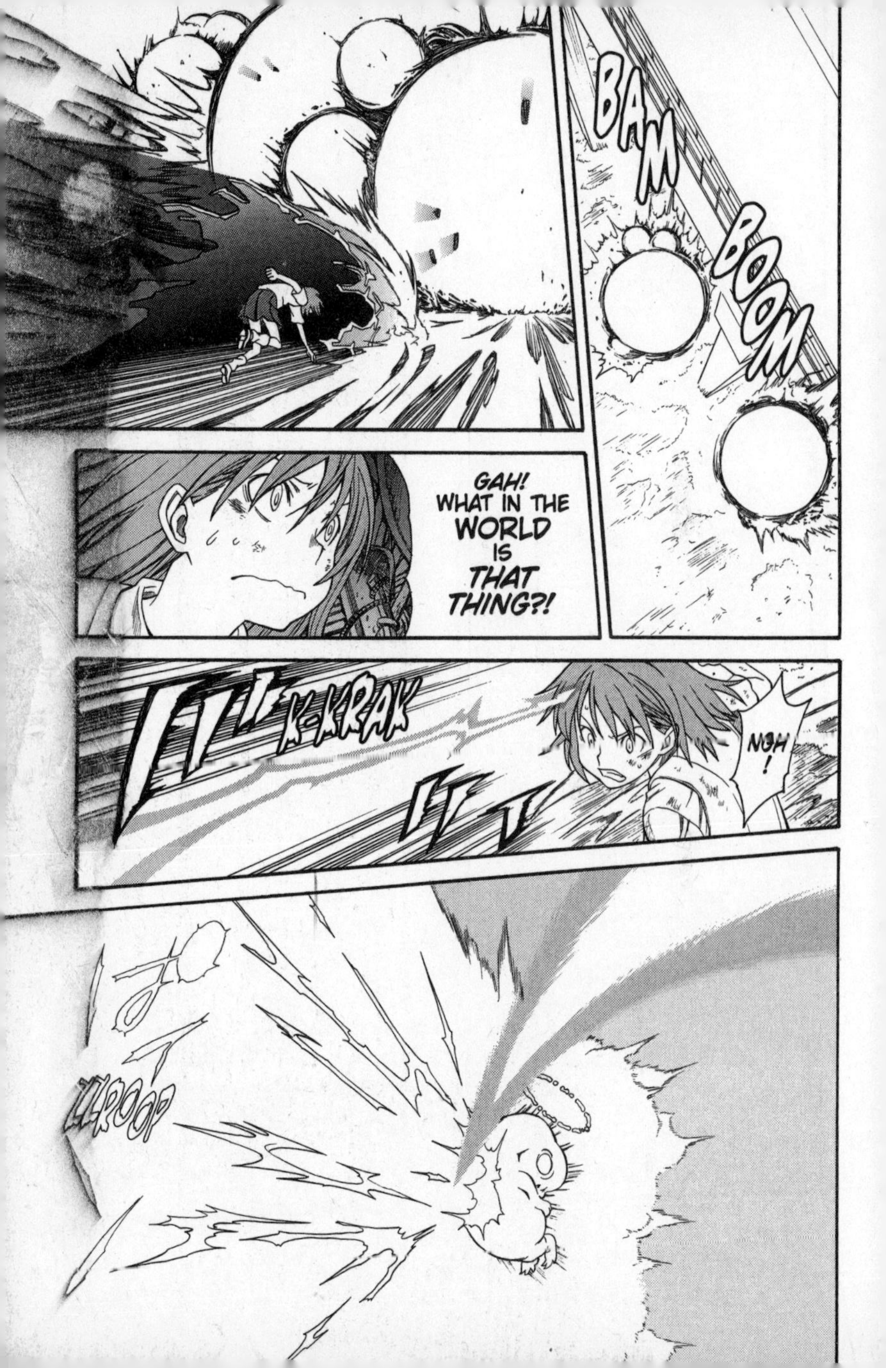
BAM
BOOM
GAH! WHAT IN THE WORLD IS THAT THING?!
NGH!
K-KRAK
ZZROOP

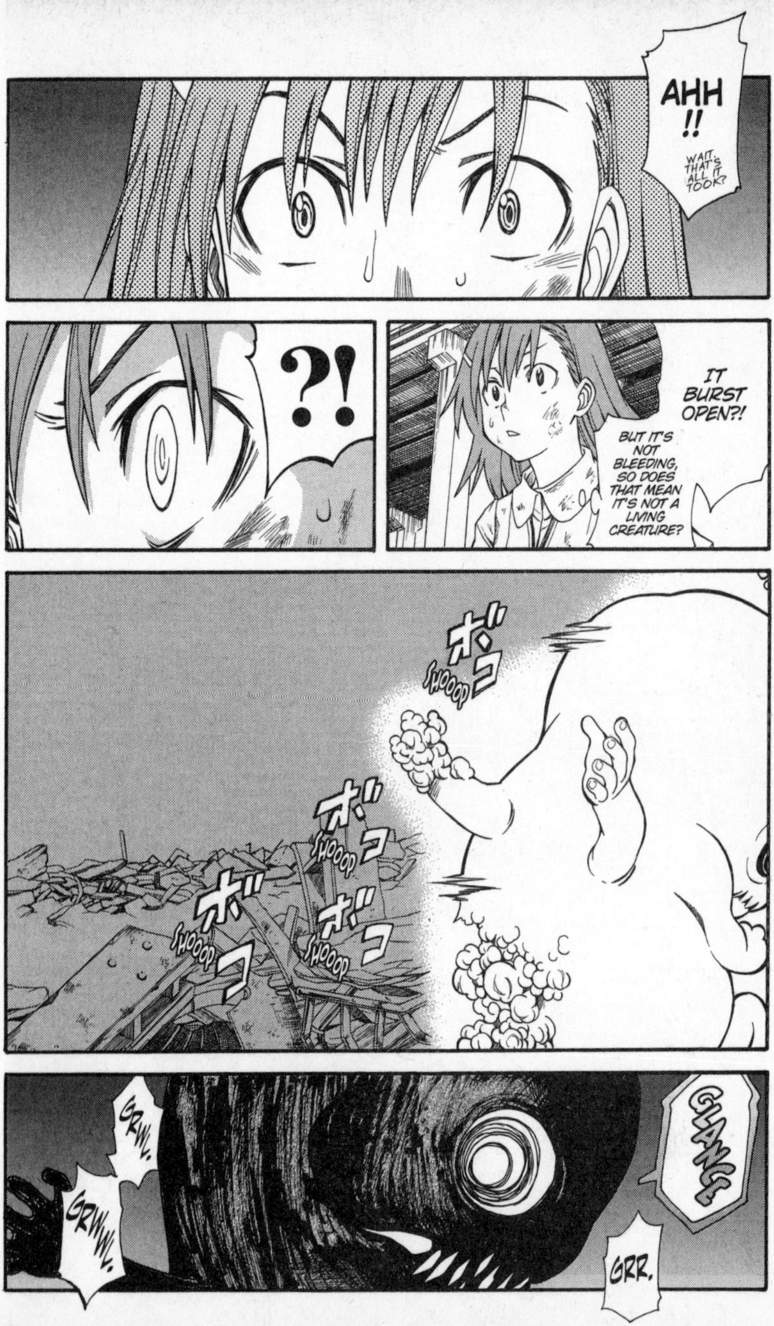
AHH!!
WAIT, THAT'S ALL IT TOOK?
IT BURST OPEN?!
BUT IT'S NOT BLEEDING, SO DOES THAT MEAN IT'S NOT A LIVING CREATURE?
?!
SHOOOP
SHOOOP
SHOOOP
SHOOOP
GLANCE
GRR.
GRWL.
GRWL.

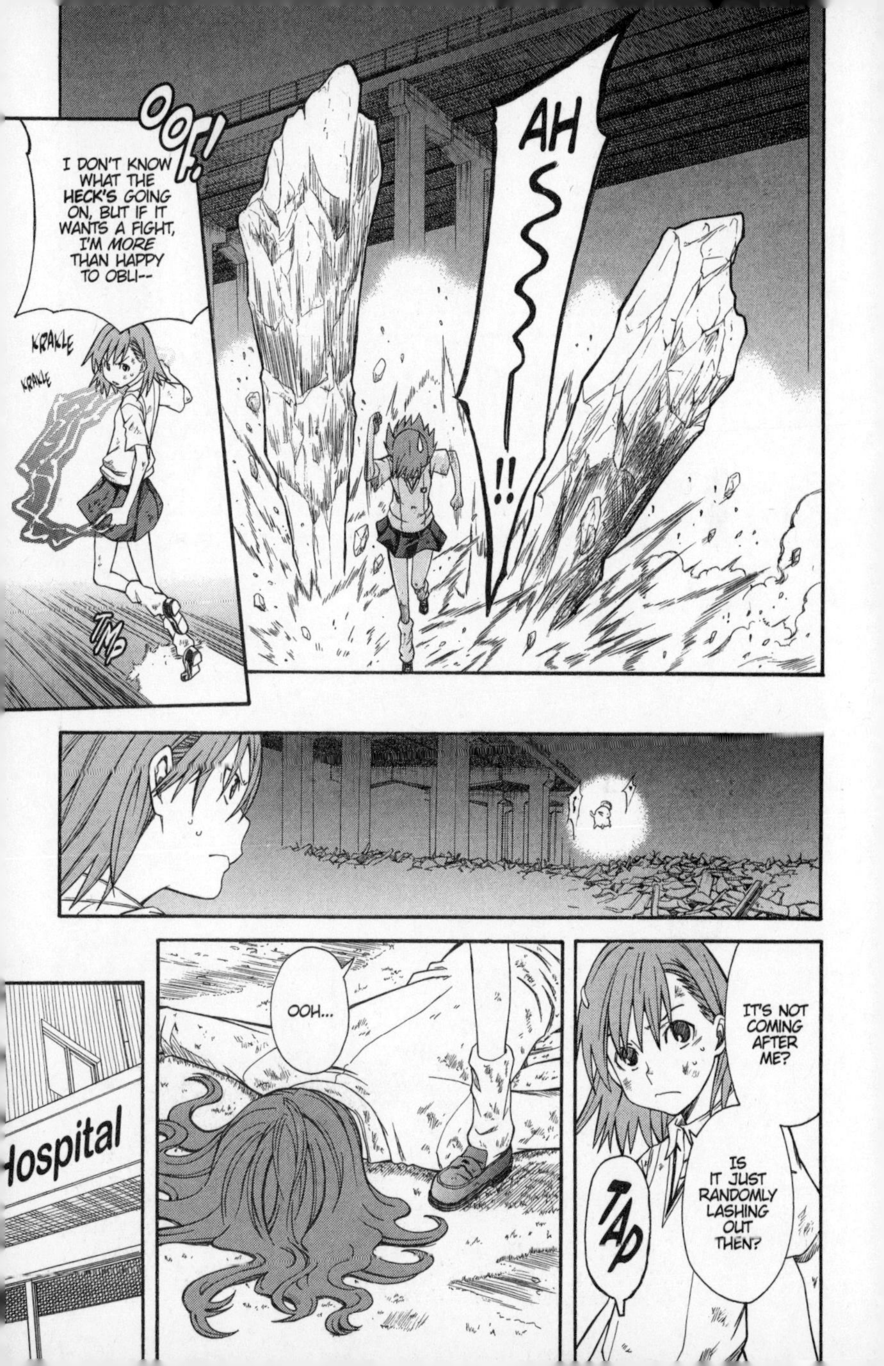
OOF!
AH~!!
I DON'T KNOW WHAT THE HECK'S GOING ON, BUT IF IT WANTS A FIGHT, I'M *MORE* THAN HAPPY TO OBLI--
KRAKLE
KRAKLE
TMP
IT'S NOT COMING AFTER ME?
TAP
IS IT JUST RANDOMLY LASHING OUT THEN?
OOH...
Hospital

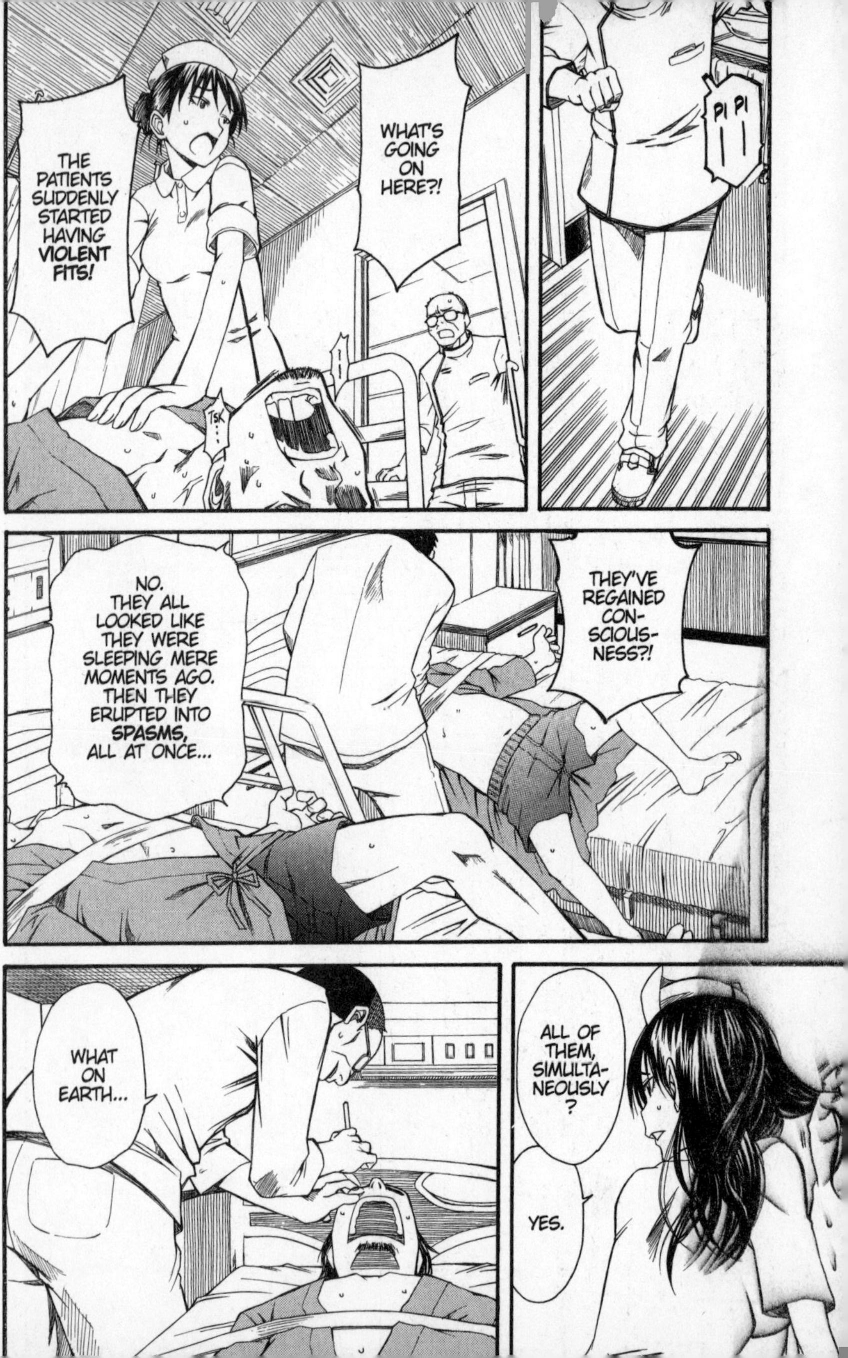
PI PI
WHAT'S GOING ON HERE?!
THE PATIENTS SUDDENLY STARTED HAVING VIOLENT FITS!
TSK...
THEY'VE REGAINED CON-SCIOUS-NESS?!
NO. THEY ALL LOOKED LIKE THEY WERE SLEEPING MERE MOMENTS AGO. THEN THEY ERUPTED INTO SPASMS, ALL AT ONCE...
ALL OF THEM, SIMULTA-NEOUSLY ?
YES.
WHAT ON EARTH...

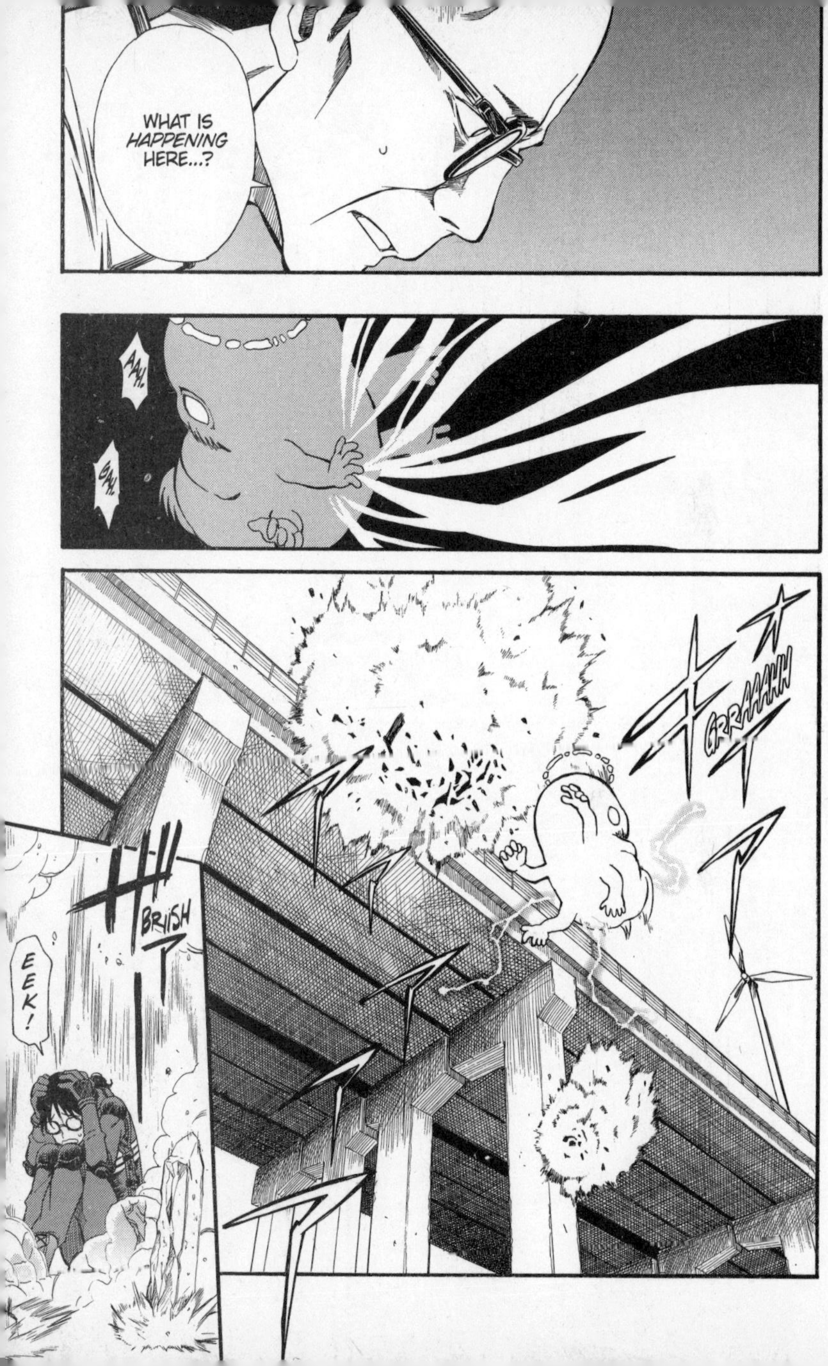
WHAT IS HAPPENING HERE...?
AAH!
BAH!
GRRAAAHH
BRIISH
EEK!

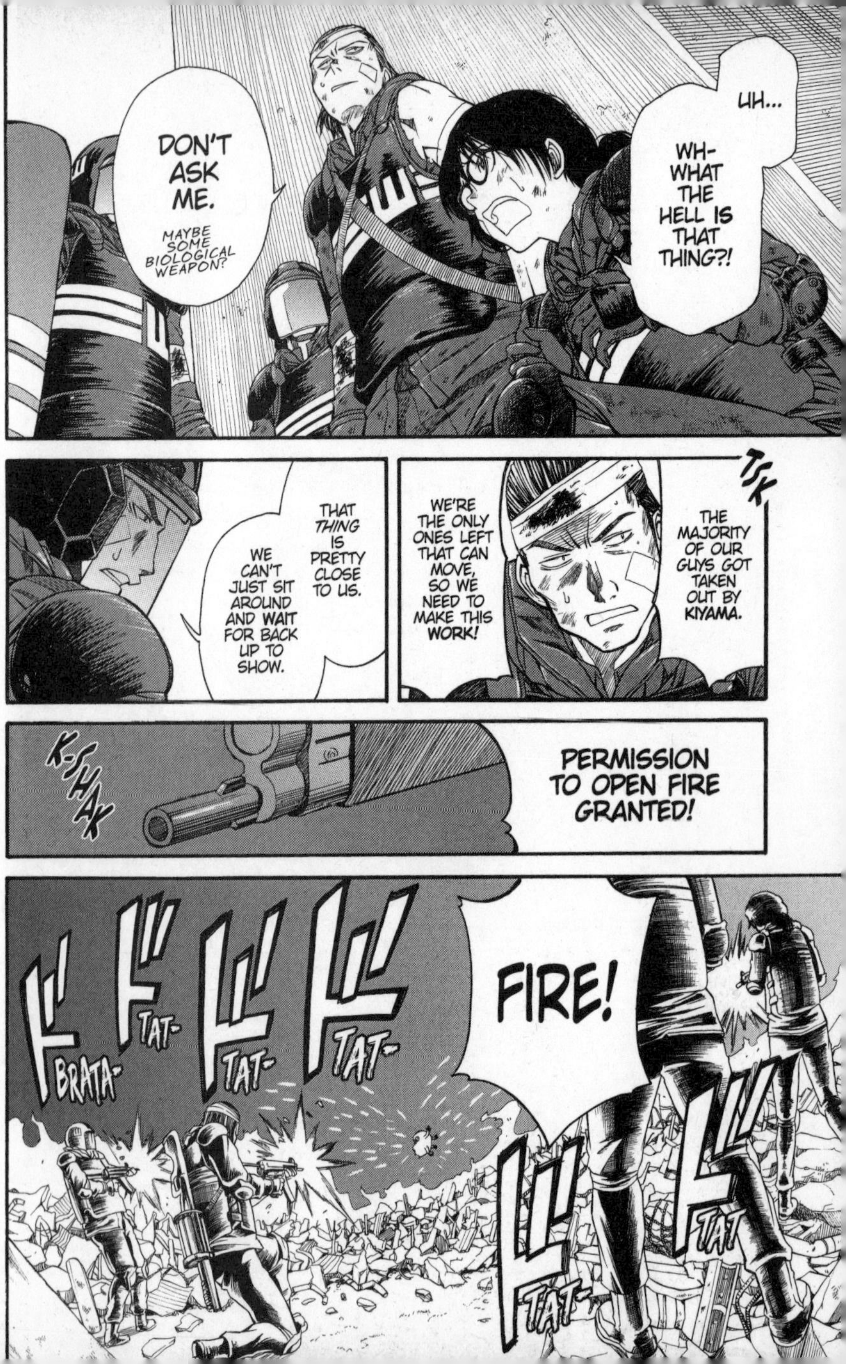
UH...
WH-WHAT THE HELL IS THAT THING?!
DON'T ASK ME.
MAYBE SOME BIOLOGICAL WEAPON?
TSK
THE MAJORITY OF OUR GUYS GOT TAKEN OUT BY KIYAMA.
WE'RE THE ONLY ONES LEFT THAT CAN MOVE, SO WE NEED TO MAKE THIS WORK!
THAT THING IS PRETTY CLOSE TO US.
WE CAN'T JUST SIT AROUND AND WAIT FOR BACK UP TO SHOW.
PERMISSION TO OPEN FIRE GRANTED!
K-SHAK
FIRE!
TAT- TAT
BRATA- TAT- TAT- TAT-

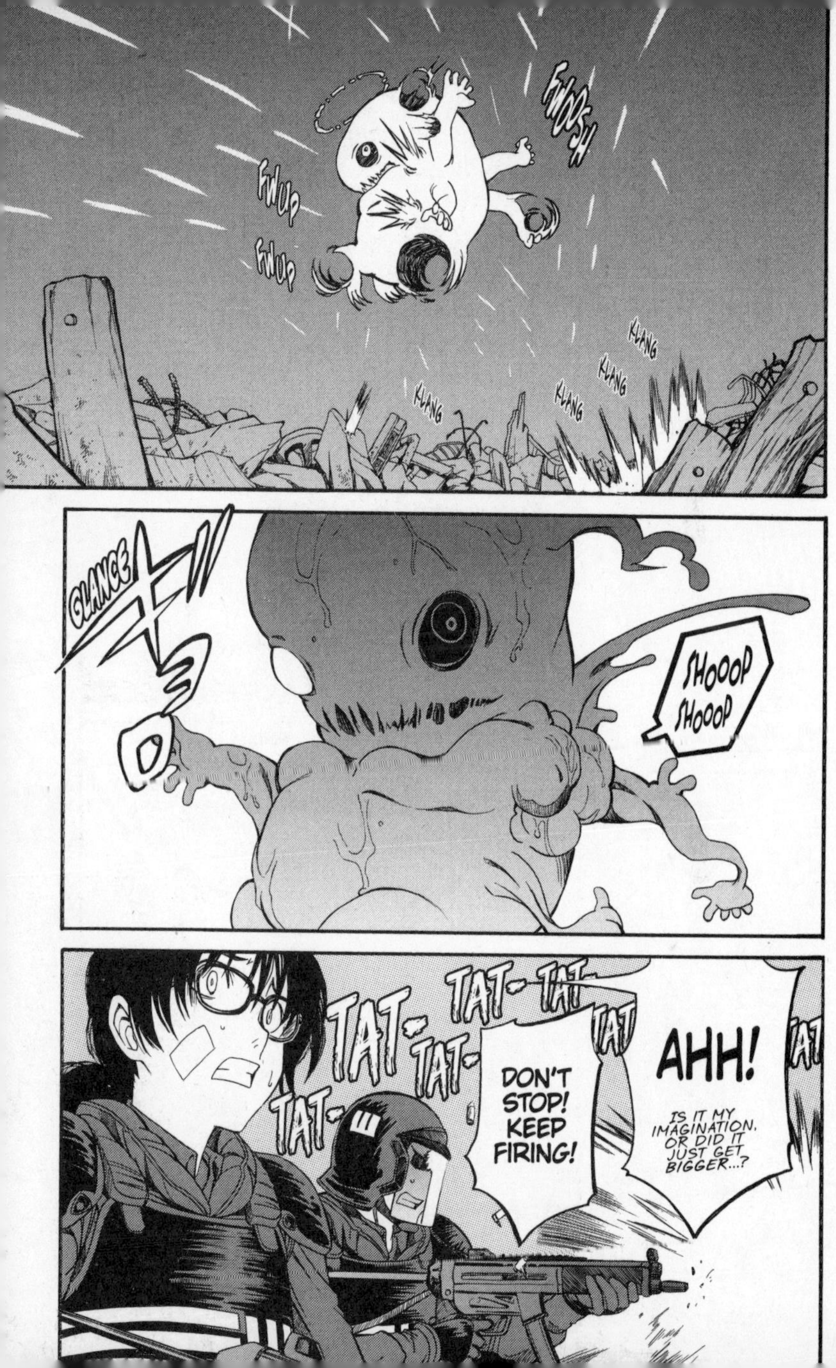
FWOOSH
FWUP
FWUP
KLANG
KLANG
KLANG
KLANG
SHOOOP SHOOOP
GLANCE
AHH!
IS IT MY IMAGINATION, OR DID IT JUST GET BIGGER...?
TAT-TAT-TAT
DON'T STOP! KEEP FIRING!
TAT-TAT-TAT-

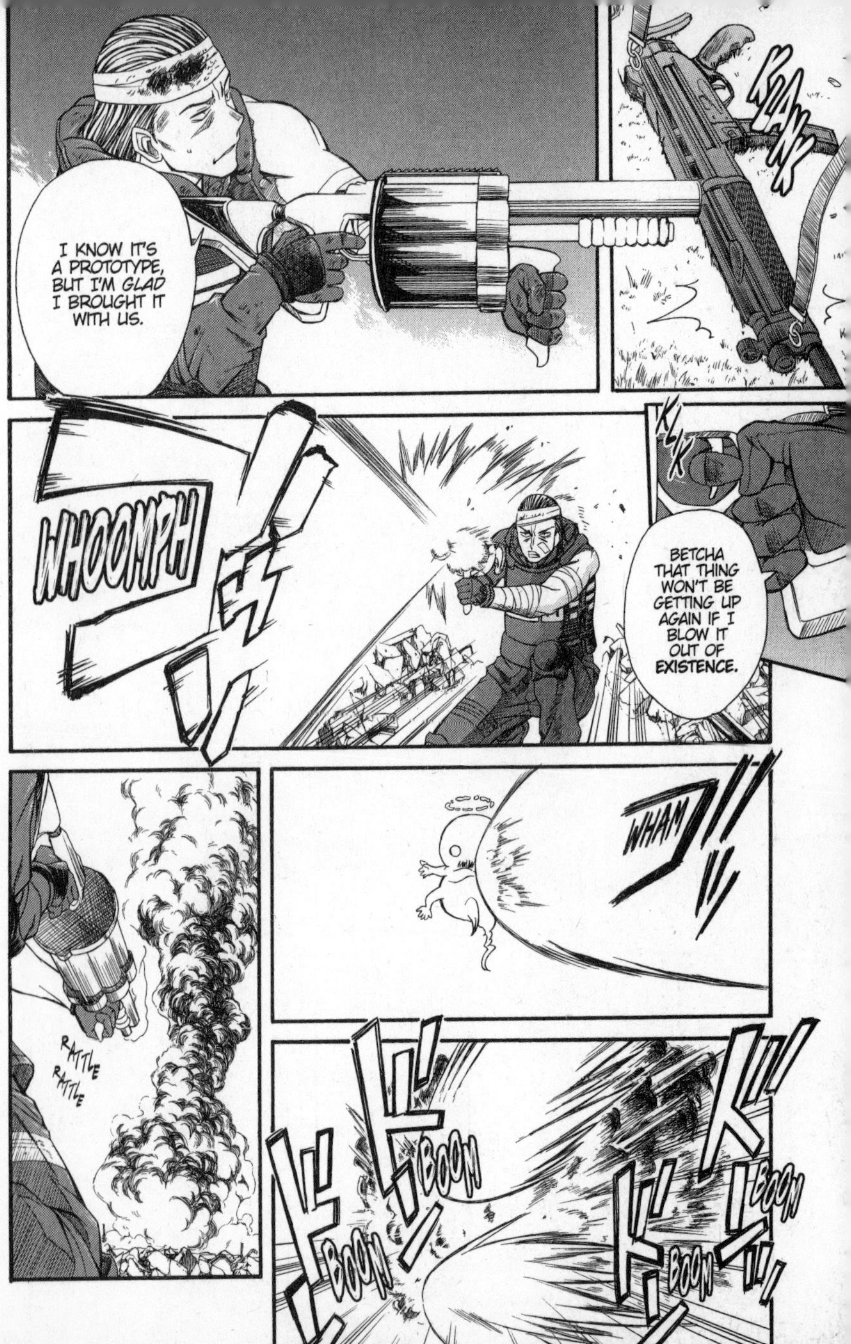
KLANK
I KNOW IT'S A PROTOTYPE, BUT I'M *GLAD* I BROUGHT IT WITH US.
KLIK
BETCHA THAT THING WON'T BE GETTING UP AGAIN IF I BLOW IT OUT OF EXISTENCE.
WHOOMPH
WHAM
BOOM
BOOM
BOOM
BOOM
RATTLE
RATTLE

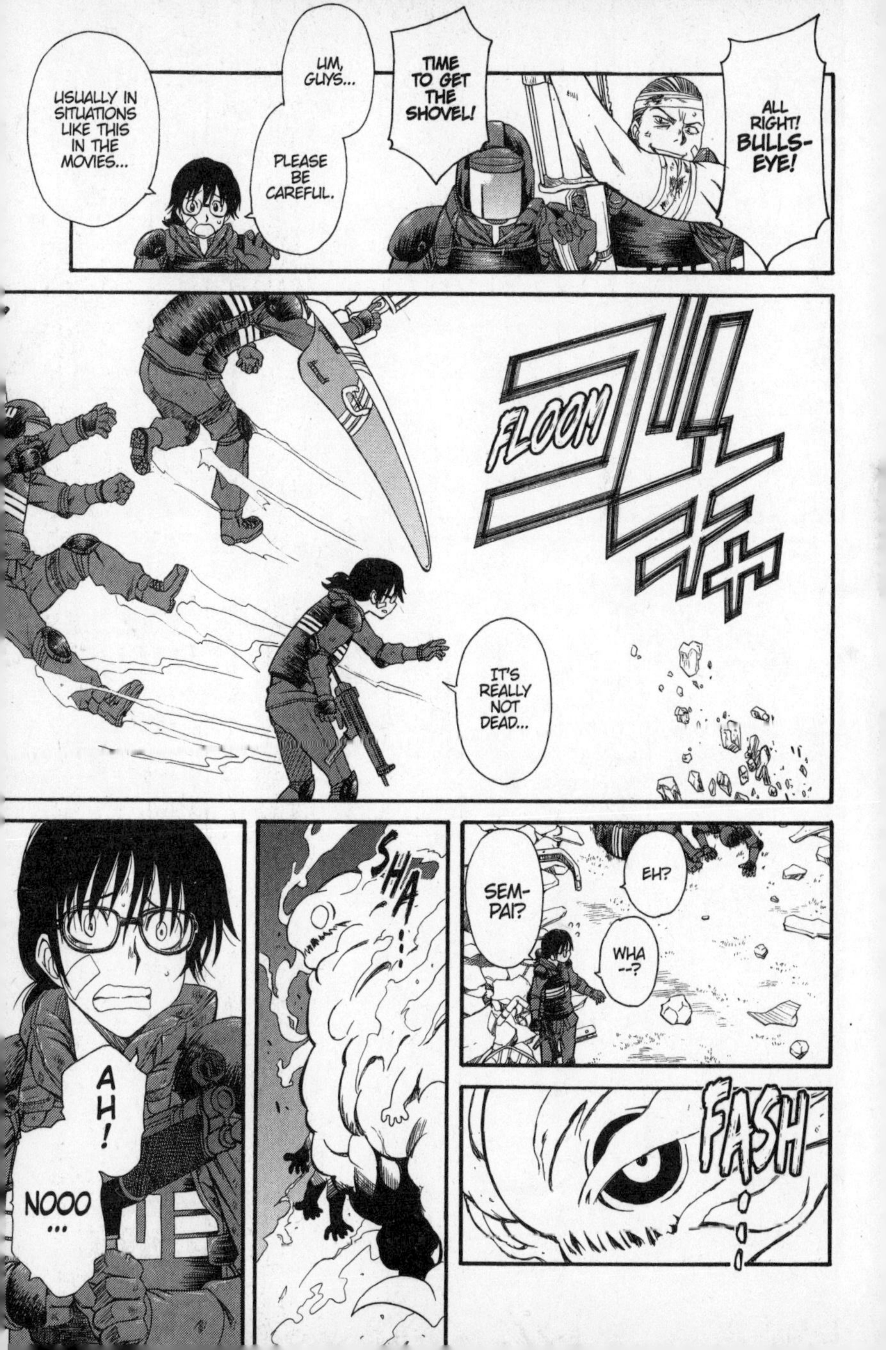
ALL RIGHT! BULLS-EYE!
TIME TO GET THE SHOVEL!
UM, GUYS... PLEASE BE CAREFUL.
USUALLY IN SITUATIONS LIKE THIS IN THE MOVIES...
FLOOM
IT'S REALLY NOT DEAD...
EH?
SEM-PAI?
WHA--?
FASH
SHA!!
AH!
NOOO...

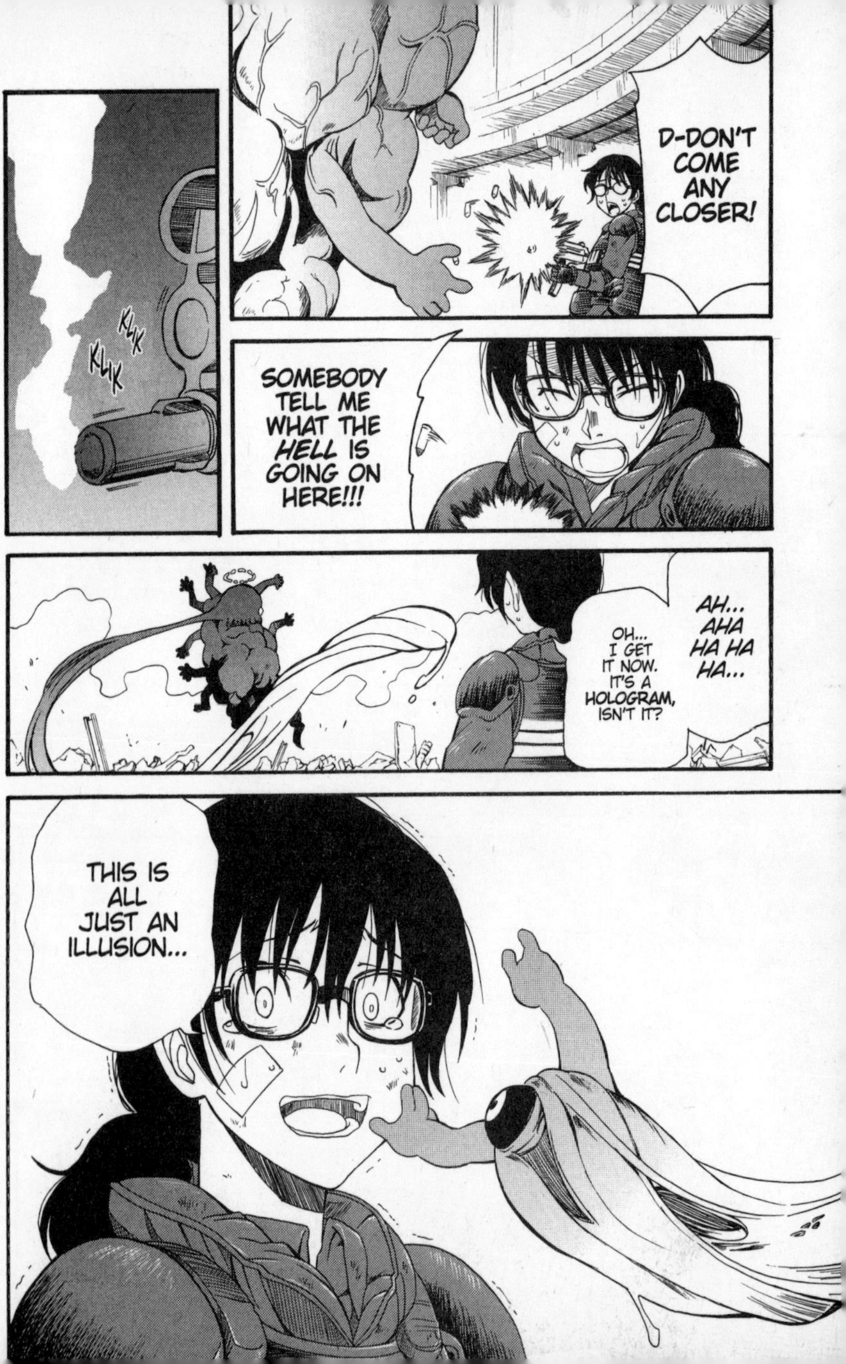
D-DON'T COME ANY CLOSER!
SOMEBODY TELL ME WHAT THE *HELL* IS GOING ON HERE!!!
KLIK KLIK
AH... AHA HA HA HA...
OH... I GET IT NOW. IT'S A HOLOGRAM, ISN'T IT?
THIS IS ALL JUST AN ILLUSION...

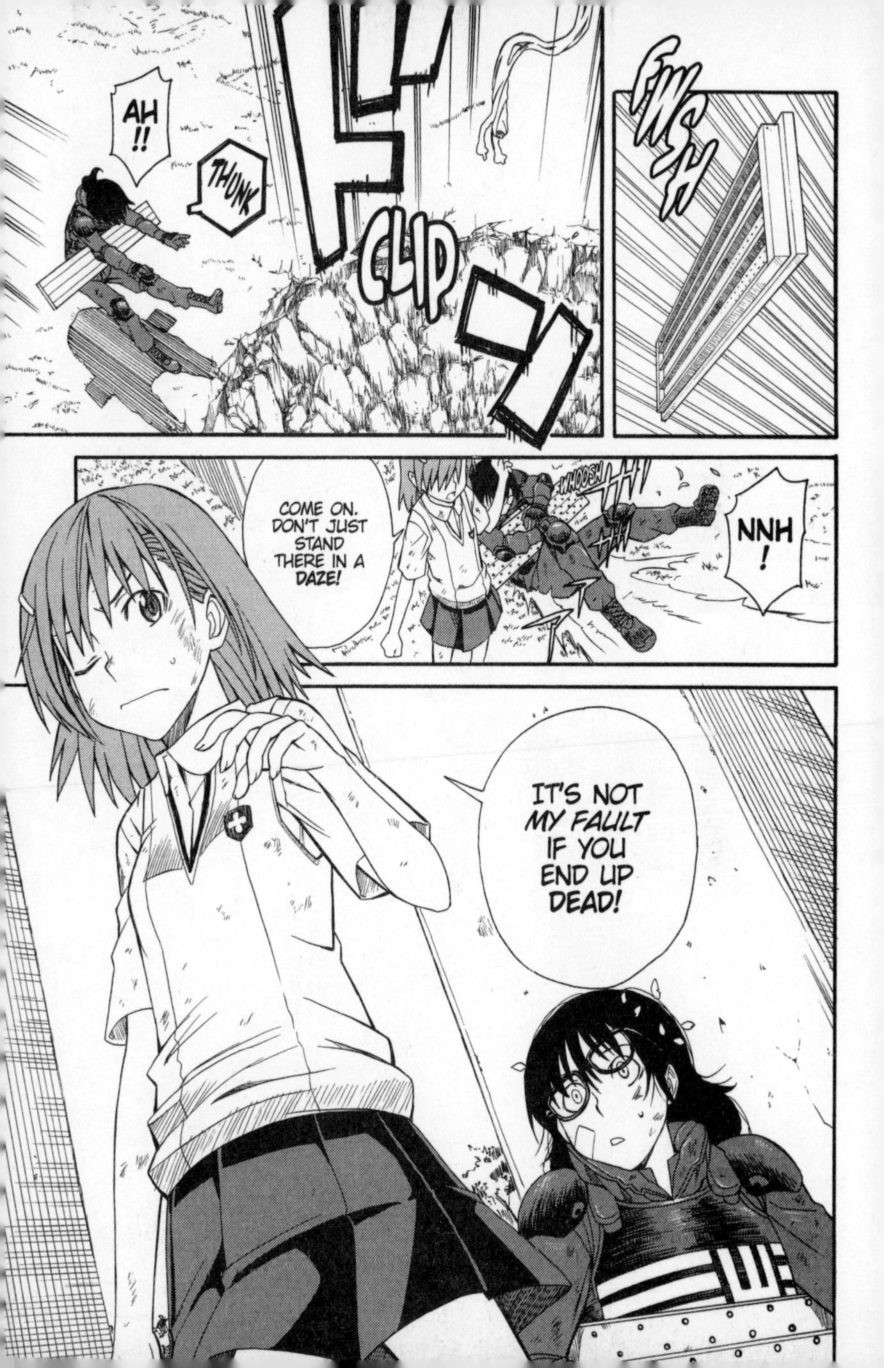
FWSH
CLIP
THUNK
AH!!
NNH!
WHOOSH
COME ON. DON'T JUST STAND THERE IN A DAZE!
IT'S NOT MY FAULT IF YOU END UP DEAD!

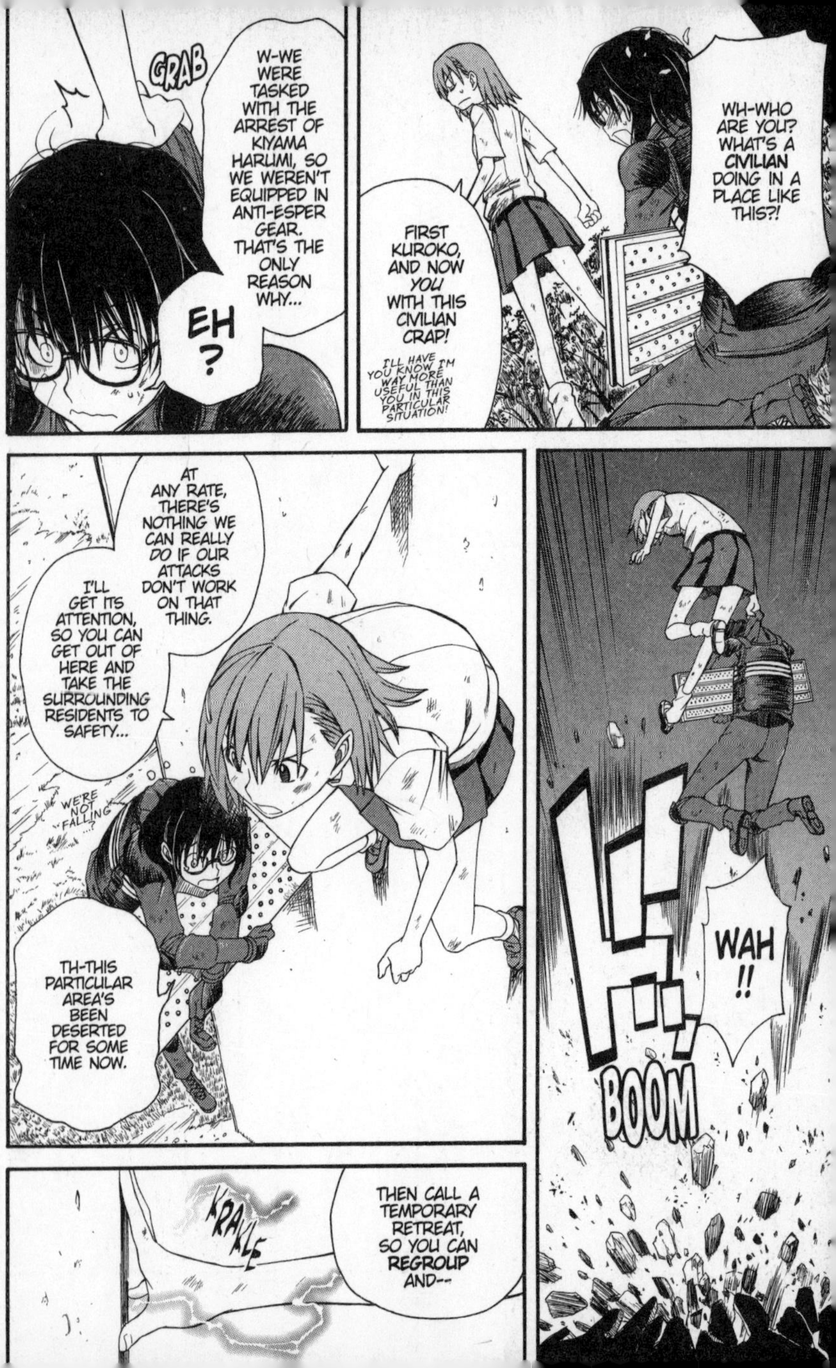
WH-WHO ARE YOU? WHAT'S A CIVILIAN DOING IN A PLACE LIKE THIS?!
FIRST KUROKO, AND NOW YOU WITH THIS CIVILIAN CRAP!
I'LL HAVE YOU KNOW I'M WAY MORE USEFUL THAN YOU IN THIS PARTICULAR SITUATION!
GRAB
W-WE WERE TASKED WITH THE ARREST OF KIYAMA HARUMI, SO WE WEREN'T EQUIPPED IN ANTI-ESPER GEAR. THAT'S THE ONLY REASON WHY...
EH?
WAH!!
BOOM
AT ANY RATE, THERE'S NOTHING WE CAN REALLY DO IF OUR ATTACKS DON'T WORK ON THAT THING.
I'LL GET ITS ATTENTION, SO YOU CAN GET OUT OF HERE AND TAKE THE SURROUNDING RESIDENTS TO SAFETY...
WE'RE NOT FALLING...?
TH-THIS PARTICULAR AREA'S BEEN DESERTED FOR SOME TIME NOW.
THEN CALL A TEMPORARY RETREAT, SO YOU CAN REGROUP AND--
KRAKLE

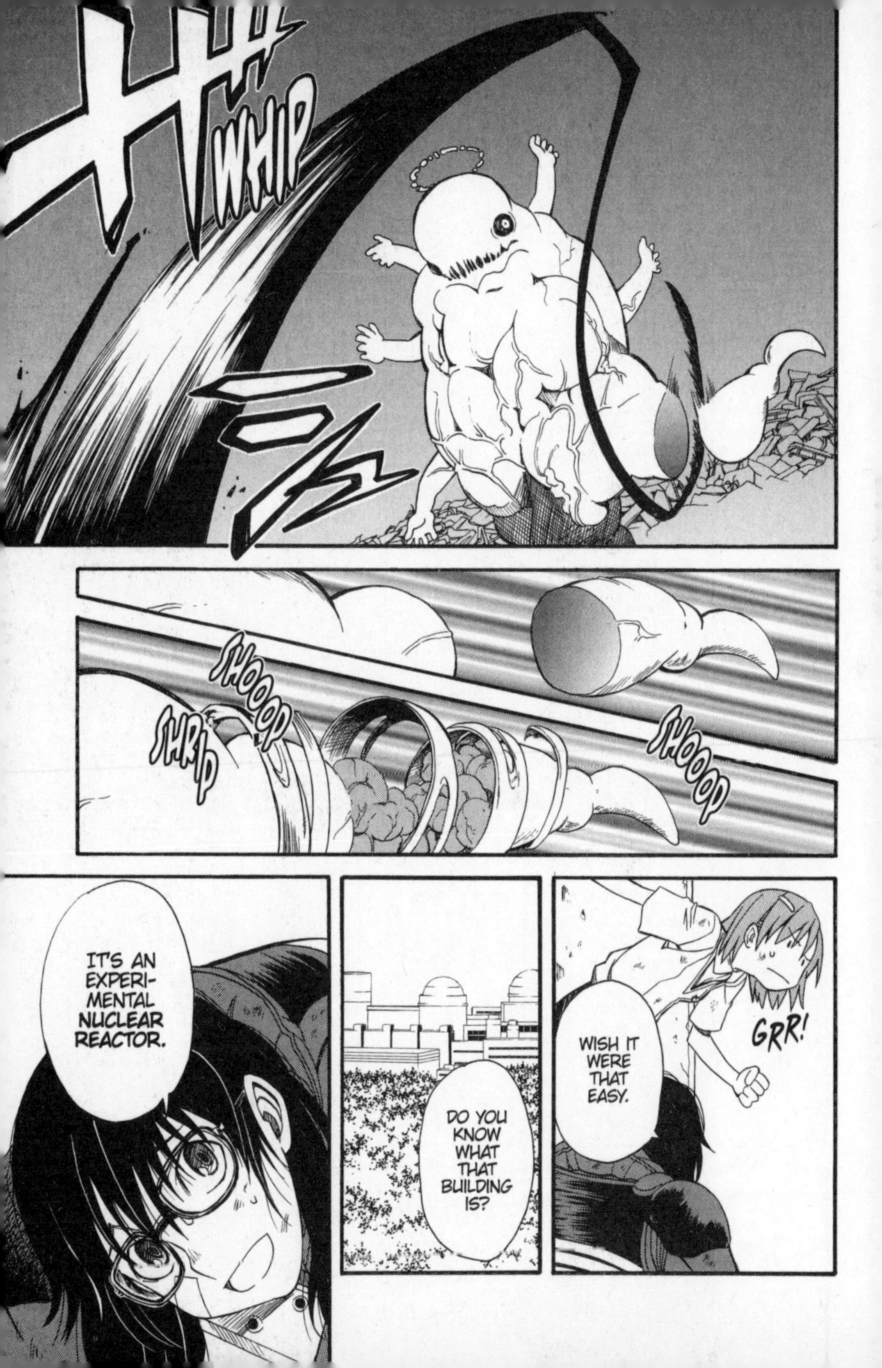
WHIP
SHOOOP
SHOOOP
SHRIP
GRR!
WISH IT WERE THAT EASY.
DO YOU KNOW WHAT THAT BUILDING IS?
IT'S AN EXPERI-MENTAL NUCLEAR REACTOR.

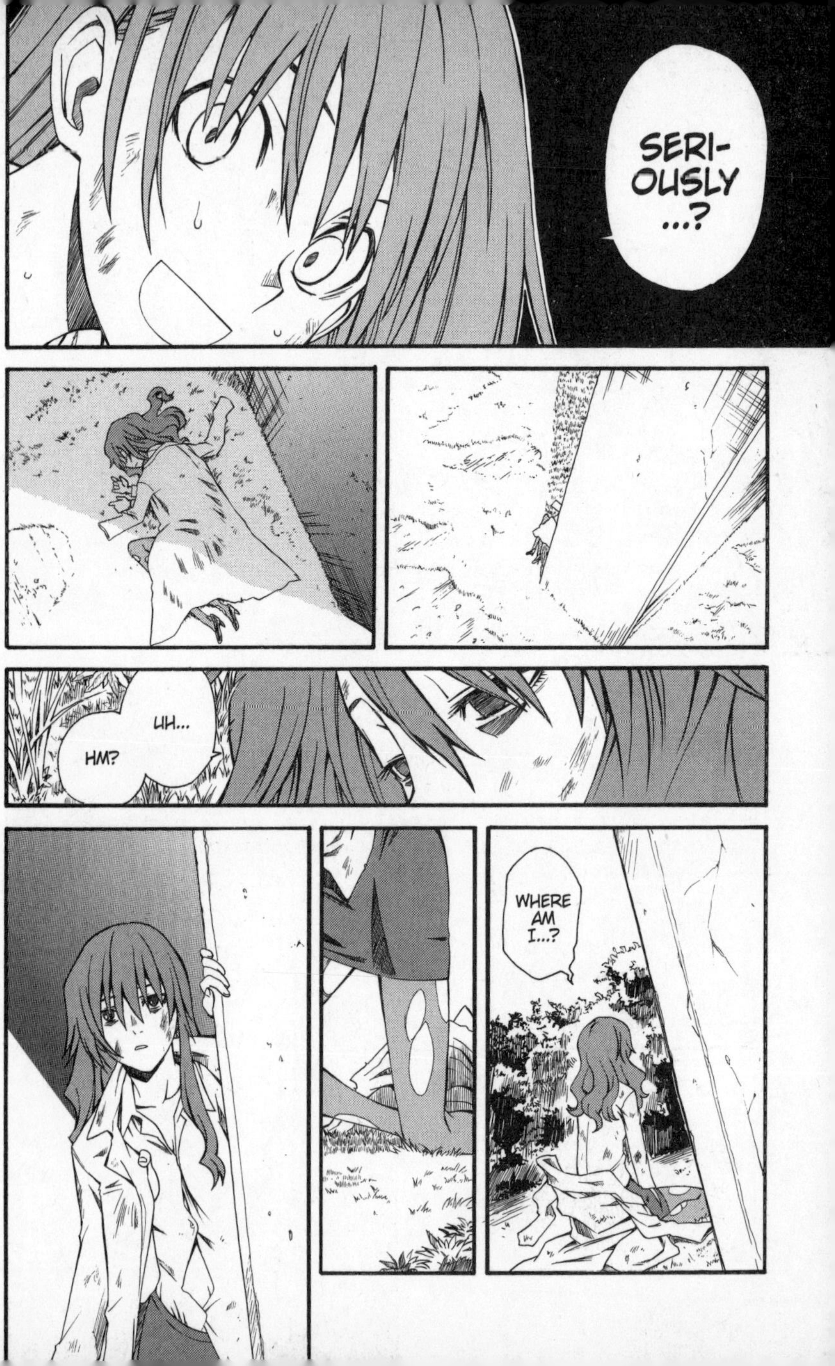
SERI-OUSLY ...?
UH... HM?
WHERE AM I...?

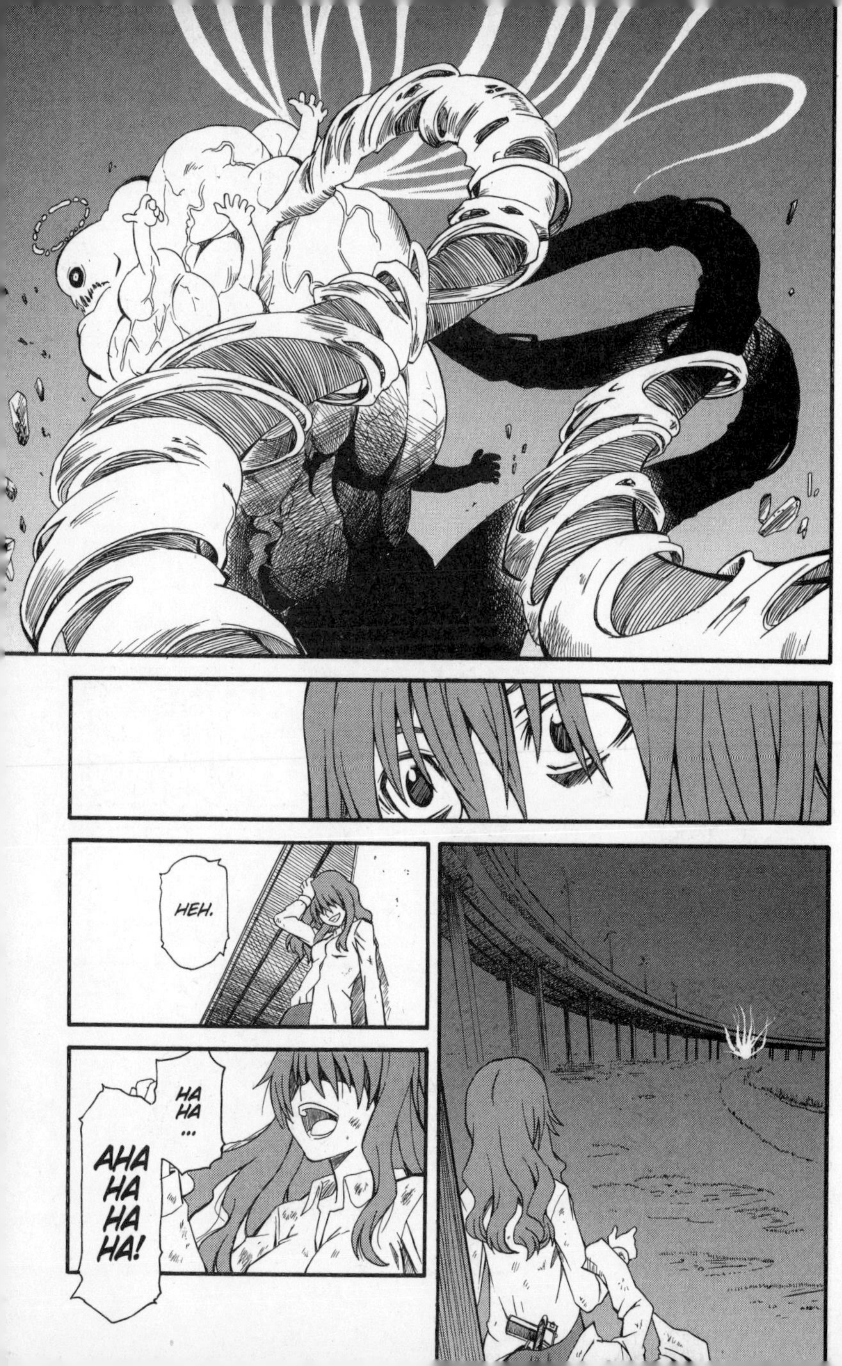
HEH.
HA HA ...
AHA HA HA HA!

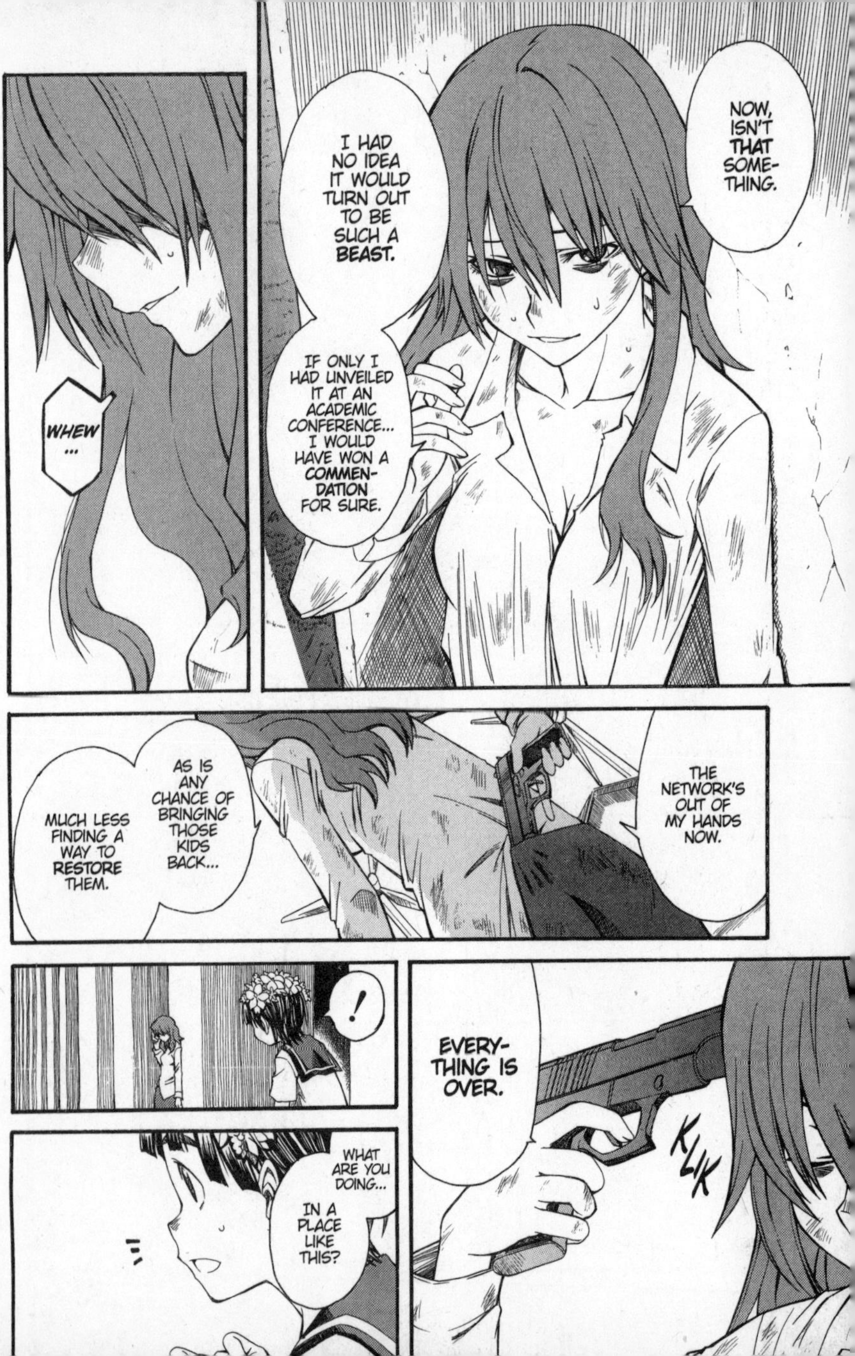
NOW, ISN'T THAT SOME-THING.
I HAD NO IDEA IT WOULD TURN OUT TO BE SUCH A BEAST.
IF ONLY I HAD UNVEILED IT AT AN ACADEMIC CONFERENCE... I WOULD HAVE WON A COMMEN-DATION FOR SURE.
WHEW ...
THE NETWORK'S OUT OF MY HANDS NOW.
AS IS ANY CHANCE OF BRINGING THOSE KIDS BACK...
MUCH LESS FINDING A WAY TO RESTORE THEM.
EVERY-THING IS OVER.
KLIK
!
WHAT ARE YOU DOING...
IN A PLACE LIKE THIS?

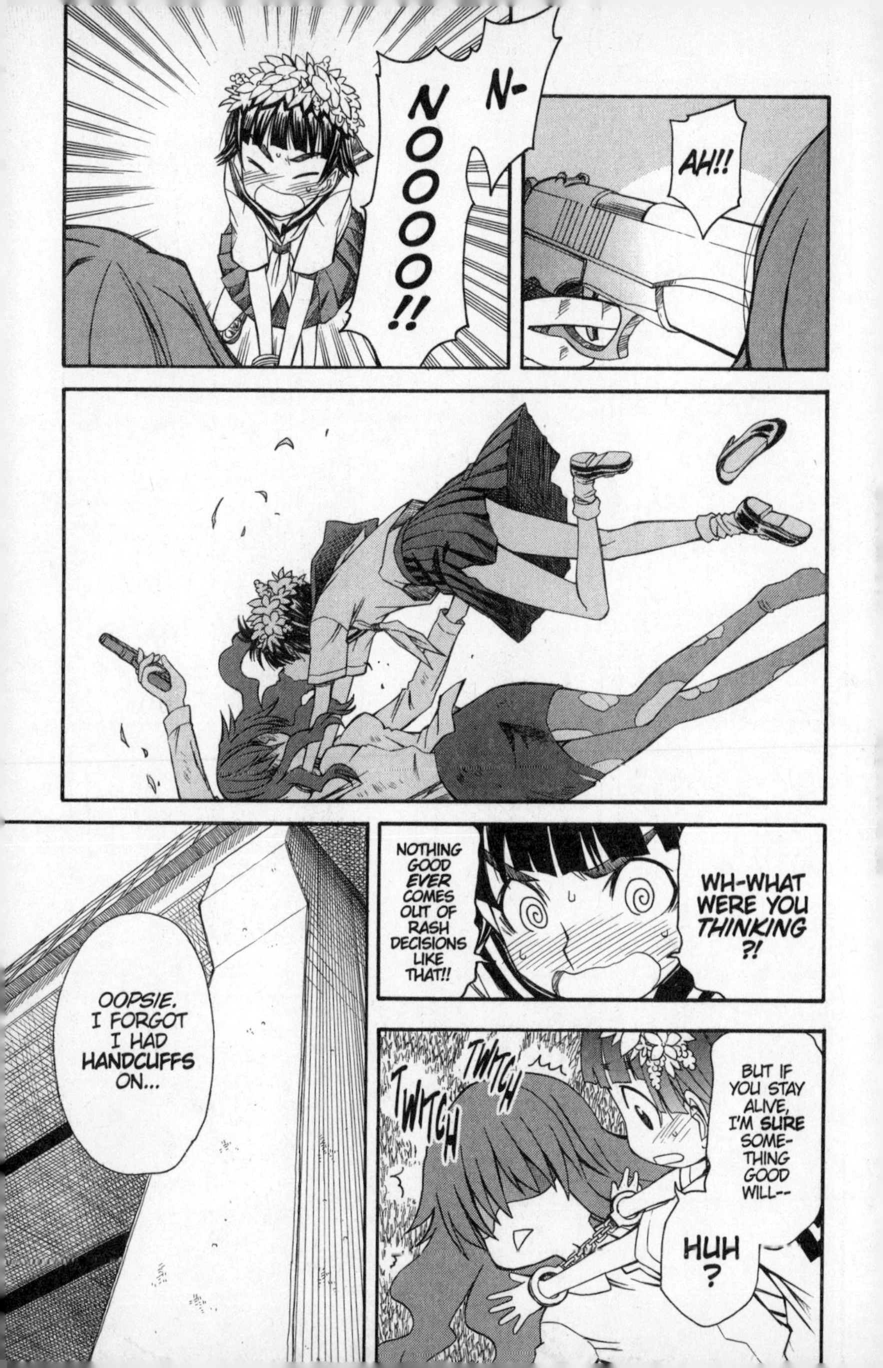
AH!!
N-NOOOOO!!
WH-WHAT WERE YOU THINKING?!
NOTHING GOOD EVER COMES OUT OF RASH DECISIONS LIKE THAT!!
BUT IF YOU STAY ALIVE, I'M SURE SOMETHING GOOD WILL--
TWITCH
TWITCH
HUH?
OOPSIE. I FORGOT I HAD HANDCUFFS ON...

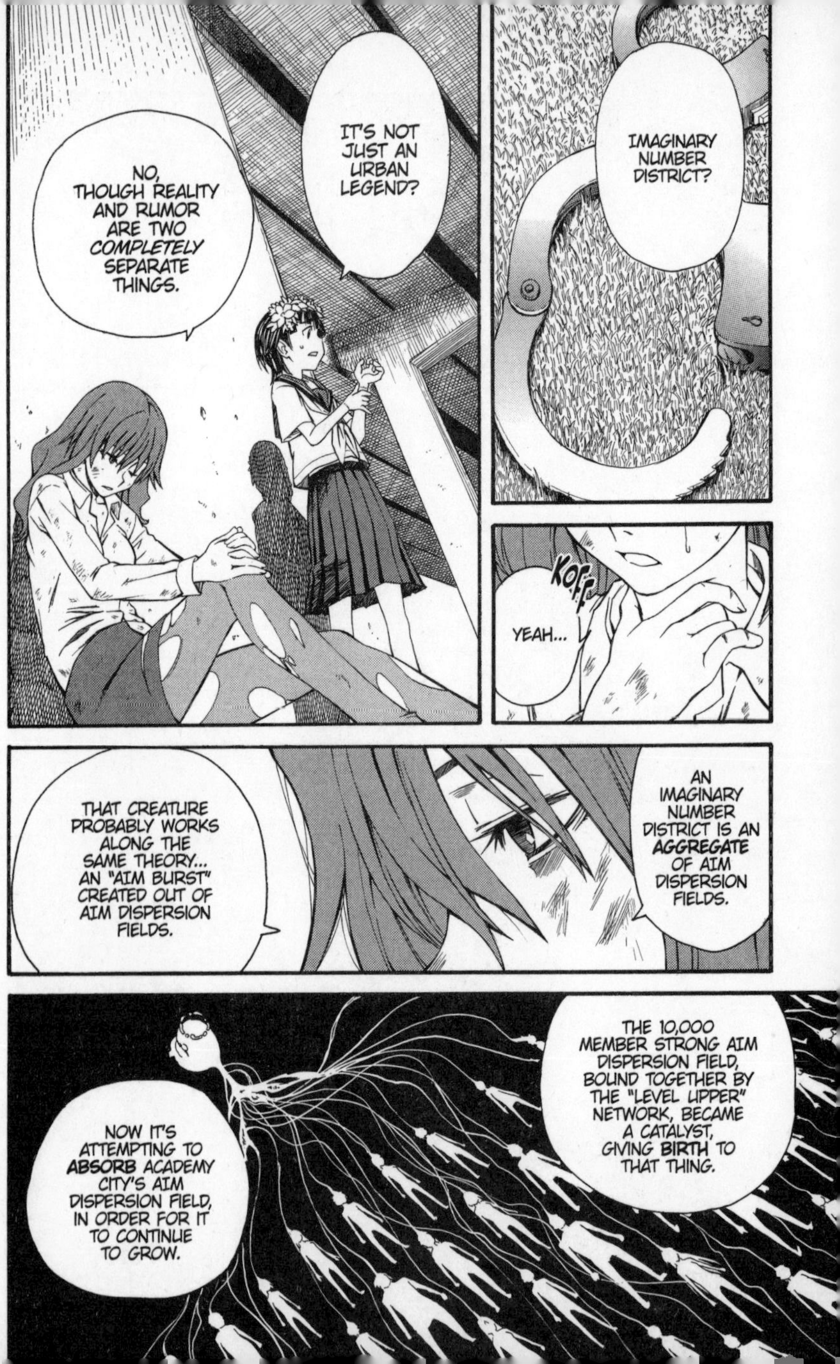
IMAGINARY NUMBER DISTRICT?
KOFF
YEAH...
IT'S NOT JUST AN URBAN LEGEND?
NO, THOUGH REALITY AND RUMOR ARE TWO COMPLETELY SEPARATE THINGS.
AN IMAGINARY NUMBER DISTRICT IS AN AGGREGATE OF AIM DISPERSION FIELDS.
THAT CREATURE PROBABLY WORKS ALONG THE SAME THEORY... AN "AIM BURST" CREATED OUT OF AIM DISPERSION FIELDS.
THE 10,000 MEMBER STRONG AIM DISPERSION FIELD, BOUND TOGETHER BY THE "LEVEL UPPER" NETWORK, BECAME A CATALYST, GIVING BIRTH TO THAT THING.
NOW IT'S ATTEMPTING TO ABSORB ACADEMY CITY'S AIM DISPERSION FIELD, IN ORDER FOR IT TO CONTINUE TO GROW.

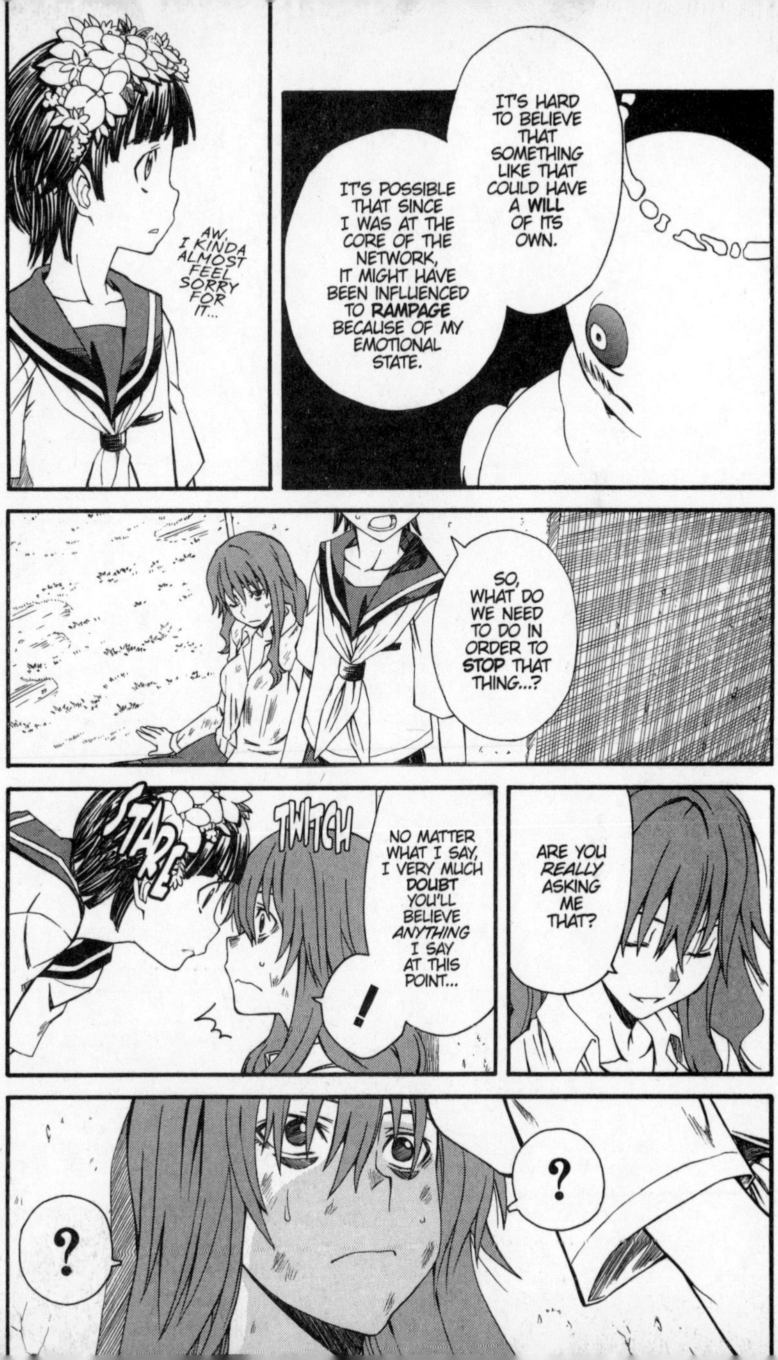
IT'S HARD TO BELIEVE THAT SOMETHING LIKE THAT COULD HAVE A **WILL** OF ITS OWN.
IT'S POSSIBLE THAT SINCE I WAS AT THE CORE OF THE NETWORK, IT MIGHT HAVE BEEN INFLUENCED TO **RAMPAGE** BECAUSE OF MY EMOTIONAL STATE.
AW, I KINDA ALMOST FEEL SORRY FOR IT...
SO, WHAT DO WE NEED TO DO IN ORDER TO **STOP** THAT THING...?
ARE YOU *REALLY* ASKING ME THAT?
NO MATTER WHAT I SAY, I VERY MUCH **DOUBT** YOU'LL BELIEVE *ANYTHING* I SAY AT THIS POINT...
TWITCH
STARE
!
?
?

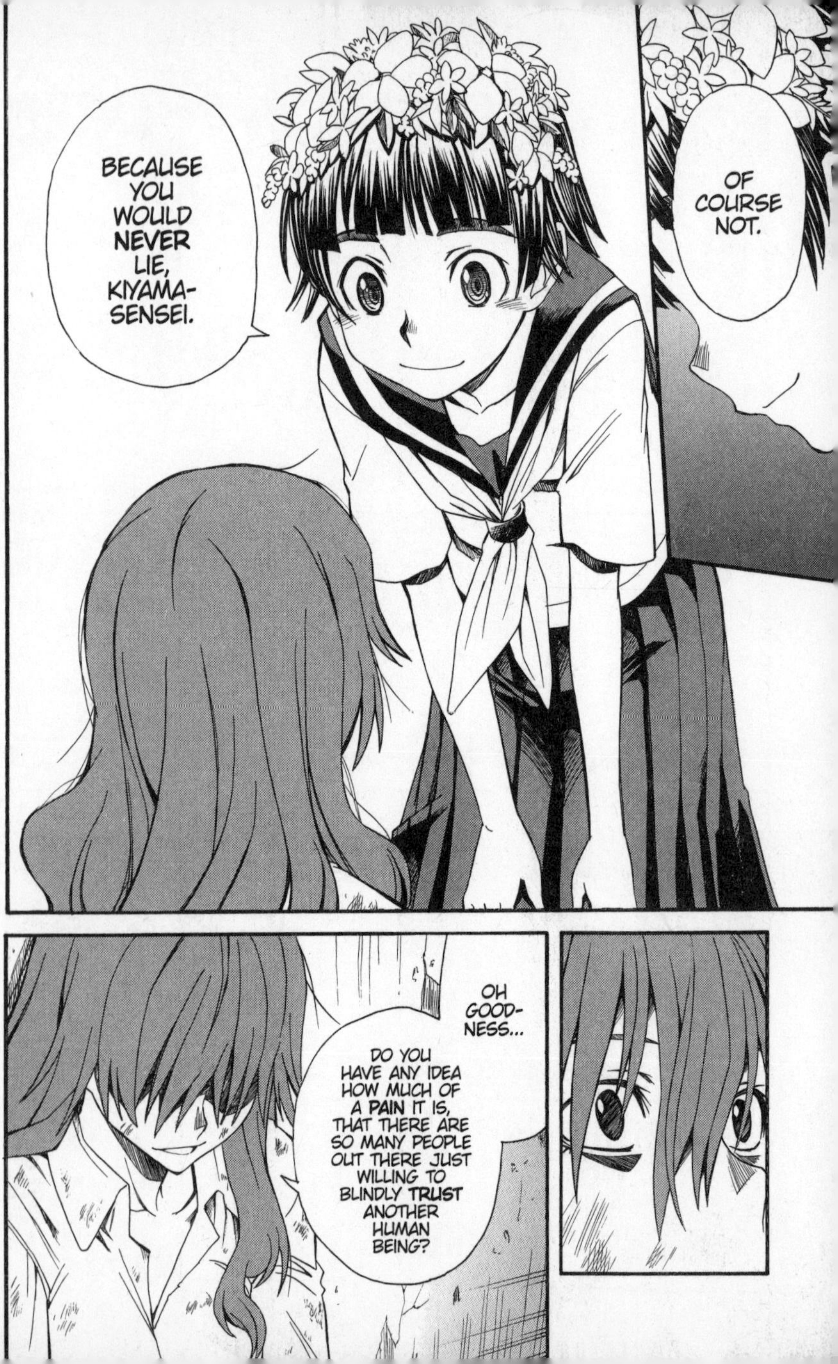
OF COURSE NOT.
BECAUSE YOU WOULD NEVER LIE, KIYAMA-SENSEI.
OH GOODNESS...
DO YOU HAVE ANY IDEA HOW MUCH OF A PAIN IT IS, THAT THERE ARE SO MANY PEOPLE OUT THERE JUST WILLING TO BLINDLY TRUST ANOTHER HUMAN BEING?

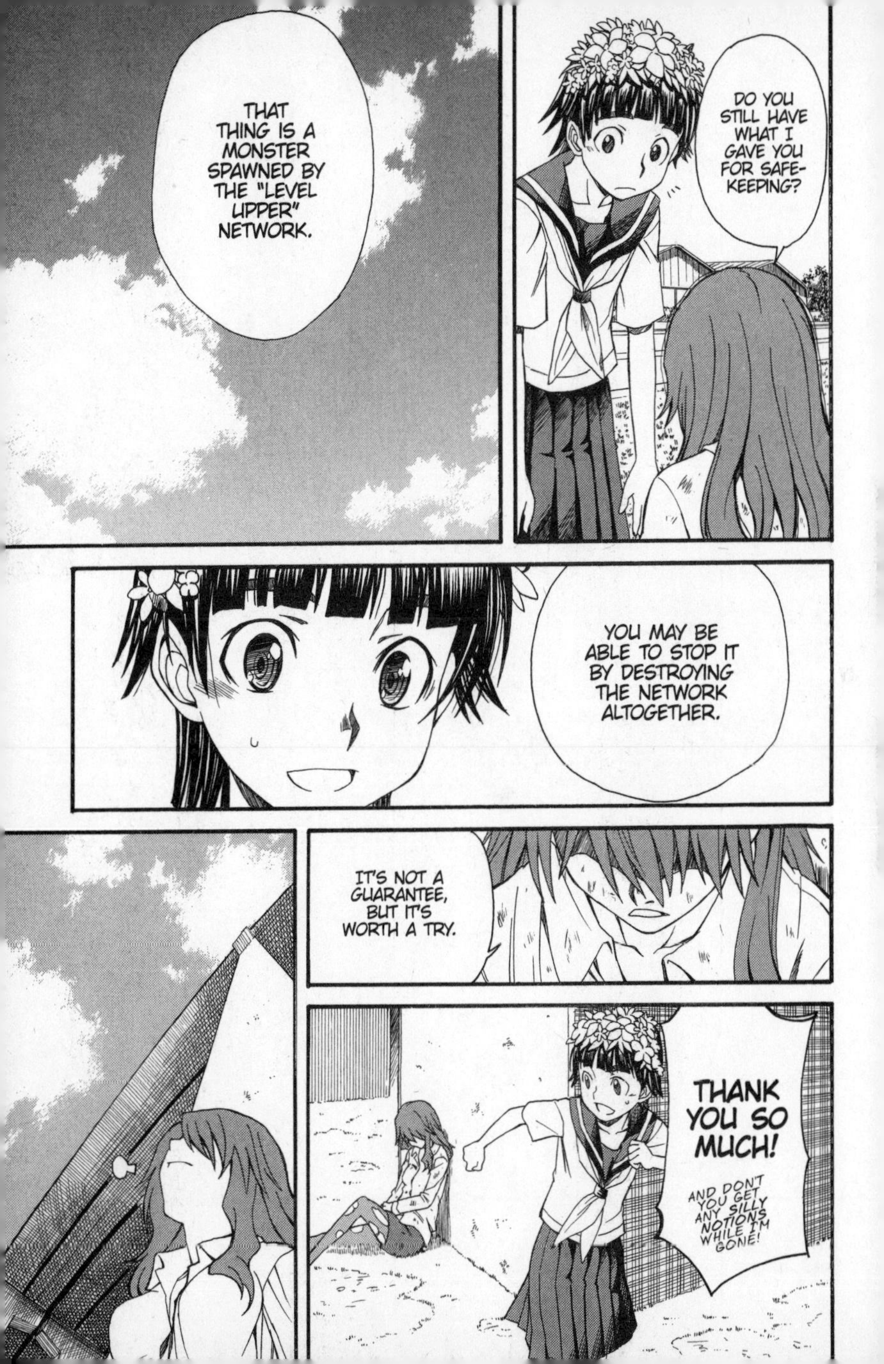

DO YOU STILL HAVE WHAT I GAVE YOU FOR SAFE-KEEPING?
THAT THING IS A MONSTER SPAWNED BY THE "LEVEL UPPER" NETWORK.
YOU MAY BE ABLE TO STOP IT BY DESTROYING THE NETWORK ALTOGETHER.
IT'S NOT A GUARANTEE, BUT IT'S WORTH A TRY.
THANK YOU SO MUCH!
AND DON'T YOU GET ANY SILLY NOTIONS WHILE I'M GONE!

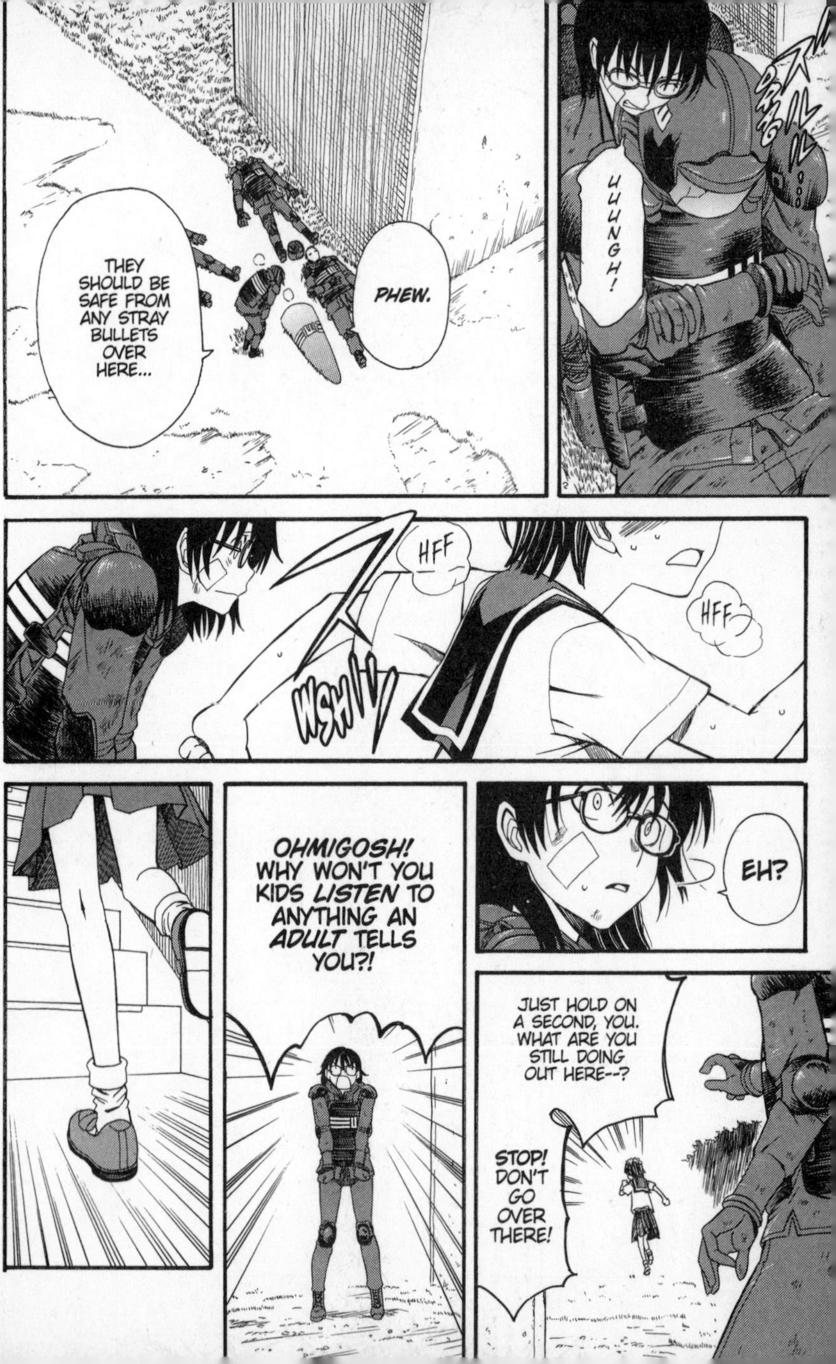
UUUNGH!
PHEW.
THEY SHOULD BE SAFE FROM ANY STRAY BULLETS OVER HERE...
HFF
HFF
WSH
EH?
JUST HOLD ON A SECOND, YOU. WHAT ARE YOU STILL DOING OUT HERE--?
STOP! DON'T GO OVER THERE!
OHMIGOSH! WHY WON'T YOU KIDS *LISTEN* TO ANYTHING AN *ADULT* TELLS YOU?!

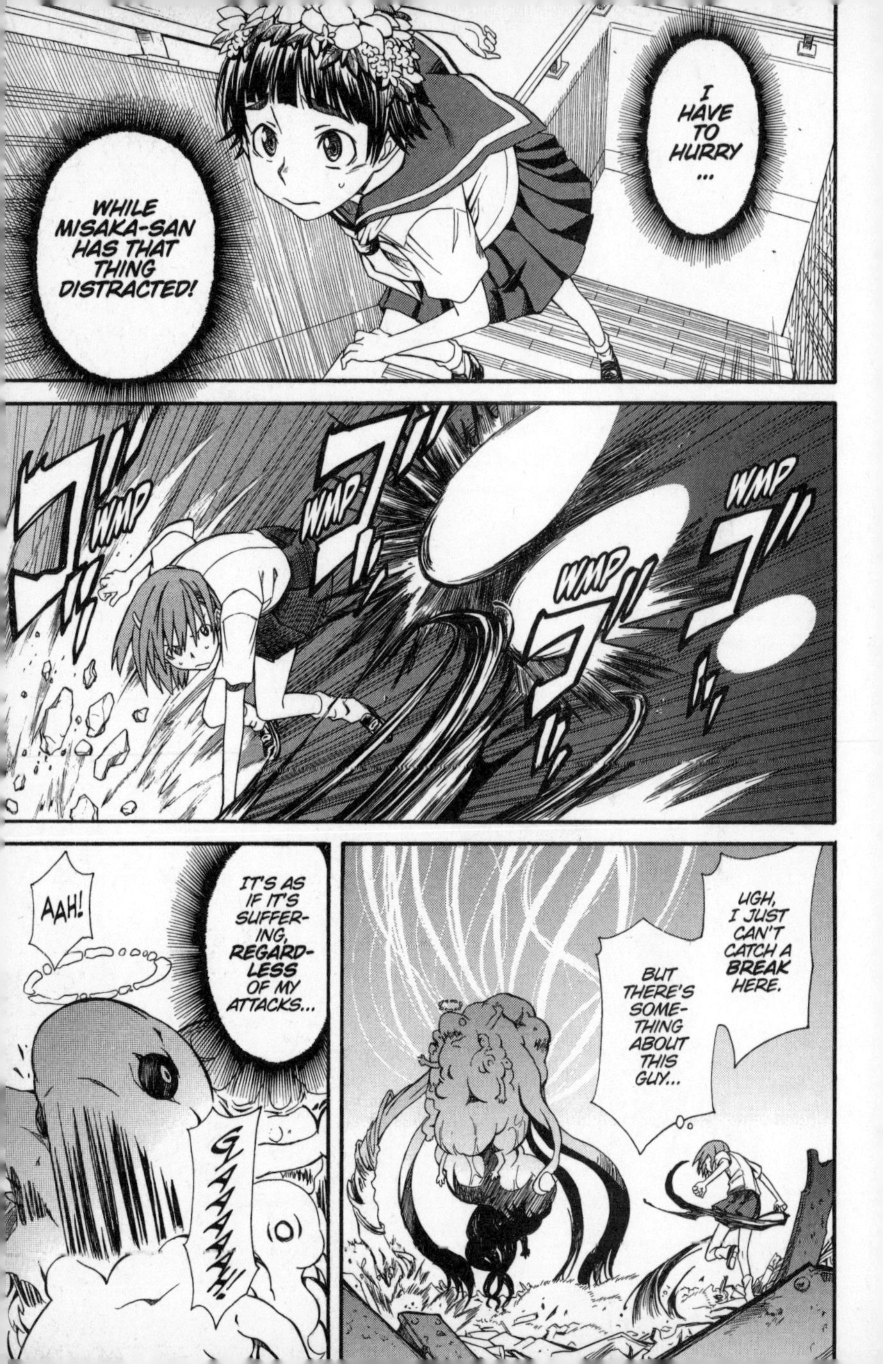
I HAVE TO HURRY ...
WHILE MISAKA-SAN HAS THAT THING DISTRACTED!
WMP
WMP
WMP
WMP
UGH, I JUST CAN'T CATCH A **BREAK** HERE.
BUT THERE'S SOMETHING ABOUT THIS GUY...
IT'S AS IF IT'S SUFFERING, **REGARDLESS OF MY ATTACKS...**
AAH!
GIAAAAAAAH!

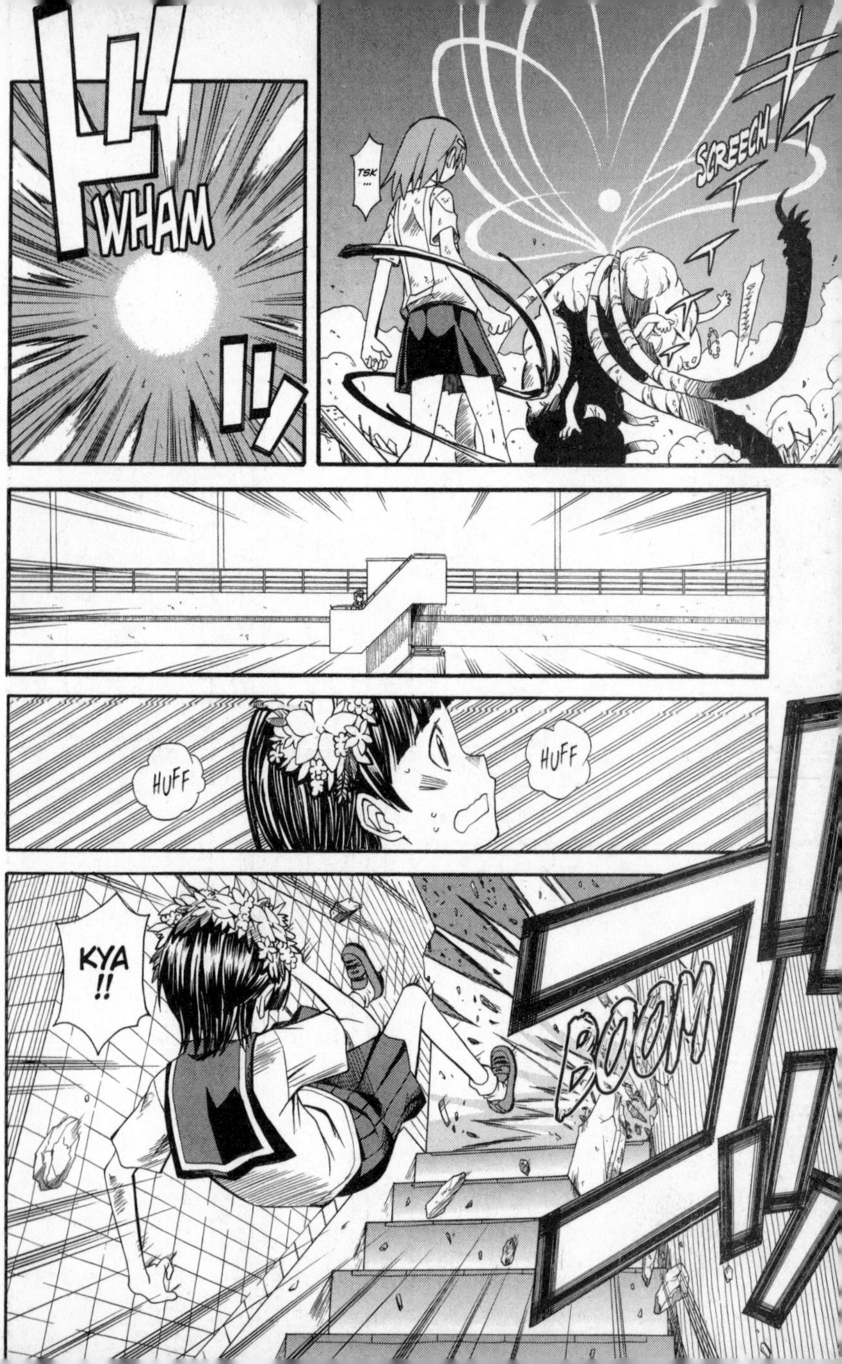

TSK
...
SCREECH
WHAM
HUFF
HUFF
KYA
!!
BOOM

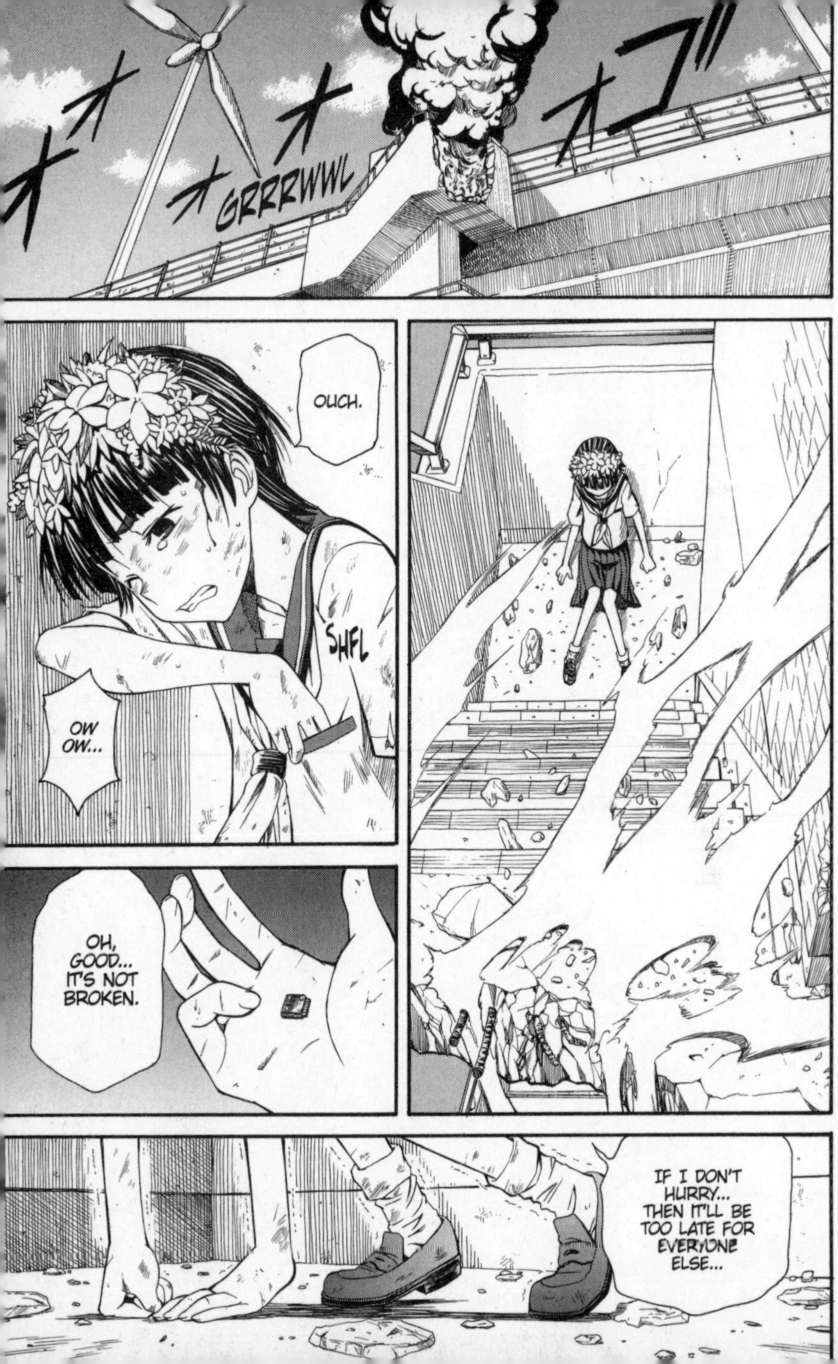
ゴオオオオオ
GRRRWWL
OUCH.
SHFL
OW OW...
OH, GOOD... IT'S NOT BROKEN.
IF I DON'T HURRY... THEN IT'LL BE TOO LATE FOR EVERYONE ELSE...

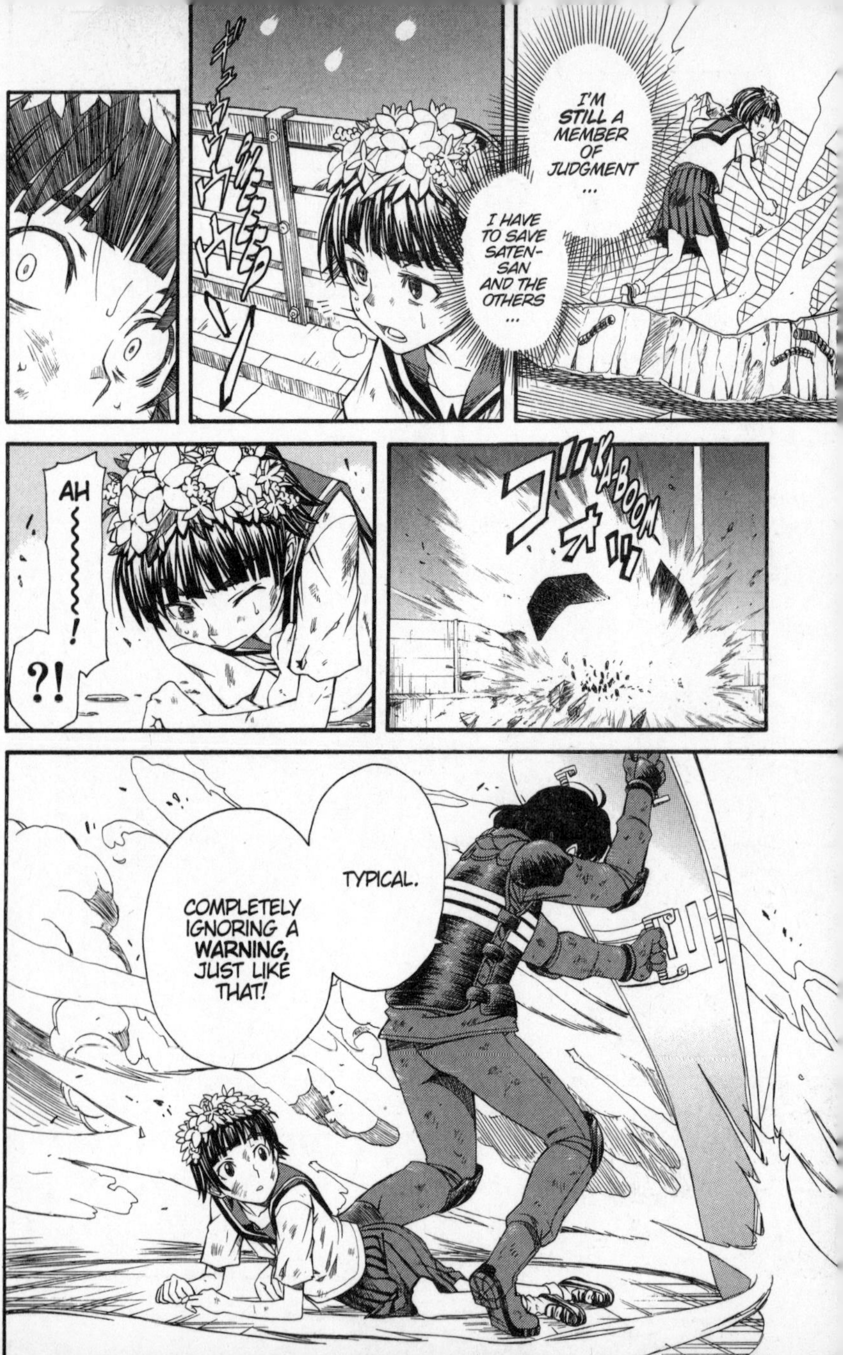
I'M STILL A MEMBER OF JUDGMENT ...
I HAVE TO SAVE SATEN-SAN AND THE OTHERS ...
KABOOM
AH ~~~~~!
?!
TYPICAL.
COMPLETELY IGNORING A WARNING, JUST LIKE THAT!

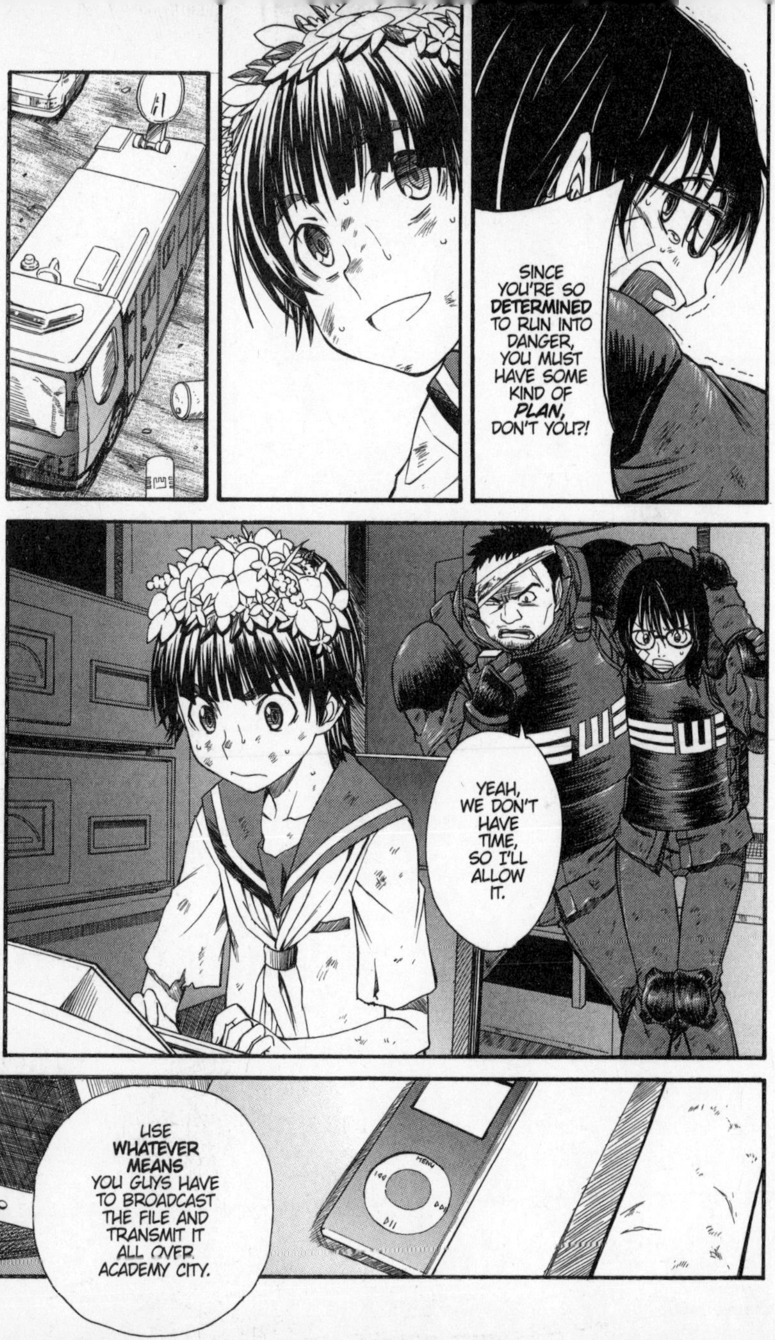
SINCE YOU'RE SO **DETERMINED** TO RUN INTO DANGER, YOU MUST HAVE SOME KIND OF ***PLAN,*** DON'T YOU?!
YEAH, WE DON'T HAVE TIME, SO I'LL ALLOW IT.
USE **WHATEVER MEANS** YOU GUYS HAVE TO BROADCAST THE FILE AND TRANSMIT IT ALL OVER ACADEMY CITY.

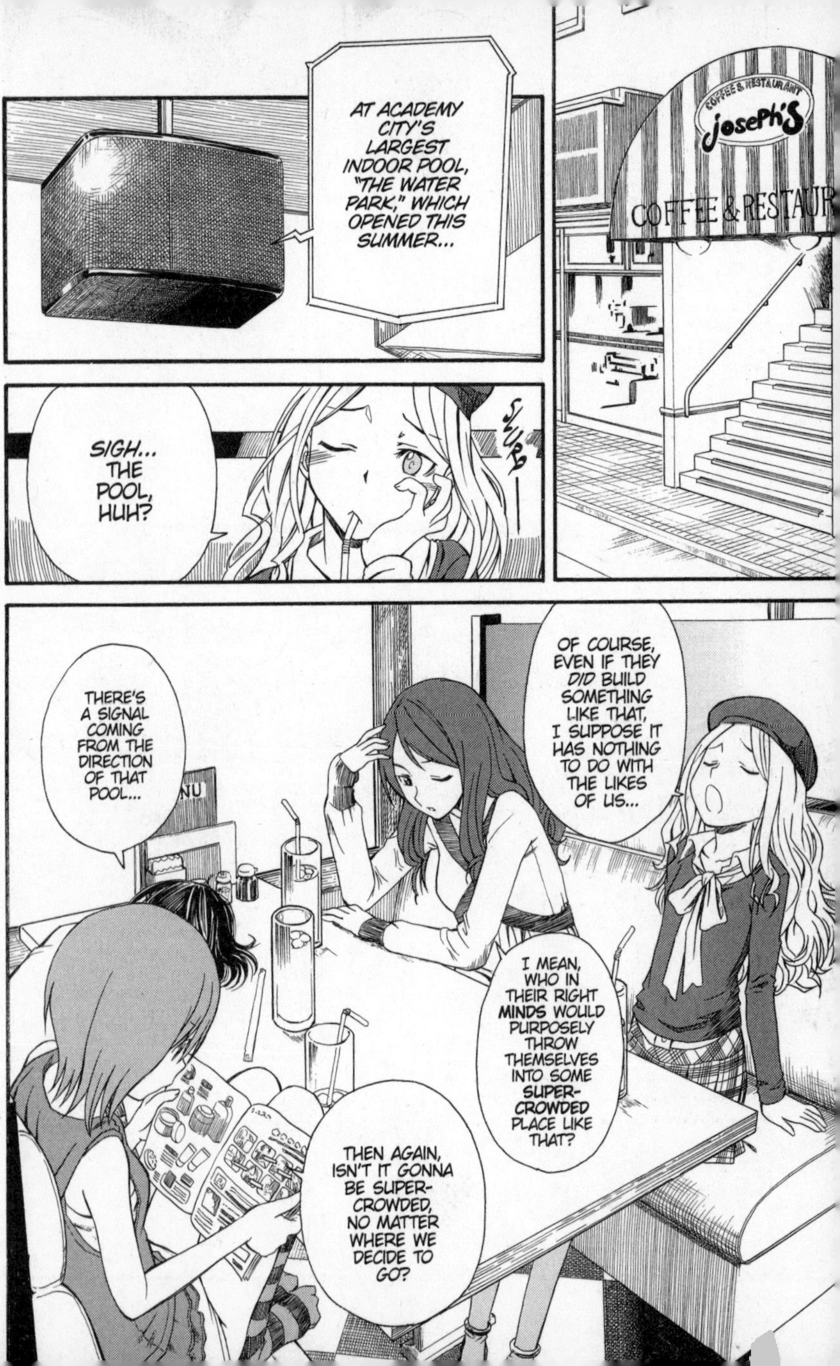
COFFEE & RESTAURANT
joseph's
COFFEE & RESTAUR
AT ACADEMY CITY'S LARGEST INDOOR POOL, "THE WATER PARK," WHICH OPENED THIS SUMMER...
SLURP—
SIGH... THE POOL, HUH?
OF COURSE, EVEN IF THEY *DID* BUILD SOMETHING LIKE THAT, I SUPPOSE IT HAS NOTHING TO DO WITH THE LIKES OF US...
THERE'S A SIGNAL COMING FROM THE DIRECTION OF THAT POOL...
I MEAN, WHO IN THEIR RIGHT **MINDS** WOULD PURPOSELY THROW THEMSELVES INTO SOME **SUPER-CROWDED** PLACE LIKE THAT?
THEN AGAIN, ISN'T IT GONNA BE SUPER-CROWDED, NO MATTER WHERE WE DECIDE TO GO?

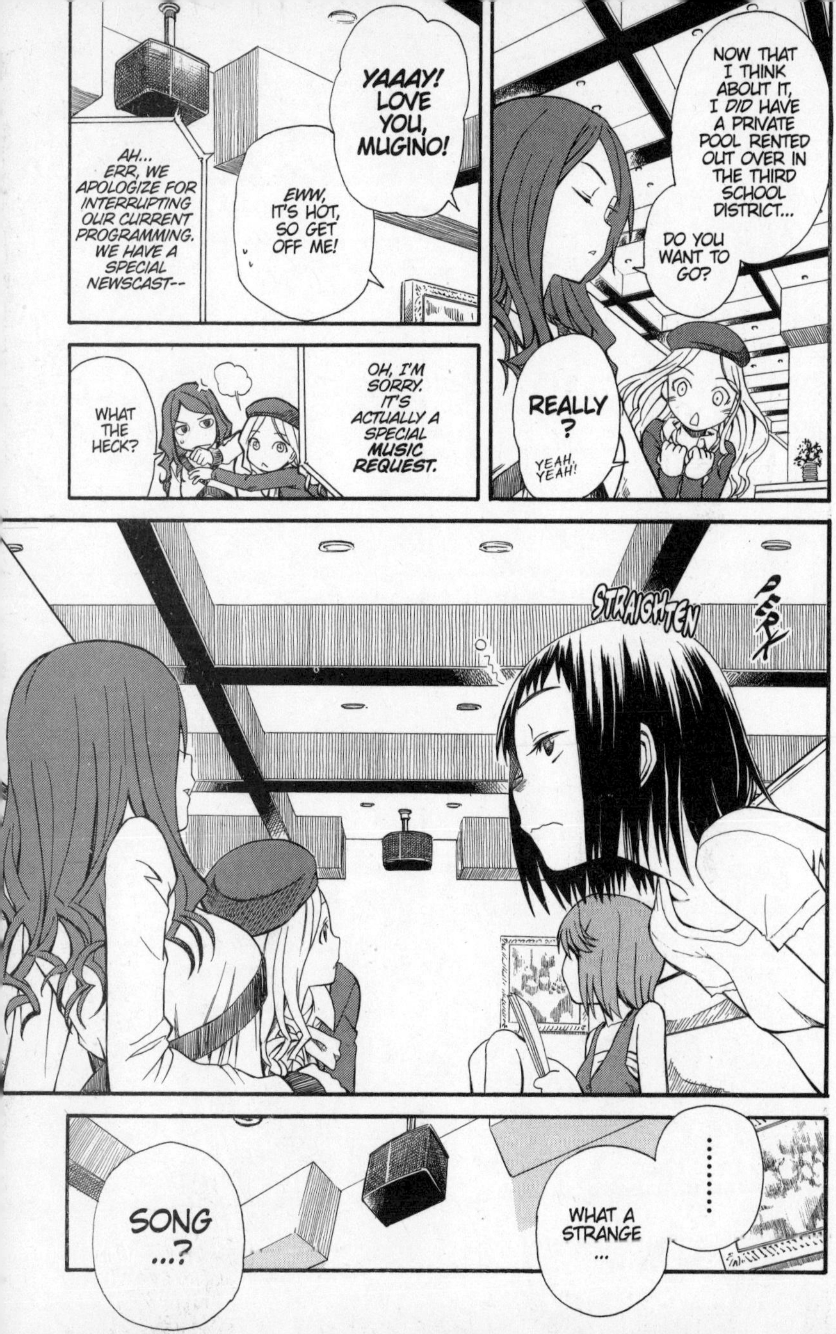

NOW THAT I THINK ABOUT IT, I *DID* HAVE A PRIVATE POOL RENTED OUT OVER IN THE THIRD SCHOOL DISTRICT...
DO YOU WANT TO GO?
REALLY?
YEAH, YEAH!
YAAAY! LOVE YOU, MUGINO!
EWW, IT'S HOT, SO GET OFF ME!
AH... ERR, WE APOLOGIZE FOR INTERRUPTING OUR CURRENT PROGRAMMING. WE HAVE A SPECIAL NEWSCAST--
OH, I'M SORRY. IT'S ACTUALLY A SPECIAL MUSIC REQUEST.
WHAT THE HECK?
PERK
STRAIGHTEN
......
WHAT A STRANGE ...
SONG ...?

AIM Burst ~ Rough Image

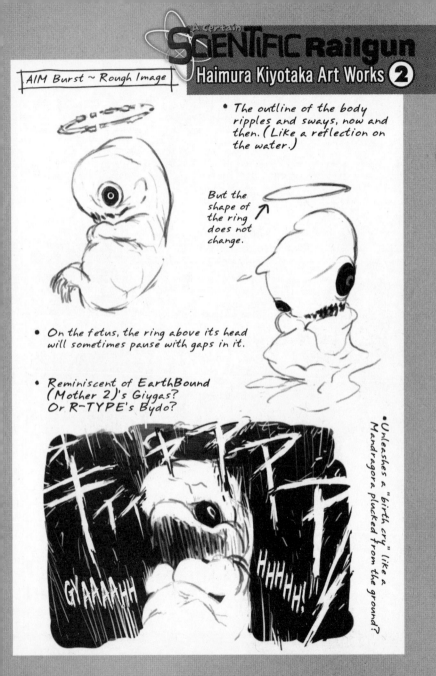

• The outline of the body ripples and sways, now and then. (Like a reflection on the water.)

But the shape of the ring does not change.

• On the fetus, the ring above its head will sometimes pause with gaps in it.

• Reminiscent of EarthBound (Mother 2)'s Giygas? Or R-TYPE's Bydo?

GYAAAAHH

HHHHH!

• Unleashes a "birth cry" like a Mandragora plucked from the ground?

CHAPTER 16: JULY 24 (6)

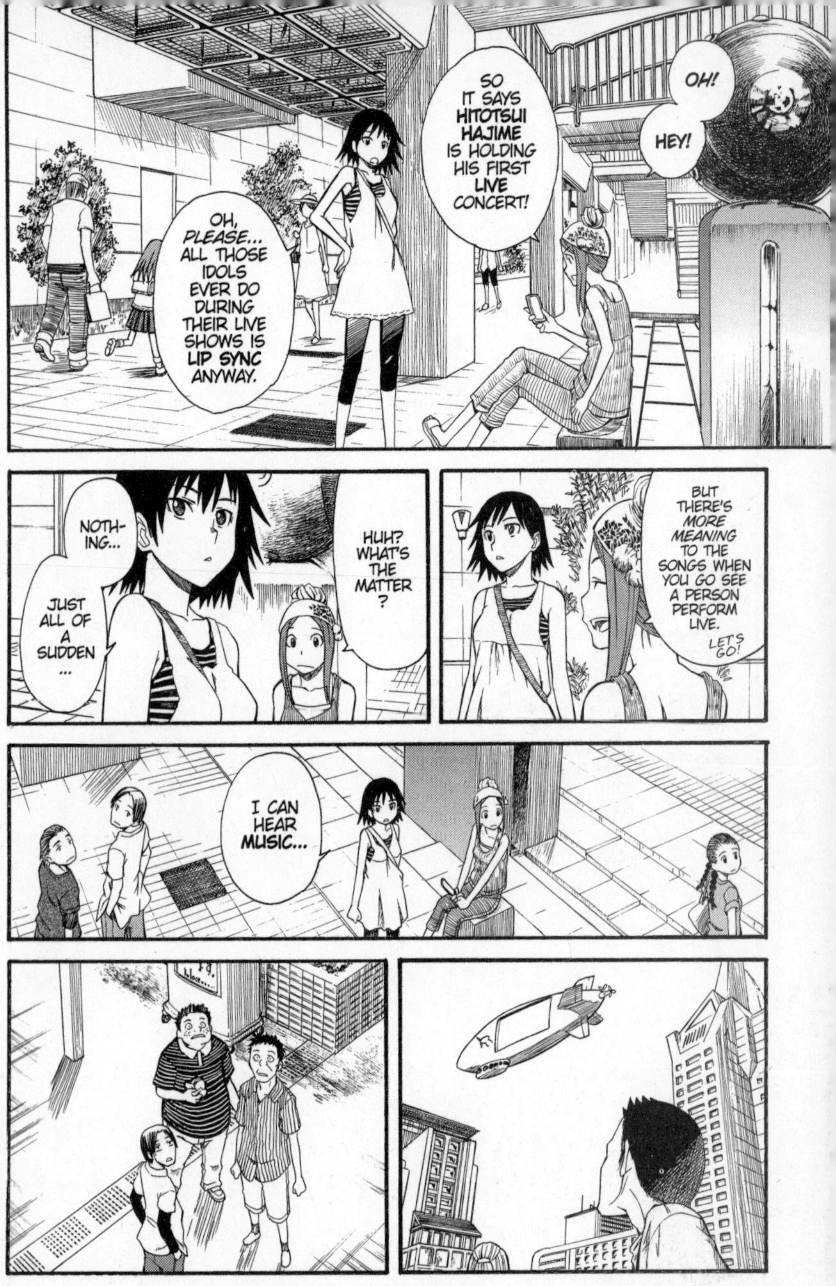
OH!
HEY!
SO IT SAYS HITOTSUI HAJIME IS HOLDING HIS FIRST LIVE CONCERT!
OH, PLEASE... ALL THOSE IDOLS EVER DO DURING THEIR LIVE SHOWS IS LIP SYNC ANYWAY.
BUT THERE'S MORE MEANING TO THE SONGS WHEN YOU GO SEE A PERSON PERFORM LIVE.
LET'S GO!
HUH? WHAT'S THE MATTER ?
NOTHING...
JUST ALL OF A SUDDEN ...
I CAN HEAR MUSIC...

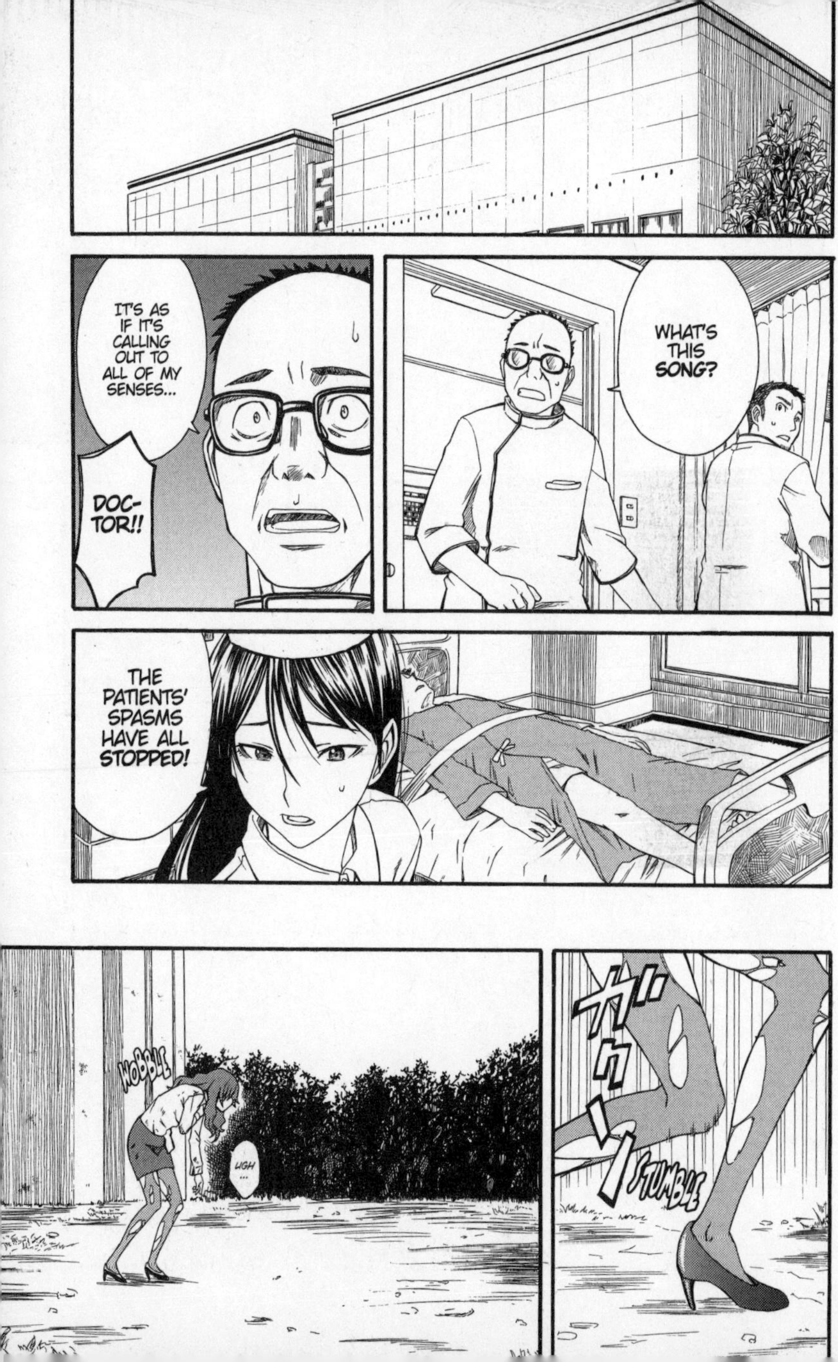

WHAT'S THIS SONG?
IT'S AS IF IT'S CALLING OUT TO ALL OF MY SENSES...
DOCTOR!!
THE PATIENTS' SPASMS HAVE ALL STOPPED!
STUMBLE
WOBBLE
UGH...

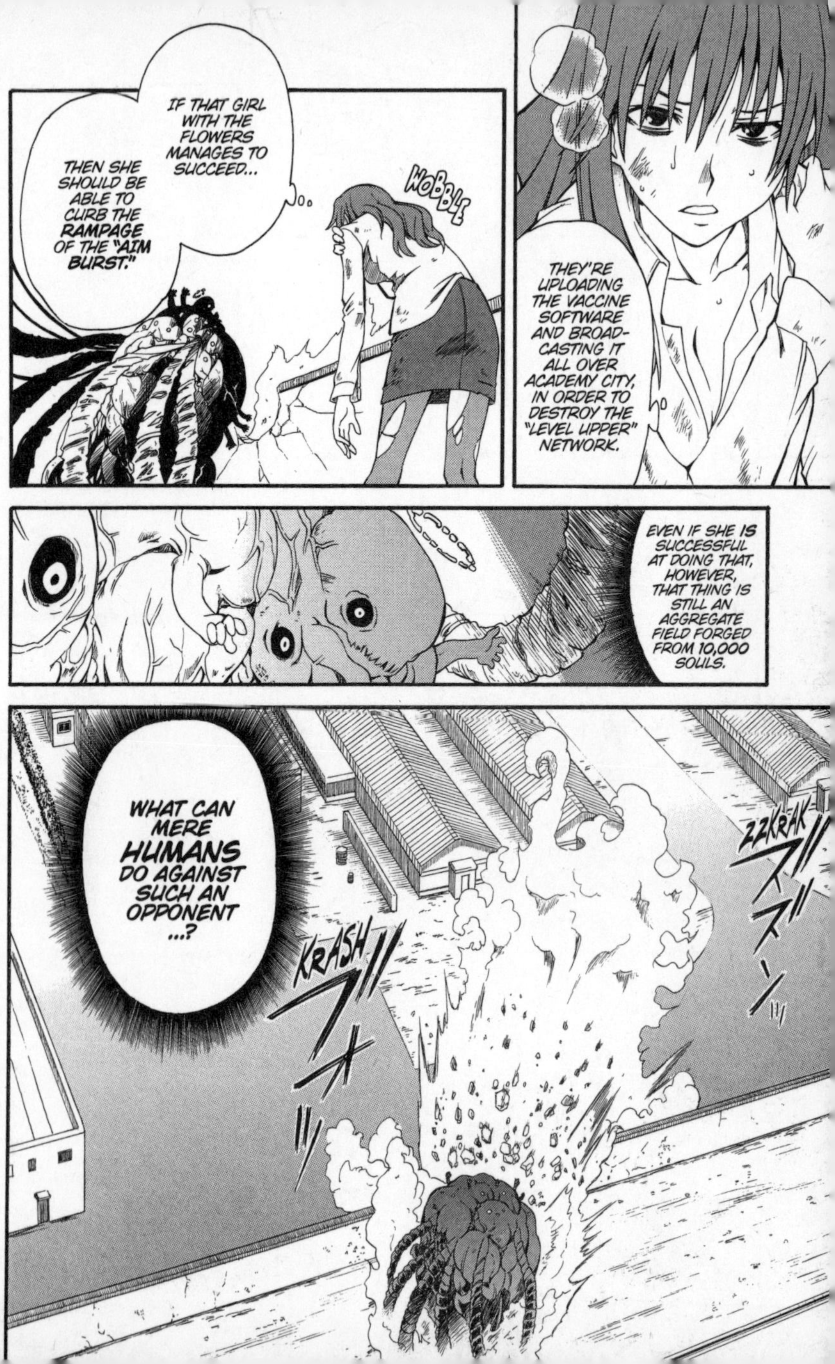
THEY'RE UPLOADING THE VACCINE SOFTWARE AND BROAD-CASTING IT ALL OVER ACADEMY CITY, IN ORDER TO DESTROY THE "LEVEL UPPER" NETWORK.
IF THAT GIRL WITH THE FLOWERS MANAGES TO SUCCEED...
THEN SHE SHOULD BE ABLE TO CURB THE RAMPAGE OF THE "AIM BURST."
WOBBLE
EVEN IF SHE IS SUCCESSFUL AT DOING THAT, HOWEVER, THAT THING IS STILL AN AGGREGATE FIELD FORGED FROM 10,000 SOULS.
ZZKRAK
WHAT CAN MERE HUMANS DO AGAINST SUCH AN OPPONENT ...?
KRASH

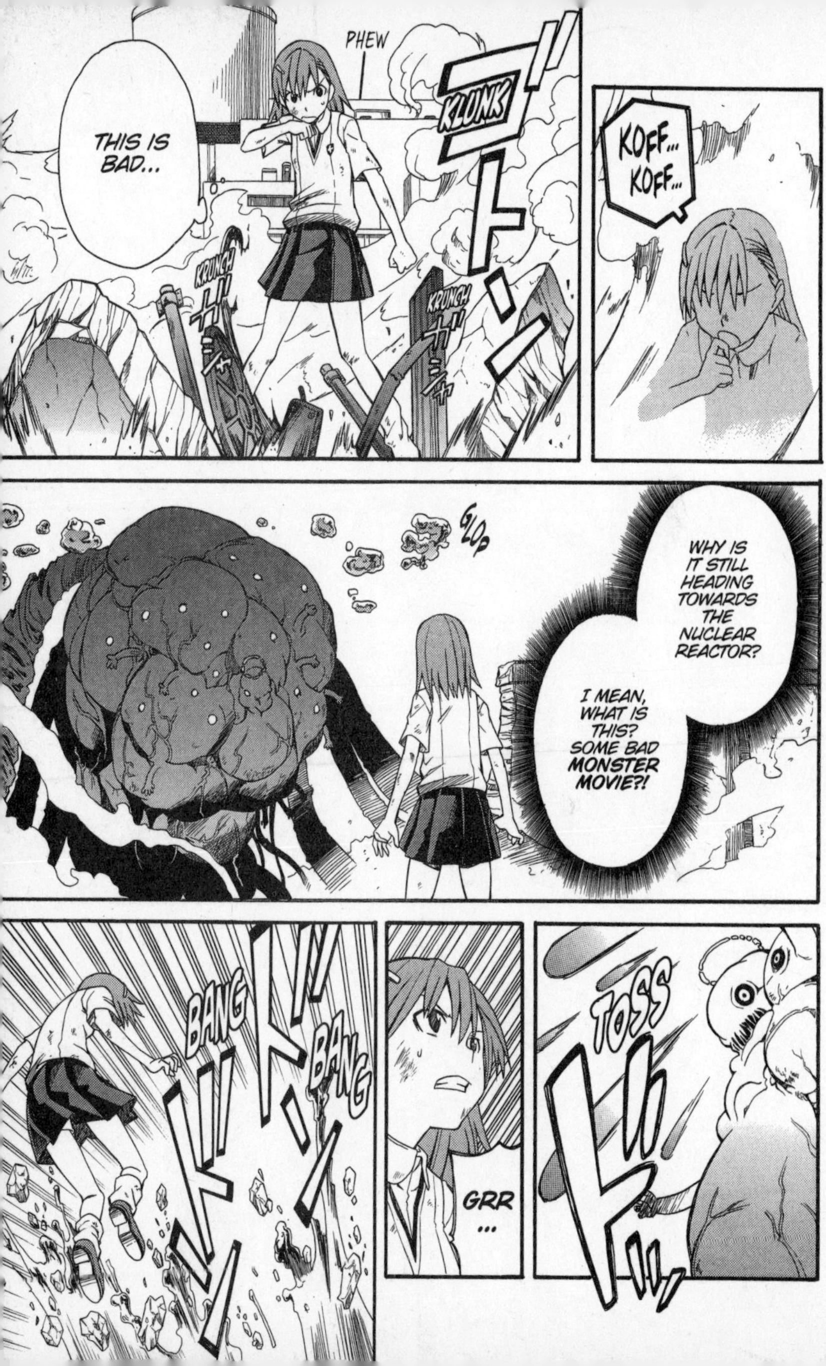
KOFF... KOFF...
KLUNK
PHEW
THIS IS BAD...
KRUNCH
KRUNCH
GLOP
WHY IS IT STILL HEADING TOWARDS THE NUCLEAR REACTOR?
I MEAN, WHAT IS THIS? SOME BAD MONSTER MOVIE?!
TOSS
GRR ...
BANG
BANG

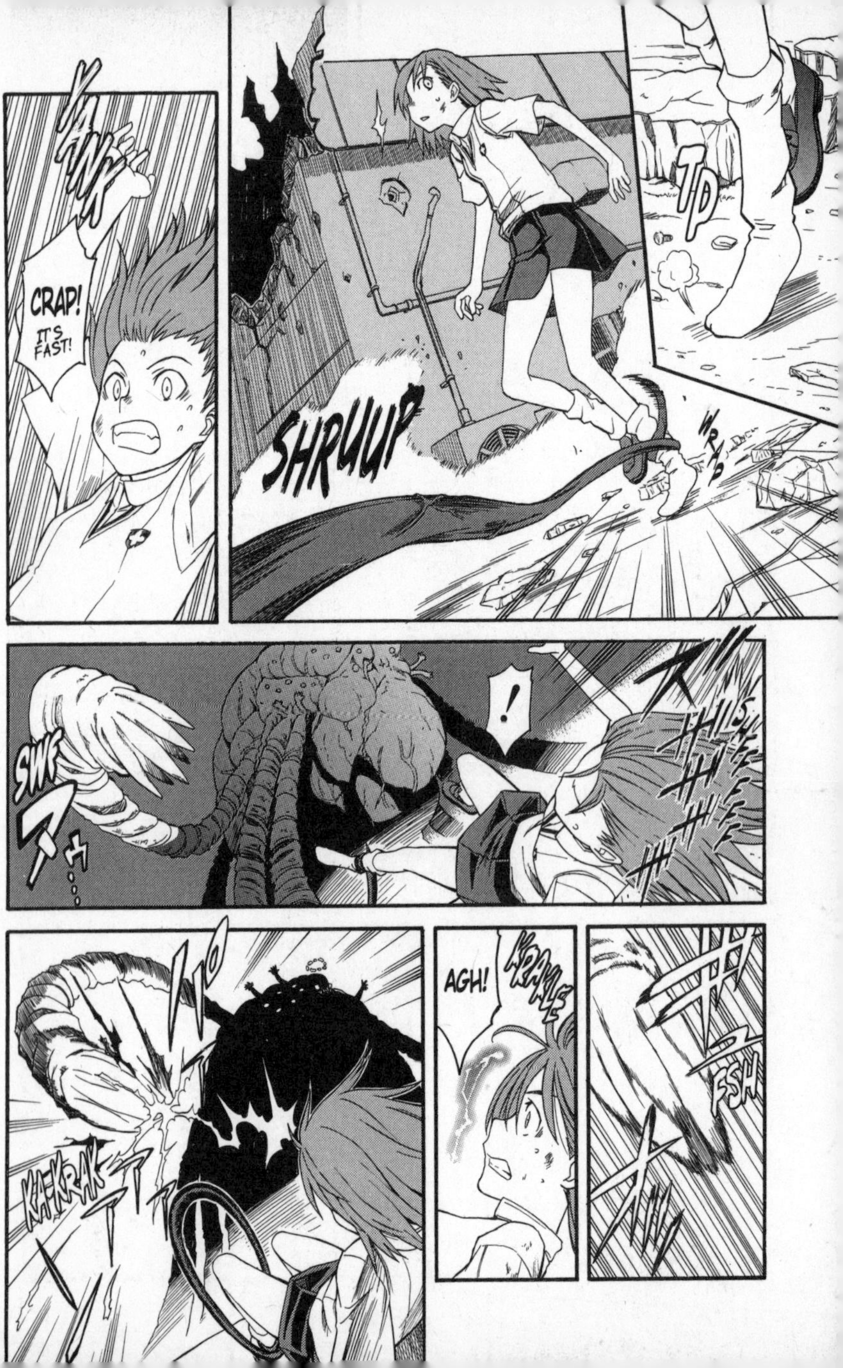
TP
SHRUUP
WRAP
YANK
CRAP!
IT'S FAST!
!
SWF
FSH
AGH!
KRAKLE
KA-KRAK

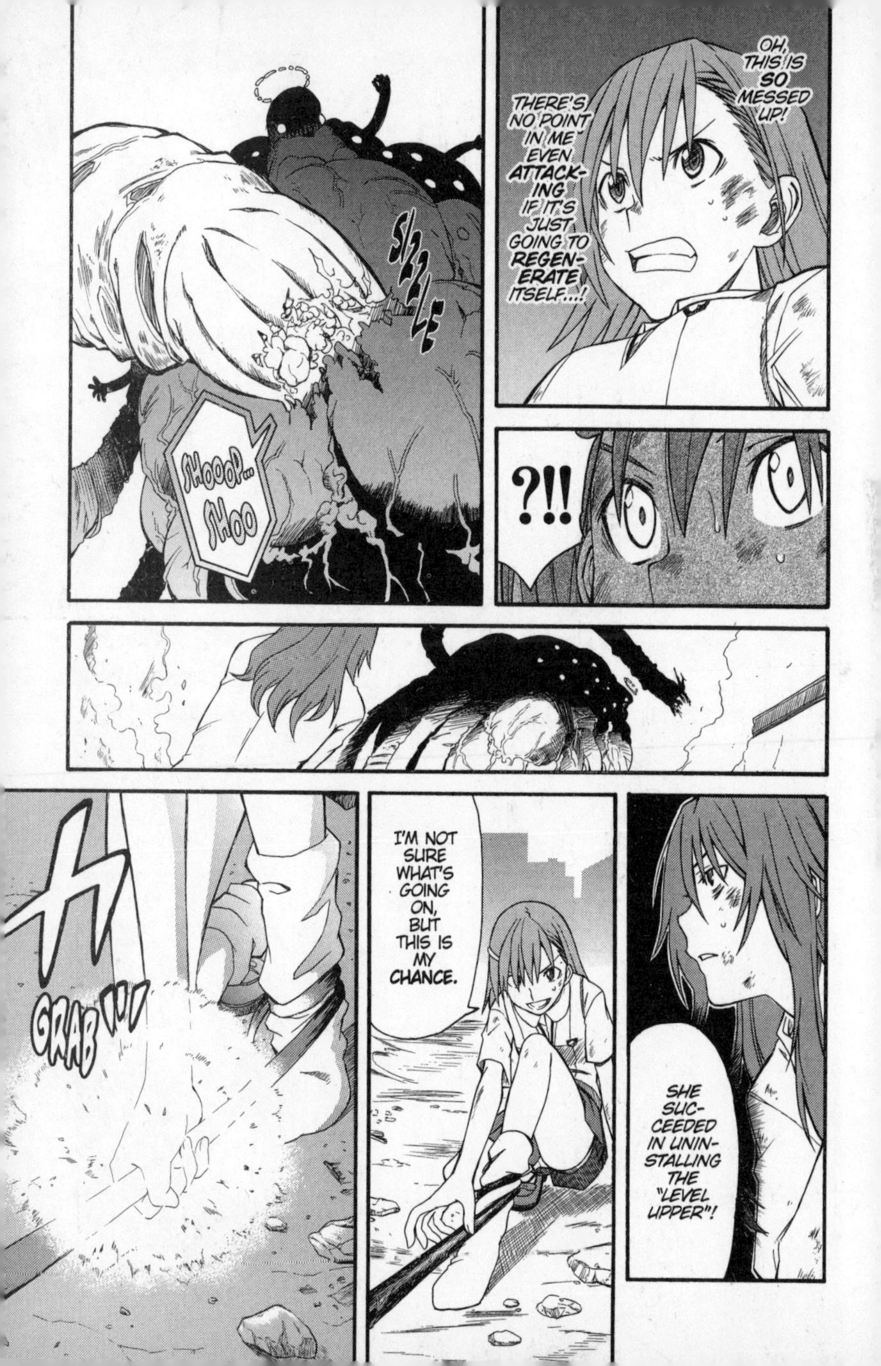
OH, THIS IS SO MESSED UP!
THERE'S NO POINT IN ME EVEN ATTACKING IF IT'S JUST GOING TO REGENERATE ITSELF...!
?!!
SIZZLE
SHOOOP... SHOO
SHE SUCCEEDED IN UNINSTALLING THE "LEVEL UPPER"!
I'M NOT SURE WHAT'S GOING ON, BUT THIS IS MY CHANCE.
GRAB !!

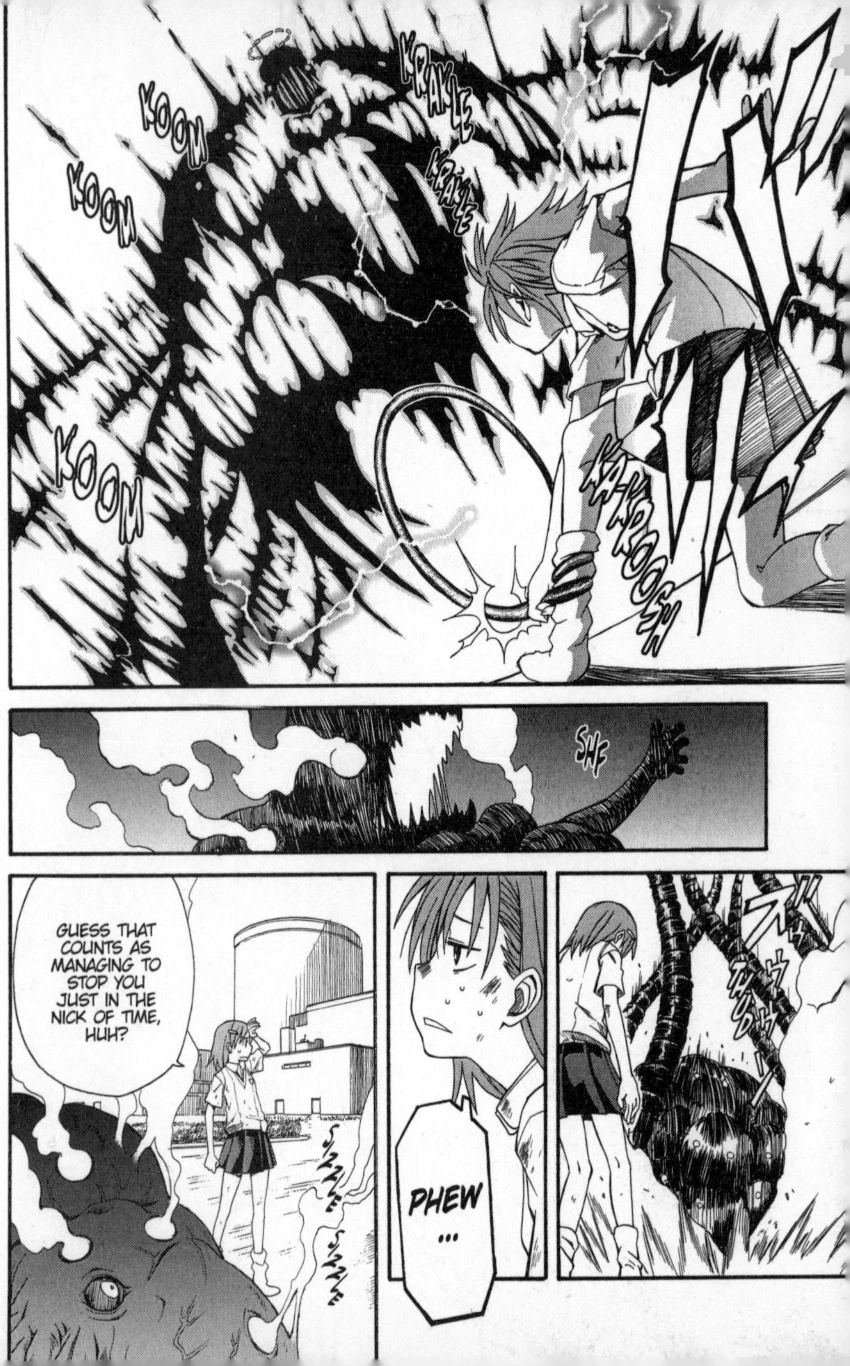
KRAKLE
KRAKLE
KOOM
KOOM
KOOM
KA-KOOSH!
SHF
THUD
PHEW ...
GUESS THAT COUNTS AS MANAGING TO STOP YOU JUST IN THE NICK OF TIME, HUH?
SIZZLE
SIZZLE

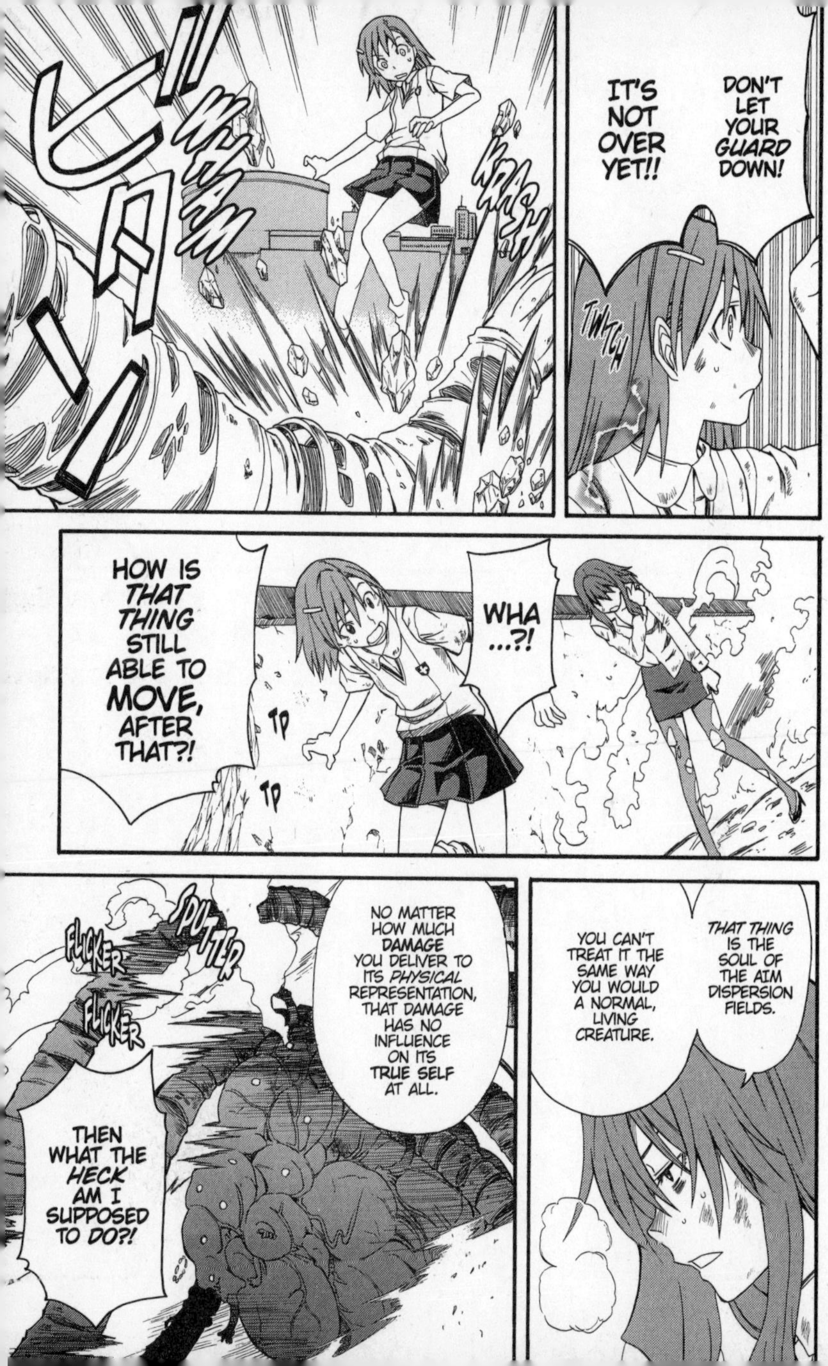
DON'T LET YOUR GUARD DOWN!
IT'S NOT OVER YET!!
TWITCH
KRASH
WHAAM
WHA ...?!
HOW IS THAT THING STILL ABLE TO MOVE, AFTER THAT?!
Tp
Tp
THAT THING IS THE SOUL OF THE AIM DISPERSION FIELDS.
YOU CAN'T TREAT IT THE SAME WAY YOU WOULD A NORMAL, LIVING CREATURE.
NO MATTER HOW MUCH DAMAGE YOU DELIVER TO ITS PHYSICAL REPRESENTATION, THAT DAMAGE HAS NO INFLUENCE ON ITS TRUE SELF AT ALL.
SPUTTER
FLICKER
FLICKER
THEN WHAT THE HECK AM I SUPPOSED TO DO?!

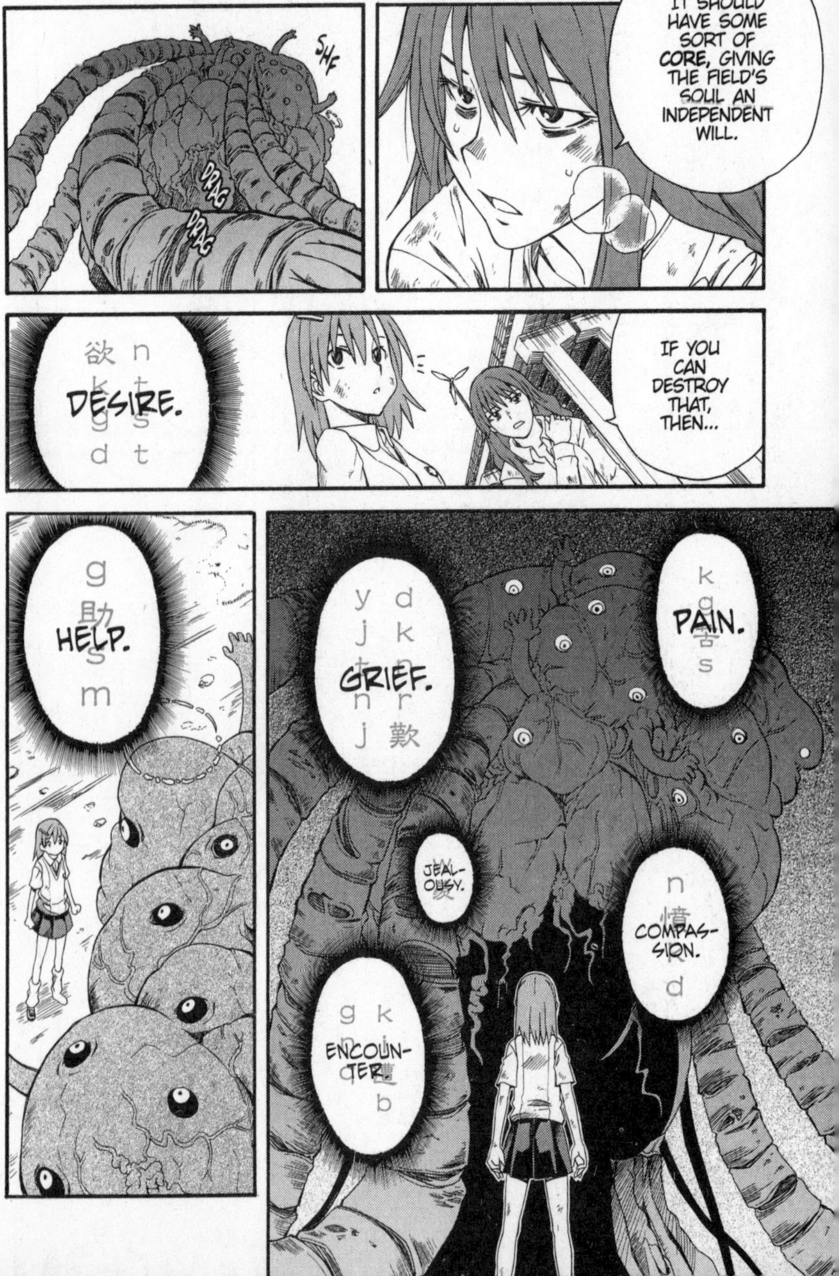
IT SHOULD HAVE SOME SORT OF CORE, GIVING THE FIELD'S SOUL AN INDEPENDENT WILL.
SHF
DRAG
DRAG
IF YOU CAN DESTROY THAT, THEN...
DESIRE.
PAIN.
GRIEF.
COMPAS-SION.
JEAL-OUSY.
ENCOUN-TER.
HELP.

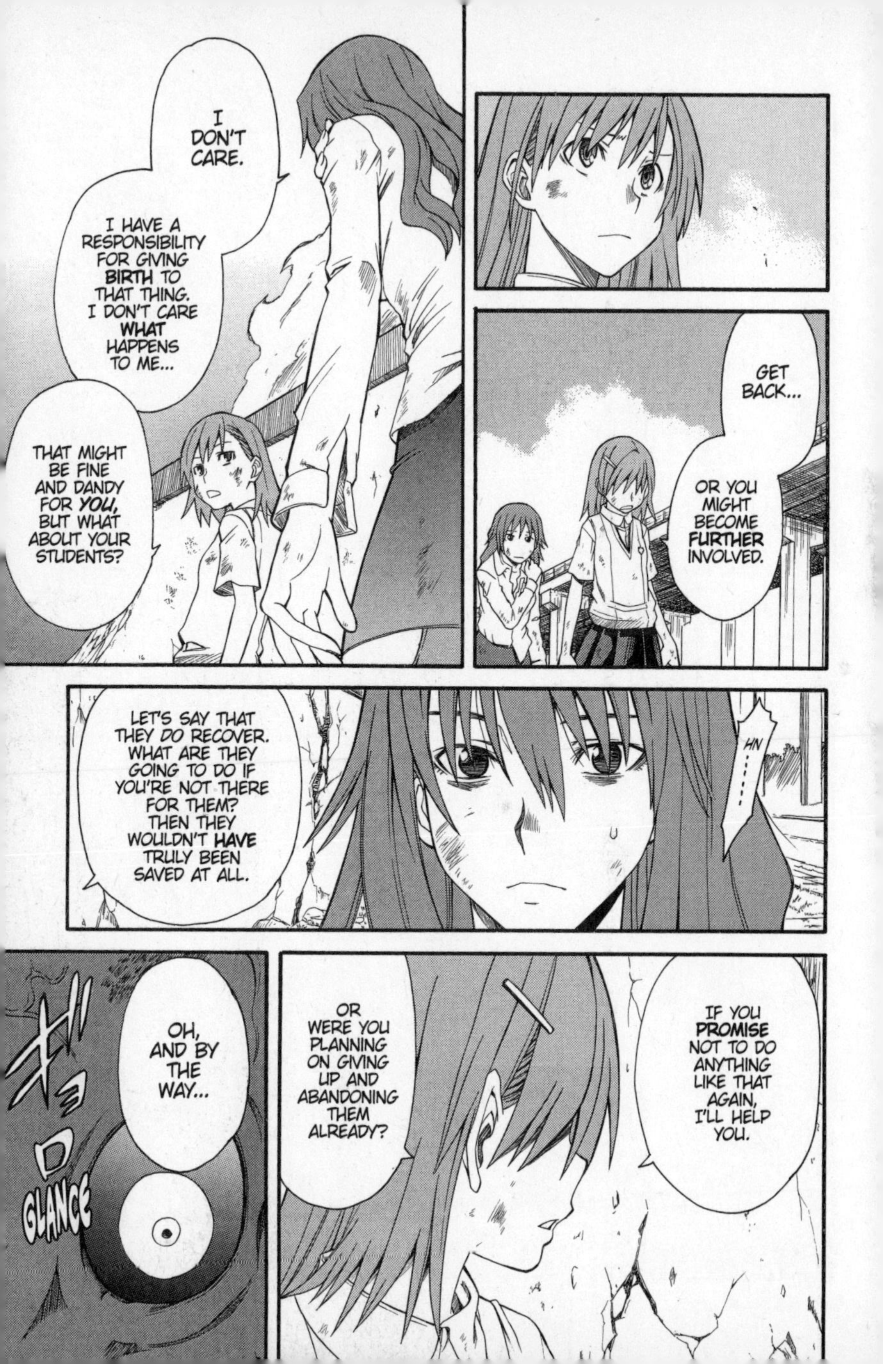
GET BACK...
OR YOU MIGHT BECOME FURTHER INVOLVED.
I DON'T CARE.
I HAVE A RESPONSIBILITY FOR GIVING BIRTH TO THAT THING. I DON'T CARE WHAT HAPPENS TO ME...
THAT MIGHT BE FINE AND DANDY FOR YOU, BUT WHAT ABOUT YOUR STUDENTS?
LET'S SAY THAT THEY DO RECOVER. WHAT ARE THEY GOING TO DO IF YOU'RE NOT THERE FOR THEM? THEN THEY WOULDN'T HAVE TRULY BEEN SAVED AT ALL.
HN......
OR WERE YOU PLANNING ON GIVING UP AND ABANDONING THEM ALREADY?
IF YOU PROMISE NOT TO DO ANYTHING LIKE THAT AGAIN, I'LL HELP YOU.
OH, AND BY THE WAY...
GLANCE

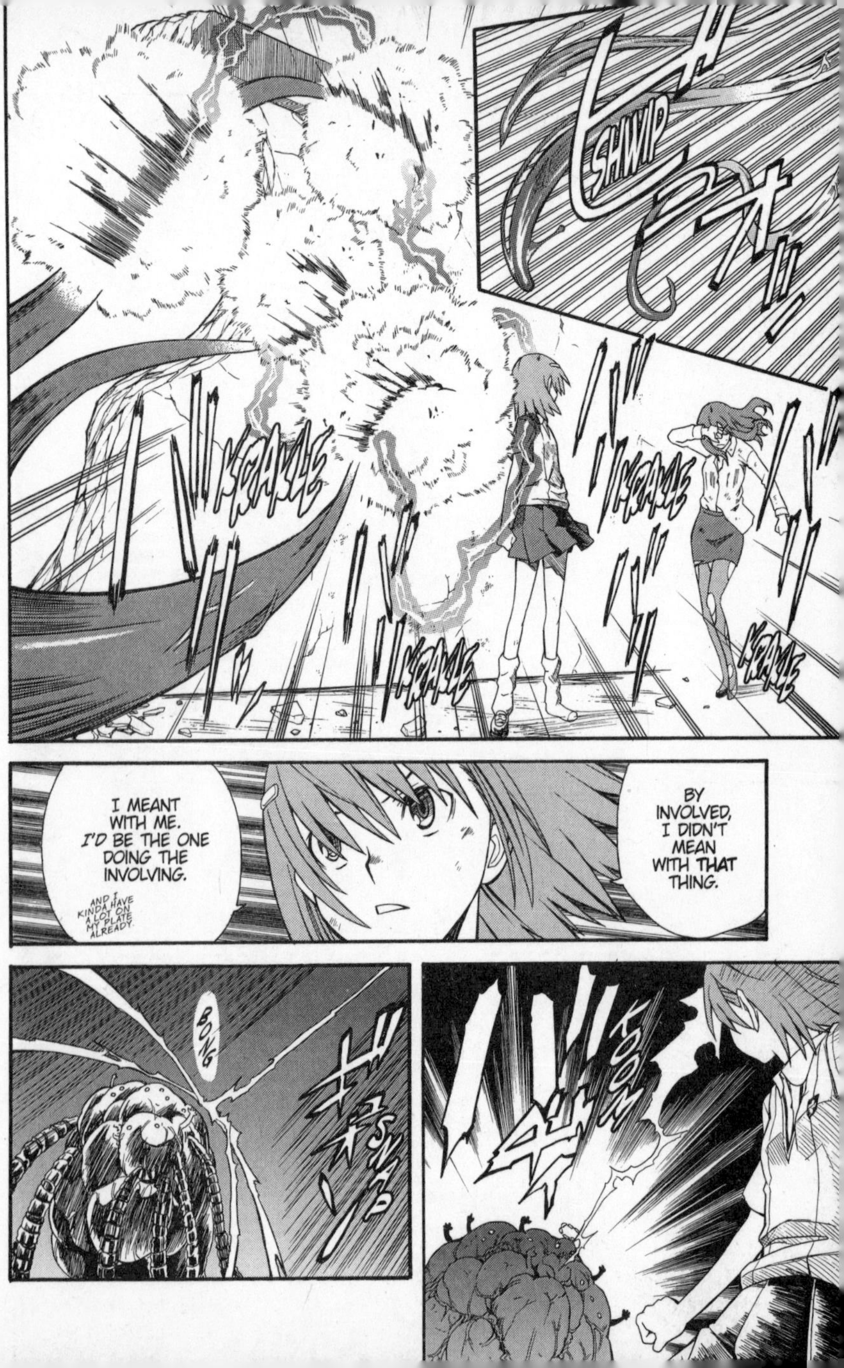
SHWIP
BY INVOLVED, I DIDN'T MEAN WITH THAT THING.
I MEANT WITH ME. I'D BE THE ONE DOING THE INVOLVING.
AND I KINDA HAVE A LOT ON MY PLATE ALREADY.
KOOOM
BONG
SNAP

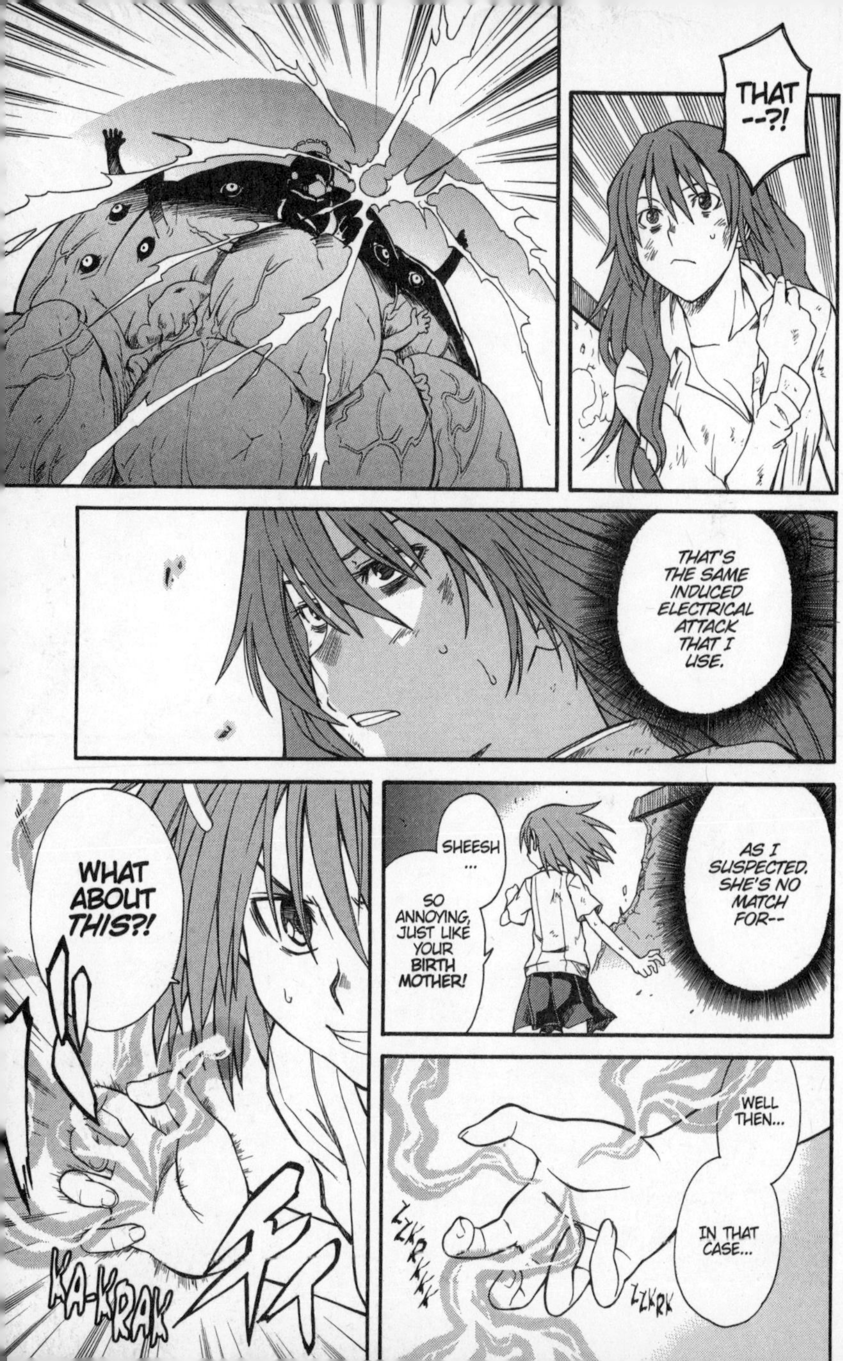
THAT --?!
THAT'S THE SAME INDUCED ELECTRICAL ATTACK THAT I USE.
AS I SUSPECTED. SHE'S NO MATCH FOR--
SHEESH ...
SO ANNOYING, JUST LIKE YOUR BIRTH MOTHER!
WELL THEN...
IN THAT CASE...
ZZKRK
ZZKRKKK
WHAT ABOUT THIS?!
KA-KRAK

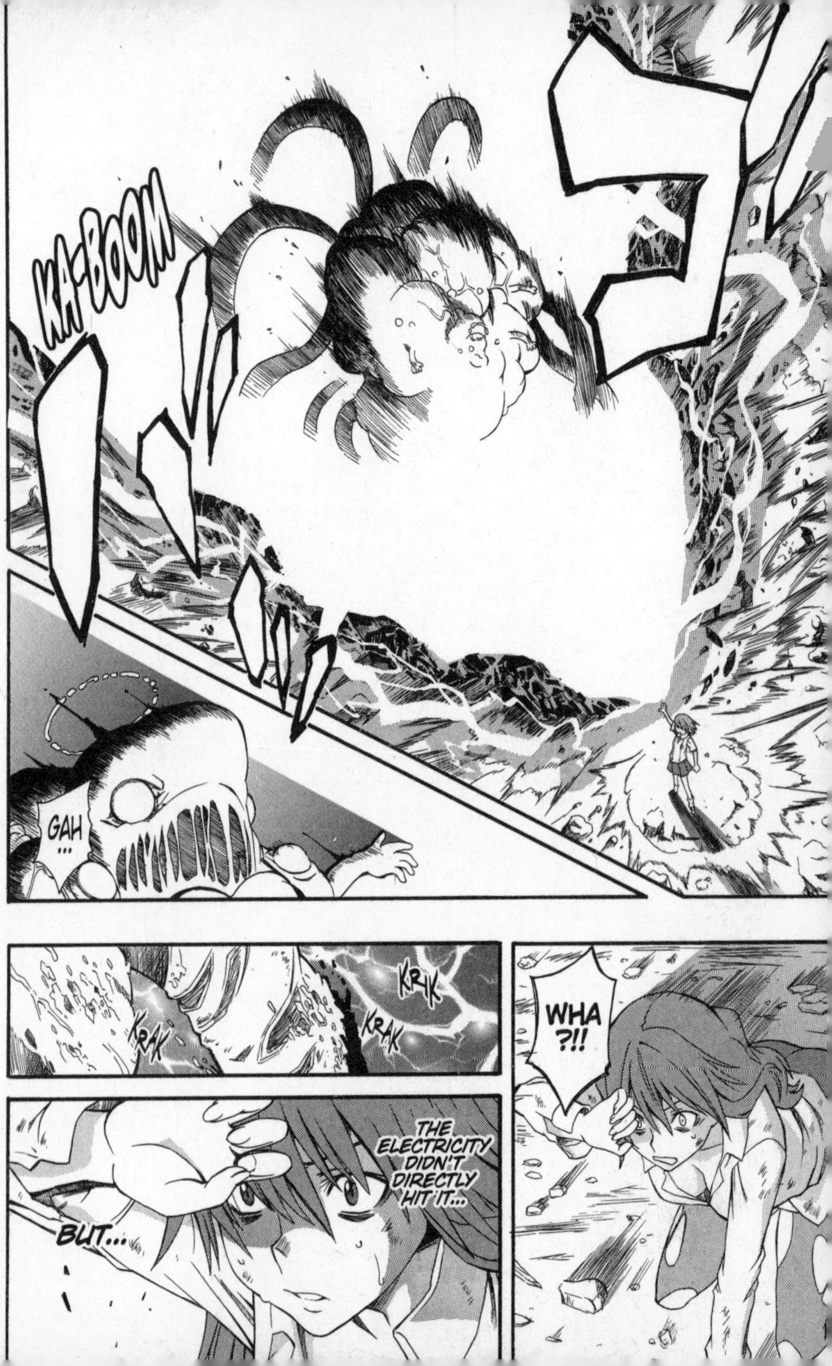
KA-BOOM
GAH ...
WHA ?!!
KRIK
KRAK
KRAK
THE ELECTRICITY DIDN'T DIRECTLY HIT IT...
BUT...

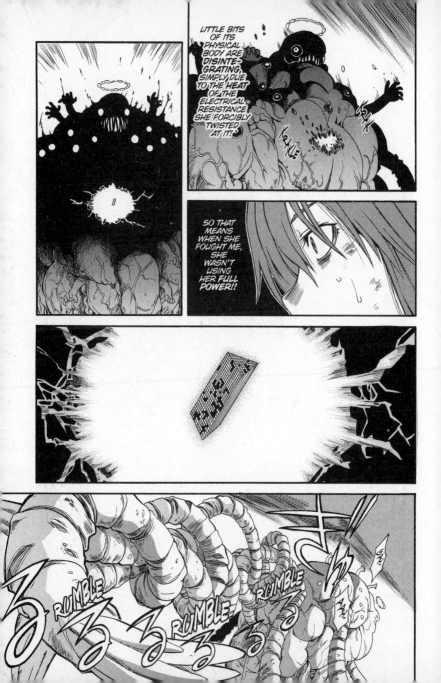

LITTLE BITS OF ITS PHYSICAL BODY ARE DISINTEGRATING, SIMPLY DUE TO THE HEAT OF THE ELECTRICAL RESISTANCE SHE FORCIBLY TWISTED AT IT!

KRAKK

KRAKLE

SO THAT MEANS WHEN SHE FOUGHT ME, SHE WASN'T USING HER FULL POWER!!

RUMBLE

RUMBLE

RUMBLE

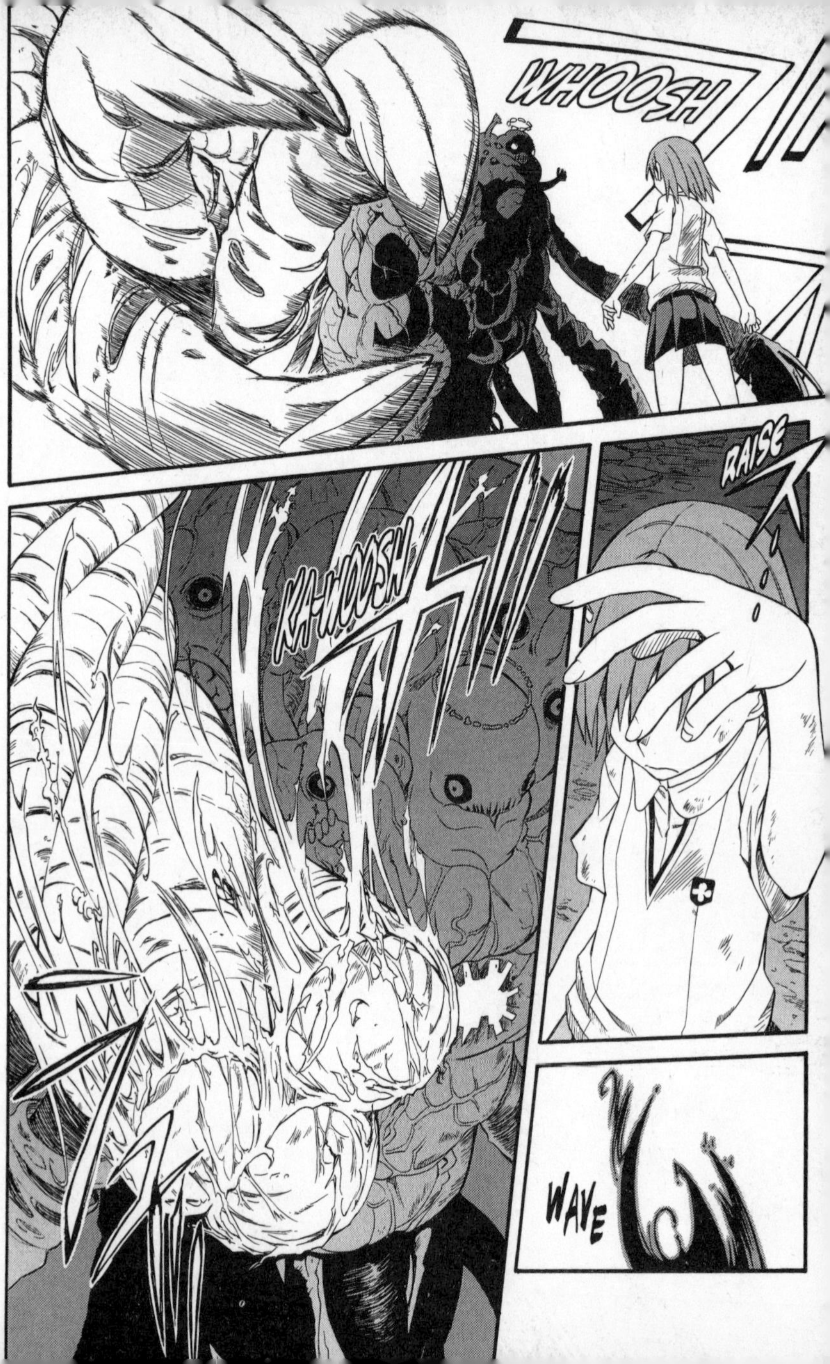
WHOOSH
RAISE
WAVE
KA-WOOSH

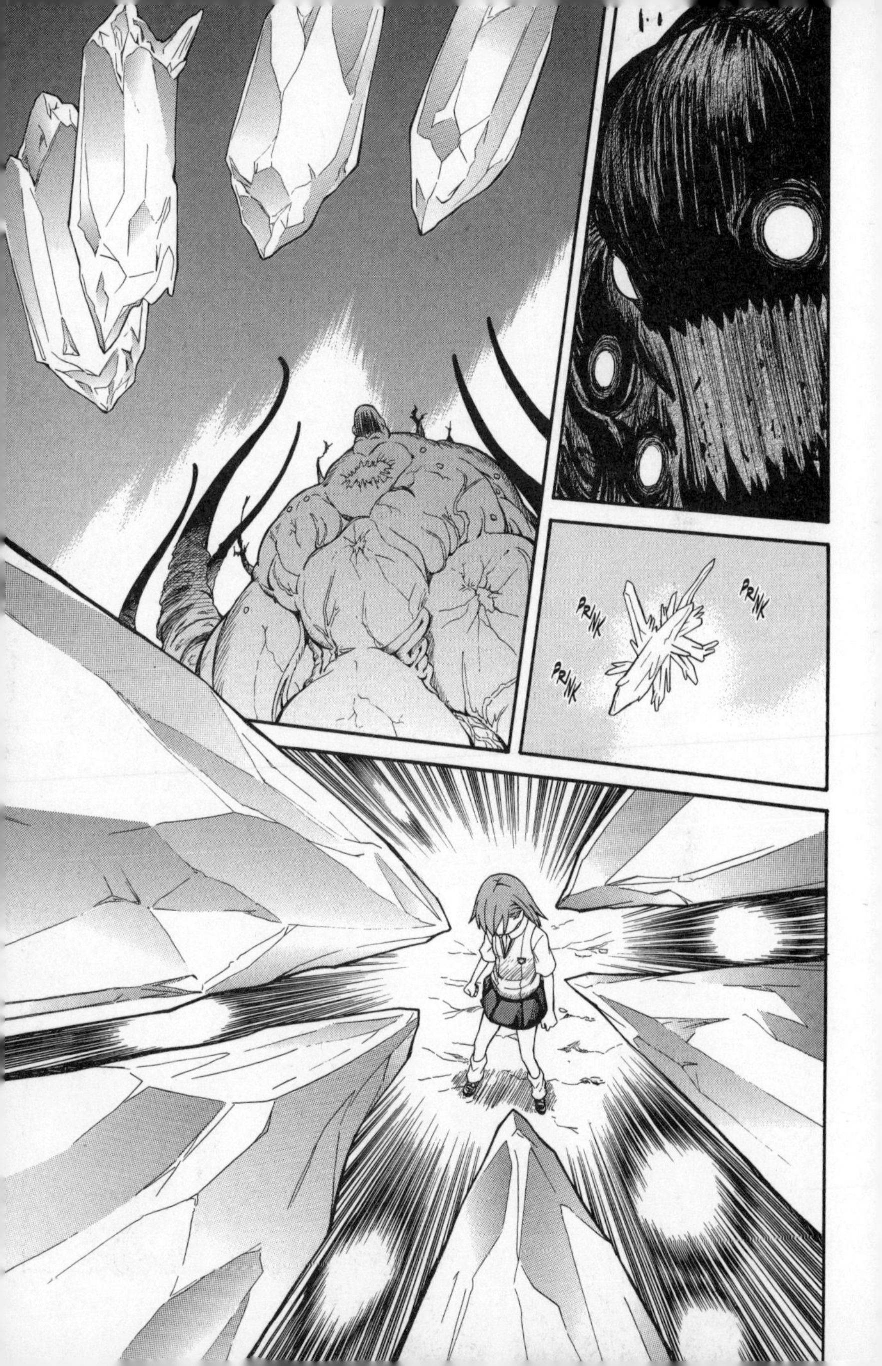
PRINK
PRINK
PRINK

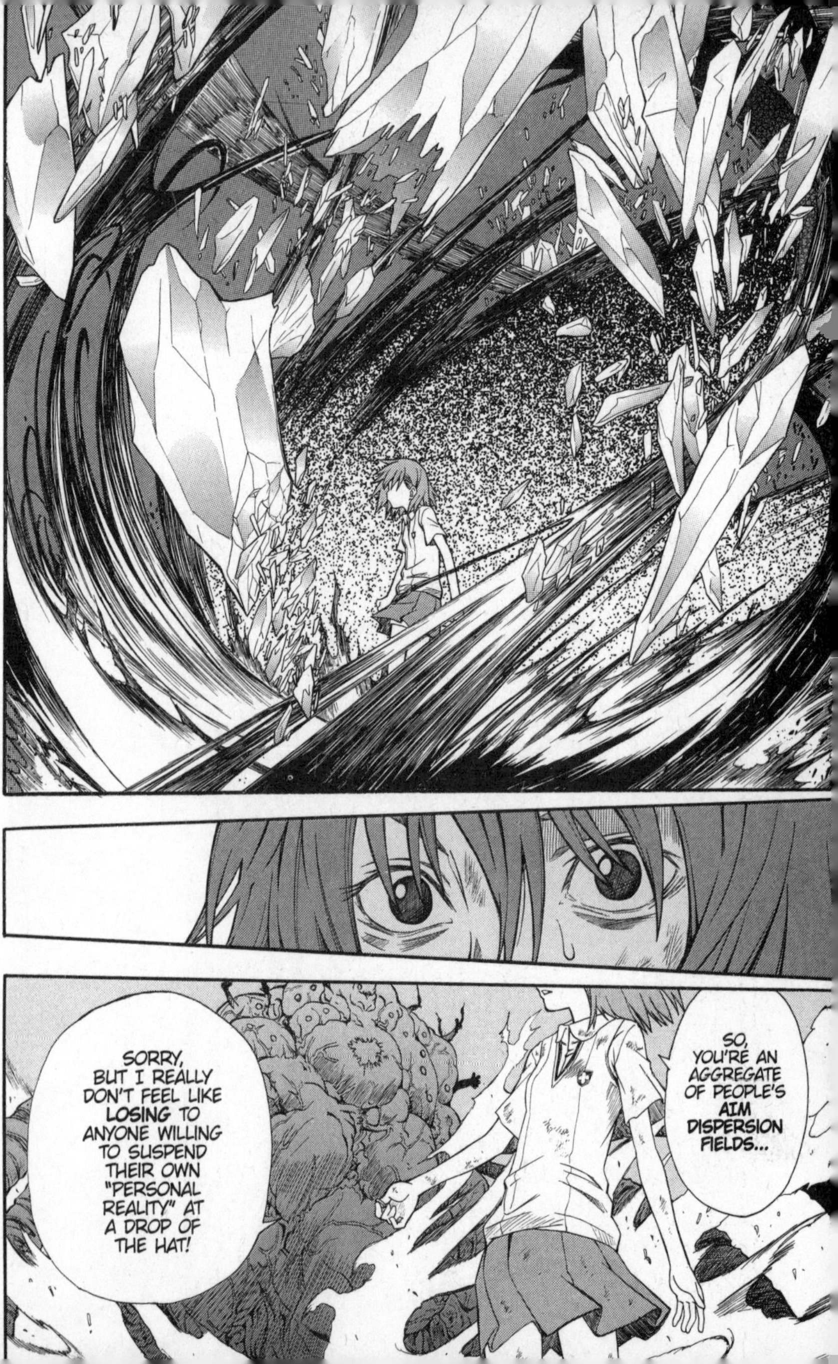
SO, YOU'RE AN AGGREGATE OF PEOPLE'S AIM DISPERSION FIELDS...
SORRY, BUT I REALLY DON'T FEEL LIKE LOSING TO ANYONE WILLING TO SUSPEND THEIR OWN "PERSONAL REALITY" AT A DROP OF THE HAT!

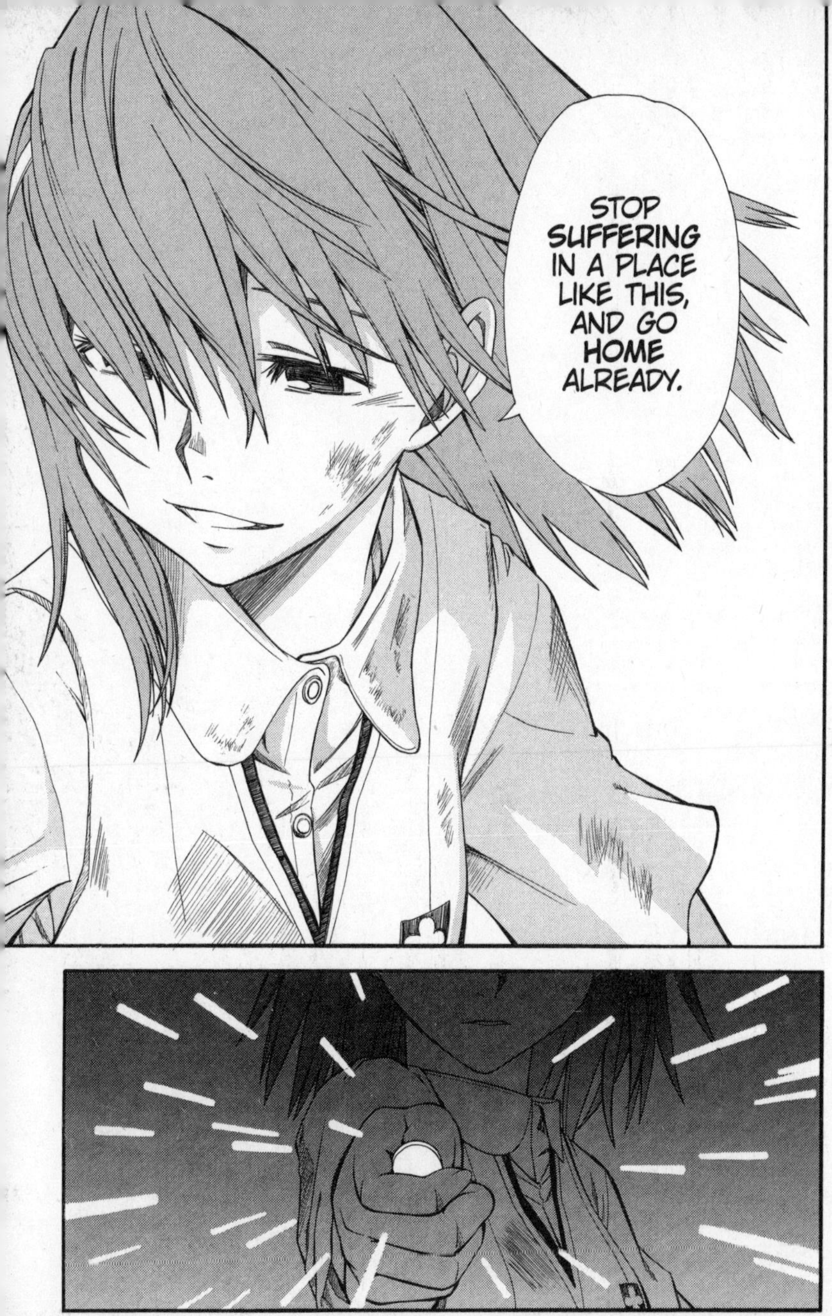
STOP SUFFERING IN A PLACE LIKE THIS, AND GO HOME ALREADY.

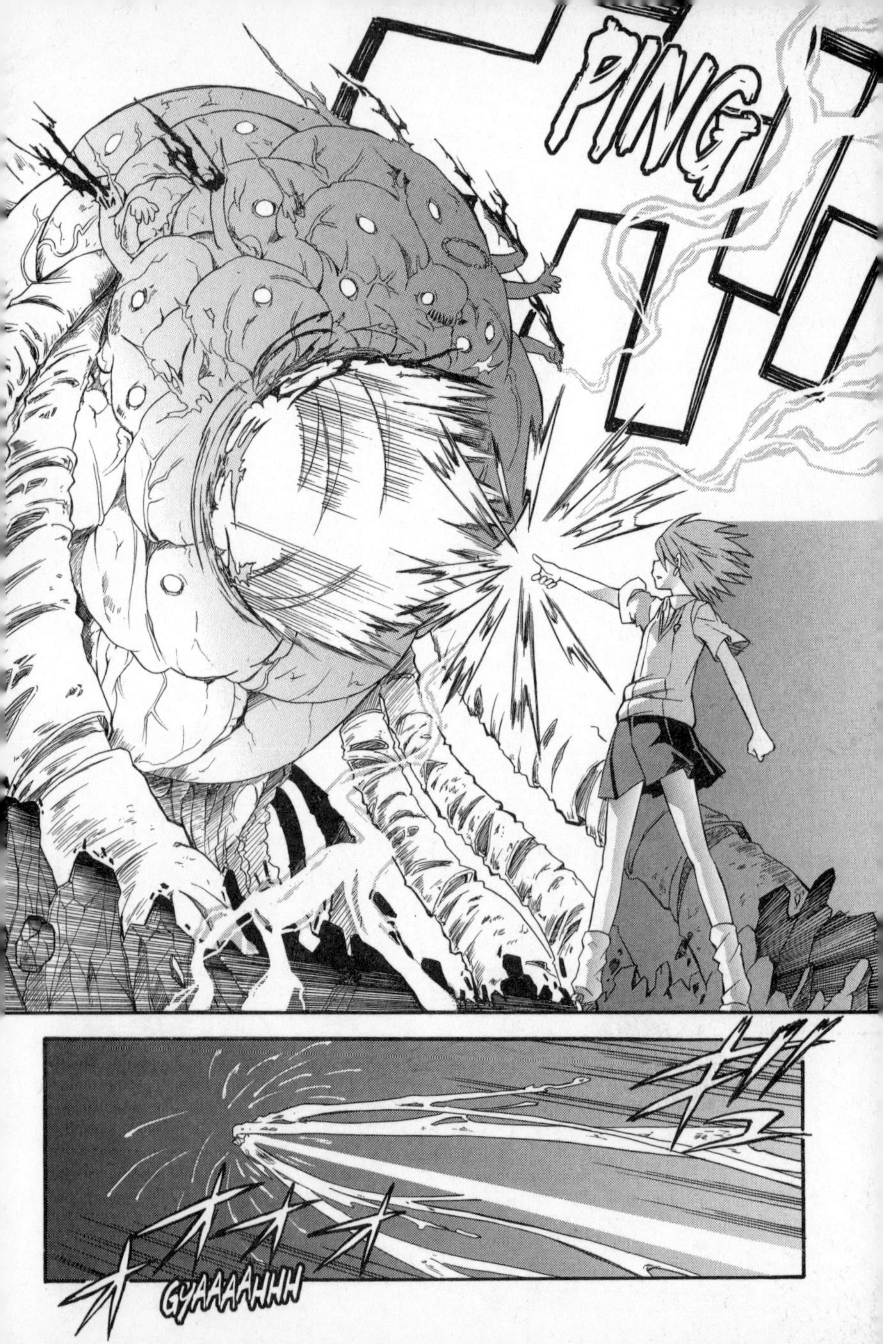
PING
GYAAAHHH

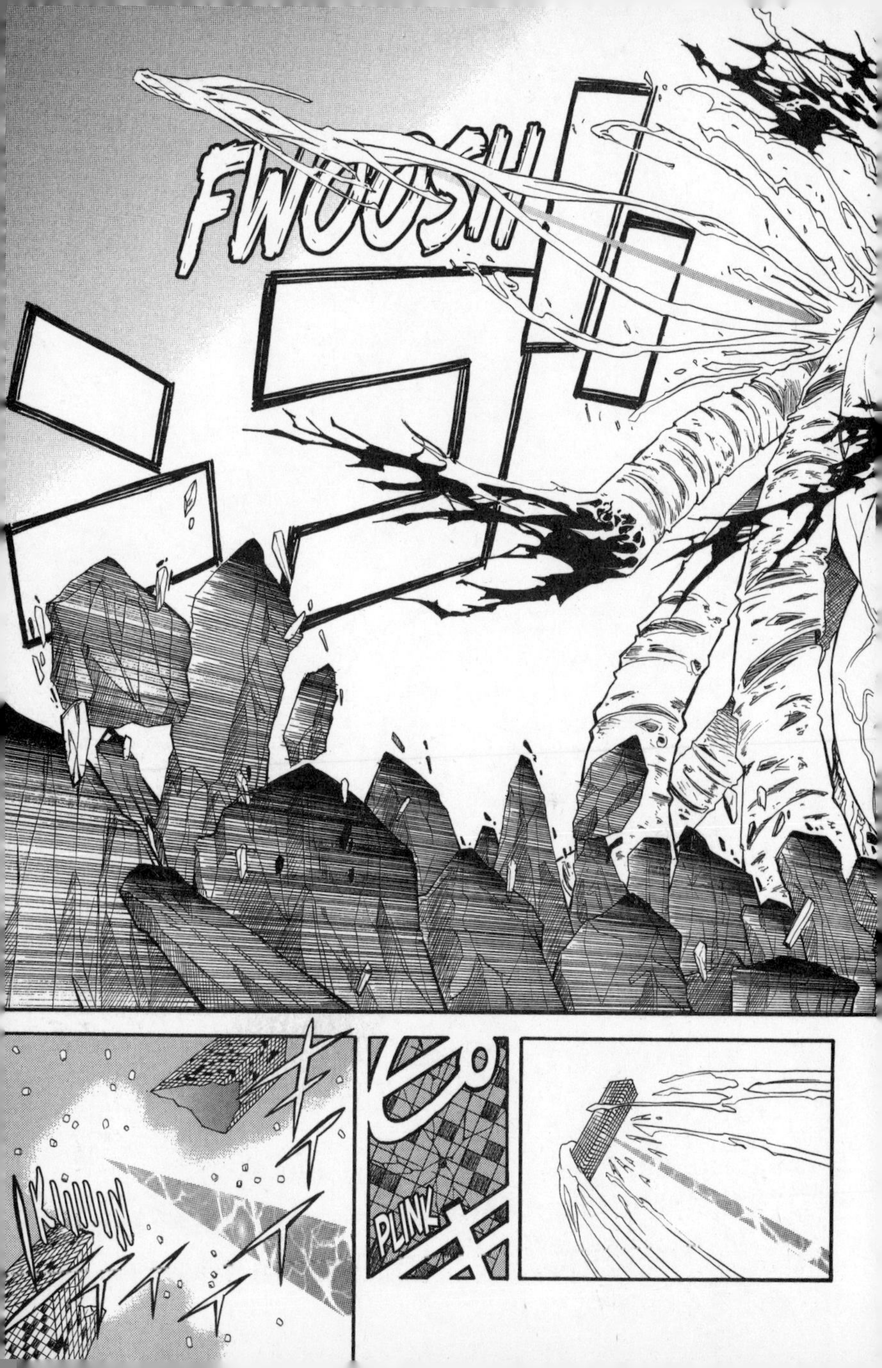
FWOOSH
PLINK
KIIIIN

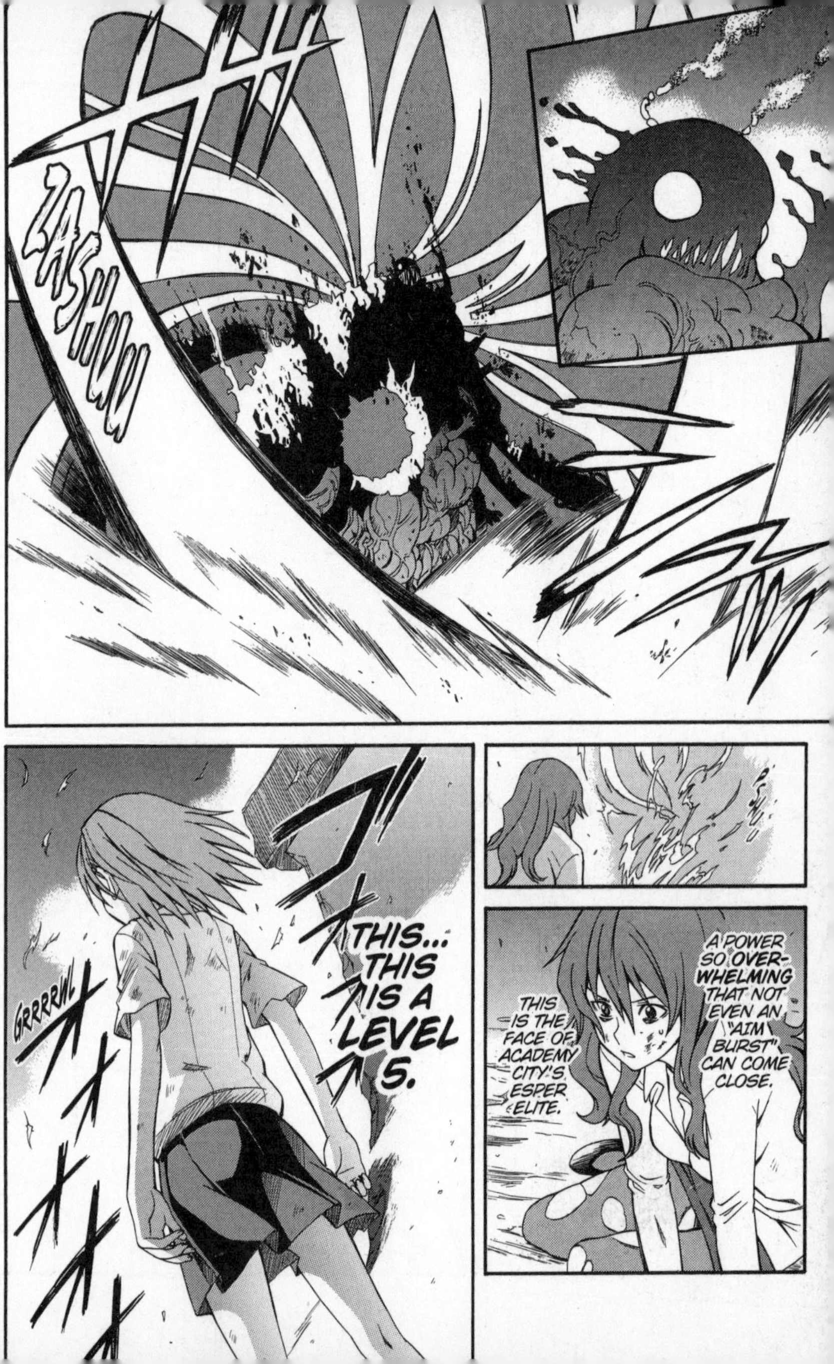
ZASHUUU
THIS... THIS IS A LEVEL 5.
A POWER SO OVERWHELMING THAT NOT EVEN AN "AIM BURST" CAN COME CLOSE.
THIS IS THE FACE OF ACADEMY CITY'S ESPER ELITE.
GRRRRWL

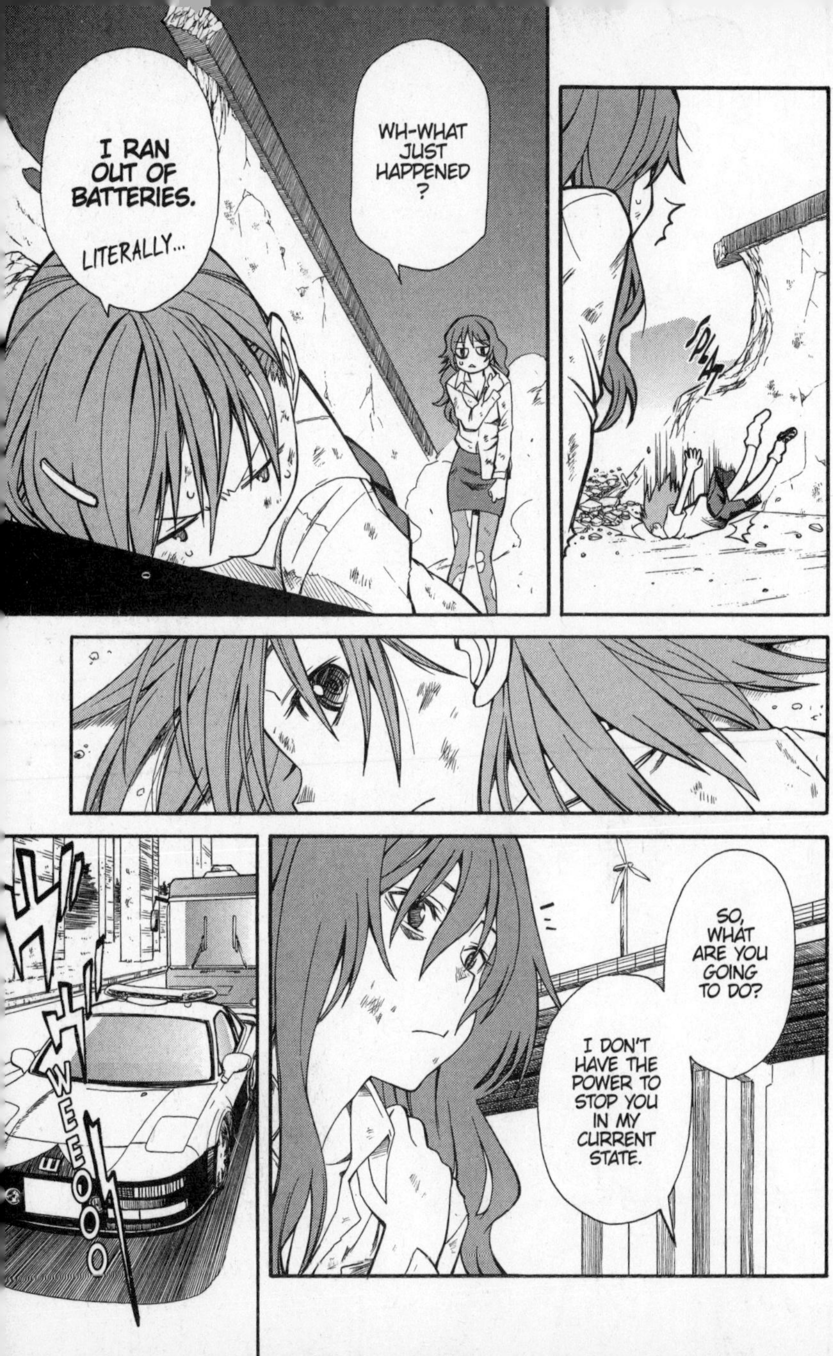
SPLAT
WH-WHAT JUST HAPPENED?
I RAN OUT OF BATTERIES.
LITERALLY...
SO, WHAT ARE YOU GOING TO DO?
I DON'T HAVE THE POWER TO STOP YOU IN MY CURRENT STATE.
WEEOOO

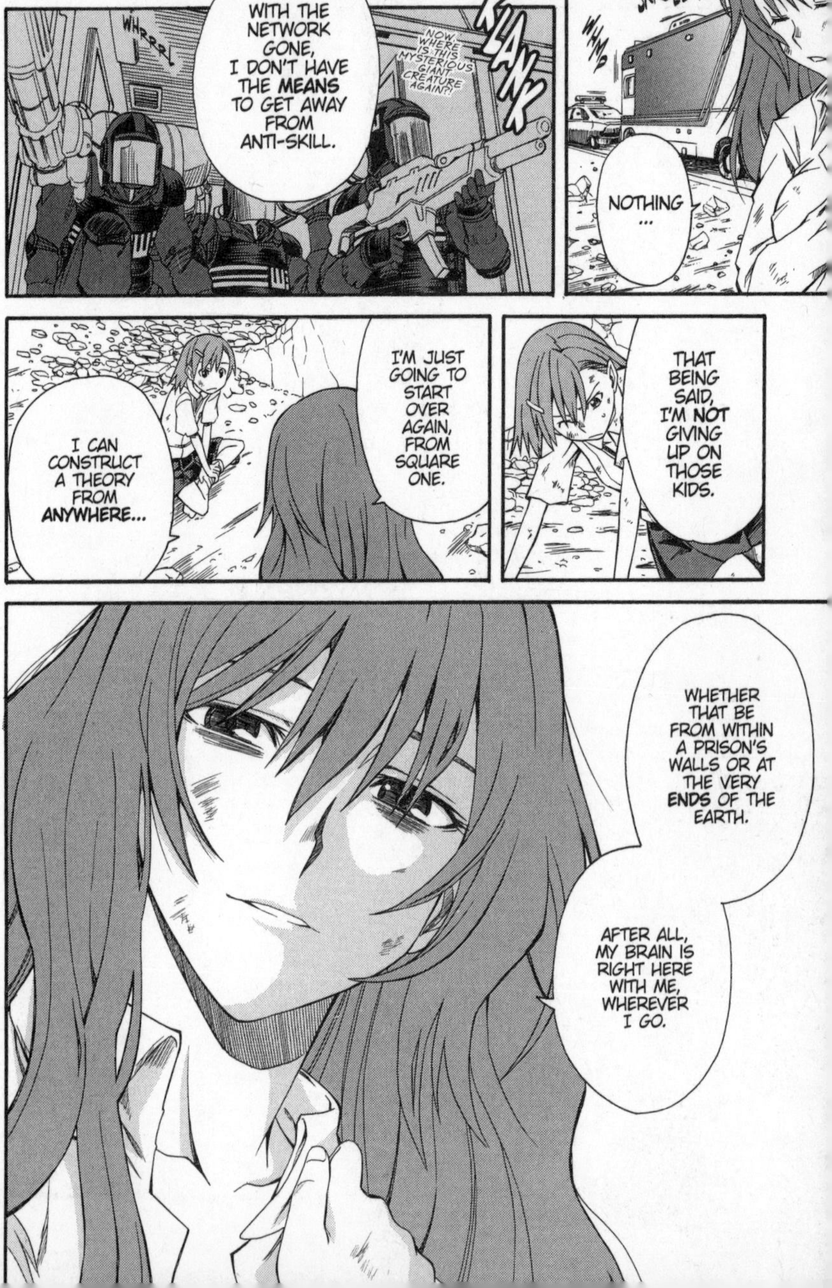
SKREEECH
WHMP
NOTHING...
KLANK
NOW, WHERE IS THIS MYSTERIOUS GIANT CREATURE AGAIN?!
WITH THE NETWORK GONE, I DON'T HAVE THE MEANS TO GET AWAY FROM ANTI-SKILL.
WHRRRL
THAT BEING SAID, I'M NOT GIVING UP ON THOSE KIDS.
I'M JUST GOING TO START OVER AGAIN, FROM SQUARE ONE.
I CAN CONSTRUCT A THEORY FROM ANYWHERE...
WHETHER THAT BE FROM WITHIN A PRISON'S WALLS OR AT THE VERY ENDS OF THE EARTH.
AFTER ALL, MY BRAIN IS RIGHT HERE WITH ME, WHEREVER I GO.

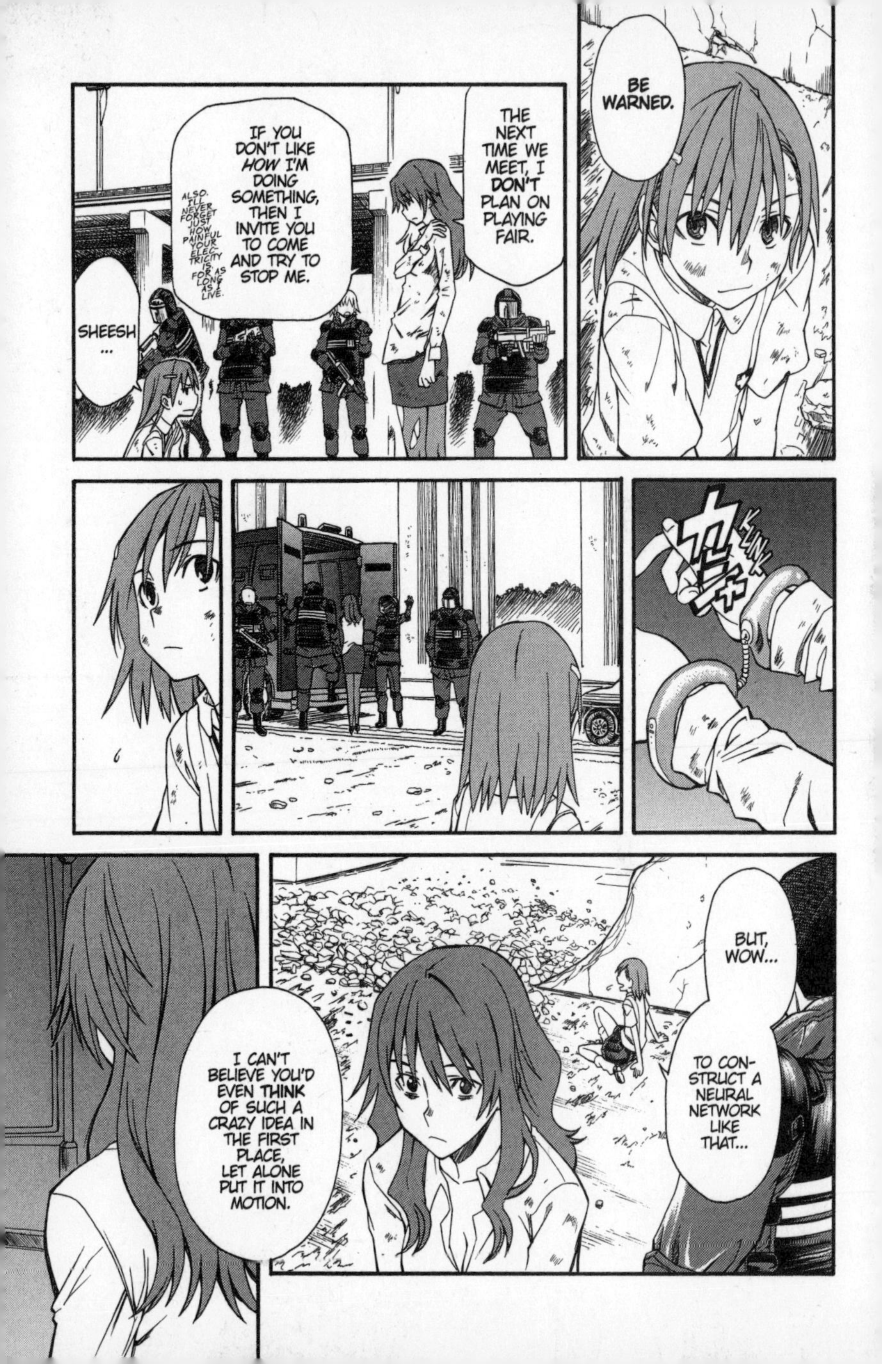
BE WARNED.
THE NEXT TIME WE MEET, I DON'T PLAN ON PLAYING FAIR.
IF YOU DON'T LIKE *HOW* I'M DOING SOMETHING, THEN I INVITE YOU TO COME AND TRY TO STOP ME.
ALSO, I'LL NEVER FORGET JUST HOW PAINFUL YOUR ELEC-TRICITY IS. FOR AS LONG AS I LIVE.
SHEESH ...
KLINK
BUT, WOW...
TO CON-STRUCT A NEURAL NETWORK LIKE THAT...
I CAN'T BELIEVE YOU'D EVEN THINK OF SUCH A CRAZY IDEA IN THE FIRST PLACE, LET ALONE PUT IT INTO MOTION.

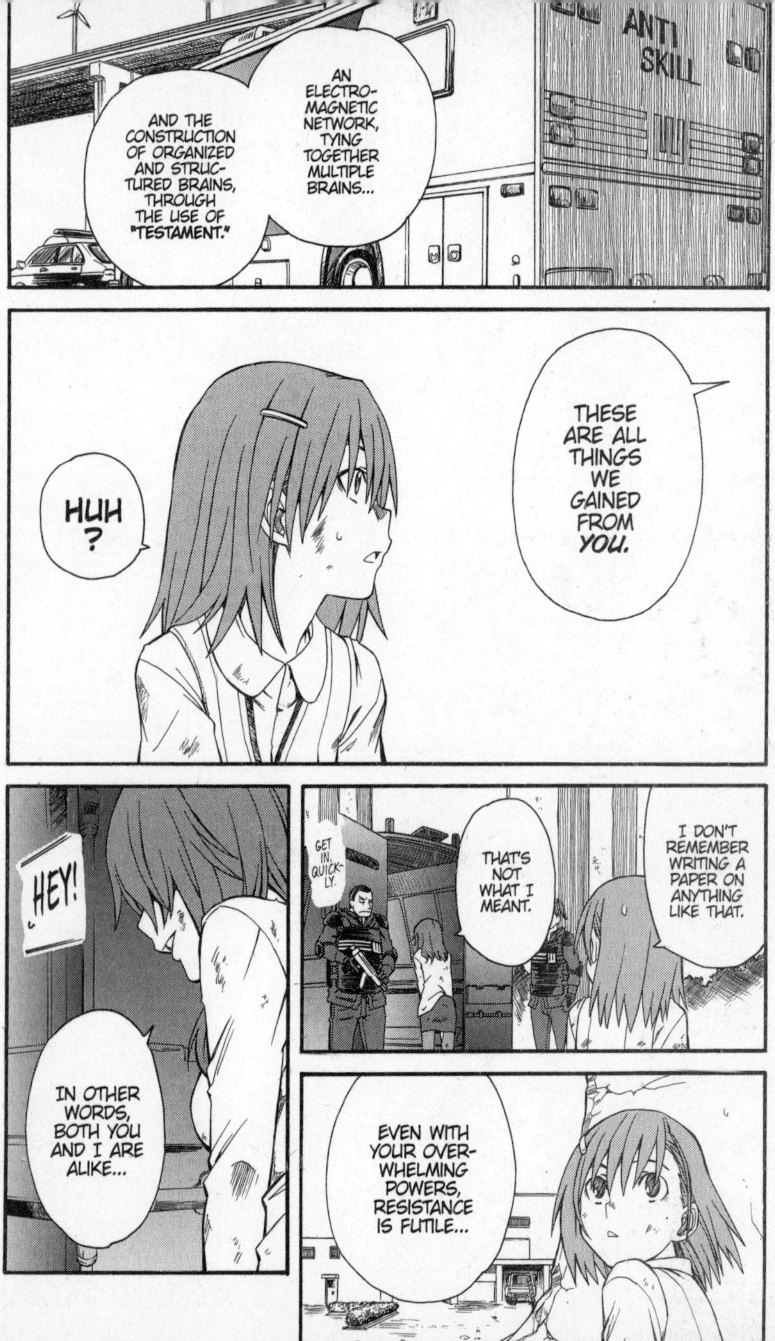
AN ELECTROMAGNETIC NETWORK, TYING TOGETHER MULTIPLE BRAINS...
AND THE CONSTRUCTION OF ORGANIZED AND STRUCTURED BRAINS, THROUGH THE USE OF "TESTAMENT."
ANTI SKILL
THESE ARE ALL THINGS WE GAINED FROM *YOU*.
HUH?
I DON'T REMEMBER WRITING A PAPER ON ANYTHING LIKE THAT.
THAT'S NOT WHAT I MEANT.
GET IN, QUICKLY.
EVEN WITH YOUR OVERWHELMING POWERS, RESISTANCE IS FUTILE...
HEY!
IN OTHER WORDS, BOTH YOU AND I ARE ALIKE...

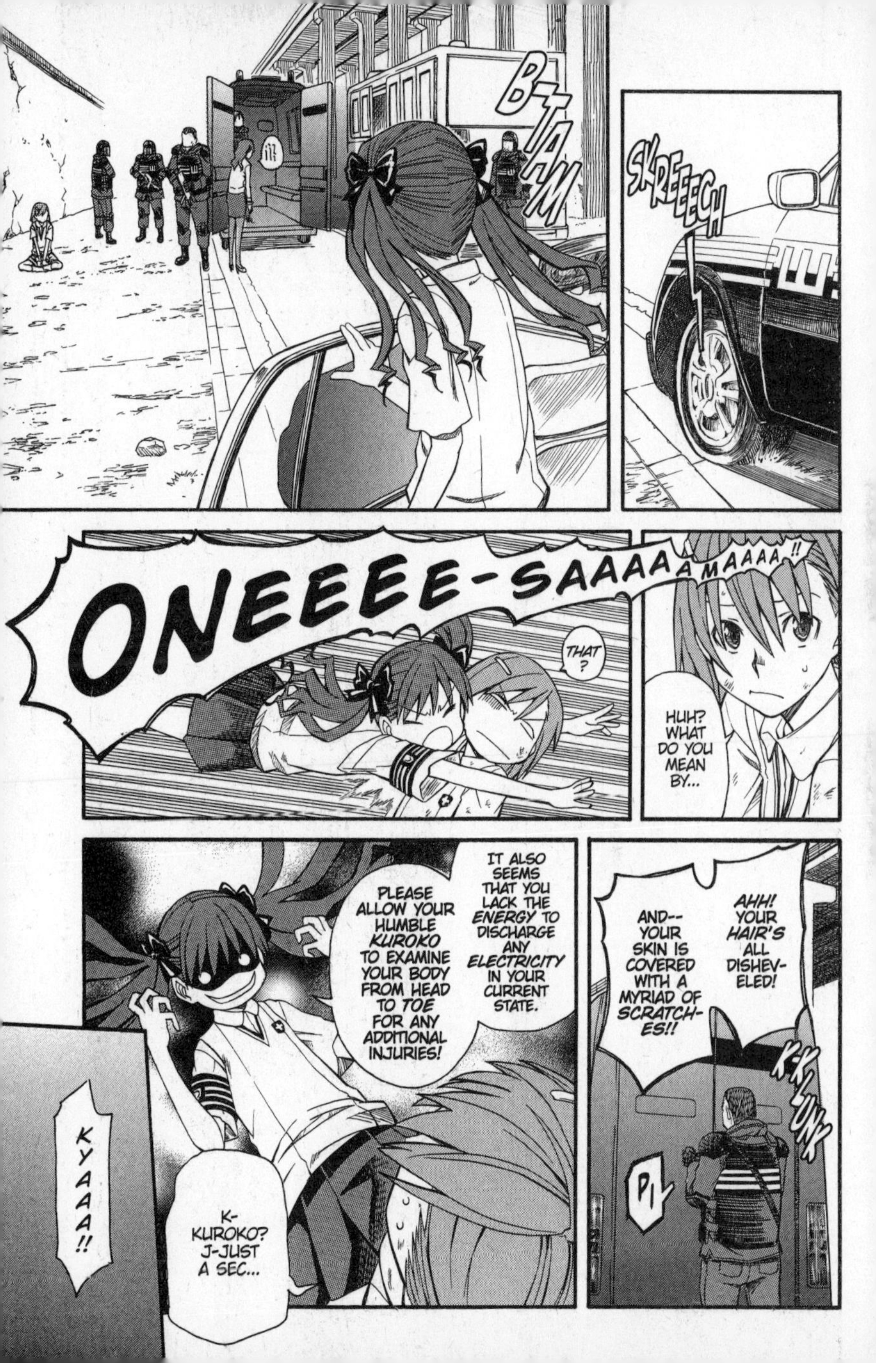
SKREEECH
B-TAM
HUH? WHAT DO YOU MEAN BY...
ONEEEE-SAAAAAMAAAA!!
THAT?
AHH! YOUR HAIR'S ALL DISHEVELED!
AND-- YOUR SKIN IS COVERED WITH A MYRIAD OF SCRATCHES!!
K-KLUNK
PI
IT ALSO SEEMS THAT YOU LACK THE ENERGY TO DISCHARGE ANY ELECTRICITY IN YOUR CURRENT STATE.
PLEASE ALLOW YOUR HUMBLE KUROKO TO EXAMINE YOUR BODY FROM HEAD TO TOE FOR ANY ADDITIONAL INJURIES!
K-KUROKO? J-JUST A SEC...
KYAAAA!!

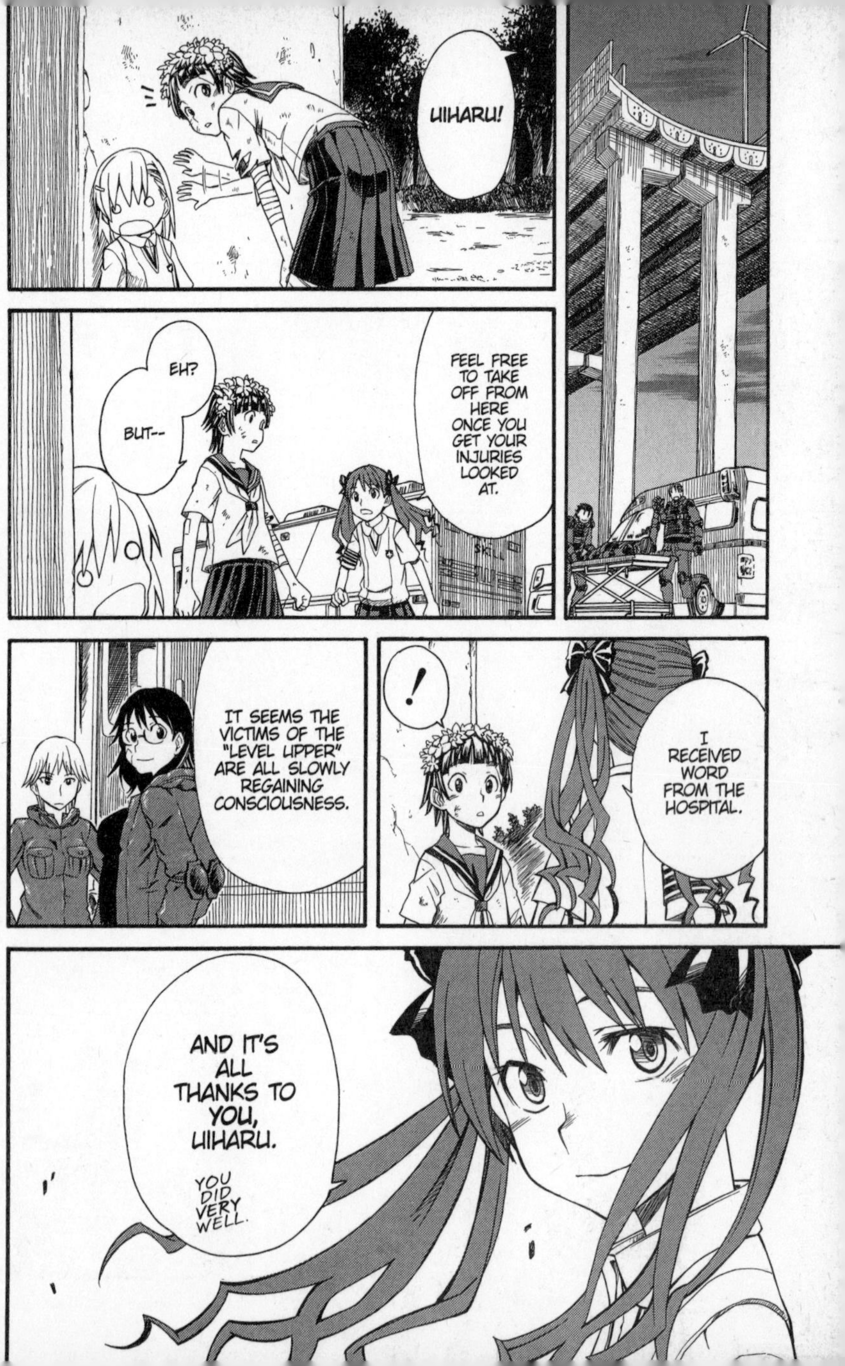
UIHARU!
FEEL FREE TO TAKE OFF FROM HERE ONCE YOU GET YOUR INJURIES LOOKED AT.
EH?
BUT--
I RECEIVED WORD FROM THE HOSPITAL.
!
IT SEEMS THE VICTIMS OF THE "LEVEL UPPER" ARE ALL SLOWLY REGAINING CONSCIOUSNESS.
AND IT'S ALL THANKS TO YOU, UIHARU.
YOU DID VERY WELL.

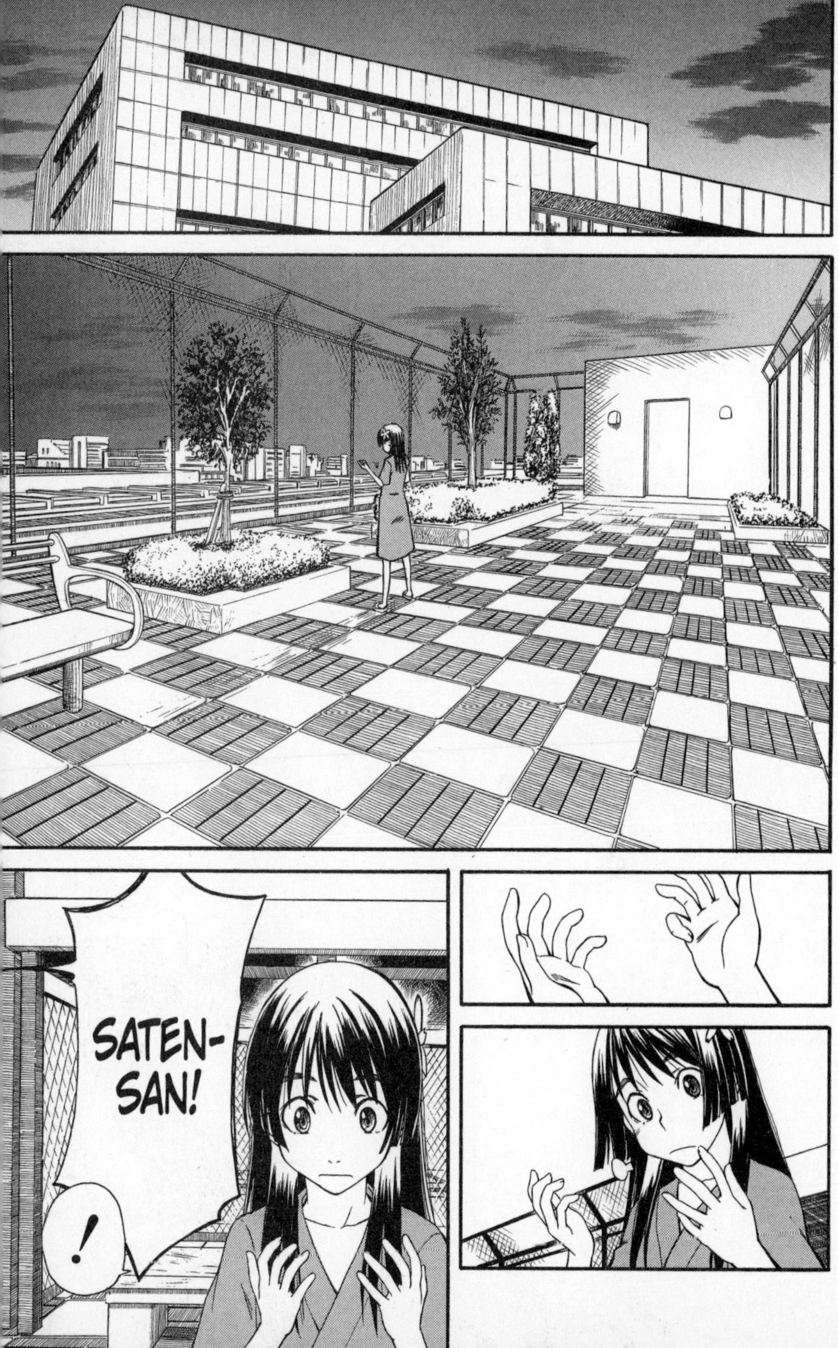
SATEN-SAN!
!

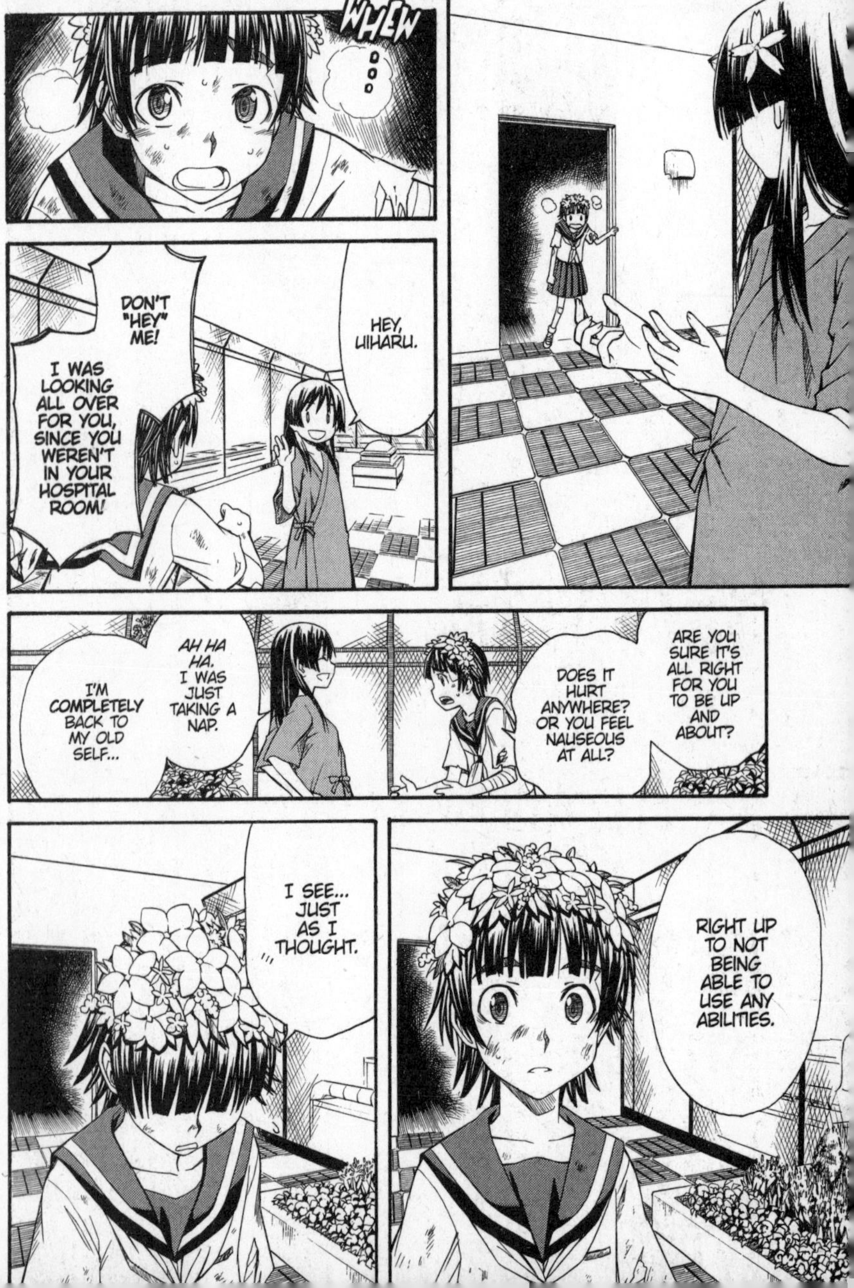
WHEW
HEY, UIHARU.
DON'T "HEY" ME!
I WAS LOOKING ALL OVER FOR YOU, SINCE YOU WEREN'T IN YOUR HOSPITAL ROOM!
ARE YOU SURE IT'S ALL RIGHT FOR YOU TO BE UP AND ABOUT?
DOES IT HURT ANYWHERE? OR YOU FEEL NAUSEOUS AT ALL?
AH HA HA. I WAS JUST TAKING A NAP.
I'M COMPLETELY BACK TO MY OLD SELF...
RIGHT UP TO NOT BEING ABLE TO USE ANY ABILITIES.
I SEE... JUST AS I THOUGHT.

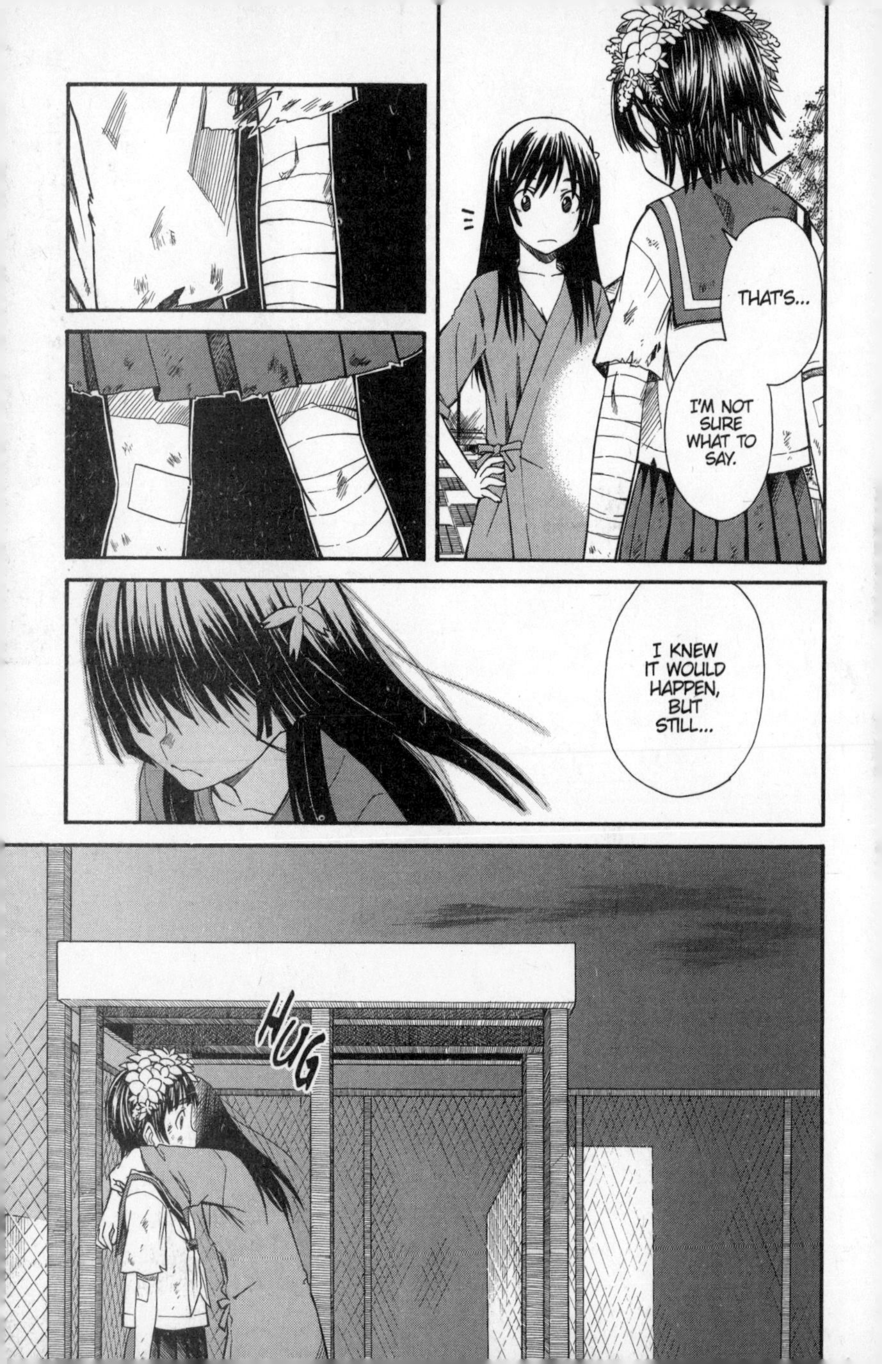
THAT'S...
I'M NOT SURE WHAT TO SAY.
I KNEW IT WOULD HAPPEN, BUT STILL...
HUG

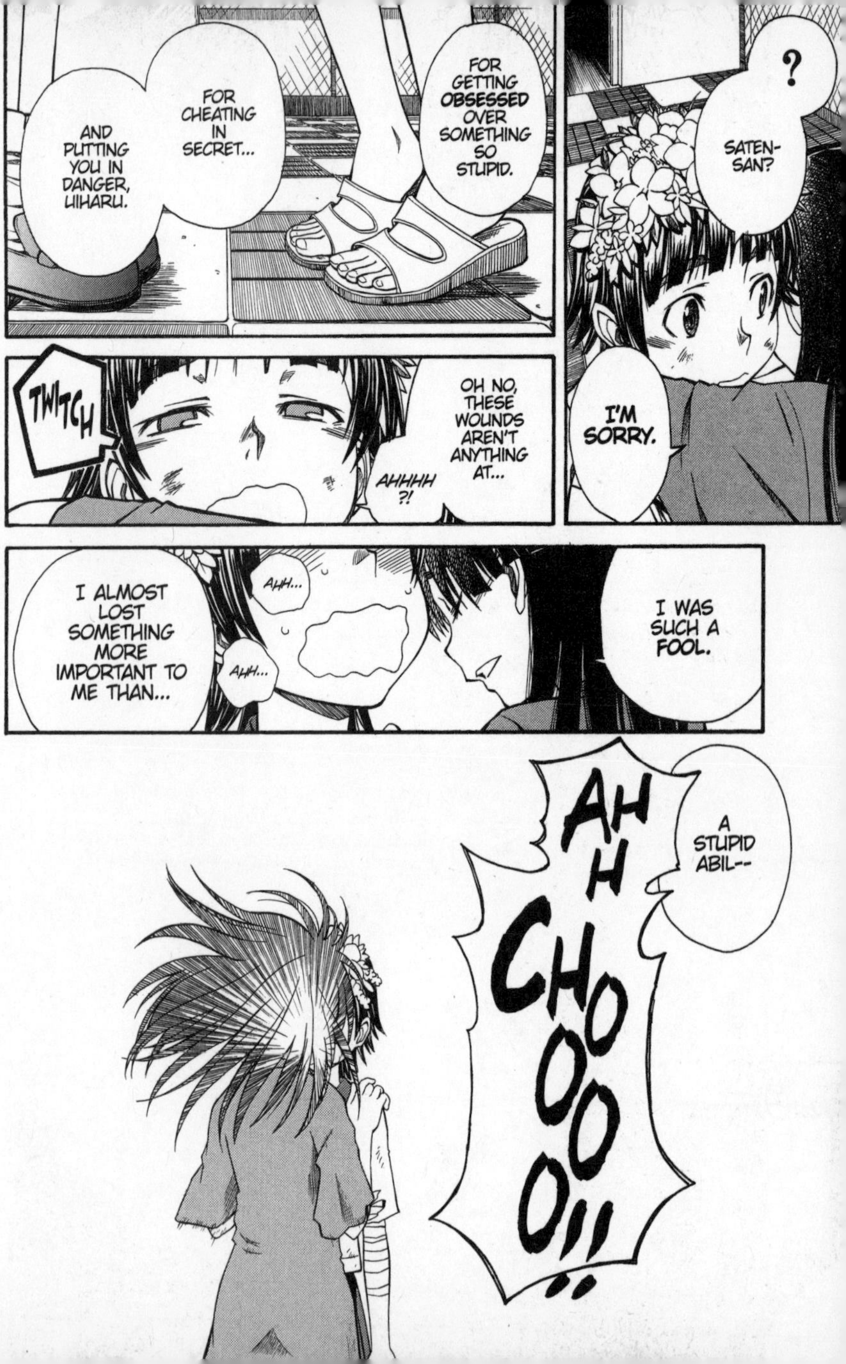
?
SATEN-SAN?
I'M SORRY.
FOR GETTING **OBSESSED** OVER SOMETHING SO STUPID.
FOR CHEATING IN SECRET...
AND PUTTING YOU IN DANGER, UIHARU.
OH NO, THESE WOUNDS AREN'T ANYTHING AT...
AHHHH ?!
TWITCH
I WAS SUCH A FOOL.
AHH...
AHH...
I ALMOST LOST SOMETHING MORE IMPORTANT TO ME THAN...
A STUPID ABIL--
AHHCHOOOO!!!!

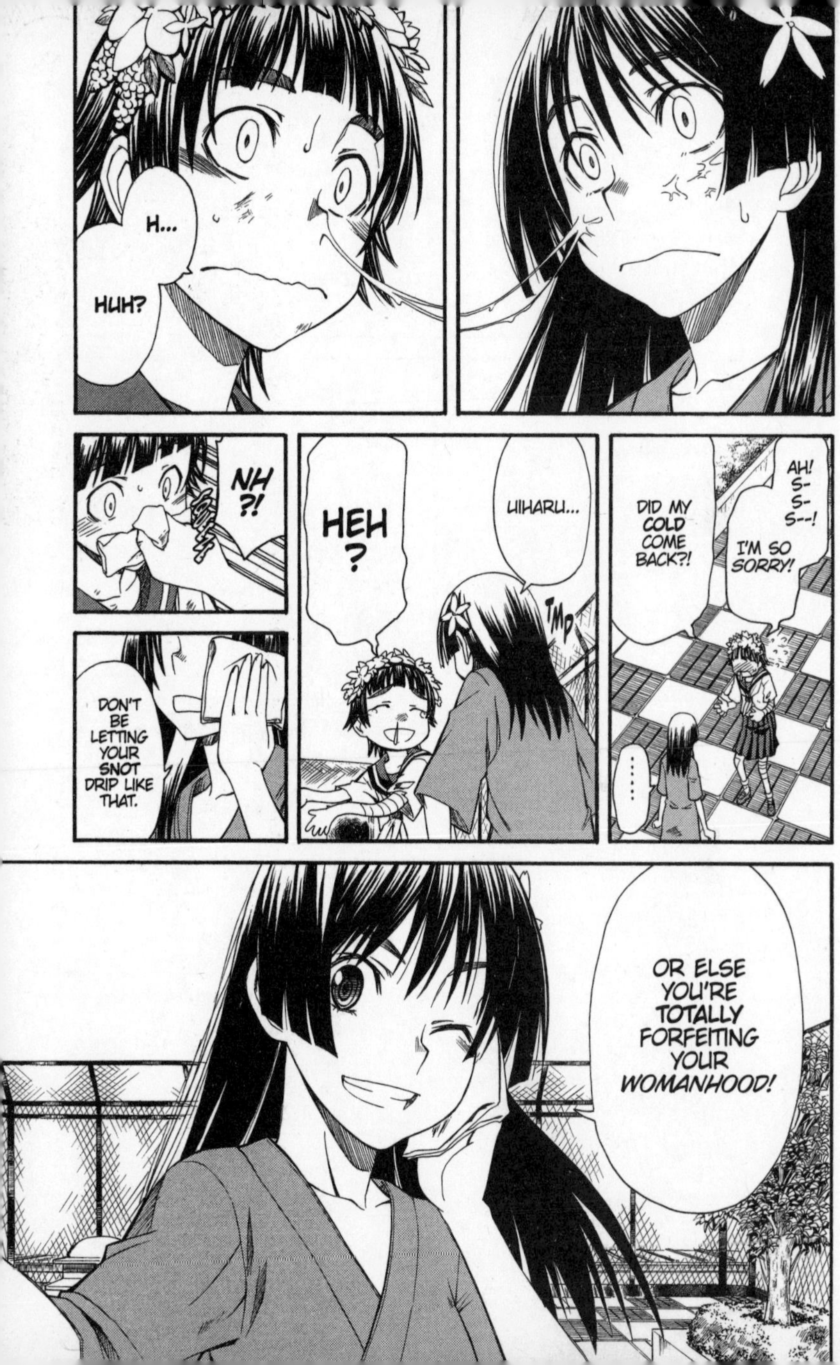
H...
HUH?
AH! S-S-S--!
I'M SO SORRY!
DID MY COLD COME BACK?!
......
UIHARU...
TMP
HEH?
NH?!
DON'T BE LETTING YOUR SNOT DRIP LIKE THAT.
OR ELSE YOU'RE TOTALLY FORFEITING YOUR WOMANHOOD!

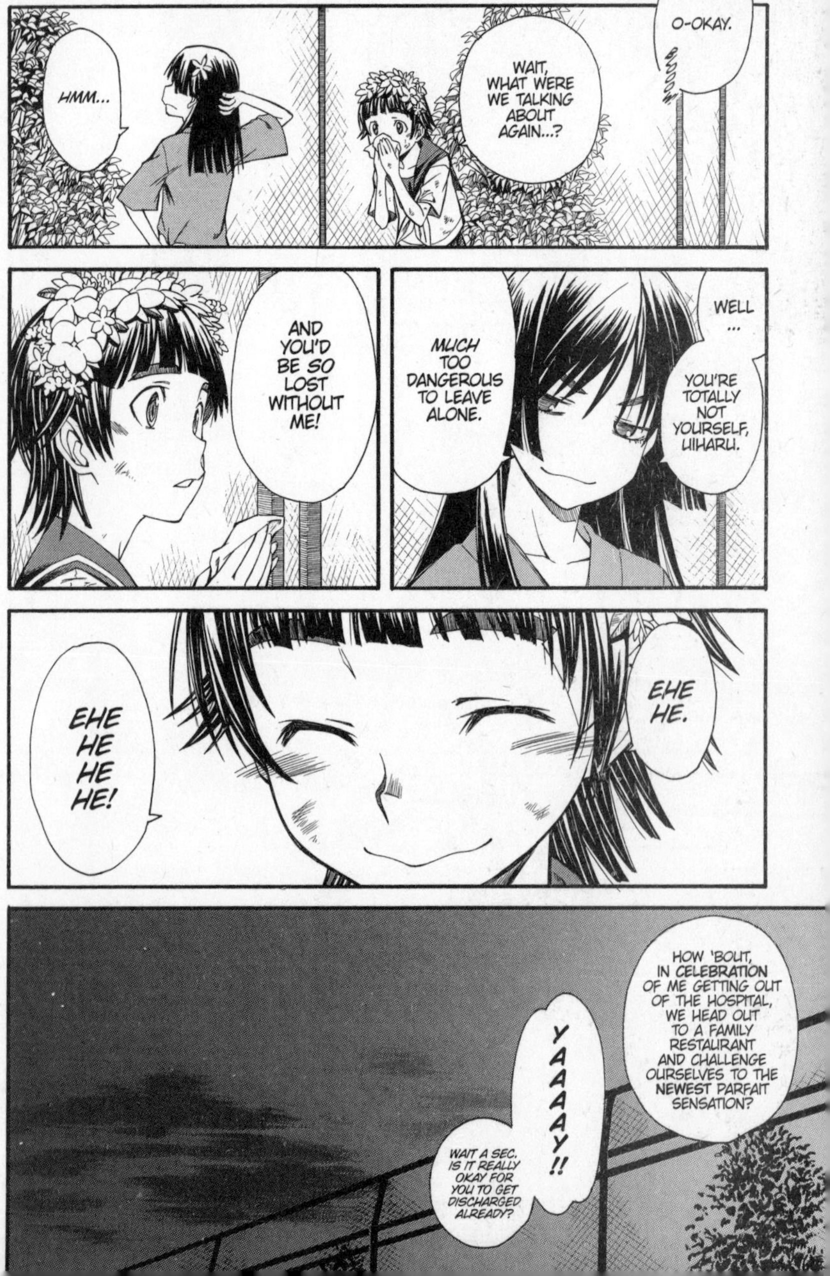
O-OKAY.
WAIT, WHAT WERE WE TALKING ABOUT AGAIN...?
HMM...
WELL ...
YOU'RE TOTALLY NOT YOURSELF, UIHARU.
MUCH TOO DANGEROUS TO LEAVE ALONE.
AND YOU'D BE SO LOST WITHOUT ME!
EHE HE.
EHE HE HE HE!
HOW 'BOUT, IN CELEBRATION OF ME GETTING OUT OF THE HOSPITAL, WE HEAD OUT TO A FAMILY RESTAURANT AND CHALLENGE OURSELVES TO THE NEWEST PARFAIT SENSATION?
YAAAAAY!!
WAIT A SEC. IS IT REALLY OKAY FOR YOU TO GET DISCHARGED ALREADY?

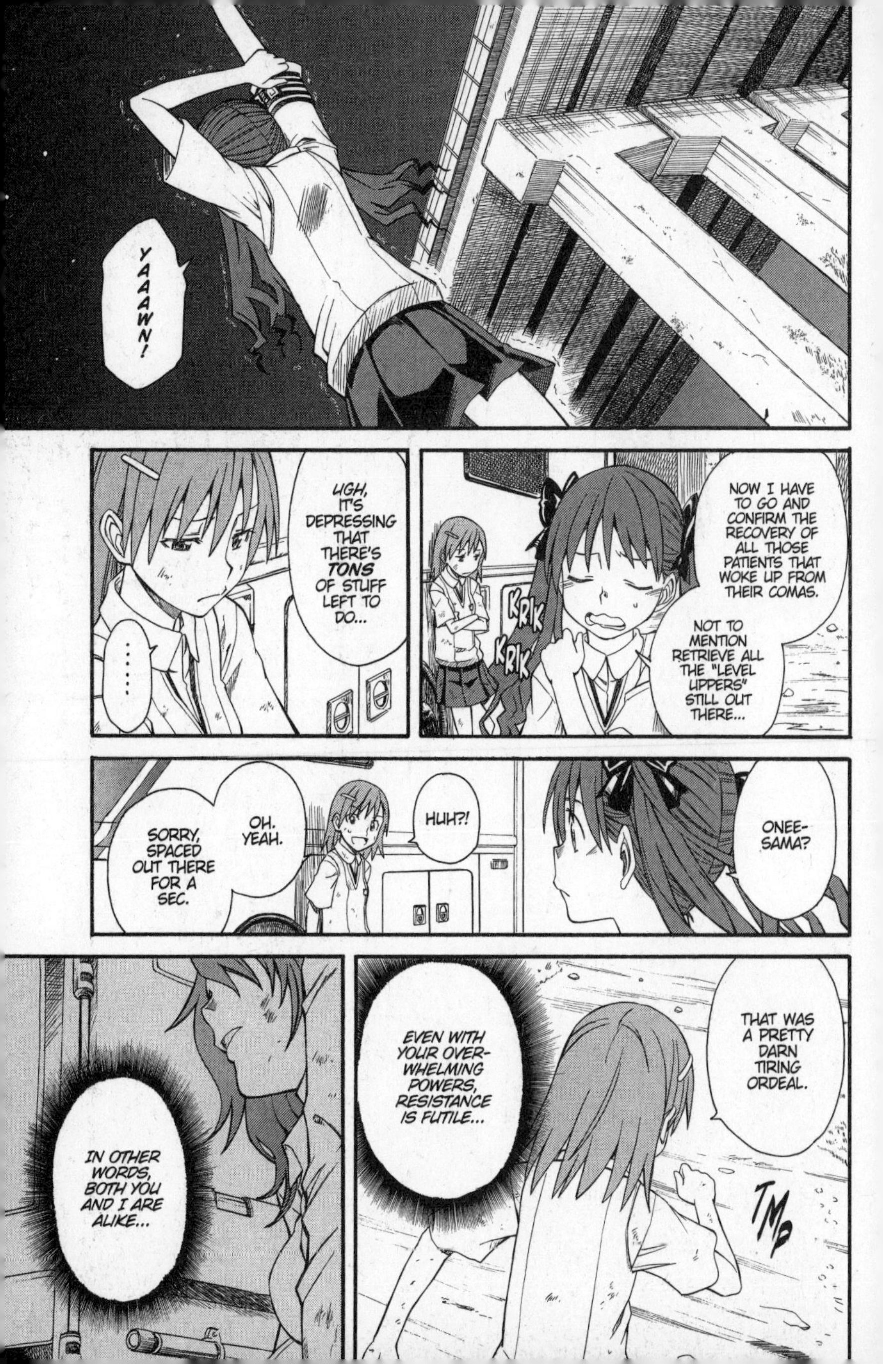
YAAAWN!
NOW I HAVE TO GO AND CONFIRM THE RECOVERY OF ALL THOSE PATIENTS THAT WOKE UP FROM THEIR COMAS.
NOT TO MENTION RETRIEVE ALL THE "LEVEL UPPERS" STILL OUT THERE...
KRIK
KRIK
UGH, IT'S DEPRESSING THAT THERE'S TONS OF STUFF LEFT TO DO...
......
ONEE-SAMA?
HUH?!
OH. YEAH.
SORRY, SPACED OUT THERE FOR A SEC.
THAT WAS A PRETTY DARN TIRING ORDEAL.
TMP
EVEN WITH YOUR OVER-WHELMING POWERS, RESISTANCE IS FUTILE...
IN OTHER WORDS, BOTH YOU AND I ARE ALIKE...

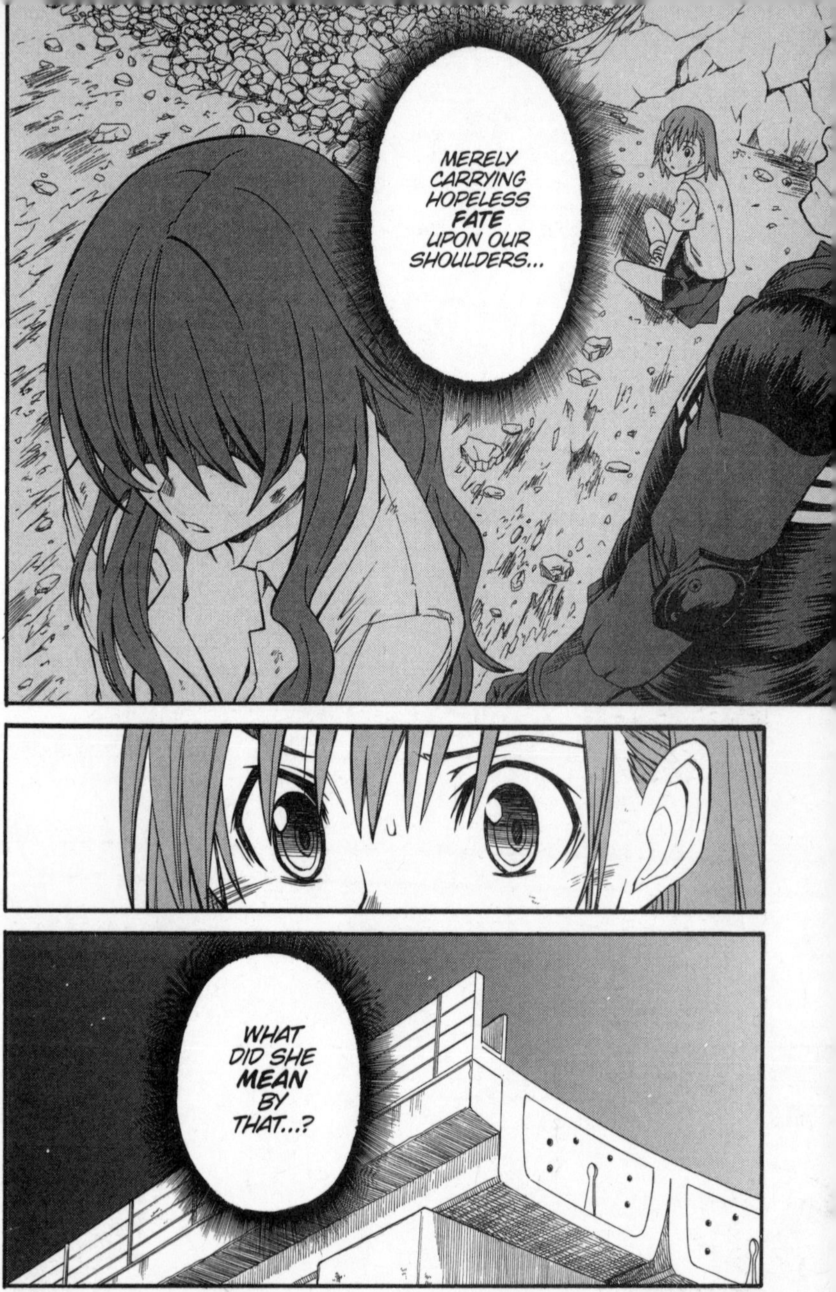
MERELY CARRYING HOPELESS FATE UPON OUR SHOULDERS...
WHAT DID SHE MEAN BY THAT...?

A Certain
SCIENTIFIC Railgun

A CERTAIN STUDENT'S EPILOGUE

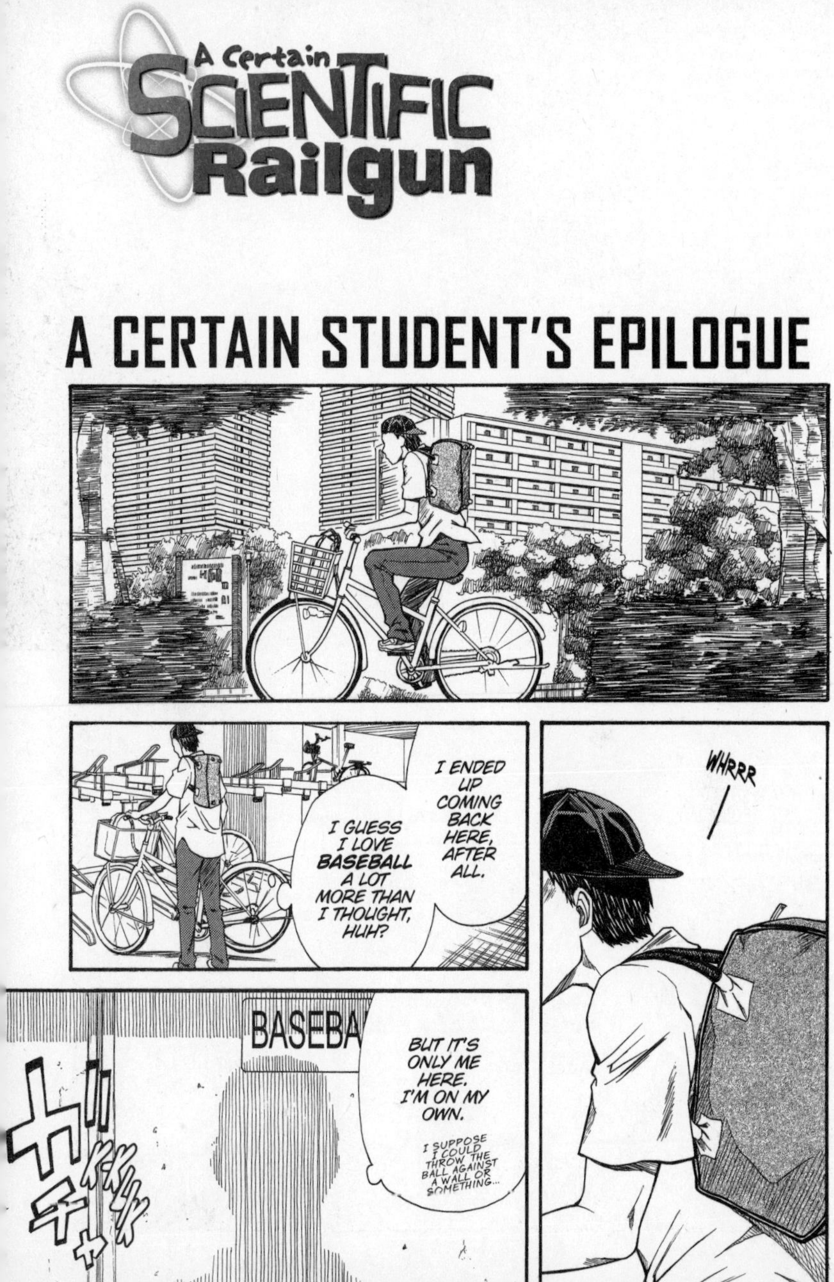
WHRRR
I ENDED UP COMING BACK HERE, AFTER ALL.
I GUESS I LOVE BASEBALL A LOT MORE THAN I THOUGHT, HUH?
BUT IT'S ONLY ME HERE. I'M ON MY OWN.
I SUPPOSE I COULD THROW THE BALL AGAINST A WALL OR SOMETHING...
BASEBA

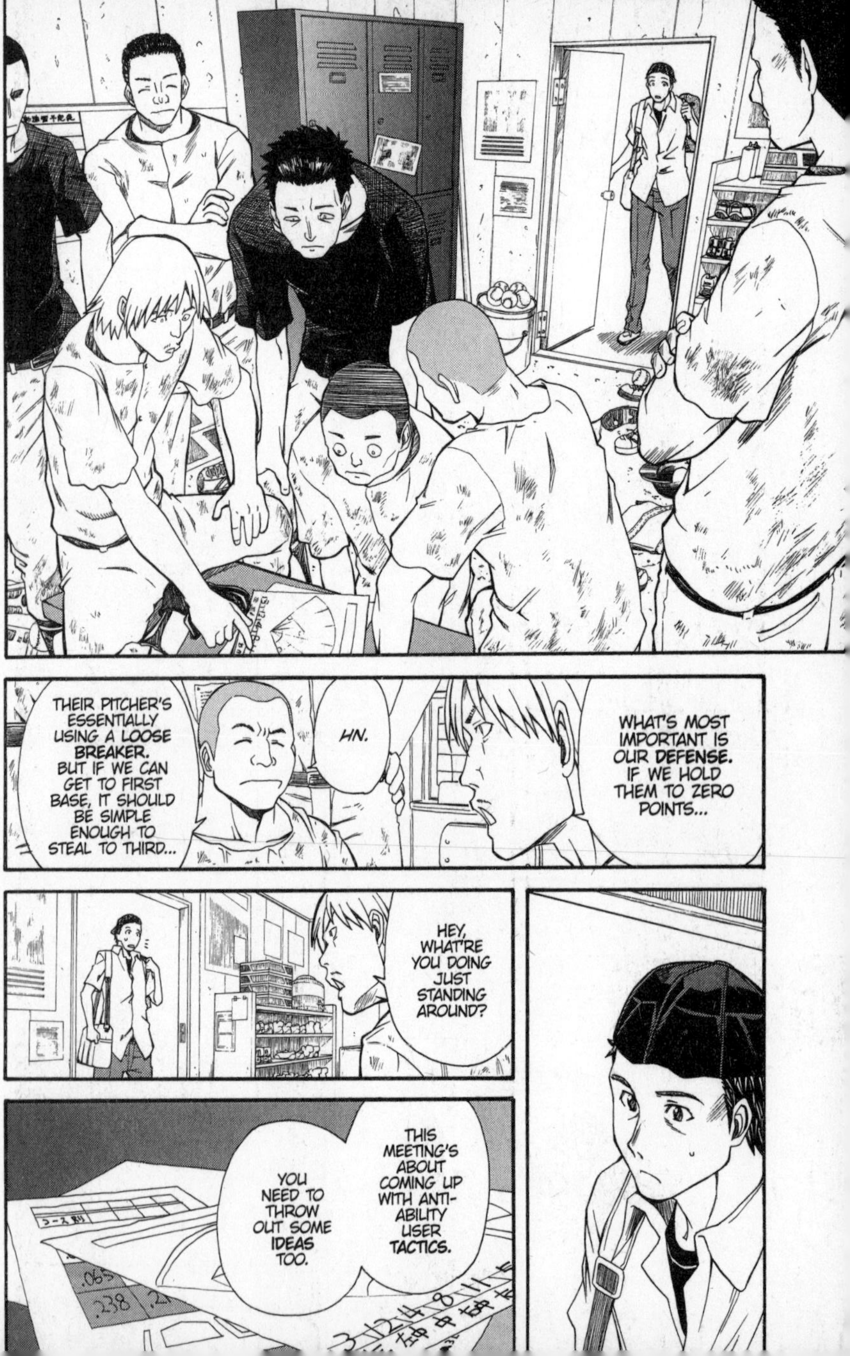
WHAT'S MOST IMPORTANT IS OUR DEFENSE. IF WE HOLD THEM TO ZERO POINTS...
HN.
THEIR PITCHER'S ESSENTIALLY USING A LOOSE BREAKER. BUT IF WE CAN GET TO FIRST BASE, IT SHOULD BE SIMPLE ENOUGH TO STEAL TO THIRD...
HEY, WHAT'RE YOU DOING JUST STANDING AROUND?
THIS MEETING'S ABOUT COMING UP WITH ANTI-ABILITY USER TACTICS.
YOU NEED TO THROW OUT SOME IDEAS TOO.

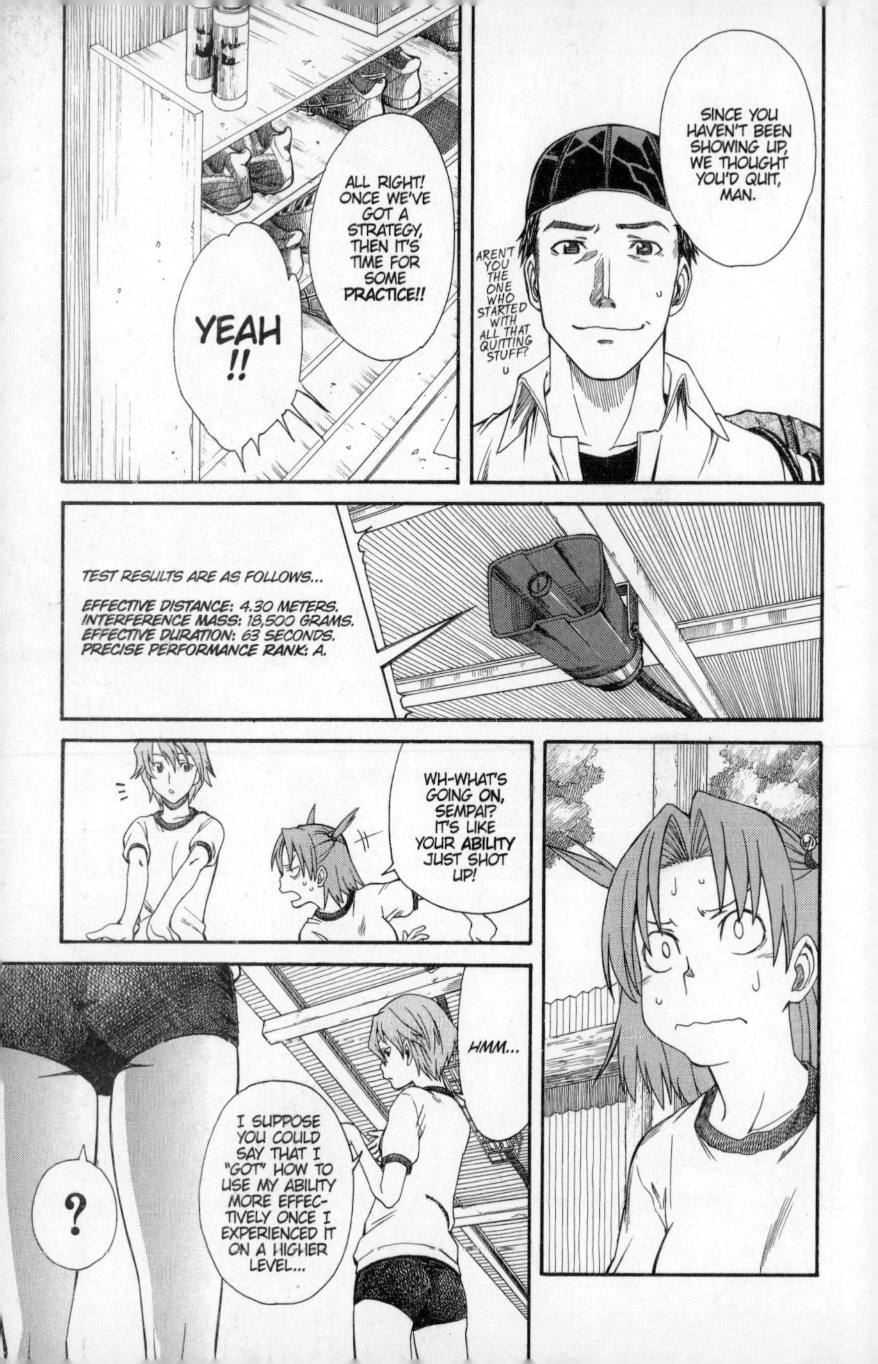
SINCE YOU HAVEN'T BEEN SHOWING UP, WE THOUGHT YOU'D QUIT, MAN.
AREN'T YOU THE ONE WHO STARTED WITH ALL THAT QUITTING STUFF?
ALL RIGHT! ONCE WE'VE GOT A STRATEGY, THEN IT'S TIME FOR SOME PRACTICE!!
YEAH !!
TEST RESULTS ARE AS FOLLOWS...
EFFECTIVE DISTANCE: 4.30 METERS.
INTERFERENCE MASS: 18,500 GRAMS.
EFFECTIVE DURATION: 63 SECONDS.
PRECISE PERFORMANCE RANK: A.
WH-WHAT'S GOING ON, SEMPAI? IT'S LIKE YOUR ABILITY JUST SHOT UP!
HMM...
I SUPPOSE YOU COULD SAY THAT I "GOT" HOW TO USE MY ABILITY MORE EFFECTIVELY ONCE I EXPERIENCED IT ON A HIGHER LEVEL...
?

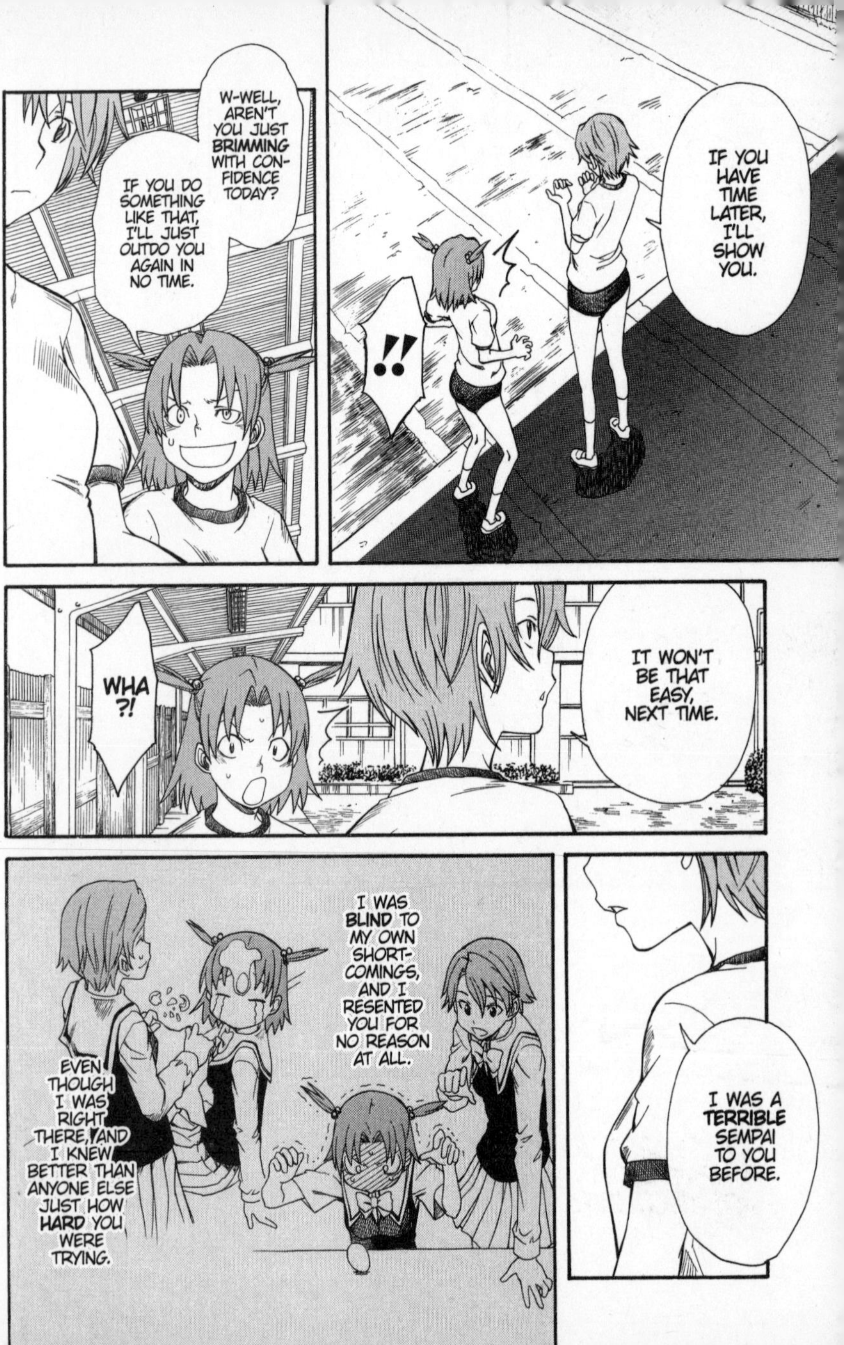
IF YOU HAVE TIME LATER, I'LL SHOW YOU.
!!
W-WELL, AREN'T YOU JUST BRIMMING WITH CONFIDENCE TODAY?
IF YOU DO SOMETHING LIKE THAT, I'LL JUST OUTDO YOU AGAIN IN NO TIME.
IT WON'T BE THAT EASY, NEXT TIME.
WHA ?!
I WAS A TERRIBLE SEMPAI TO YOU BEFORE.
I WAS BLIND TO MY OWN SHORTCOMINGS, AND I RESENTED YOU FOR NO REASON AT ALL.
EVEN THOUGH I WAS RIGHT THERE, AND I KNEW BETTER THAN ANYONE ELSE JUST HOW HARD YOU WERE TRYING.

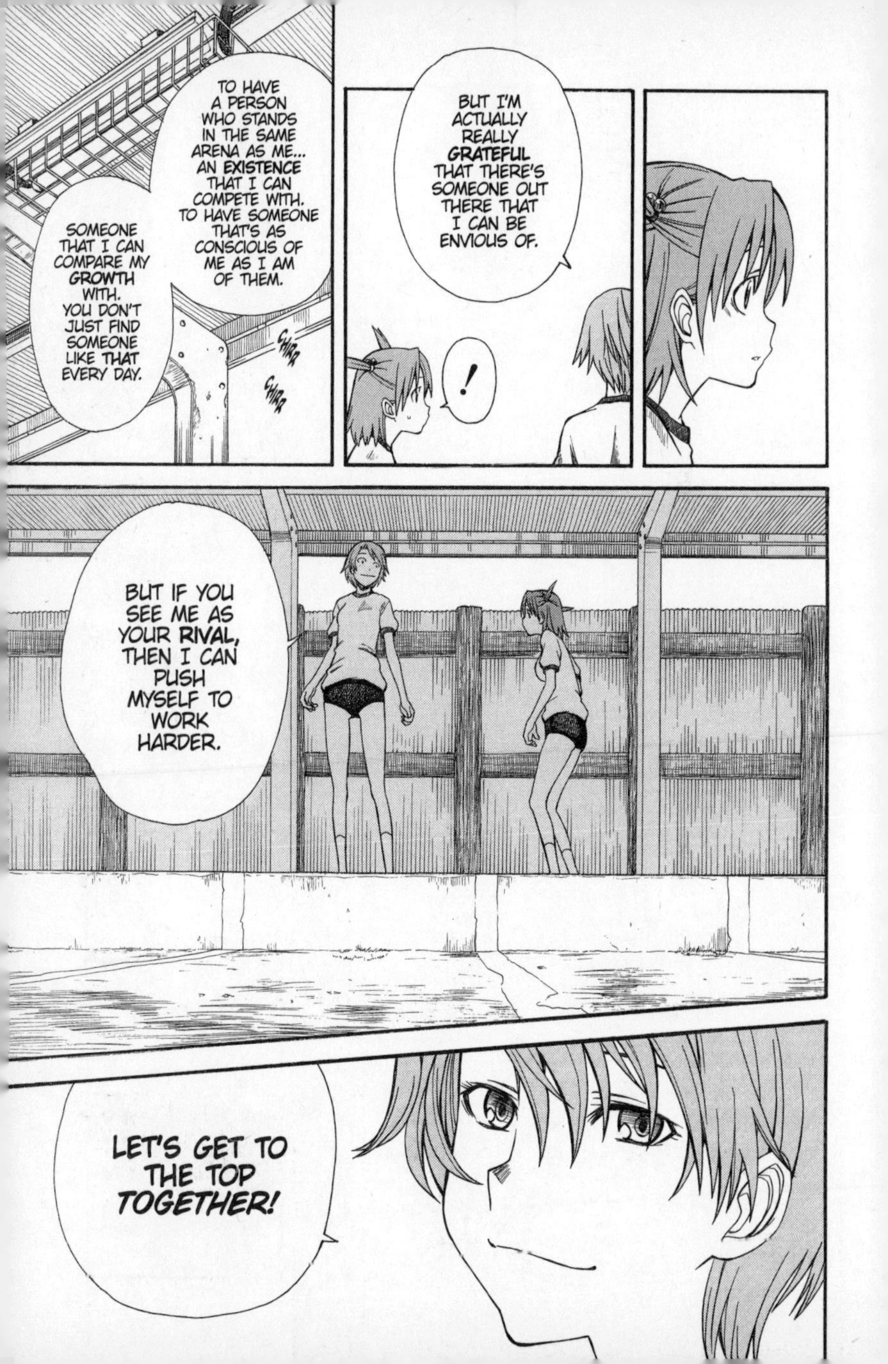
BUT I'M ACTUALLY REALLY GRATEFUL THAT THERE'S SOMEONE OUT THERE THAT I CAN BE ENVIOUS OF.
!
TO HAVE A PERSON WHO STANDS IN THE SAME ARENA AS ME... AN EXISTENCE THAT I CAN COMPETE WITH. TO HAVE SOMEONE THAT'S AS CONSCIOUS OF ME AS I AM OF THEM.
SOMEONE THAT I CAN COMPARE MY GROWTH WITH. YOU DON'T JUST FIND SOMEONE LIKE THAT EVERY DAY.
CHIRA
CHIRA
BUT IF YOU SEE ME AS YOUR RIVAL, THEN I CAN PUSH MYSELF TO WORK HARDER.
LET'S GET TO THE TOP TOGETHER!

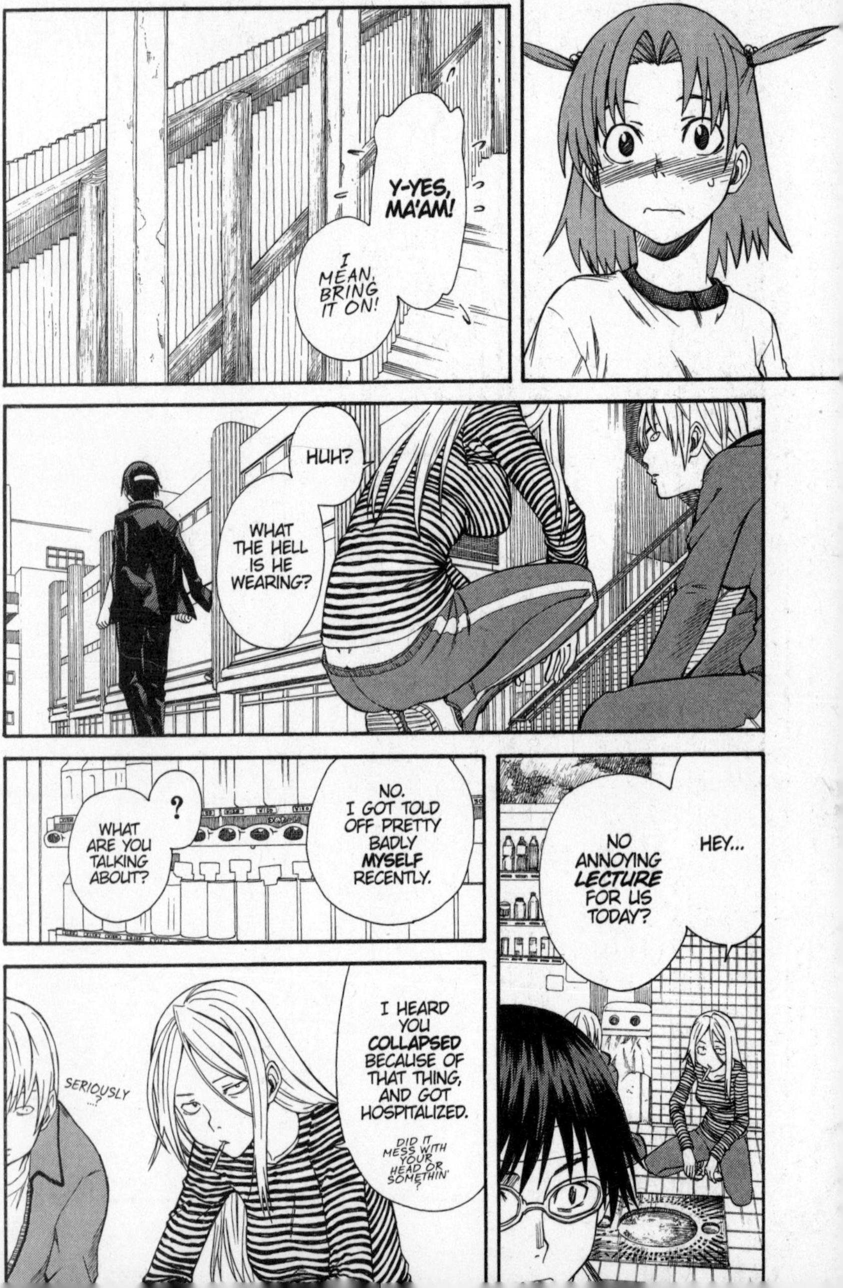
Y-YES, MA'AM!
I MEAN, BRING IT ON!
HUH?
WHAT THE HELL IS HE WEARING?
HEY...
NO ANNOYING LECTURE FOR US TODAY?
NO. I GOT TOLD OFF PRETTY BADLY MYSELF RECENTLY.
?
WHAT ARE YOU TALKING ABOUT?
I HEARD YOU COLLAPSED BECAUSE OF THAT THING, AND GOT HOSPITALIZED.
DID IT MESS WITH YOUR HEAD OR SOMETHIN'?
SERIOUSLY...?

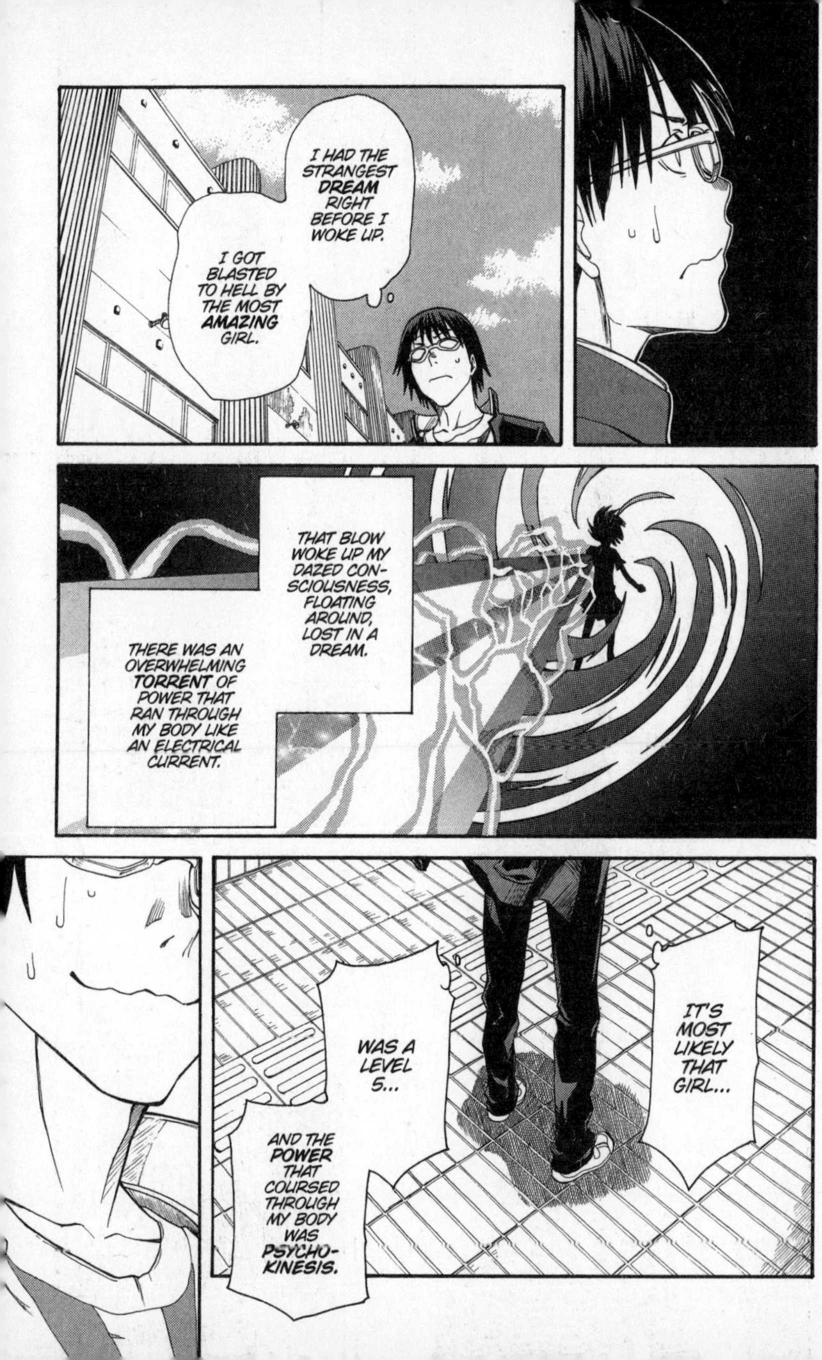
I HAD THE STRANGEST DREAM RIGHT BEFORE I WOKE UP.
I GOT BLASTED TO HELL BY THE MOST AMAZING GIRL.
THAT BLOW WOKE UP MY DAZED CON-SCIOUSNESS, FLOATING AROUND, LOST IN A DREAM.
THERE WAS AN OVERWHELMING TORRENT OF POWER THAT RAN THROUGH MY BODY LIKE AN ELECTRICAL CURRENT.
IT'S MOST LIKELY THAT GIRL...
WAS A LEVEL 5...
AND THE POWER THAT COURSED THROUGH MY BODY WAS PSYCHO-KINESIS.

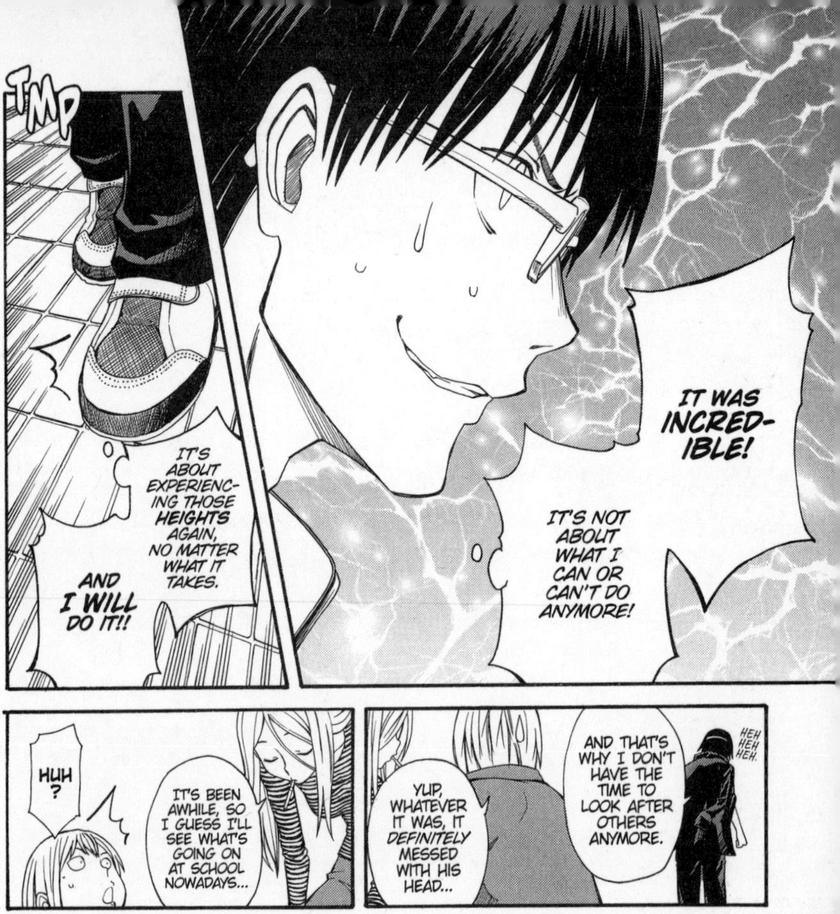
IT WAS INCREDIBLE!
IT'S NOT ABOUT WHAT I CAN OR CAN'T DO ANYMORE!
TMP
IT'S ABOUT EXPERIENCING THOSE HEIGHTS AGAIN, NO MATTER WHAT IT TAKES.
AND I WILL DO IT!!
HEH HEH HEH.
AND THAT'S WHY I DON'T HAVE THE TIME TO LOOK AFTER OTHERS ANYMORE.
YUP, WHATEVER IT WAS, IT DEFINITELY MESSED WITH HIS HEAD...
IT'S BEEN AWHILE, SO I GUESS I'LL SEE WHAT'S GOING ON AT SCHOOL NOWADAYS...
HUH?

THE CHILDREN OF THIS CITY AREN'T SO SOFT AS TO REMAIN *BROKEN* FOREVER.

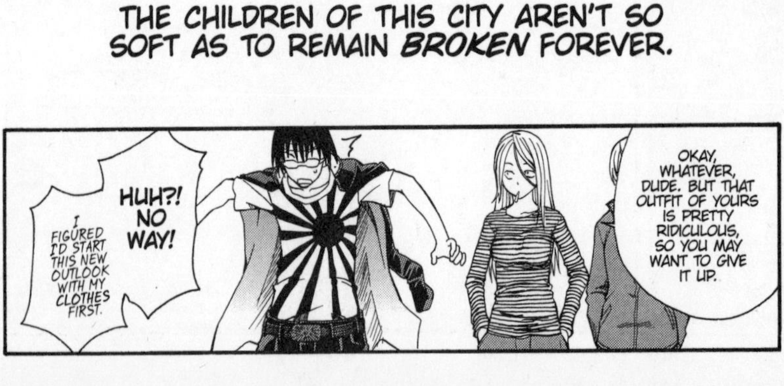
OKAY, WHATEVER, DUDE. BUT THAT OUTFIT OF YOURS IS PRETTY RIDICULOUS, SO YOU MAY WANT TO GIVE IT UP.
HUH?! NO WAY!
I FIGURED I'D START THIS NEW OUTLOOK WITH MY CLOTHES FIRST.

CHAPTER 17: JULY 25

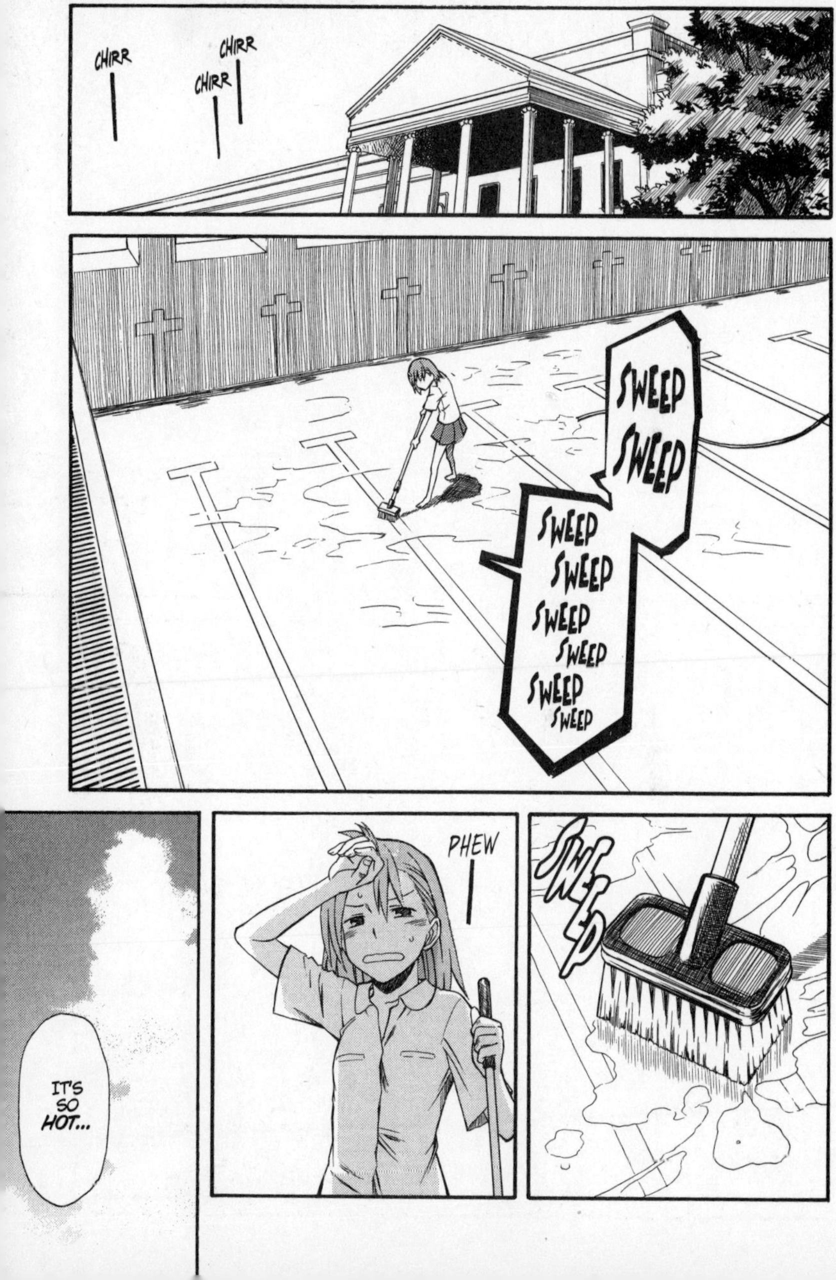
CHIRR
CHIRR
CHIRR
SWEEP SWEEP
SWEEP SWEEP SWEEP SWEEP SWEEP SWEEP
SWEEP
PHEW
IT'S SO HOT...

CHAPTER 17: JULY 25

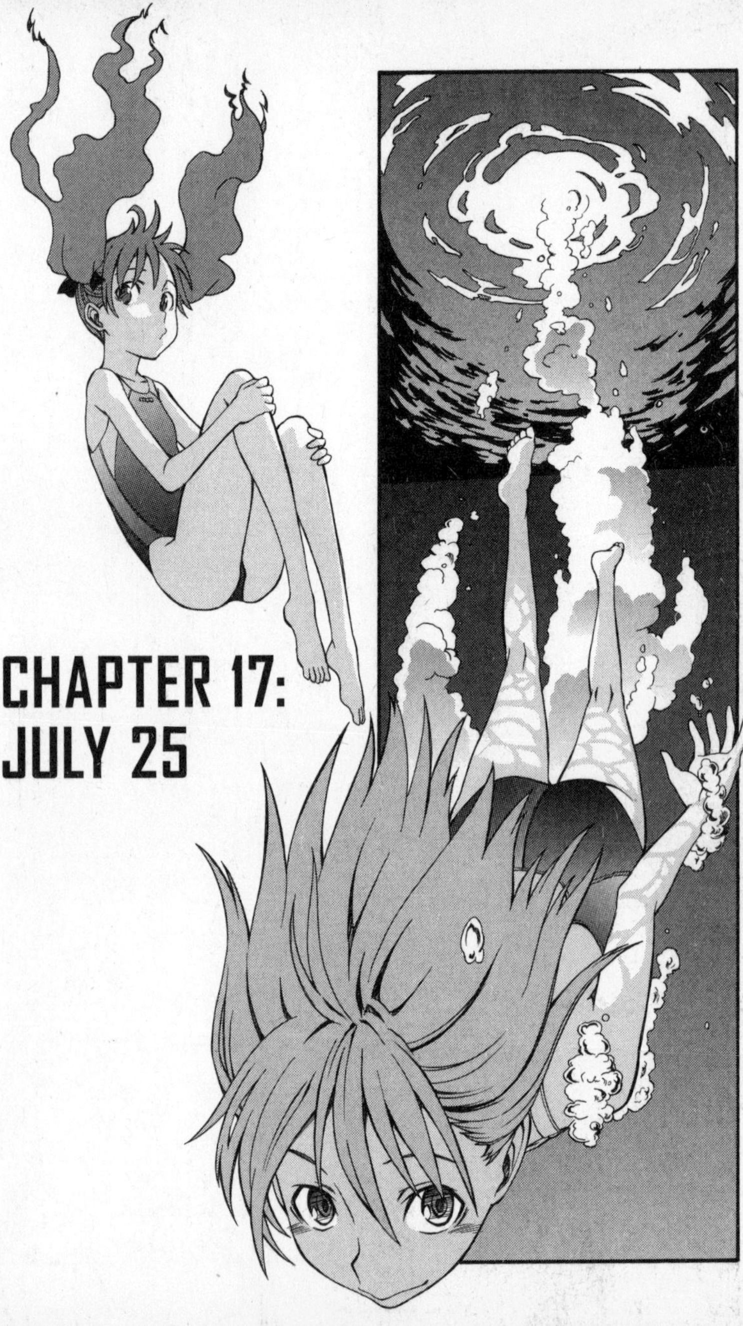

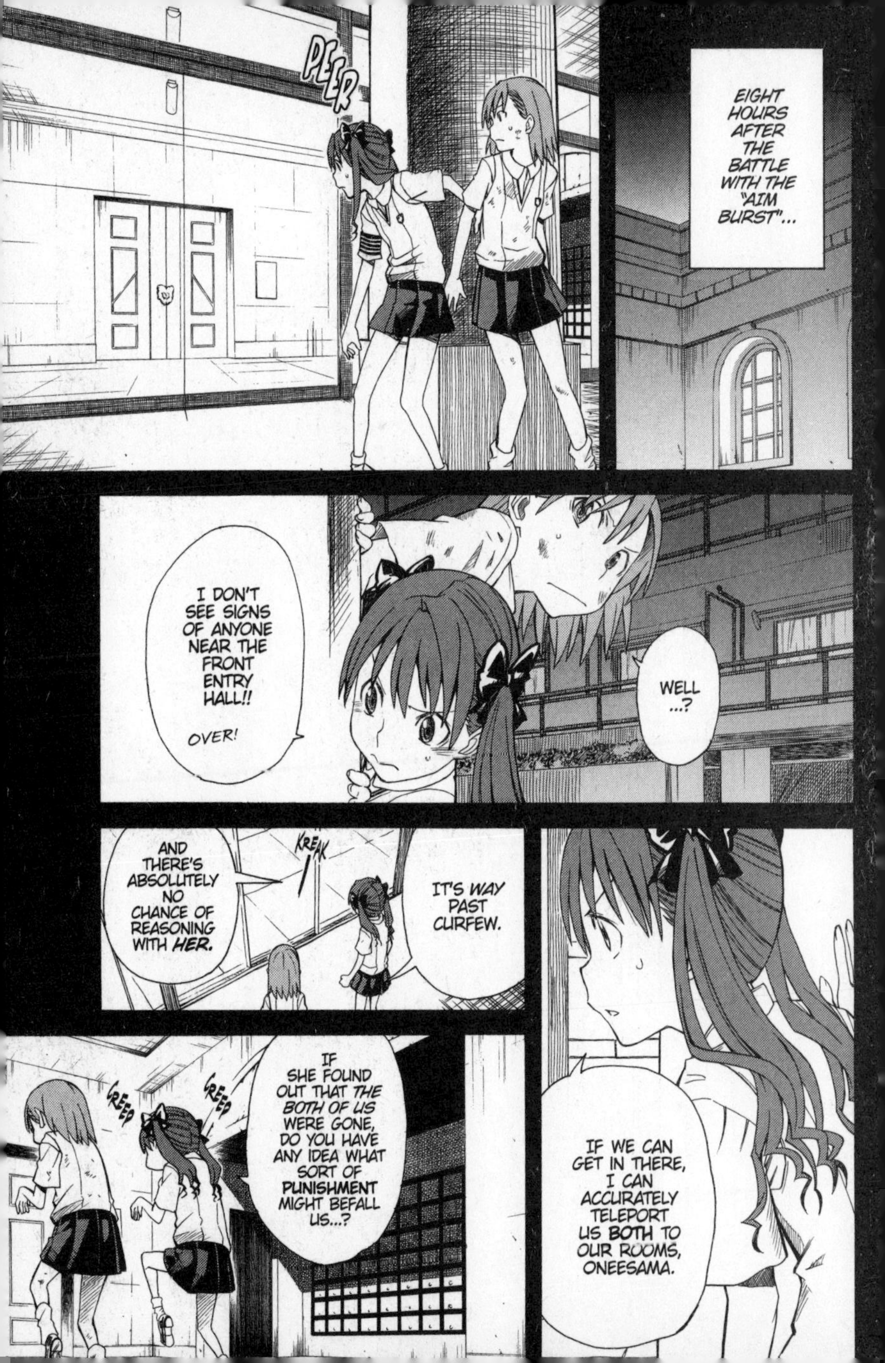
EIGHT HOURS AFTER THE BATTLE WITH THE "AIM BURST"...
PEER
WELL ...?
I DON'T SEE SIGNS OF ANYONE NEAR THE FRONT ENTRY HALL!! OVER!
IF WE CAN GET IN THERE, I CAN ACCURATELY TELEPORT US BOTH TO OUR ROOMS, ONEESAMA.
IT'S WAY PAST CURFEW.
KREAK
AND THERE'S ABSOLUTELY NO CHANCE OF REASONING WITH HER.
IF SHE FOUND OUT THAT THE BOTH OF US WERE GONE, DO YOU HAVE ANY IDEA WHAT SORT OF PUNISHMENT MIGHT BEFALL US...?
CREEP
CREEP

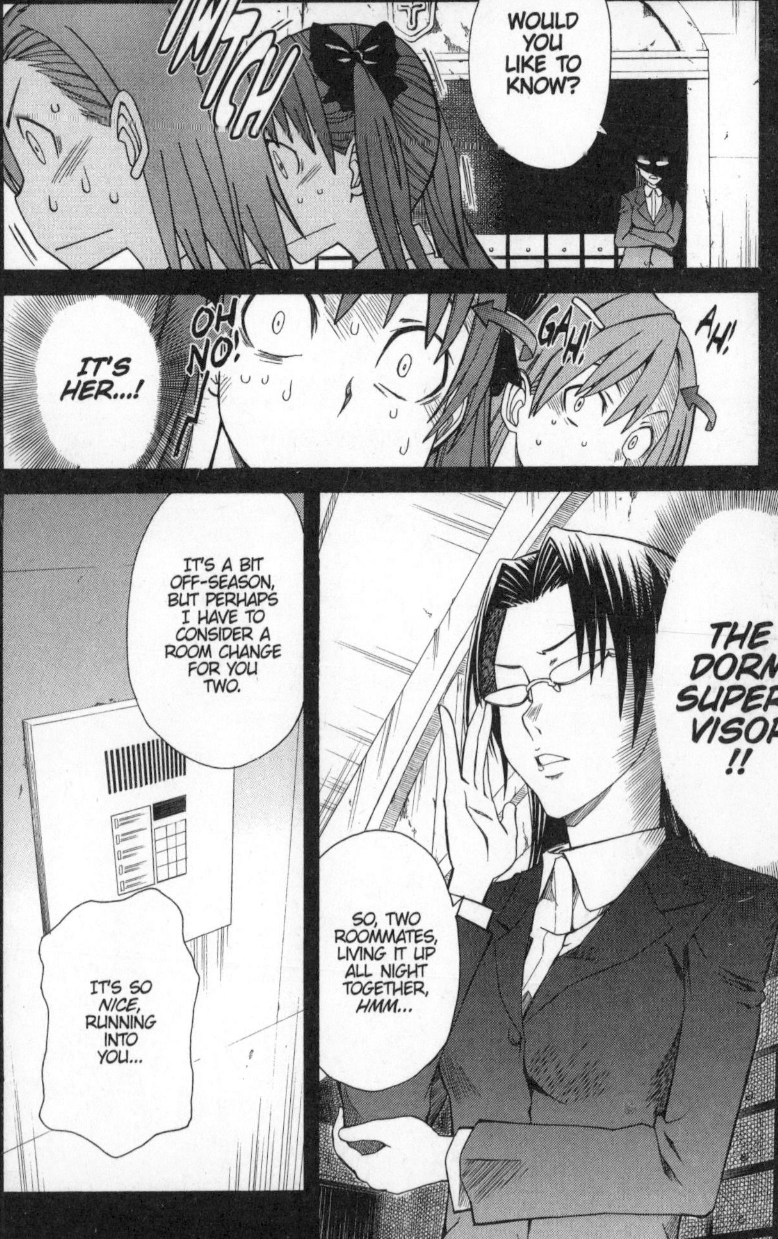
WOULD YOU LIKE TO KNOW?
TWITCH
AH!
GAH!
OH NO!
IT'S HER...!
THE DORM SUPER-VISOR!!
SO, TWO ROOMMATES, LIVING IT UP ALL NIGHT TOGETHER, *HMM...*
IT'S A BIT OFF-SEASON, BUT PERHAPS I HAVE TO CONSIDER A ROOM CHANGE FOR YOU TWO.
IT'S SO *NICE*, RUNNING INTO YOU...

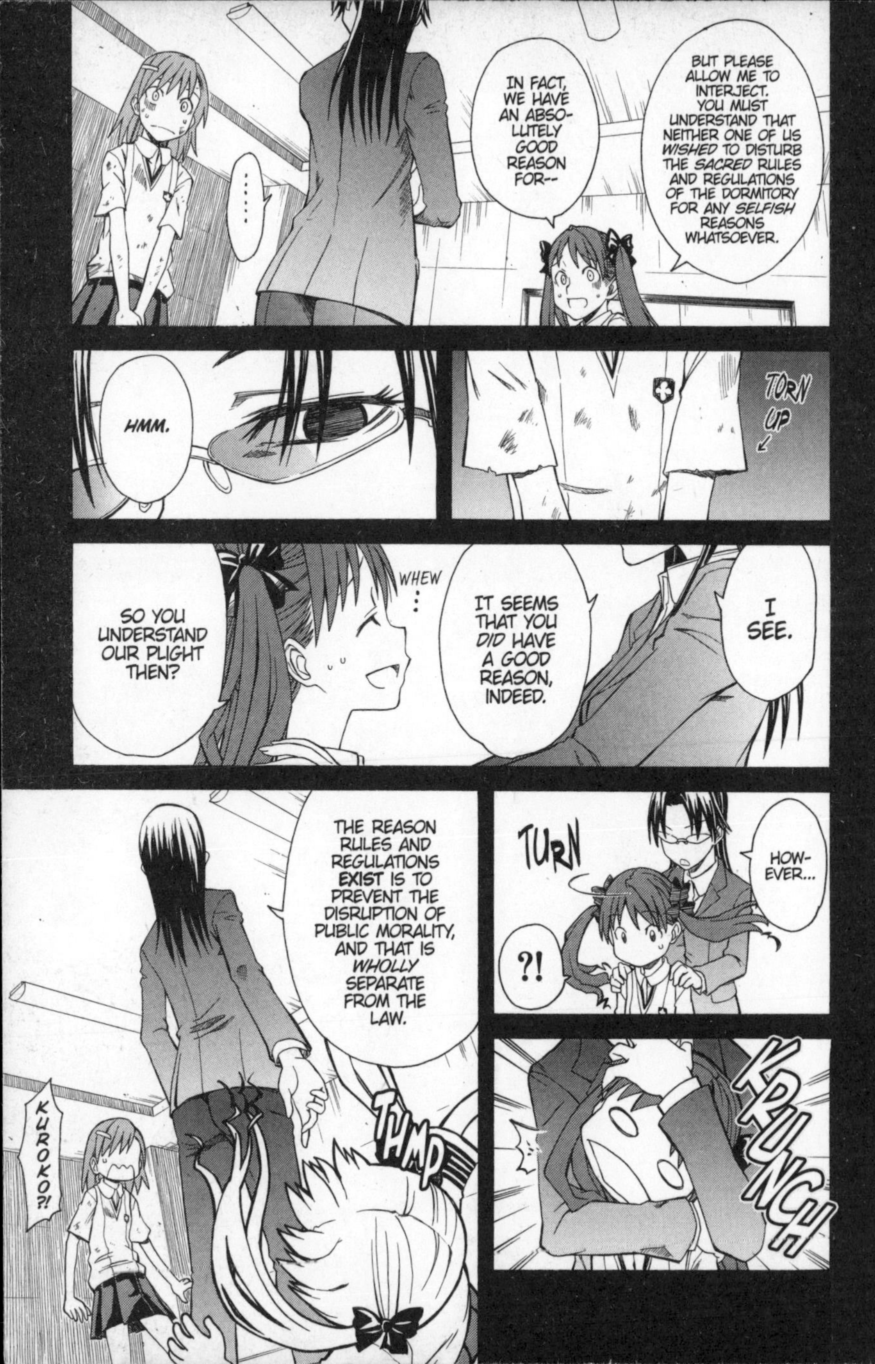
BUT PLEASE ALLOW ME TO INTERJECT. YOU MUST UNDERSTAND THAT NEITHER ONE OF US WISHED TO DISTURB THE SACRED RULES AND REGULATIONS OF THE DORMITORY FOR ANY SELFISH REASONS WHATSOEVER.
IN FACT, WE HAVE AN ABSOLUTELY GOOD REASON FOR--
......
TORN UP
HMM.
I SEE.
IT SEEMS THAT YOU DID HAVE A GOOD REASON, INDEED.
WHEW...
SO YOU UNDERSTAND OUR PLIGHT THEN?
HOW-EVER...
TURN
?!
KRUNCH
THE REASON RULES AND REGULATIONS EXIST IS TO PREVENT THE DISRUPTION OF PUBLIC MORALITY, AND THAT IS WHOLLY SEPARATE FROM THE LAW.
THUMP
KUROKO?!

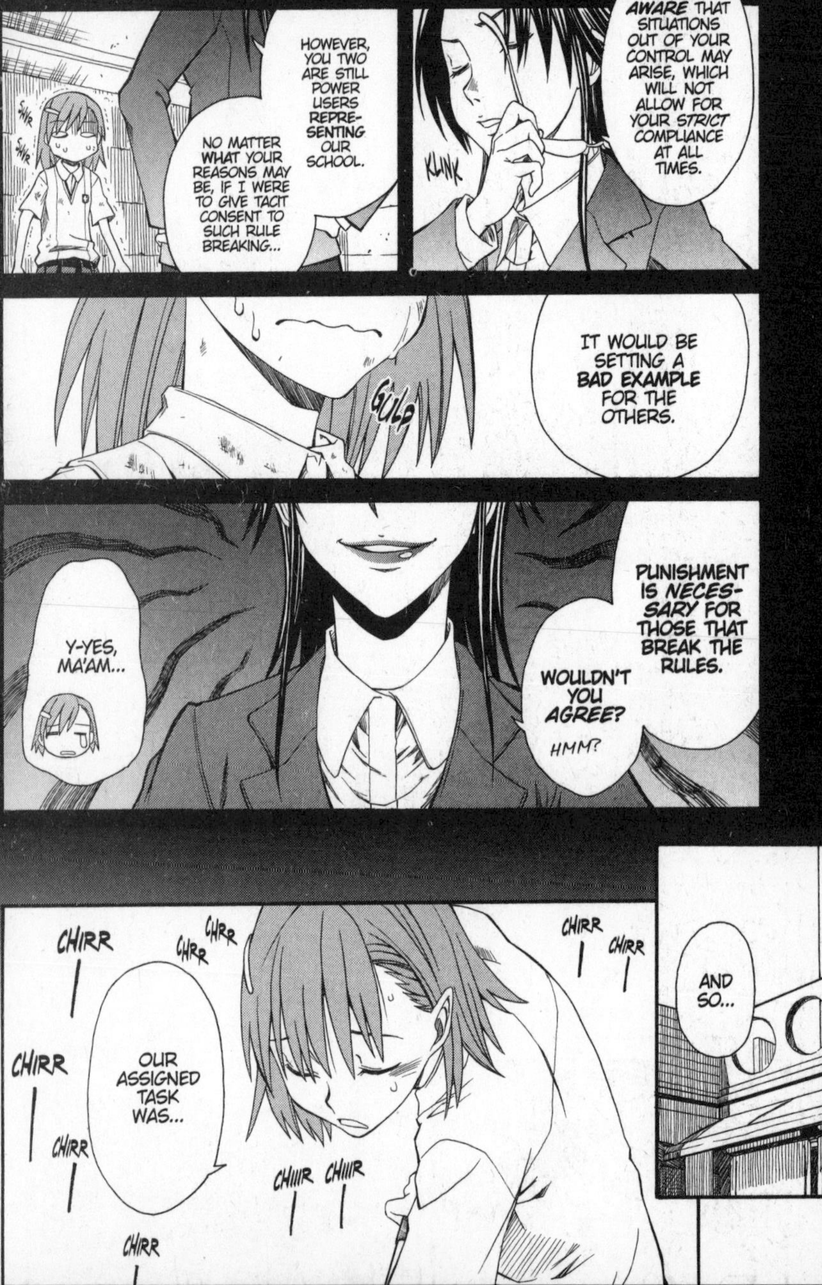
I AM WELL AWARE THAT SITUATIONS OUT OF YOUR CONTROL MAY ARISE, WHICH WILL NOT ALLOW FOR YOUR STRICT COMPLIANCE AT ALL TIMES.
KLINK
HOWEVER, YOU TWO ARE STILL POWER USERS REPRESENTING OUR SCHOOL.
NO MATTER WHAT YOUR REASONS MAY BE, IF I WERE TO GIVE TACIT CONSENT TO SUCH RULE BREAKING...
SHVR
SHVR
IT WOULD BE SETTING A BAD EXAMPLE FOR THE OTHERS.
GULP
PUNISHMENT IS NECESSARY FOR THOSE THAT BREAK THE RULES.
WOULDN'T YOU AGREE?
HMM?
Y-YES, MA'AM...
AND SO...
CHIRR
CHIRR
CHIRR
CHIRR
CHIRR
OUR ASSIGNED TASK WAS...
CHIRR
CHIRR
CHIIIR
CHIIIR
CHIRR

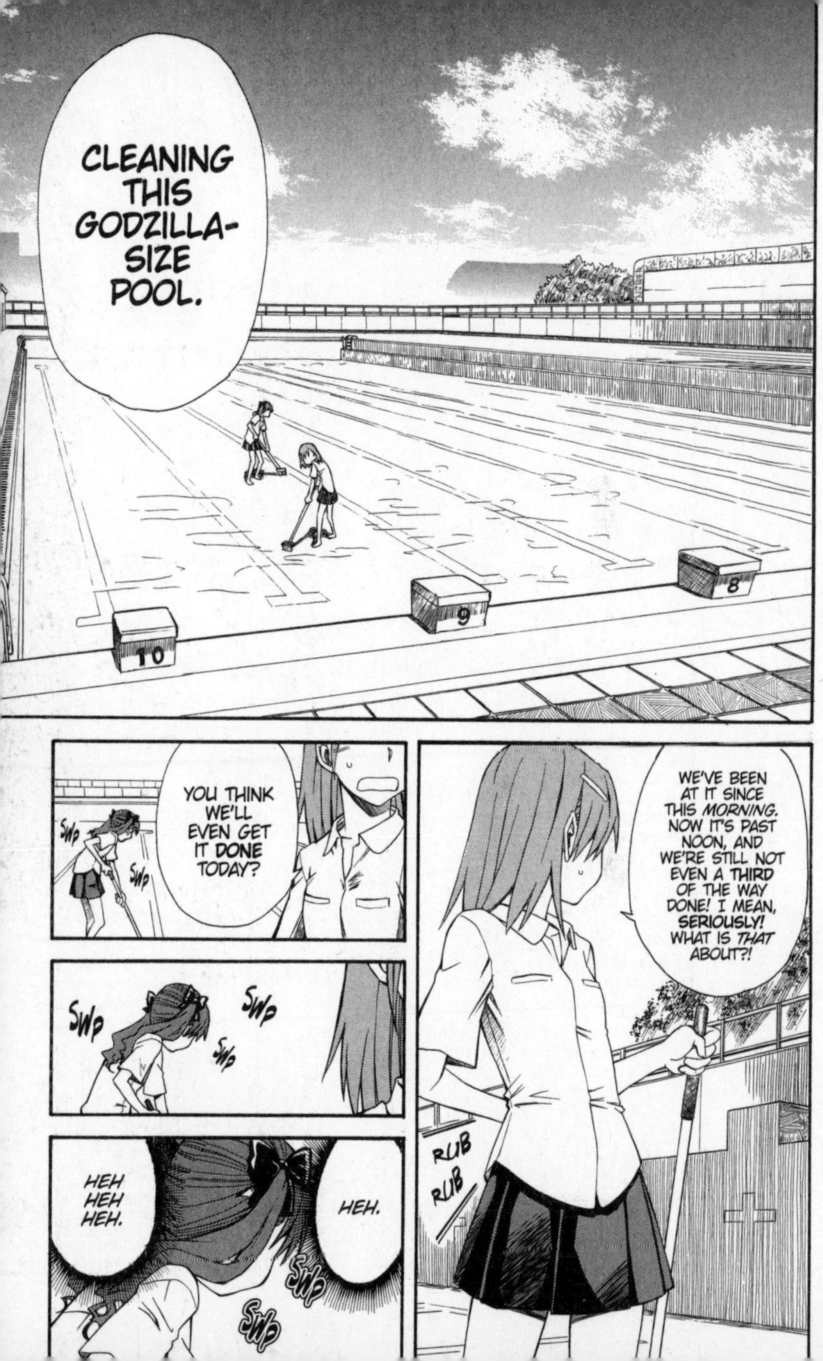
CLEANING THIS GODZILLA-SIZE POOL.
10
9
8
WE'VE BEEN AT IT SINCE THIS *MORNING*. NOW IT'S PAST NOON, AND WE'RE STILL NOT EVEN A **THIRD** OF THE WAY DONE! I MEAN, **SERIOUSLY!** WHAT IS *THAT* ABOUT?!
RUB RUB
YOU THINK WE'LL EVEN GET IT **DONE** TODAY?
SWP SWP
SWP SWP SWP
HEH.
HEH HEH HEH.
SWP SWP

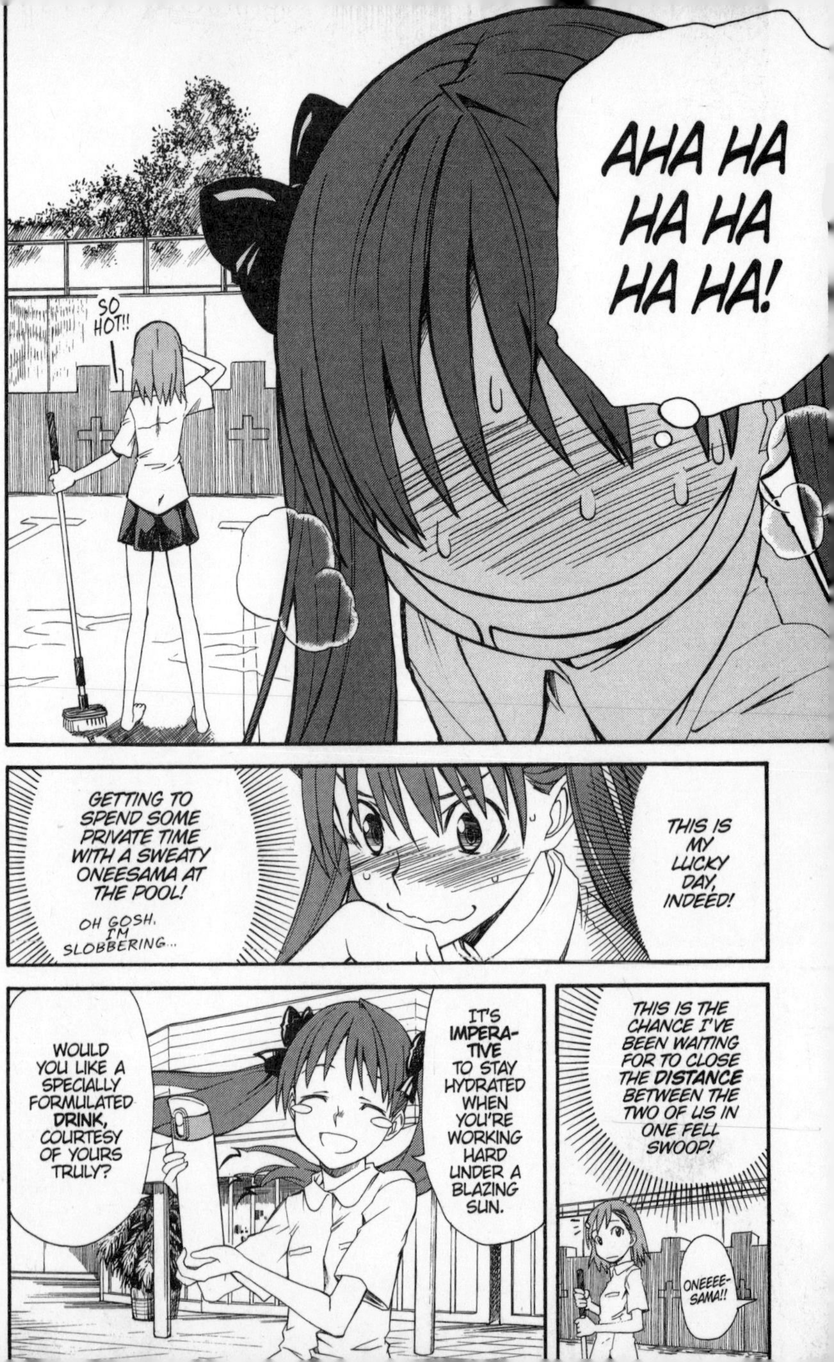
AHA HA HA HA HA HA!
SO HOT!!
THIS IS MY LUCKY DAY, INDEED!
GETTING TO SPEND SOME PRIVATE TIME WITH A SWEATY ONEESAMA AT THE POOL!
OH GOSH. I'M SLOBBERING...
THIS IS THE CHANCE I'VE BEEN WAITING FOR TO CLOSE THE DISTANCE BETWEEN THE TWO OF US IN ONE FELL SWOOP!
ONEEEE-SAMA!!
IT'S IMPERATIVE TO STAY HYDRATED WHEN YOU'RE WORKING HARD UNDER A BLAZING SUN.
WOULD YOU LIKE A SPECIALLY FORMULATED DRINK, COURTESY OF YOURS TRULY?

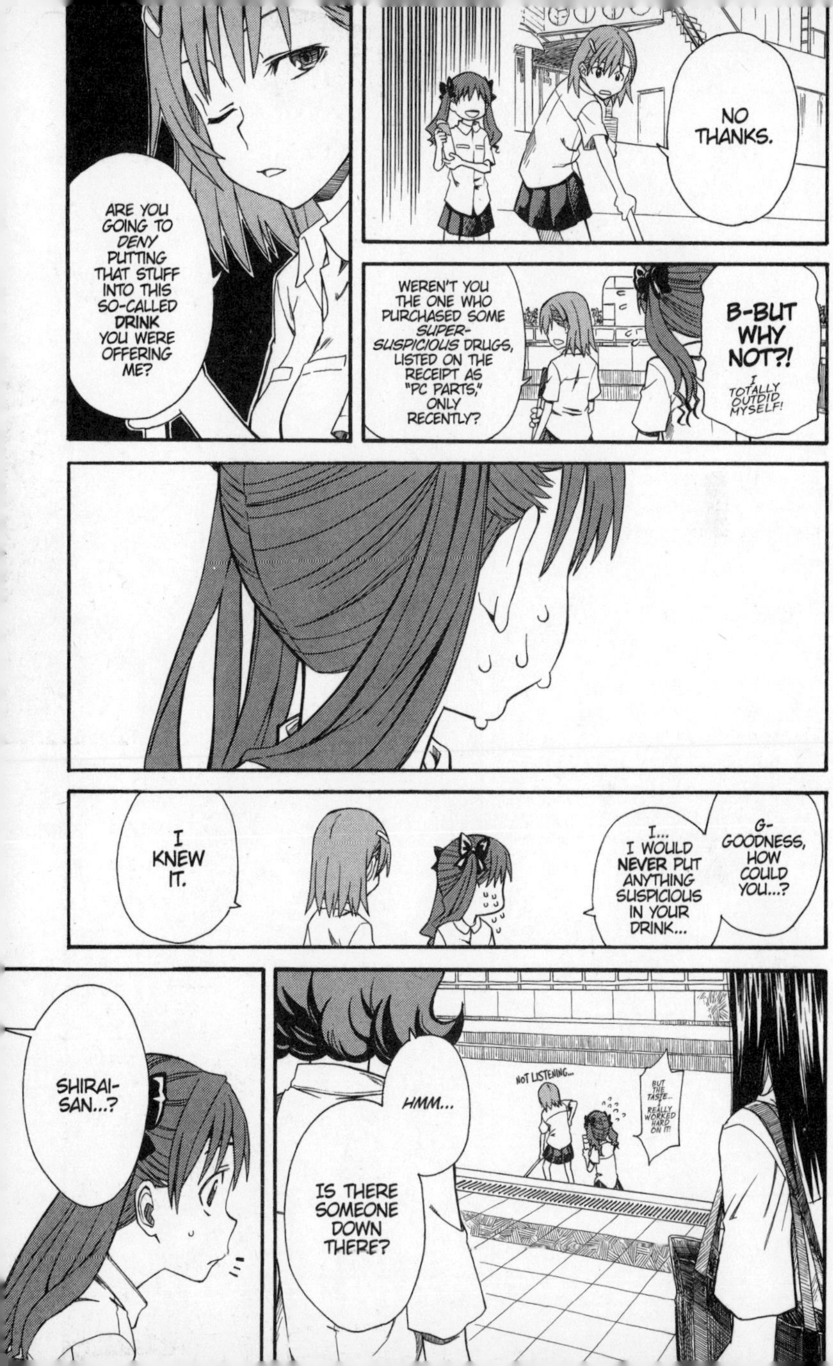
NO THANKS.
B-BUT WHY NOT?!
I TOTALLY OUTDID MYSELF!
WEREN'T YOU THE ONE WHO PURCHASED SOME SUPER-SUSPICIOUS DRUGS, LISTED ON THE RECEIPT AS "PC PARTS," ONLY RECENTLY?
ARE YOU GOING TO DENY PUTTING THAT STUFF INTO THIS SO-CALLED DRINK YOU WERE OFFERING ME?
G-GOODNESS, HOW COULD YOU...?
I... I WOULD NEVER PUT ANYTHING SUSPICIOUS IN YOUR DRINK...
I KNEW IT.
HMM...
IS THERE SOMEONE DOWN THERE?
BUT THE TASTE... I REALLY WORKED HARD ON IT!
NOT LISTENING...
SHIRAI-SAN...?

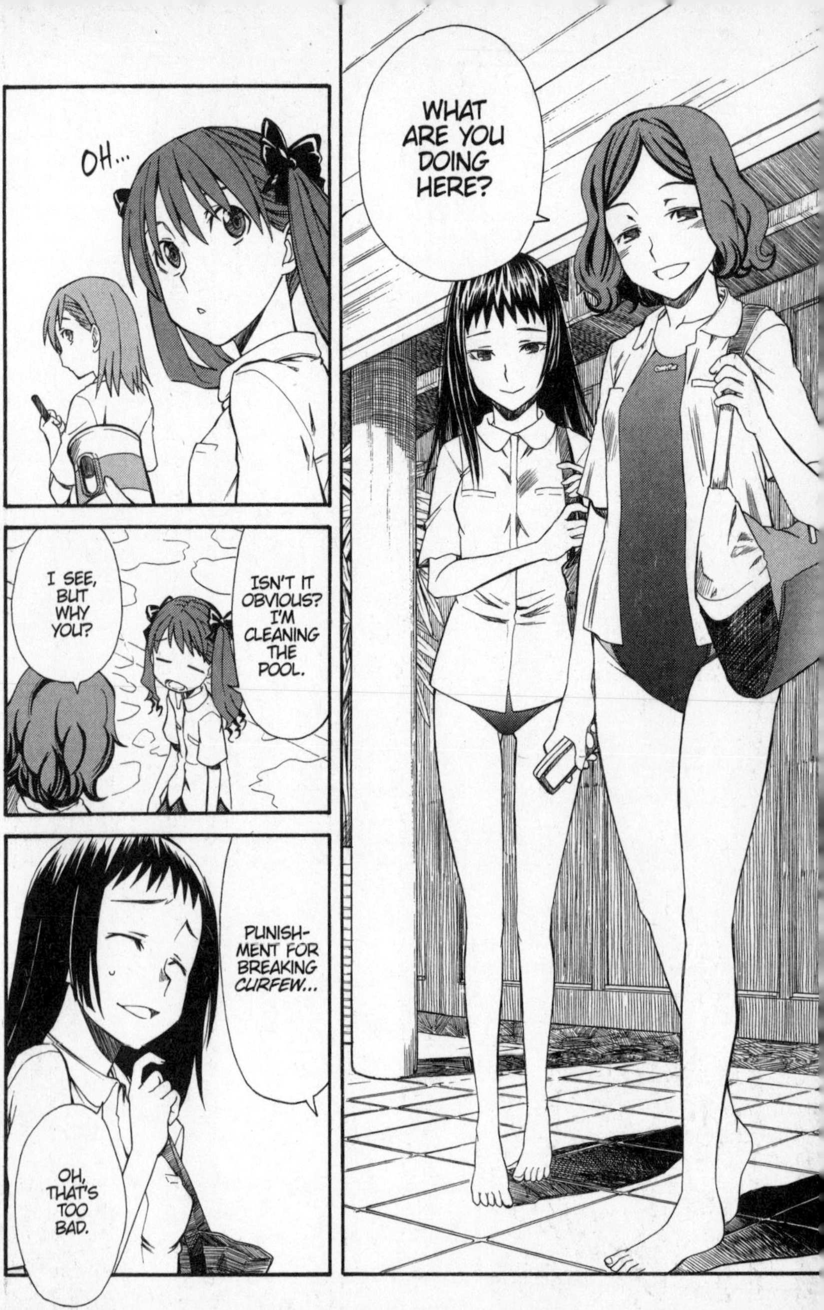
WHAT ARE YOU DOING HERE?
OH...
ISN'T IT OBVIOUS? I'M CLEANING THE POOL.
I SEE, BUT WHY YOU?
PUNISH-MENT FOR BREAKING CURFEW...
OH, THAT'S TOO BAD.

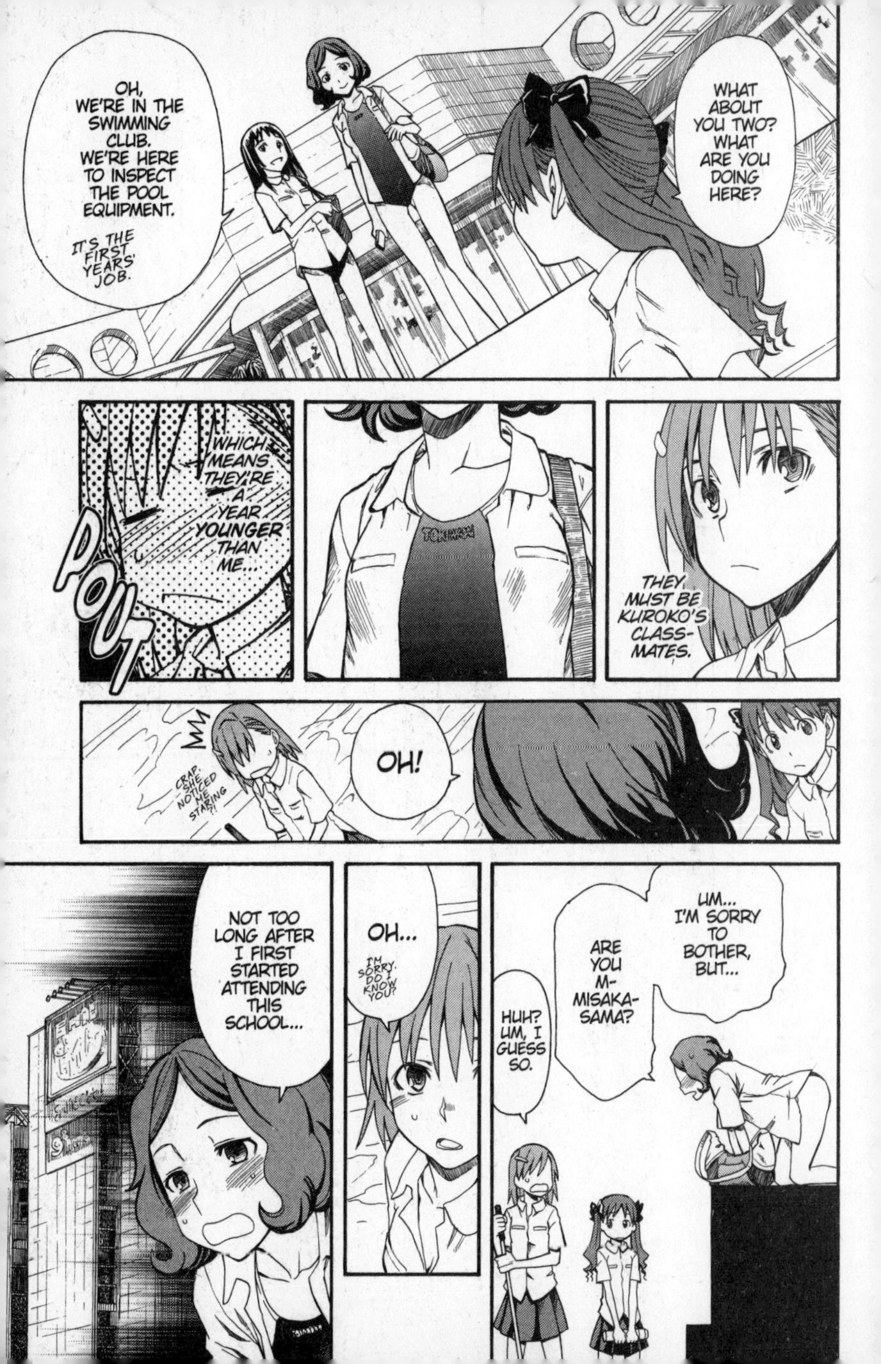
WHAT ABOUT YOU TWO? WHAT ARE YOU DOING HERE?
OH, WE'RE IN THE SWIMMING CLUB. WE'RE HERE TO INSPECT THE POOL EQUIPMENT.
IT'S THE FIRST YEARS' JOB.
THEY MUST BE KUROKO'S CLASS-MATES.
WHICH MEANS THEY'RE A YEAR YOUNGER THAN ME...
POUT
OH!
CRAP. SHE NOTICED ME STARING?!
UM... I'M SORRY TO BOTHER, BUT...
ARE YOU M-MISAKA-SAMA?
HUH? UM, I GUESS SO.
OH...
I'M SORRY. DO I KNOW YOU?
NOT TOO LONG AFTER I FIRST STARTED ATTENDING THIS SCHOOL...

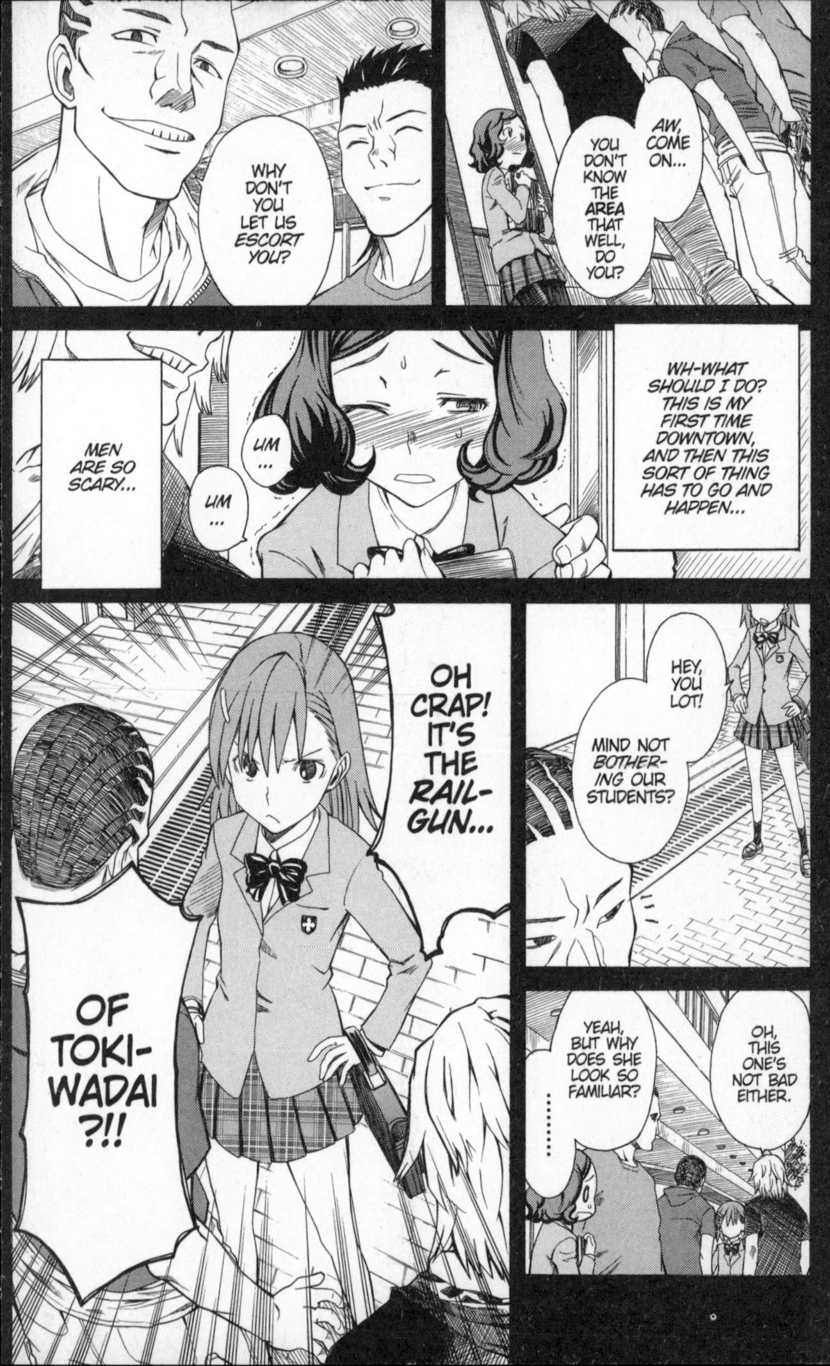
AW, COME ON... YOU DON'T KNOW THE AREA THAT WELL, DO YOU?
WHY DON'T YOU LET US ESCORT YOU?
WH-WHAT SHOULD I DO? THIS IS MY FIRST TIME DOWNTOWN, AND THEN THIS SORT OF THING HAS TO GO AND HAPPEN...
UM...
UM...
MEN ARE SO SCARY...
HEY, YOU LOT!
MIND NOT BOTHERING OUR STUDENTS?
OH, THIS ONE'S NOT BAD EITHER.
YEAH, BUT WHY DOES SHE LOOK SO FAMILIAR?
......
OH CRAP! IT'S THE RAIL-GUN...
OF TOKI-WADAI?!!

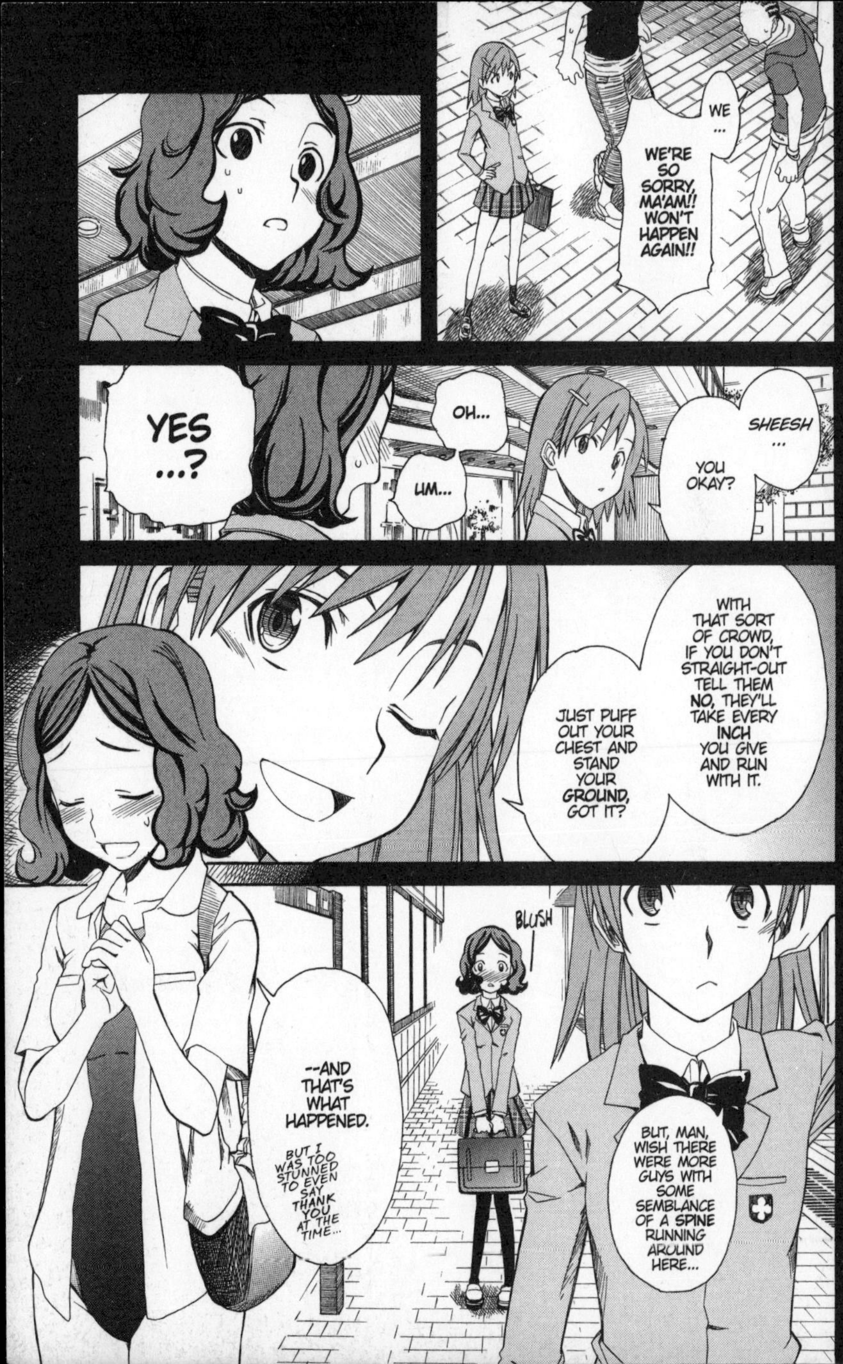
WE ...
WE'RE SO SORRY, MA'AM!! WON'T HAPPEN AGAIN!!
SHEESH ...
YOU OKAY?
OH...
UM...
YES ...?
WITH THAT SORT OF CROWD, IF YOU DON'T STRAIGHT-OUT TELL THEM NO, THEY'LL TAKE EVERY INCH YOU GIVE AND RUN WITH IT.
JUST PUFF OUT YOUR CHEST AND STAND YOUR GROUND, GOT IT?
BUT, MAN, WISH THERE WERE MORE GUYS WITH SOME SEMBLANCE OF A SPINE RUNNING AROUND HERE...
BLUSH
--AND THAT'S WHAT HAPPENED.
BUT I WAS TOO STUNNED TO EVEN SAY THANK YOU AT THE TIME...

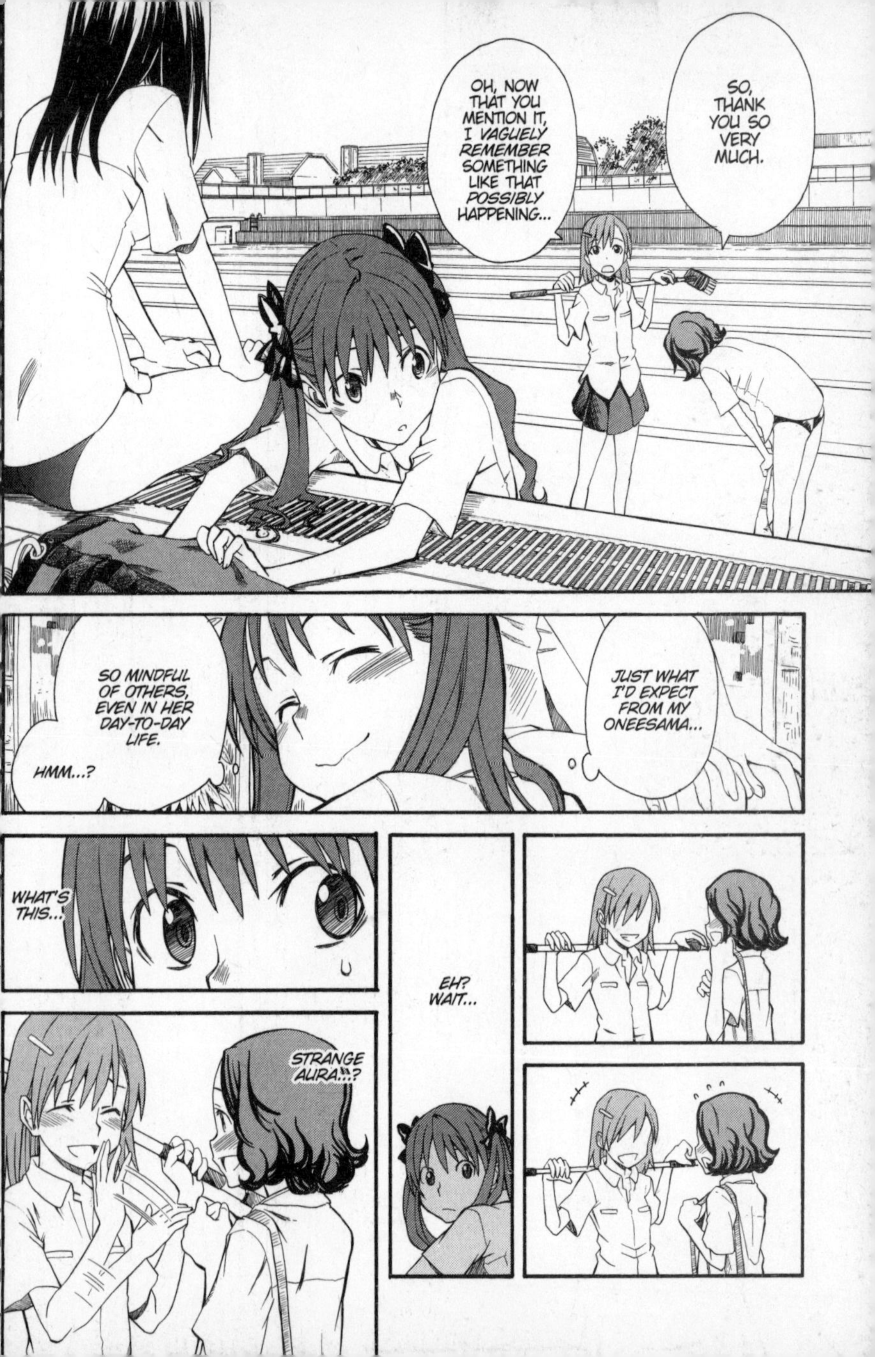
SO, THANK YOU SO VERY MUCH.
OH, NOW THAT YOU MENTION IT, I *VAGUELY REMEMBER* SOMETHING LIKE THAT *POSSIBLY* HAPPENING...
JUST WHAT I'D EXPECT FROM MY ONEESAMA...
SO MINDFUL OF OTHERS, EVEN IN HER DAY-TO-DAY LIFE.
HMM...?
EH? WAIT...
WHAT'S THIS...
STRANGE AURA...?

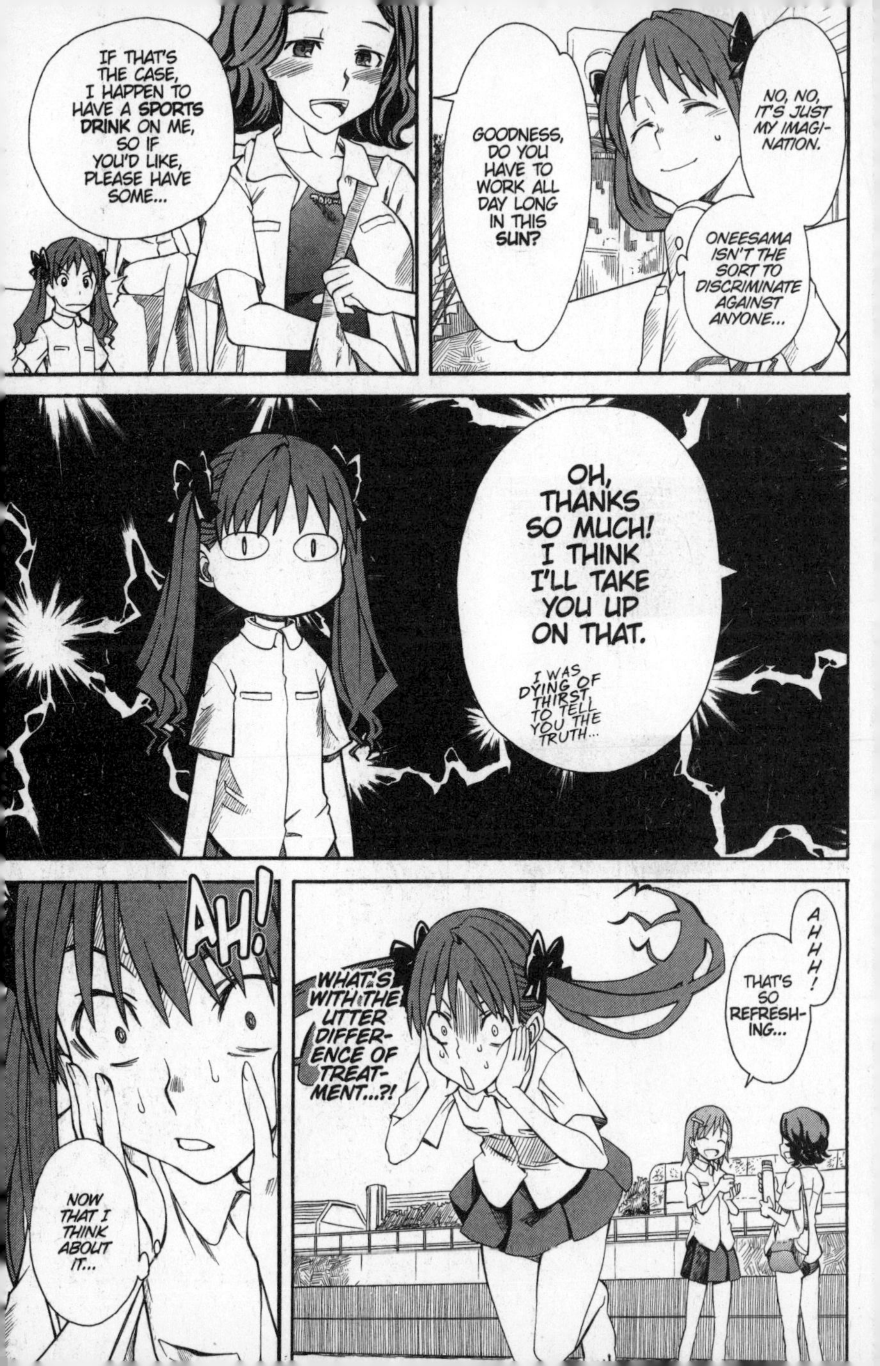
NO, NO, IT'S JUST MY IMAGINATION.
ONEESAMA ISN'T THE SORT TO DISCRIMINATE AGAINST ANYONE...
GOODNESS, DO YOU HAVE TO WORK ALL DAY LONG IN THIS SUN?
IF THAT'S THE CASE, I HAPPEN TO HAVE A SPORTS DRINK ON ME, SO IF YOU'D LIKE, PLEASE HAVE SOME...
OH, THANKS SO MUCH! I THINK I'LL TAKE YOU UP ON THAT.
I WAS DYING OF THIRST, TO TELL YOU THE TRUTH...
AHHH! THAT'S SO REFRESHING...
WHAT'S WITH THE UTTER DIFFERENCE OF TREATMENT...?!
AH!
NOW THAT I THINK ABOUT IT...

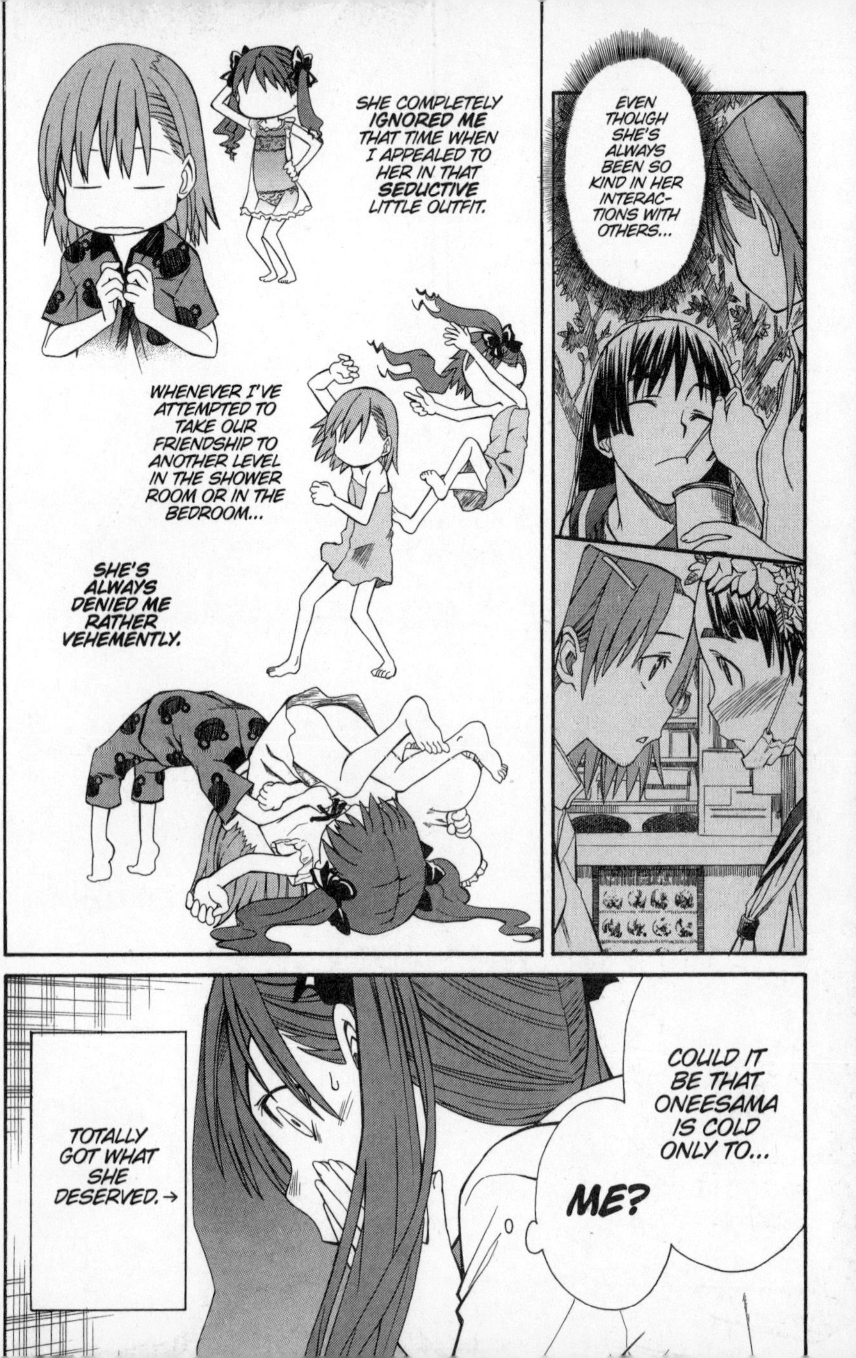
EVEN THOUGH SHE'S ALWAYS BEEN SO KIND IN HER INTERACTIONS WITH OTHERS...
SHE COMPLETELY IGNORED ME THAT TIME WHEN I APPEALED TO HER IN THAT SEDUCTIVE LITTLE OUTFIT.
WHENEVER I'VE ATTEMPTED TO TAKE OUR FRIENDSHIP TO ANOTHER LEVEL IN THE SHOWER ROOM OR IN THE BEDROOM...
SHE'S ALWAYS DENIED ME RATHER VEHEMENTLY.
COULD IT BE THAT ONEESAMA IS COLD ONLY TO...
ME?
TOTALLY GOT WHAT SHE DESERVED.→

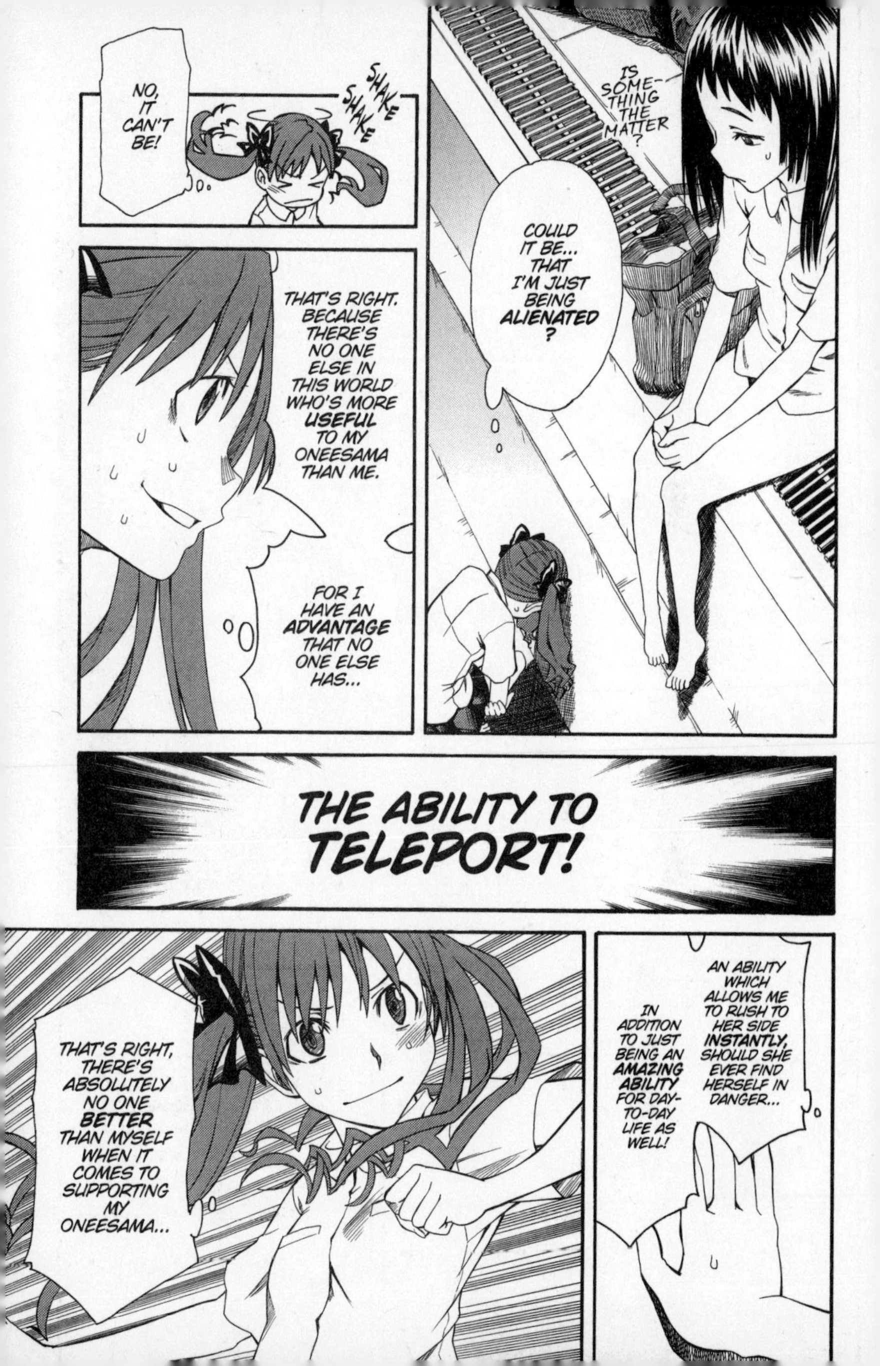
IS SOMETHING THE MATTER?
COULD IT BE... THAT I'M JUST BEING ALIENATED?
SHAKE SHAKE
NO, IT CAN'T BE!
THAT'S RIGHT. BECAUSE THERE'S NO ONE ELSE IN THIS WORLD WHO'S MORE USEFUL TO MY ONEESAMA THAN ME.
FOR I HAVE AN ADVANTAGE THAT NO ONE ELSE HAS...
THE ABILITY TO TELEPORT!
AN ABILITY WHICH ALLOWS ME TO RUSH TO HER SIDE INSTANTLY, SHOULD SHE EVER FIND HERSELF IN DANGER...
IN ADDITION TO JUST BEING AN AMAZING ABILITY FOR DAY-TO-DAY LIFE AS WELL!
THAT'S RIGHT, THERE'S ABSOLUTELY NO ONE BETTER THAN MYSELF WHEN IT COMES TO SUPPORTING MY ONEESAMA...

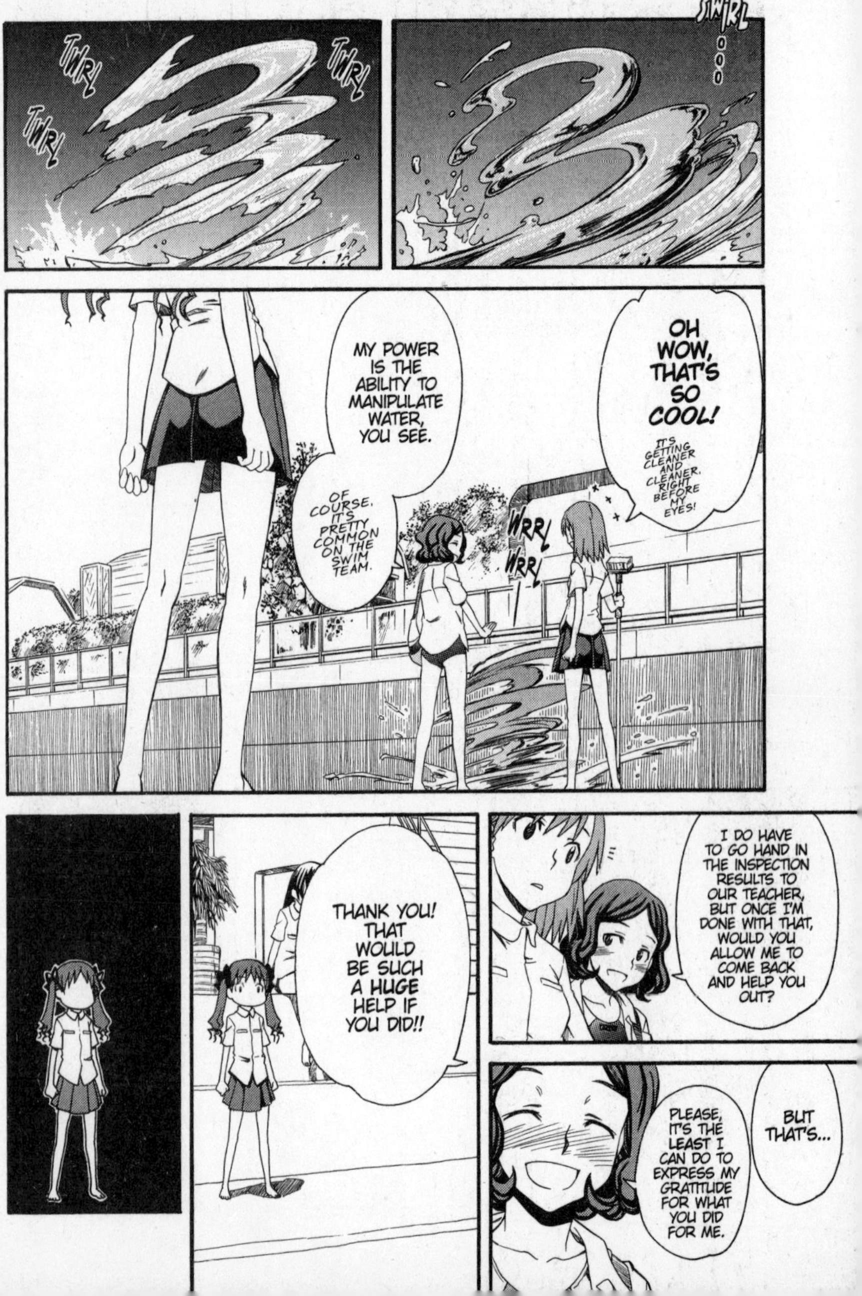
SWIRL
TWIRL
TWIRL
TWIRL
OH WOW, THAT'S SO COOL!
IT'S GETTING CLEANER AND CLEANER, RIGHT BEFORE MY EYES!
WRRL
WRRL
MY POWER IS THE ABILITY TO MANIPULATE WATER, YOU SEE.
OF COURSE, IT'S PRETTY COMMON ON THE SWIM TEAM.
I DO HAVE TO GO HAND IN THE INSPECTION RESULTS TO OUR TEACHER, BUT ONCE I'M DONE WITH THAT, WOULD YOU ALLOW ME TO COME BACK AND HELP YOU OUT?
BUT THAT'S...
PLEASE, IT'S THE LEAST I CAN DO TO EXPRESS MY GRATITUDE FOR WHAT YOU DID FOR ME.
THANK YOU! THAT WOULD BE SUCH A HUGE HELP IF YOU DID!!

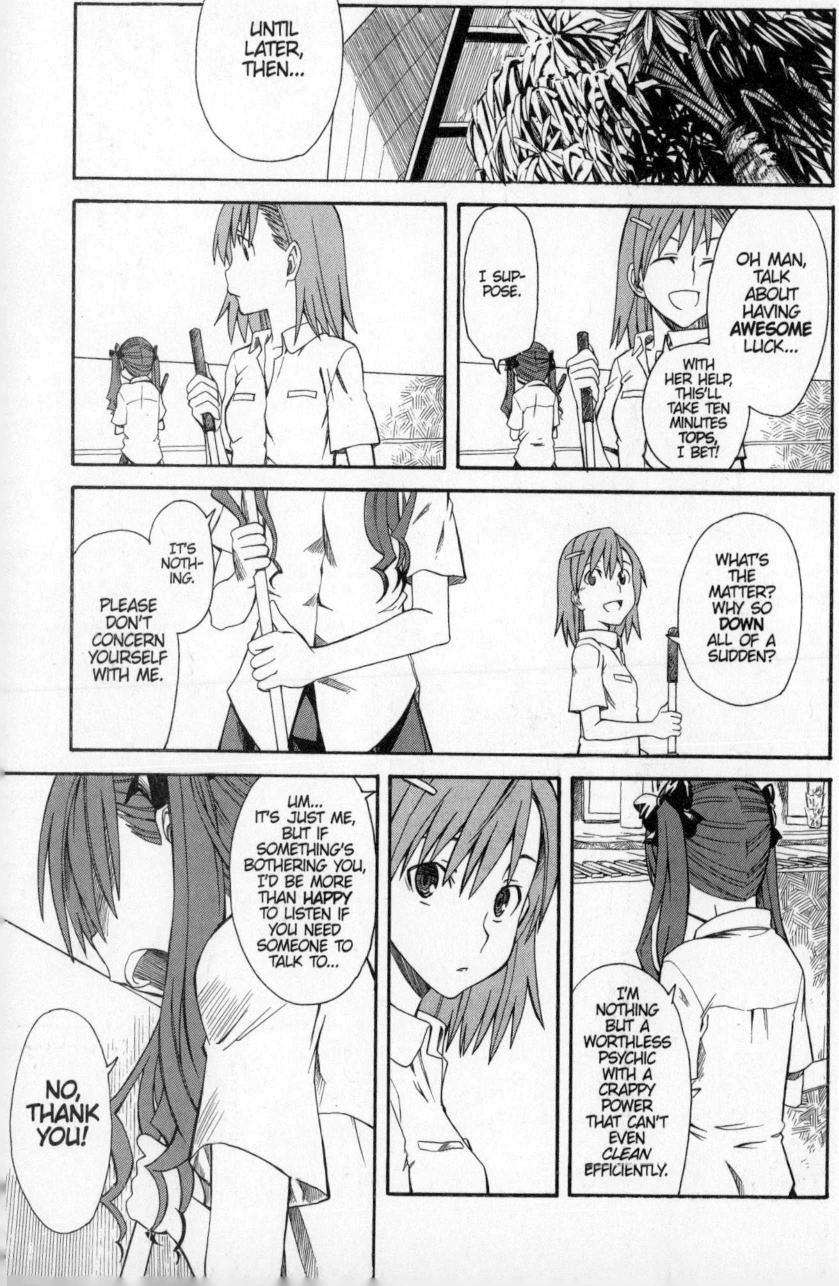
UNTIL LATER, THEN...
OH MAN, TALK ABOUT HAVING AWESOME LUCK...
WITH HER HELP, THIS'LL TAKE TEN MINUTES TOPS, I BET!
I SUP-POSE.
WHAT'S THE MATTER? WHY SO DOWN ALL OF A SUDDEN?
IT'S NOTH-ING.
PLEASE DON'T CONCERN YOURSELF WITH ME.
I'M NOTHING BUT A WORTHLESS PSYCHIC WITH A CRAPPY POWER THAT CAN'T EVEN CLEAN EFFICIENTLY.
UM... IT'S JUST ME, BUT IF SOMETHING'S BOTHERING YOU, I'D BE MORE THAN HAPPY TO LISTEN IF YOU NEED SOMEONE TO TALK TO...
NO, THANK YOU!

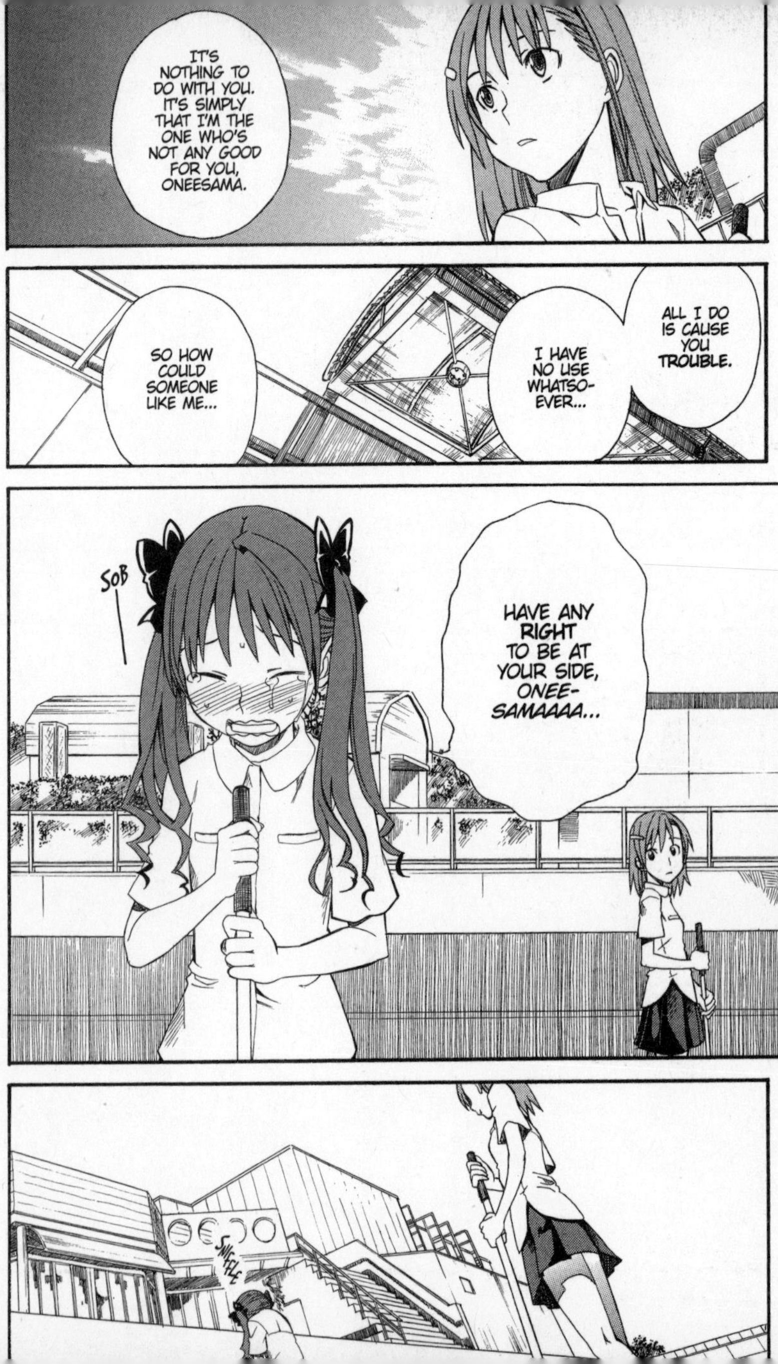
IT'S NOTHING TO DO WITH YOU. IT'S SIMPLY THAT I'M THE ONE WHO'S NOT ANY GOOD FOR YOU, ONEESAMA.
ALL I DO IS CAUSE YOU TROUBLE.
I HAVE NO USE WHATSO-EVER...
SO HOW COULD SOMEONE LIKE ME...
HAVE ANY RIGHT TO BE AT YOUR SIDE, ONEE-SAMAAAA...
SOB
SNIFFLE

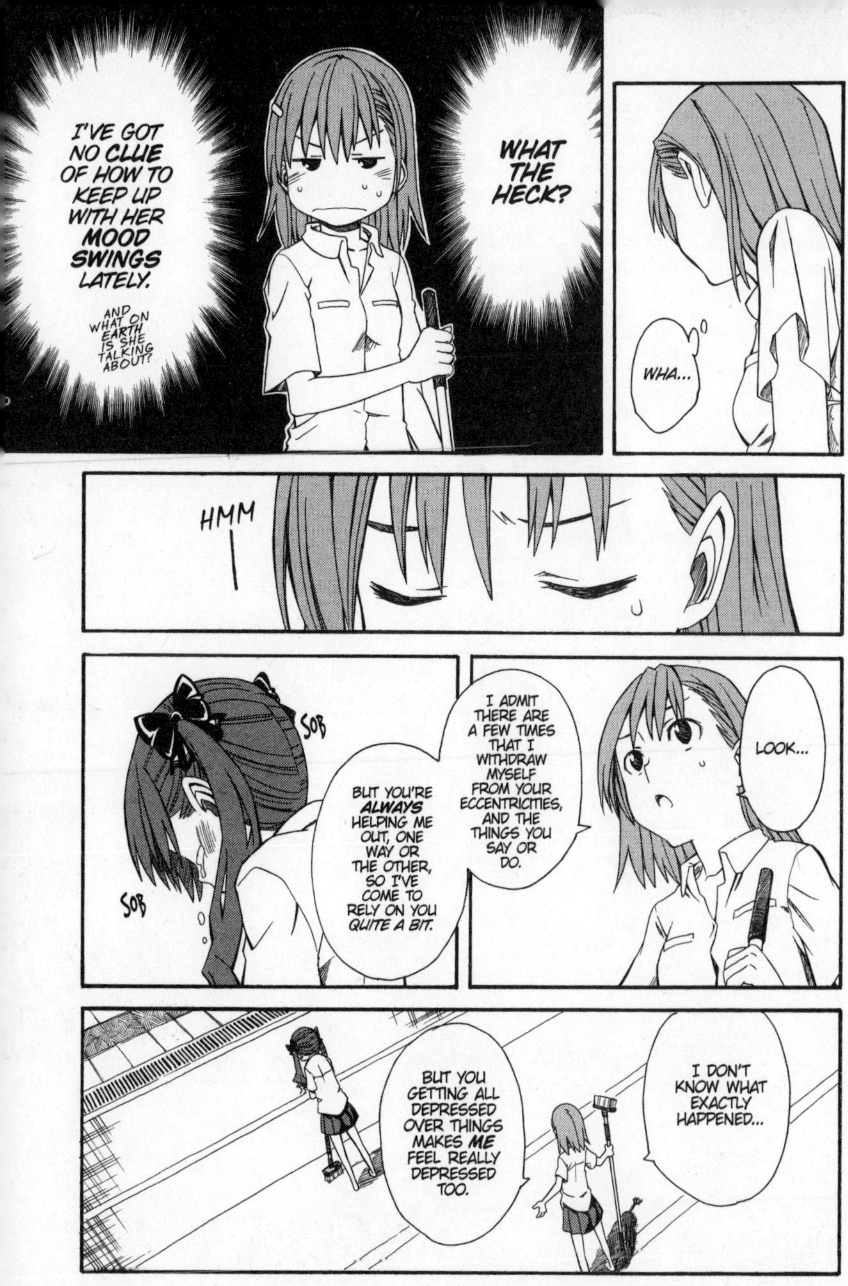
WHA...
WHAT THE HECK?
I'VE GOT NO CLUE OF HOW TO KEEP UP WITH HER MOOD SWINGS LATELY.
AND WHAT ON EARTH IS SHE TALKING ABOUT?
HMM
LOOK...
I ADMIT THERE ARE A FEW TIMES THAT I WITHDRAW MYSELF FROM YOUR ECCENTRICITIES, AND THE THINGS YOU SAY OR DO.
BUT YOU'RE ALWAYS HELPING ME OUT, ONE WAY OR THE OTHER, SO I'VE COME TO RELY ON YOU QUITE A BIT.
SOB
SOB
I DON'T KNOW WHAT EXACTLY HAPPENED...
BUT YOU GETTING ALL DEPRESSED OVER THINGS MAKES ME FEEL REALLY DEPRESSED TOO.

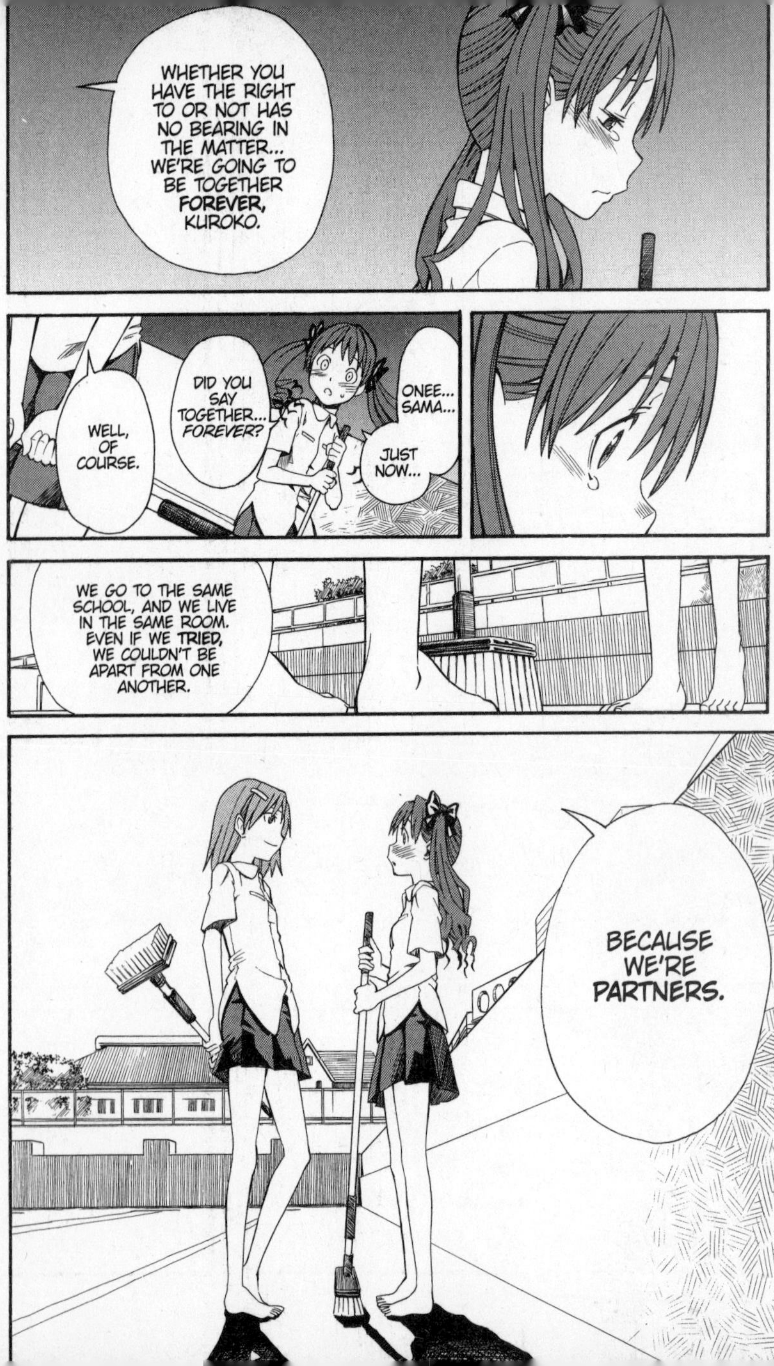
WHETHER YOU HAVE THE RIGHT TO OR NOT HAS NO BEARING IN THE MATTER... WE'RE GOING TO BE TOGETHER **FOREVER**, KUROKO.
ONEE... SAMA...
JUST NOW...
DID YOU SAY TOGETHER... *FOREVER?*
WELL, OF COURSE.
WE GO TO THE SAME SCHOOL, AND WE LIVE IN THE SAME ROOM. EVEN IF WE **TRIED**, WE COULDN'T BE APART FROM ONE ANOTHER.
BECAUSE WE'RE PARTNERS.

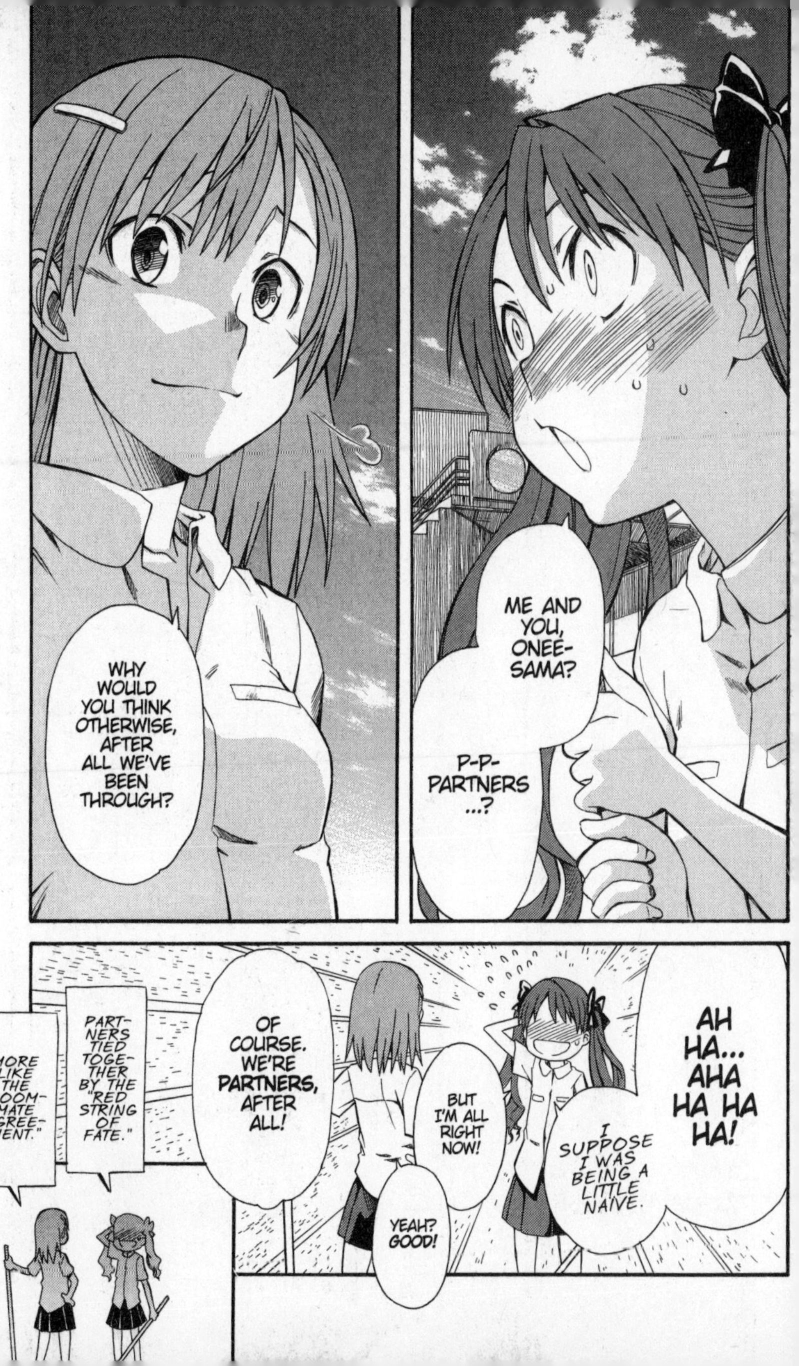
ME AND YOU, ONEE-SAMA?
P-P-PARTNERS ...?
WHY WOULD YOU THINK OTHERWISE, AFTER ALL WE'VE BEEN THROUGH?
AH HA... AHA HA HA HA!
OF COURSE. WE'RE **PARTNERS**, AFTER ALL!
I SUPPOSE I WAS BEING A LITTLE NAÏVE.
BUT I'M ALL RIGHT NOW!
YEAH? GOOD!
PARTNERS TIED TOGETHER BY THE "RED STRING OF FATE."
MORE LIKE THE "ROOMMATE AGREEMENT."

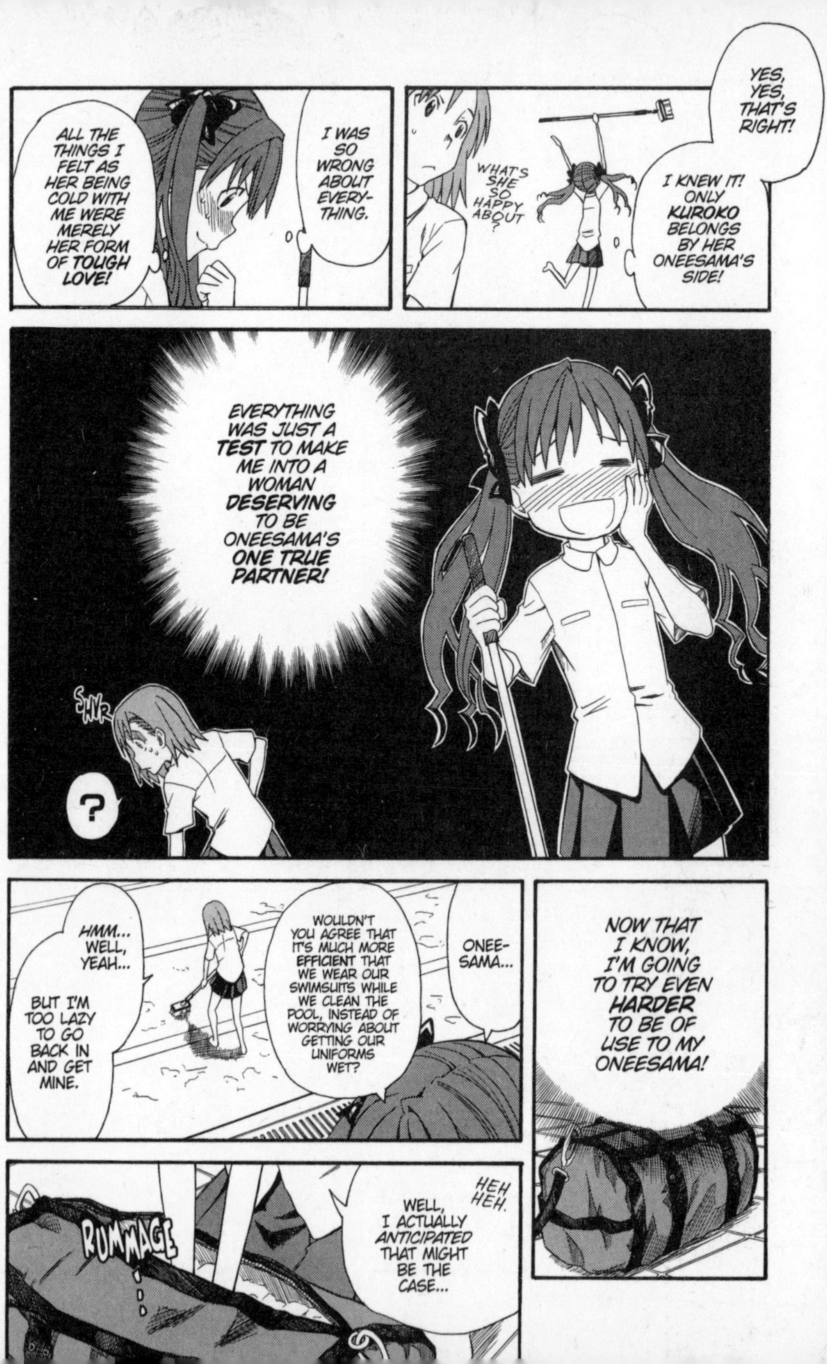
YES, YES, THAT'S RIGHT!
I KNEW IT! ONLY KUROKO BELONGS BY HER ONEESAMA'S SIDE!
WHAT'S SHE SO HAPPY ABOUT?
I WAS SO WRONG ABOUT EVERY-THING.
ALL THE THINGS I FELT AS HER BEING COLD WITH ME WERE MERELY HER FORM OF TOUGH LOVE!
EVERYTHING WAS JUST A TEST TO MAKE ME INTO A WOMAN DESERVING TO BE ONEESAMA'S ONE TRUE PARTNER!
SHVR
?
NOW THAT I KNOW, I'M GOING TO TRY EVEN HARDER TO BE OF USE TO MY ONEESAMA!
ONEE-SAMA...
WOULDN'T YOU AGREE THAT IT'S MUCH MORE EFFICIENT THAT WE WEAR OUR SWIMSUITS WHILE WE CLEAN THE POOL, INSTEAD OF WORRYING ABOUT GETTING OUR UNIFORMS WET?
HMM... WELL, YEAH...
BUT I'M TOO LAZY TO GO BACK IN AND GET MINE.
HEH HEH.
WELL, I ACTUALLY ANTICIPATED THAT MIGHT BE THE CASE...
RUMMAGE

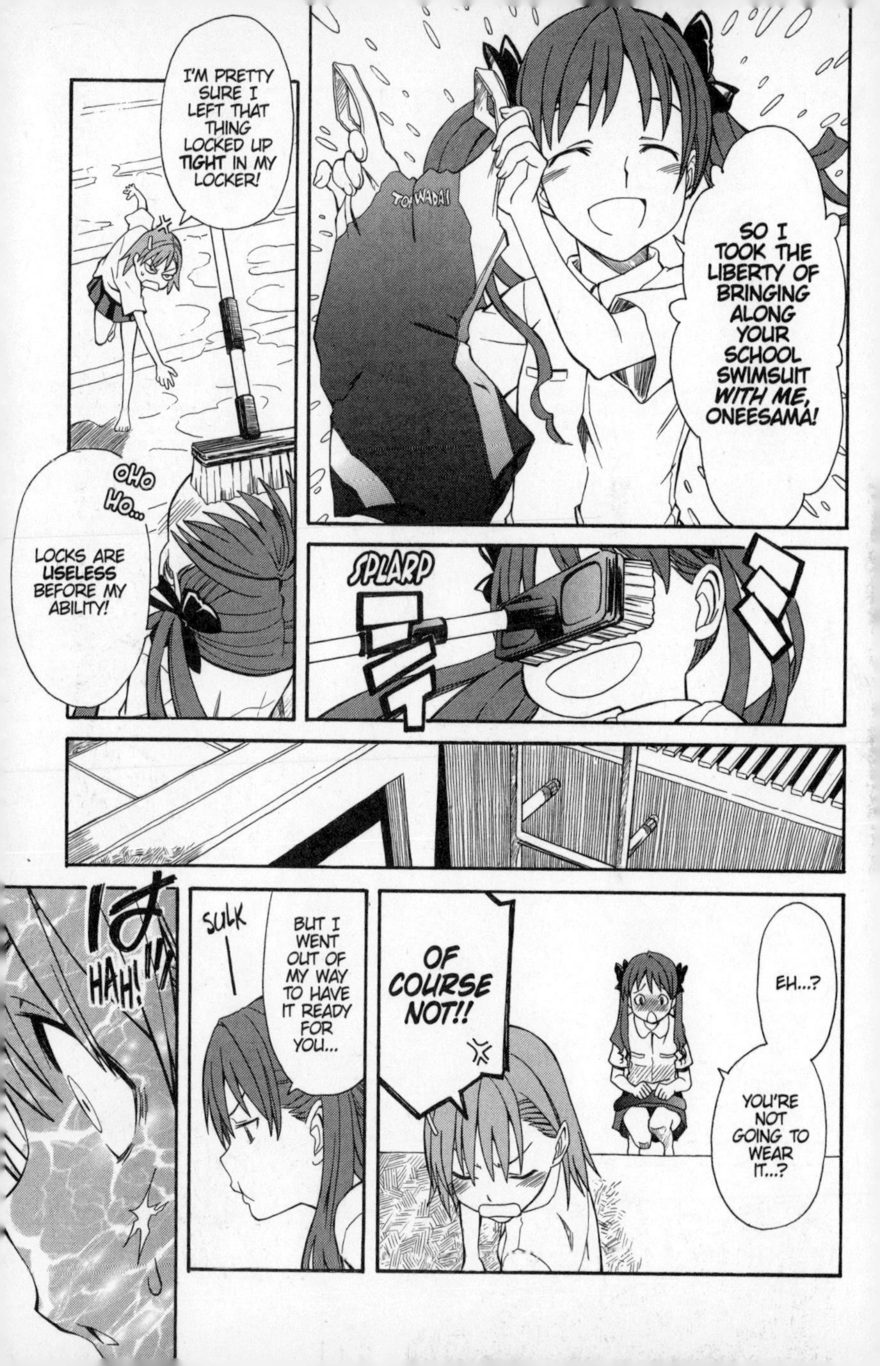

SO I TOOK THE LIBERTY OF BRINGING ALONG YOUR SCHOOL SWIMSUIT WITH ME, ONEESAMA!
TOKIWADAI
I'M PRETTY SURE I LEFT THAT THING LOCKED UP TIGHT IN MY LOCKER!
OHO HO...
LOCKS ARE USELESS BEFORE MY ABILITY!
SPLARP
EH...?
YOU'RE NOT GOING TO WEAR IT...?
OF COURSE NOT!!
SULK
BUT I WENT OUT OF MY WAY TO HAVE IT READY FOR YOU...
HAH!

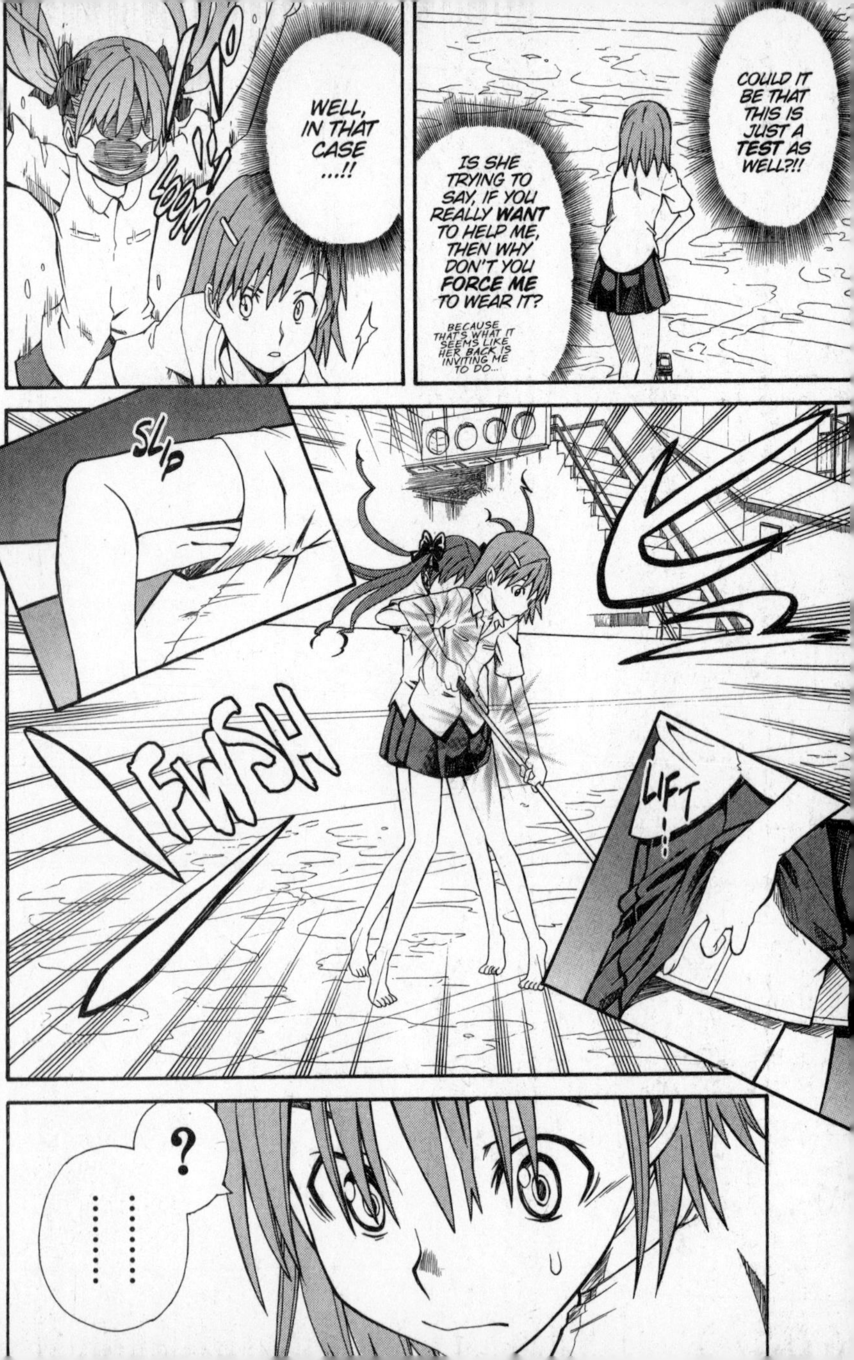
COULD IT BE THAT THIS IS JUST A TEST AS WELL?!!
IS SHE TRYING TO SAY, IF YOU REALLY WANT TO HELP ME, THEN WHY DON'T YOU FORCE ME TO WEAR IT?
BECAUSE THAT'S WHAT IT SEEMS LIKE HER BACK IS INVITING ME TO DO...
WELL, IN THAT CASE ...!!
VOOM!!
SLIP
LIFT...
FWSH
......?

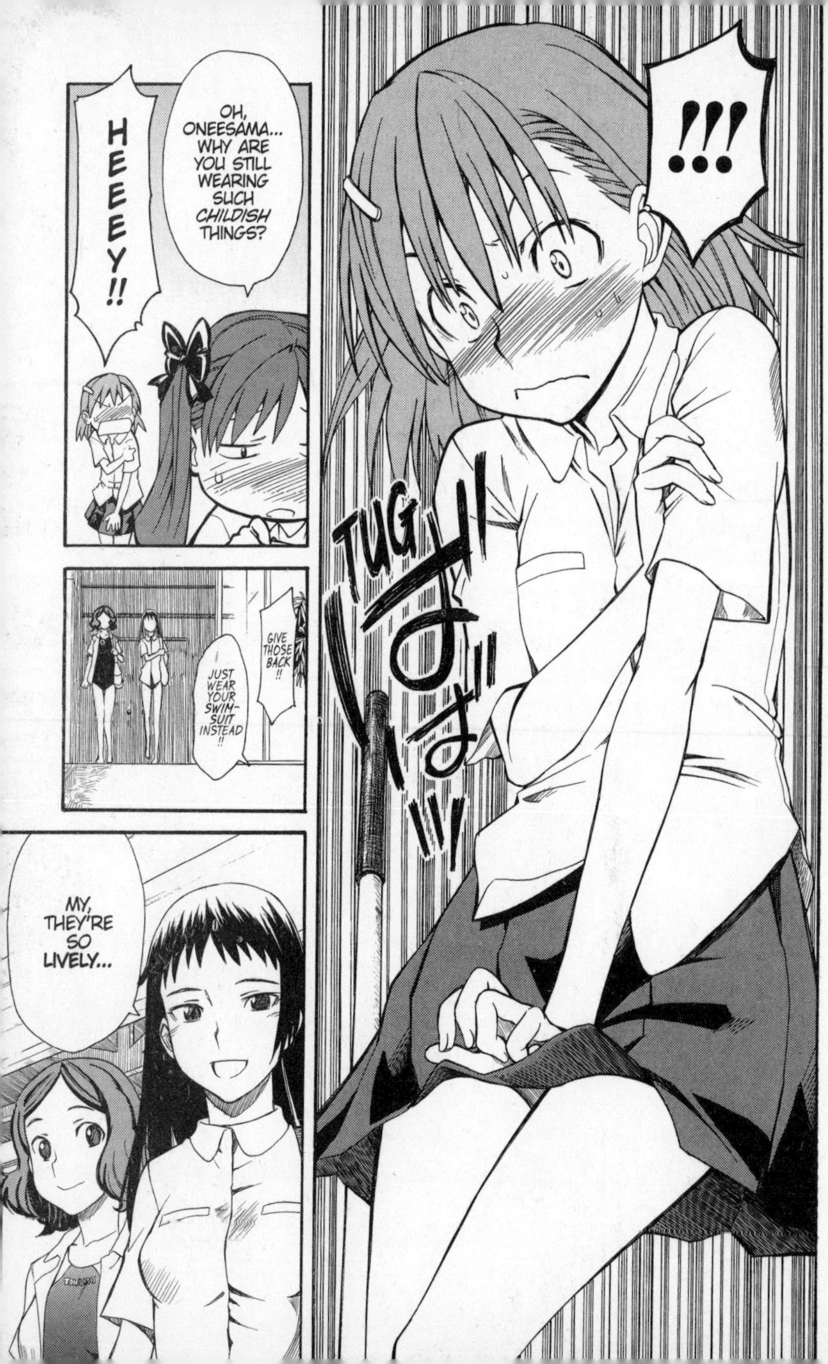
!!!
TUG
OH, ONEESAMA... WHY ARE YOU STILL WEARING SUCH CHILDISH THINGS?
HEEEEY!!
GIVE THOSE BACK!!
JUST WEAR YOUR SWIM-SUIT INSTEAD!!
MY, THEY'RE SO LIVELY...

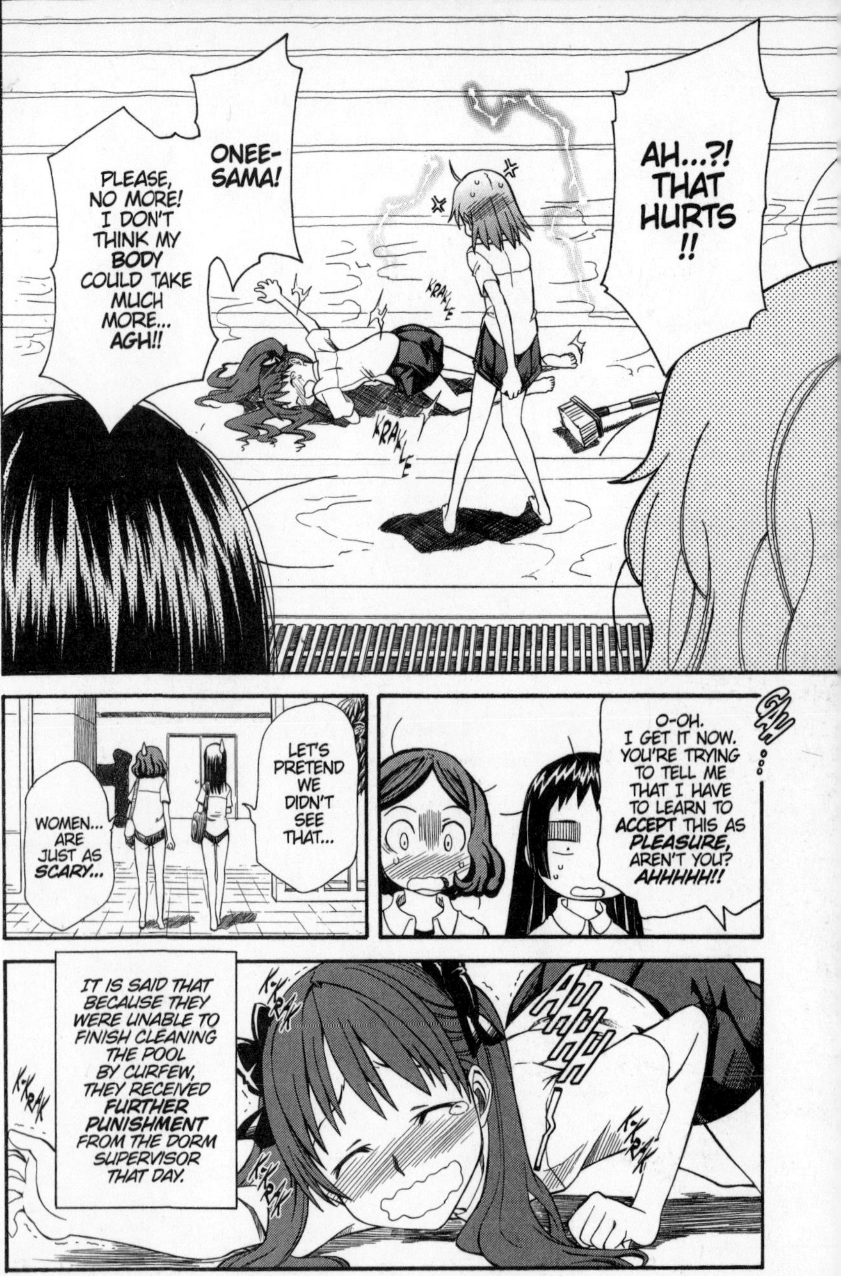
AH...?! THAT HURTS !!
ONEE-SAMA!
PLEASE, NO MORE! I DON'T THINK MY BODY COULD TAKE MUCH MORE... AGH!!
KRAKLE
KRAKLE
GAH...
O-OH. I GET IT NOW. YOU'RE TRYING TO TELL ME THAT I HAVE TO LEARN TO ACCEPT THIS AS PLEASURE, AREN'T YOU? AHHHHH!!
LET'S PRETEND WE DIDN'T SEE THAT...
WOMEN... ARE JUST AS SCARY...
K-KRAK
K-KRAK
IT IS SAID THAT BECAUSE THEY WERE UNABLE TO FINISH CLEANING THE POOL BY CURFEW, THEY RECEIVED FURTHER PUNISHMENT FROM THE DORM SUPERVISOR THAT DAY.
K-KRAK
K-KRAK

A Certain SCIENTIFIC Railgun

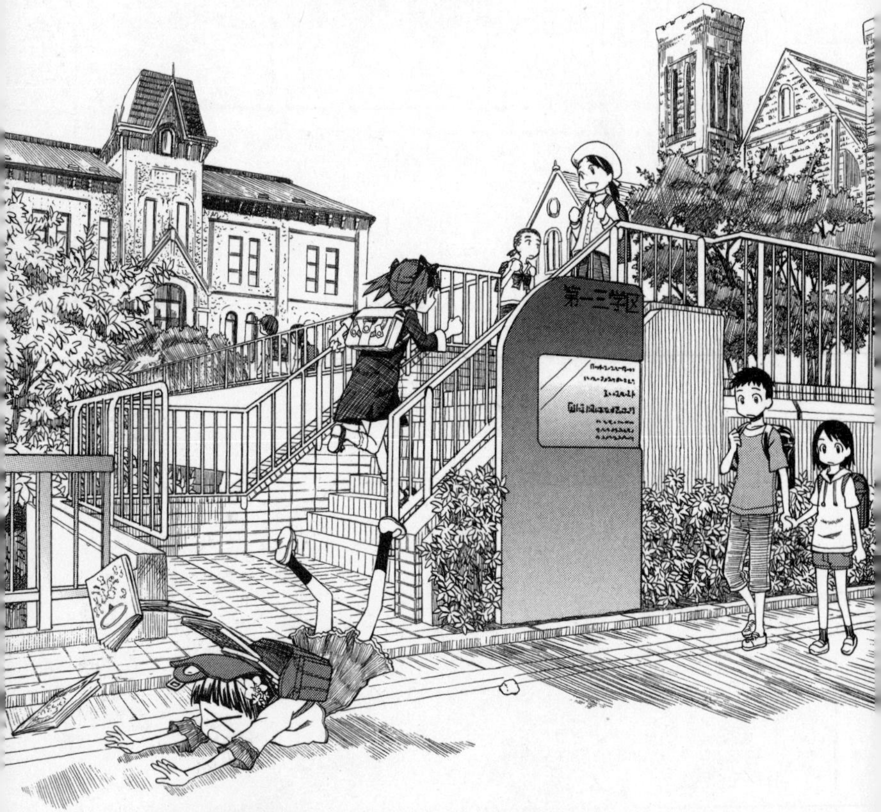

SIDE STORY:

A CERTAIN PAIR'S JOB TRAINING (PART 1 OF 2)

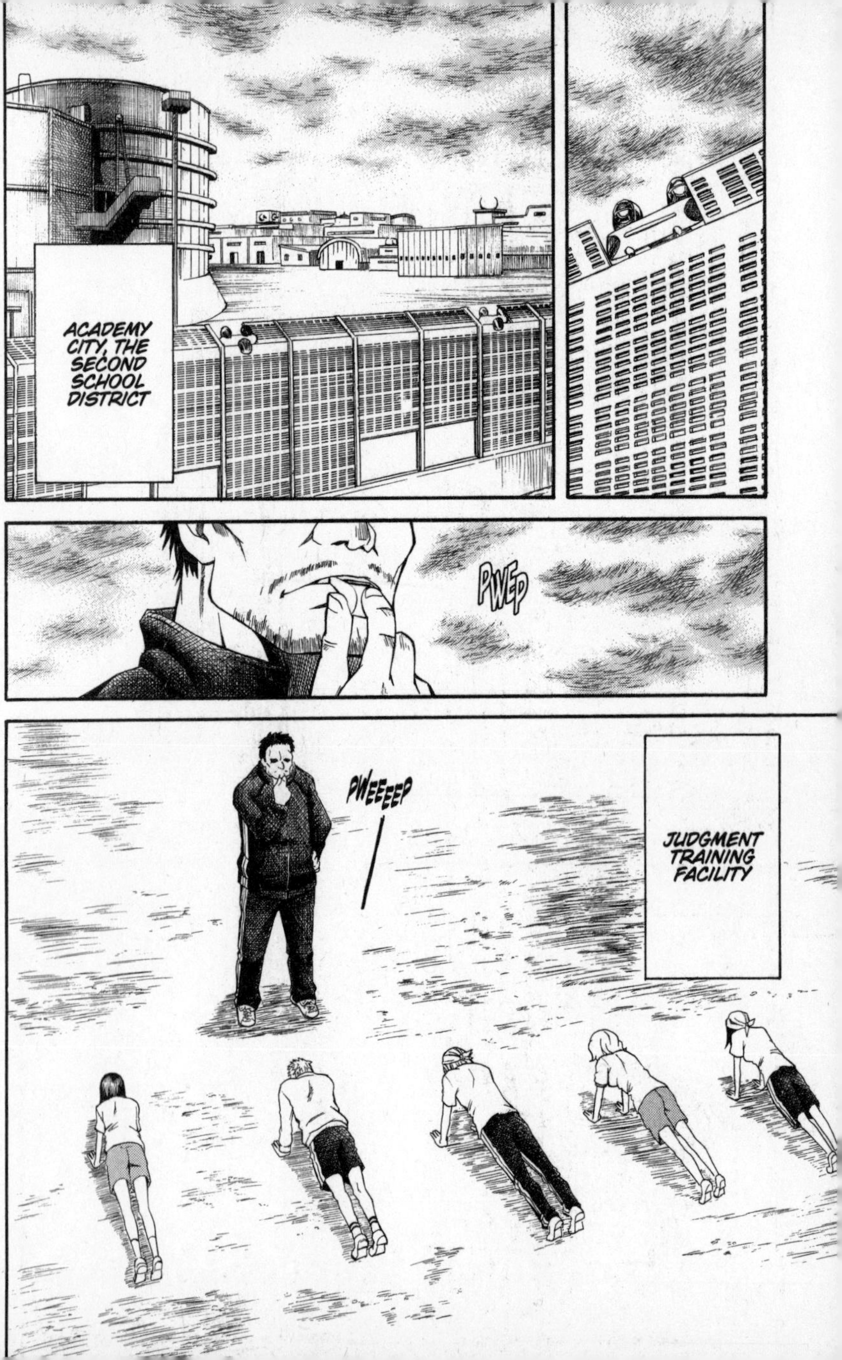
ACADEMY CITY, THE SECOND SCHOOL DISTRICT
PWEP
JUDGMENT TRAINING FACILITY
PWEEEEP

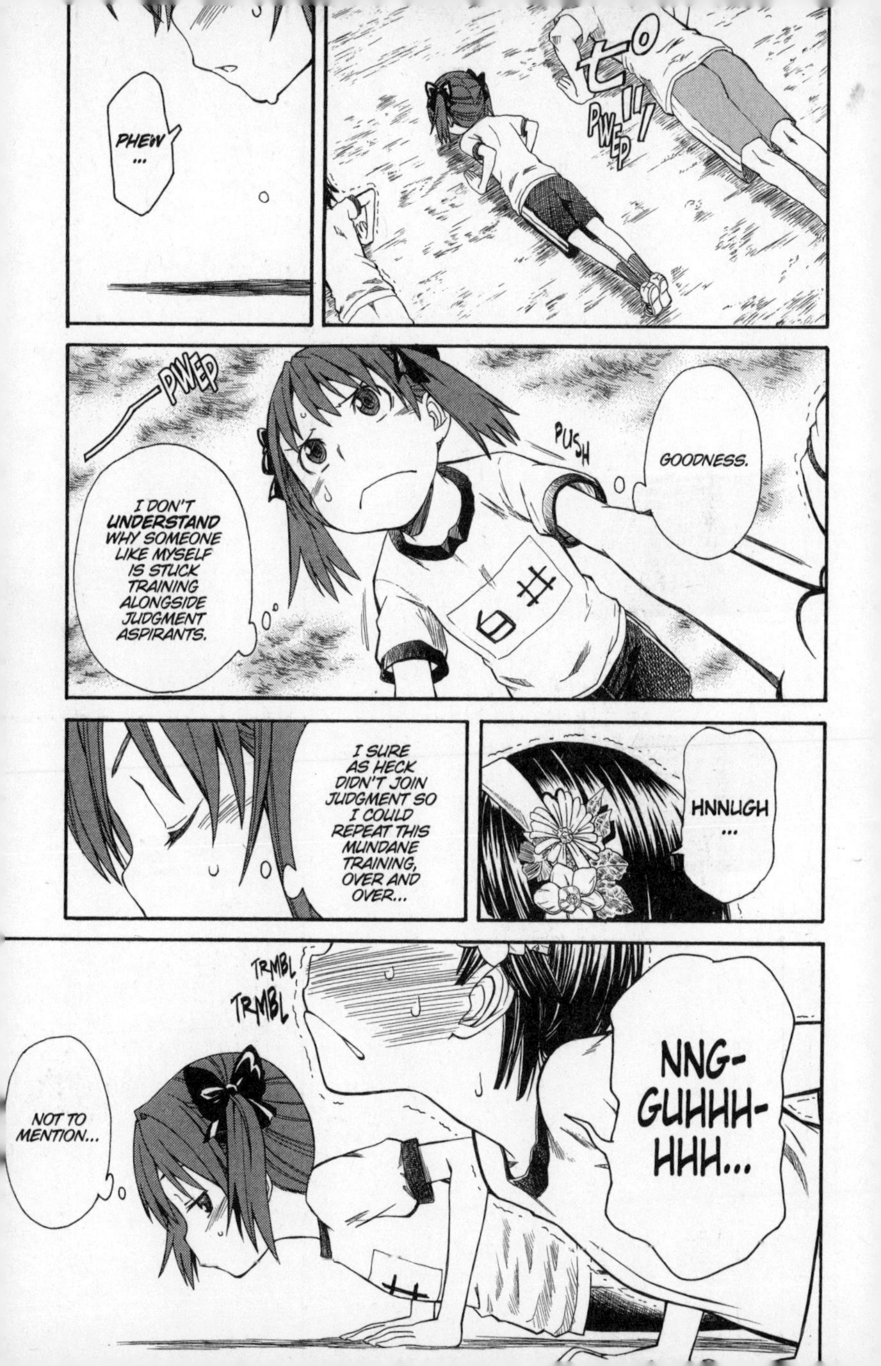
PWEP
PHEW ...
GOODNESS.
PUSH
PWEP
I DON'T UNDERSTAND WHY SOMEONE LIKE MYSELF IS STUCK TRAINING ALONGSIDE JUDGMENT ASPIRANTS.
HNNUGH ...
I SURE AS HECK DIDN'T JOIN JUDGMENT SO I COULD REPEAT THIS MUNDANE TRAINING, OVER AND OVER...
NNG-GUHHHH-HHH...
TRMBL
TRMBL
NOT TO MENTION...

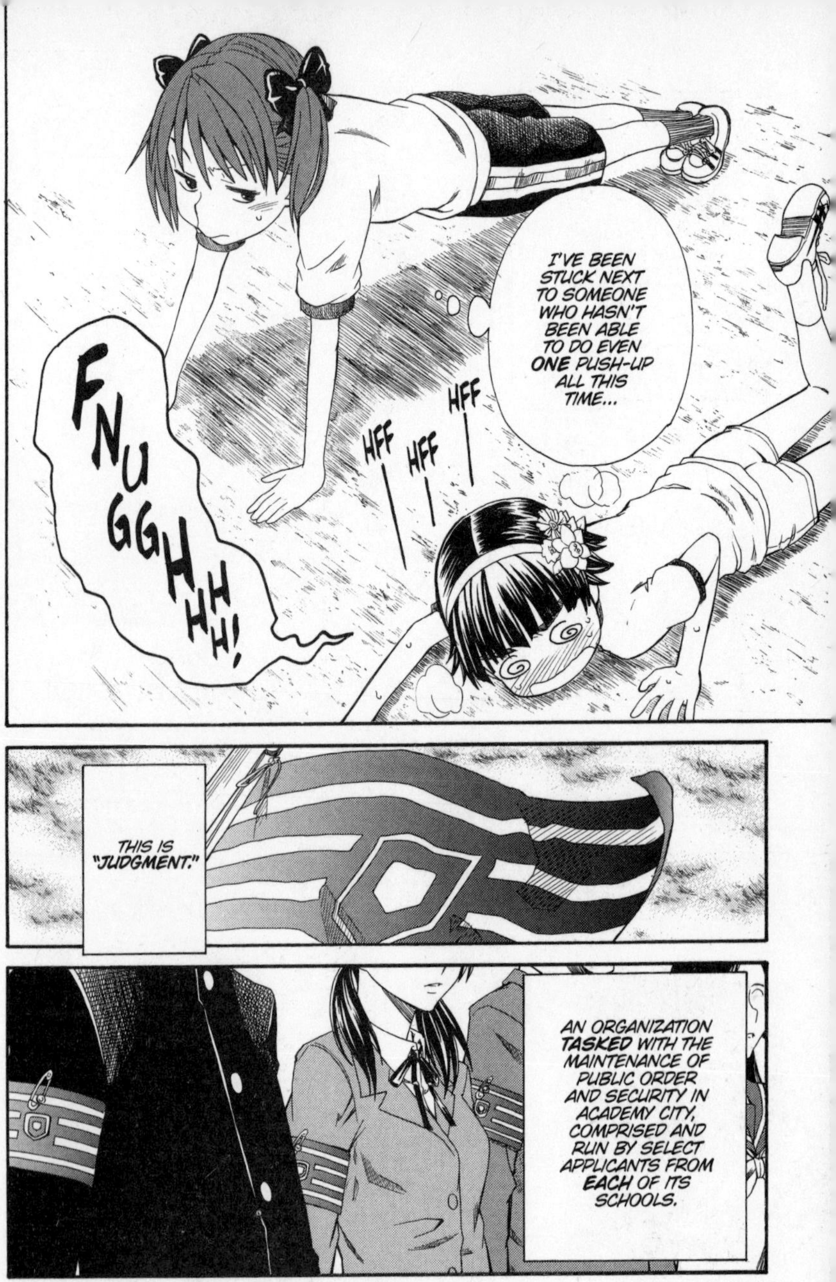
I'VE BEEN STUCK NEXT TO SOMEONE WHO HASN'T BEEN ABLE TO DO EVEN ONE PUSH-UP ALL THIS TIME...
HFF
HFF
HFF
FNUGGHHHH!
THIS IS "JUDGMENT."
AN ORGANIZATION TASKED WITH THE MAINTENANCE OF PUBLIC ORDER AND SECURITY IN ACADEMY CITY, COMPRISED AND RUN BY SELECT APPLICANTS FROM EACH OF ITS SCHOOLS.

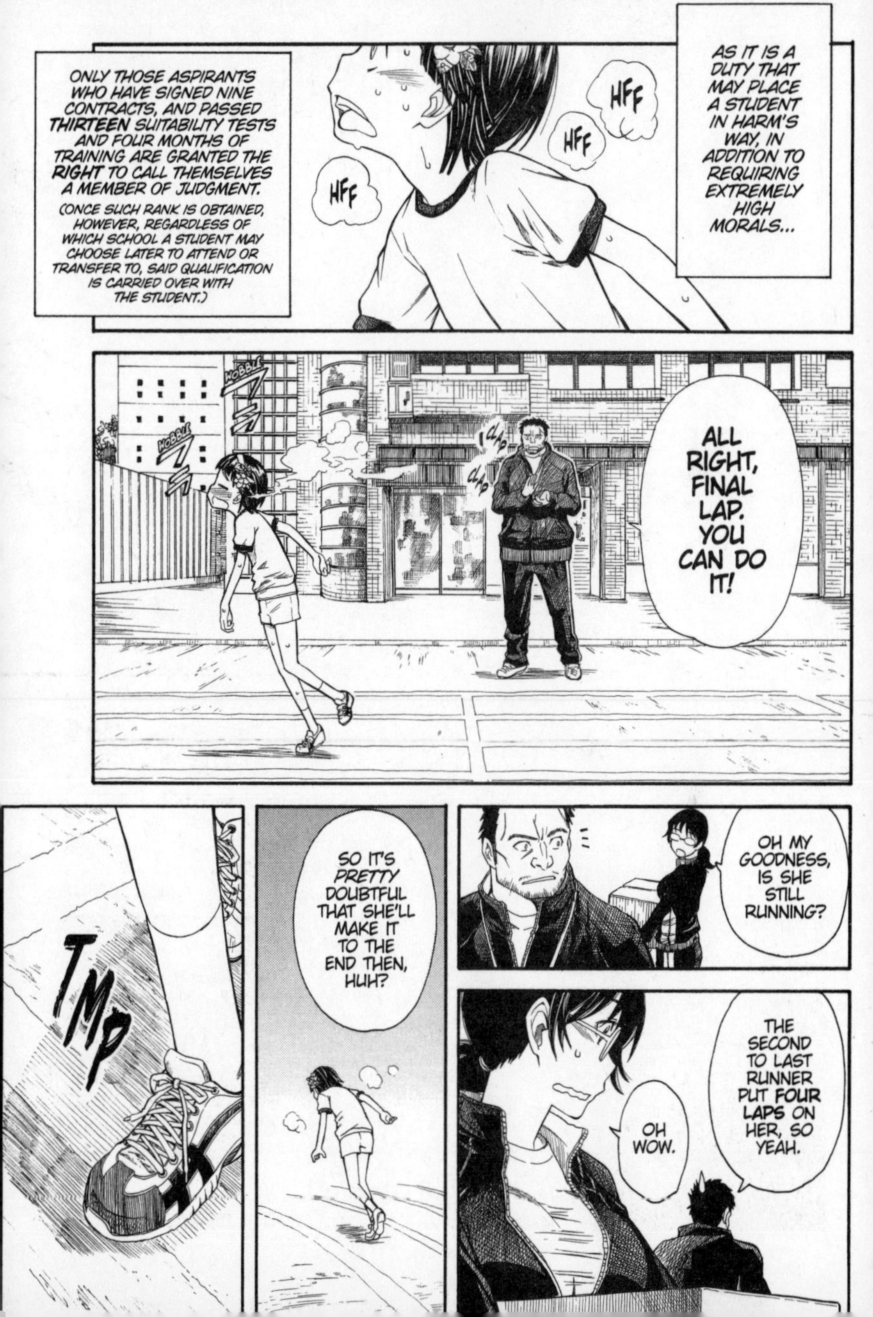
AS IT IS A DUTY THAT MAY PLACE A STUDENT IN HARM'S WAY, IN ADDITION TO REQUIRING EXTREMELY HIGH MORALS...
HFF
HFF
HFF
ONLY THOSE ASPIRANTS WHO HAVE SIGNED NINE CONTRACTS, AND PASSED **THIRTEEN** SUITABILITY TESTS AND FOUR MONTHS OF TRAINING ARE GRANTED THE **RIGHT** TO CALL THEMSELVES A MEMBER OF JUDGMENT.
(ONCE SUCH RANK IS OBTAINED, HOWEVER, REGARDLESS OF WHICH SCHOOL A STUDENT MAY CHOOSE LATER TO ATTEND OR TRANSFER TO, SAID QUALIFICATION IS CARRIED OVER WITH THE STUDENT.)
ALL RIGHT, FINAL LAP. YOU CAN DO IT!
CLAP
CLAP
WOBBLE
WOBBLE
OH MY GOODNESS, IS SHE STILL RUNNING?
THE SECOND TO LAST RUNNER PUT **FOUR LAPS** ON HER, SO YEAH.
OH WOW.
SO IT'S *PRETTY* DOUBTFUL THAT SHE'LL MAKE IT TO THE END THEN, HUH?
TMP

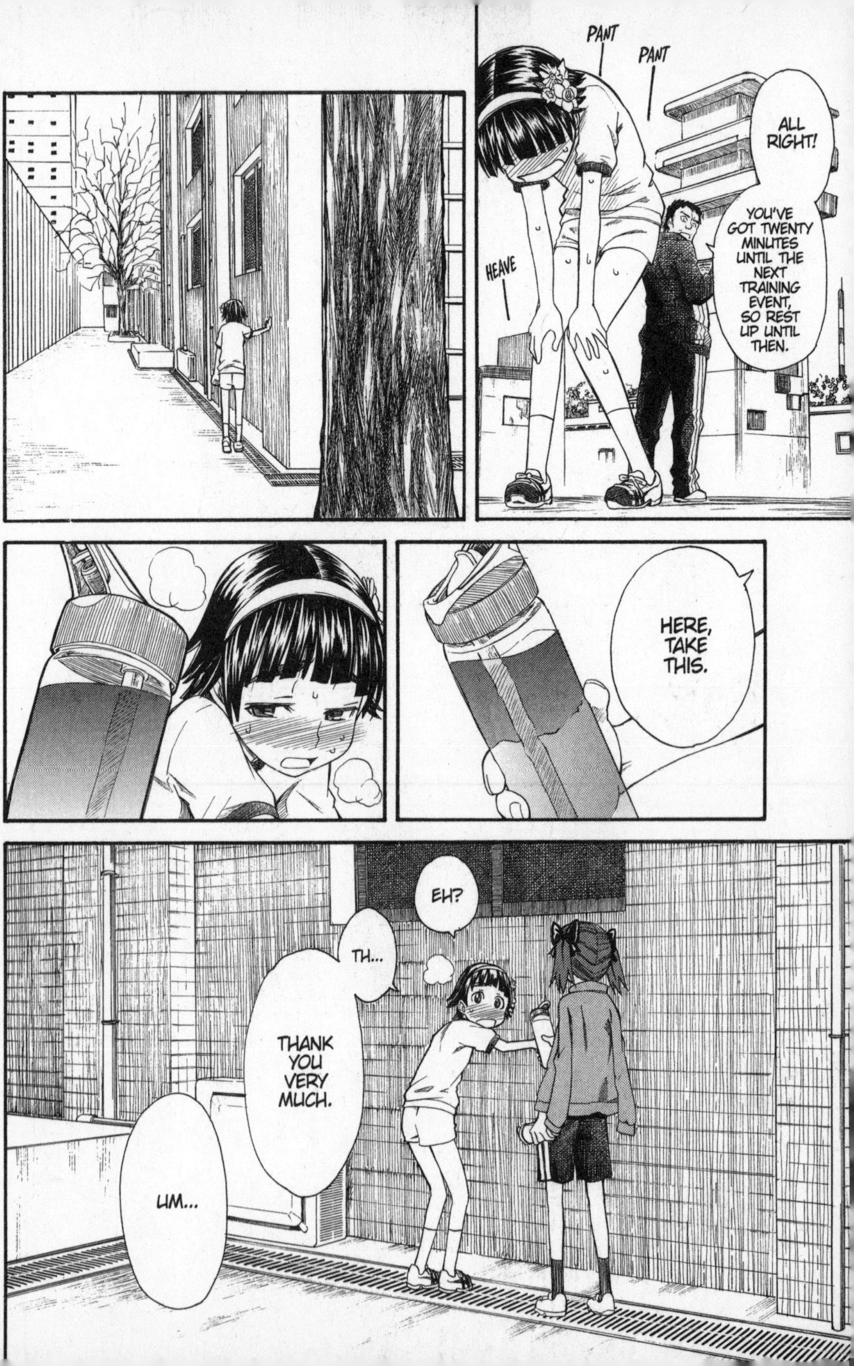
PANT
PANT
ALL RIGHT!
YOU'VE GOT TWENTY MINUTES UNTIL THE NEXT TRAINING EVENT, SO REST UP UNTIL THEN.
HEAVE
HERE, TAKE THIS.
EH?
TH...
THANK YOU VERY MUCH.
UM...

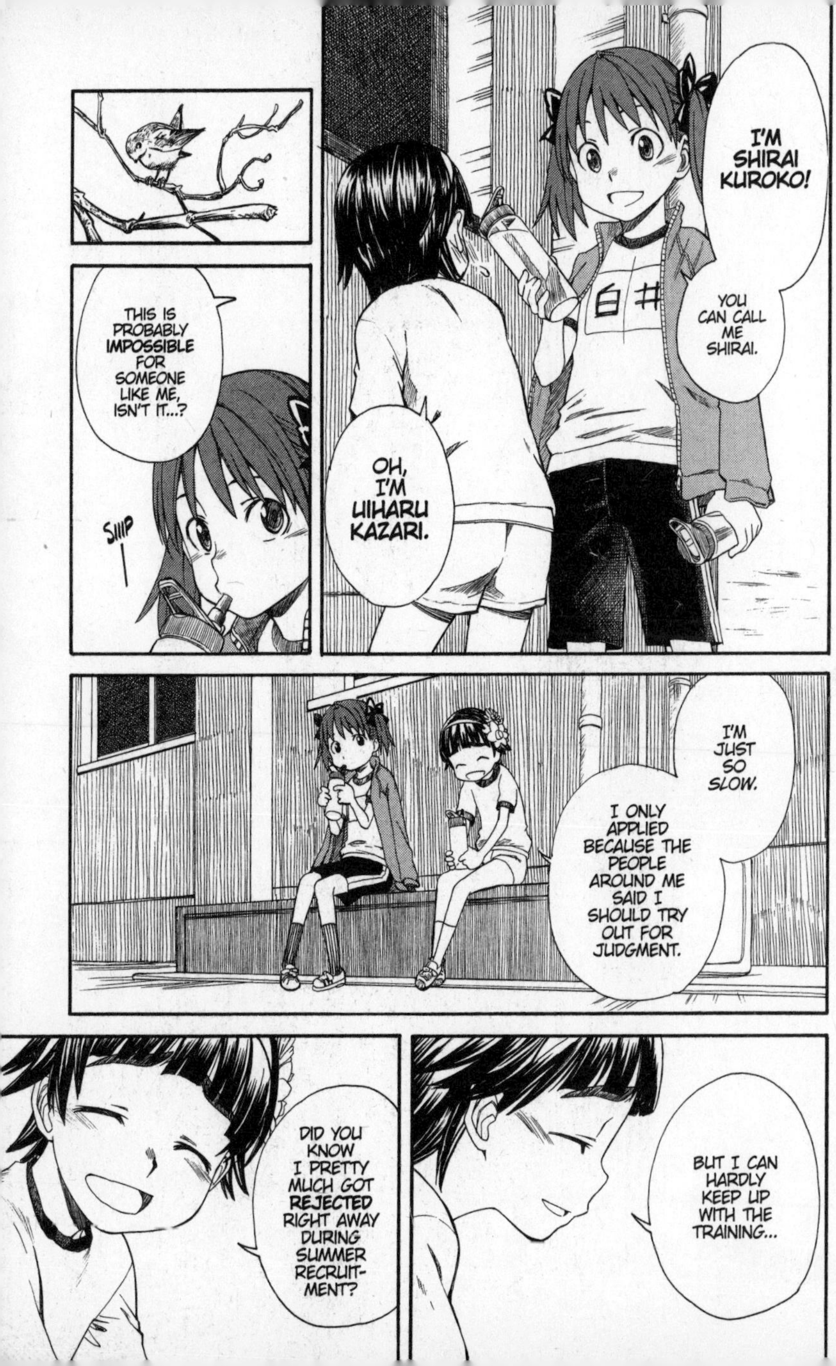

I'M SHIRAI KUROKO!
白井
YOU CAN CALL ME SHIRAI.
OH, I'M UIHARU KAZARI.
THIS IS PROBABLY IMPOSSIBLE FOR SOMEONE LIKE ME, ISN'T IT...?
SIIIP
I'M JUST SO SLOW.
I ONLY APPLIED BECAUSE THE PEOPLE AROUND ME SAID I SHOULD TRY OUT FOR JUDGMENT.
BUT I CAN HARDLY KEEP UP WITH THE TRAINING...
DID YOU KNOW I PRETTY MUCH GOT REJECTED RIGHT AWAY DURING SUMMER RECRUIT-MENT?

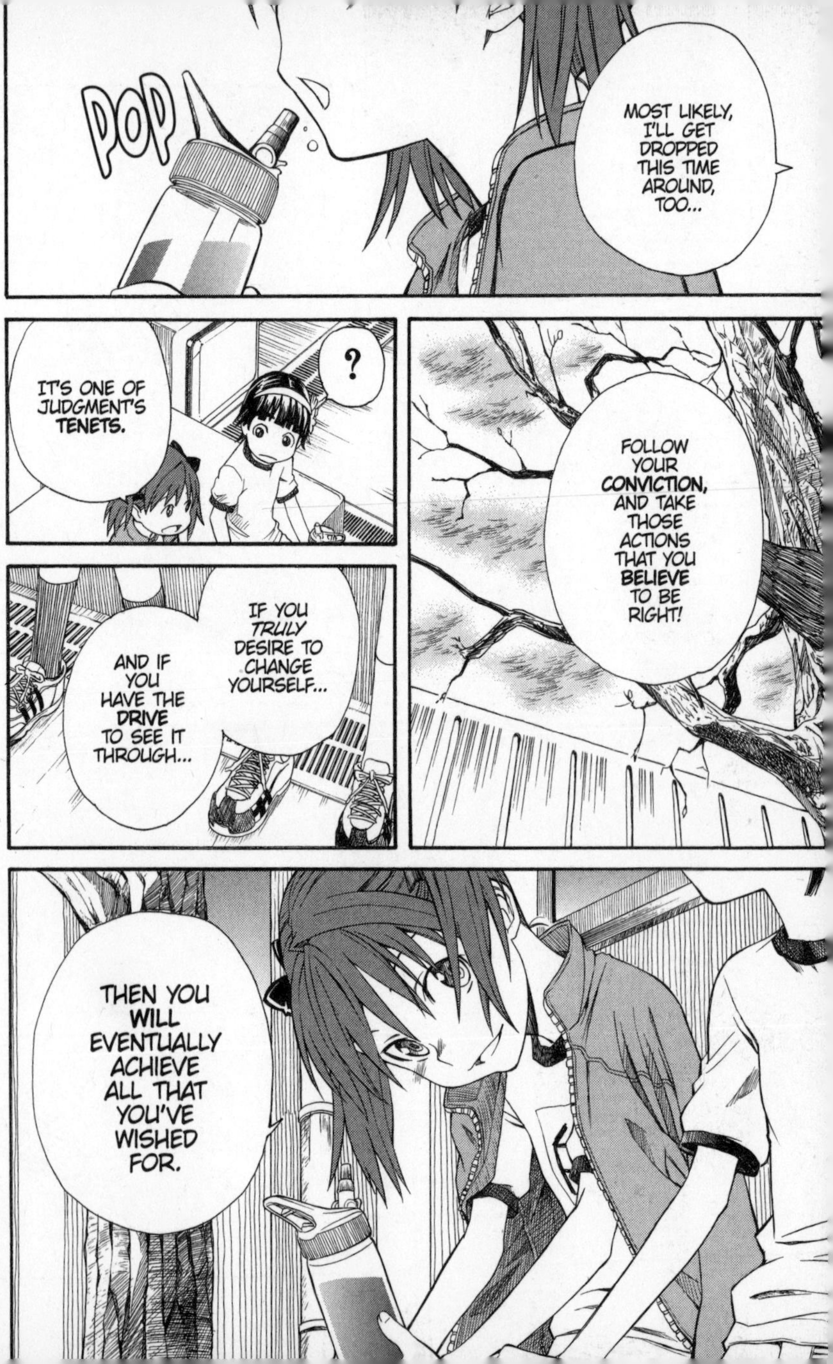

MOST LIKELY, I'LL GET DROPPED THIS TIME AROUND, TOO...
POP
FOLLOW YOUR CONVICTION, AND TAKE THOSE ACTIONS THAT YOU BELIEVE TO BE RIGHT!
?
IT'S ONE OF JUDGMENT'S TENETS.
IF YOU TRULY DESIRE TO CHANGE YOURSELF...
AND IF YOU HAVE THE DRIVE TO SEE IT THROUGH...
THEN YOU WILL EVENTUALLY ACHIEVE ALL THAT YOU'VE WISHED FOR.

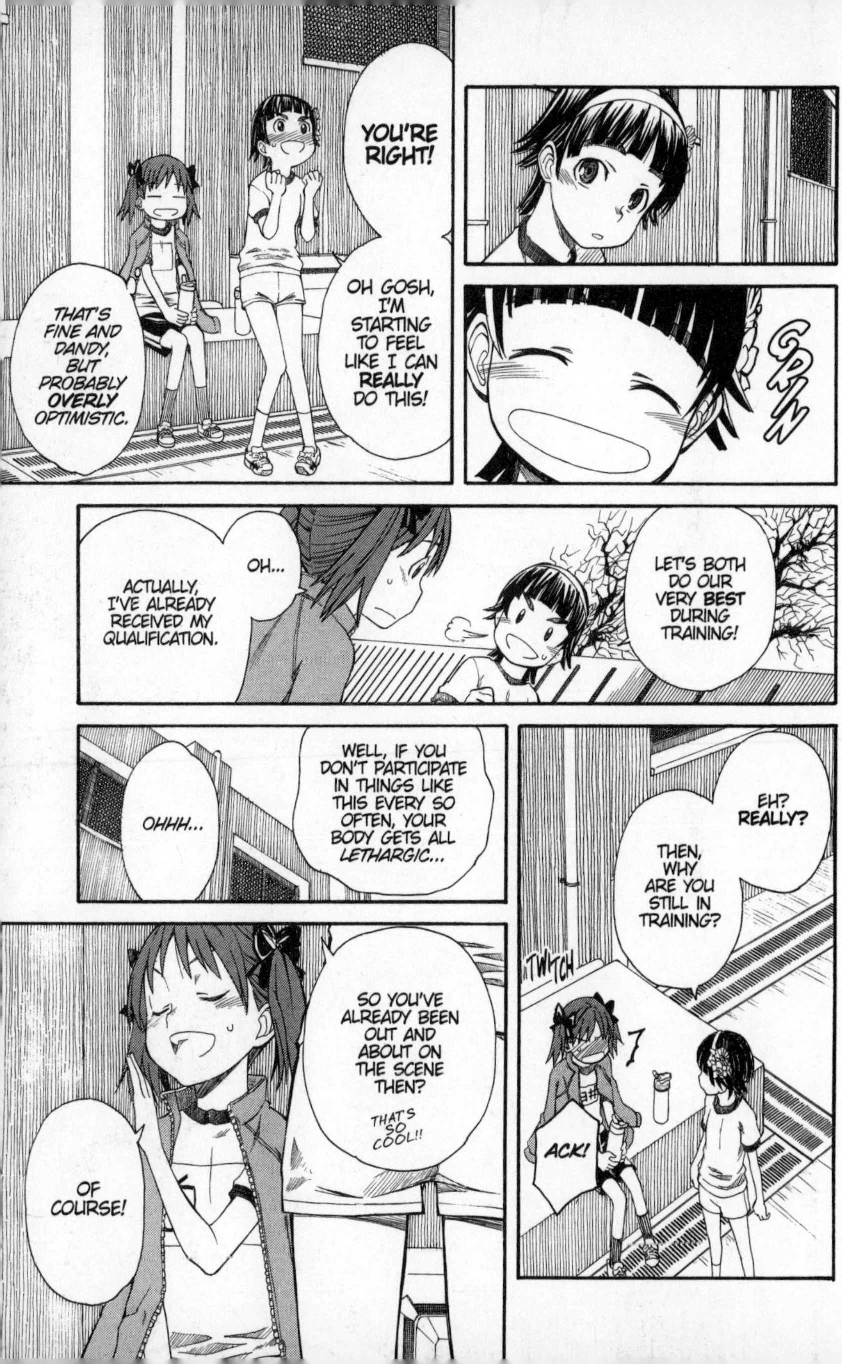
GRIN
YOU'RE RIGHT!
OH GOSH, I'M STARTING TO FEEL LIKE I CAN REALLY DO THIS!
THAT'S FINE AND DANDY, BUT PROBABLY OVERLY OPTIMISTIC.
LET'S BOTH DO OUR VERY BEST DURING TRAINING!
OH...
ACTUALLY, I'VE ALREADY RECEIVED MY QUALIFICATION.
EH? REALLY?
THEN, WHY ARE YOU STILL IN TRAINING?
TWITCH
ACK!
WELL, IF YOU DON'T PARTICIPATE IN THINGS LIKE THIS EVERY SO OFTEN, YOUR BODY GETS ALL LETHARGIC...
OHHH...
SO YOU'VE ALREADY BEEN OUT AND ABOUT ON THE SCENE THEN?
THAT'S SO COOL!!
OF COURSE!

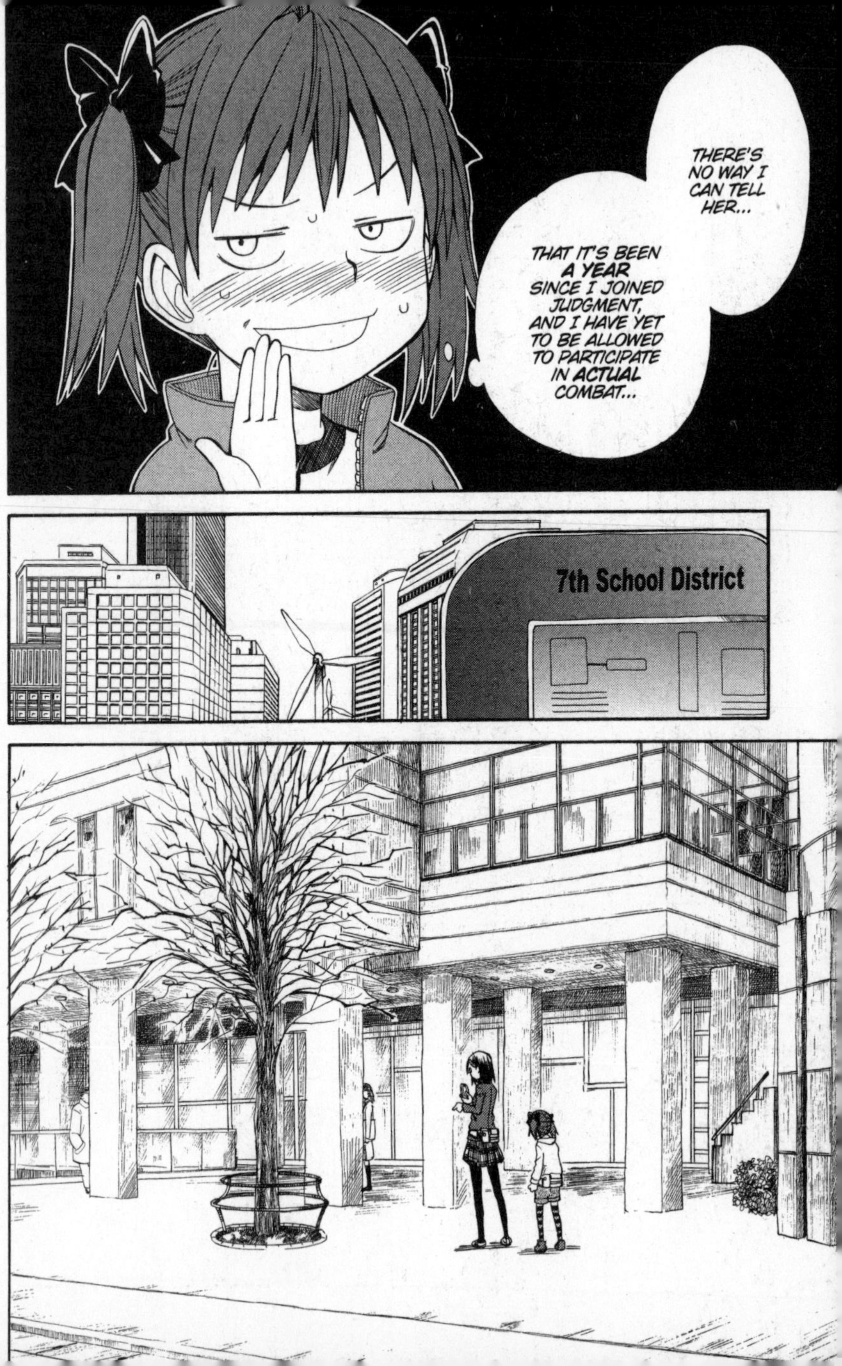
THERE'S NO WAY I CAN TELL HER...
THAT IT'S BEEN A YEAR SINCE I JOINED JUDGMENT, AND I HAVE YET TO BE ALLOWED TO PARTICIPATE IN ACTUAL COMBAT...
7th School District

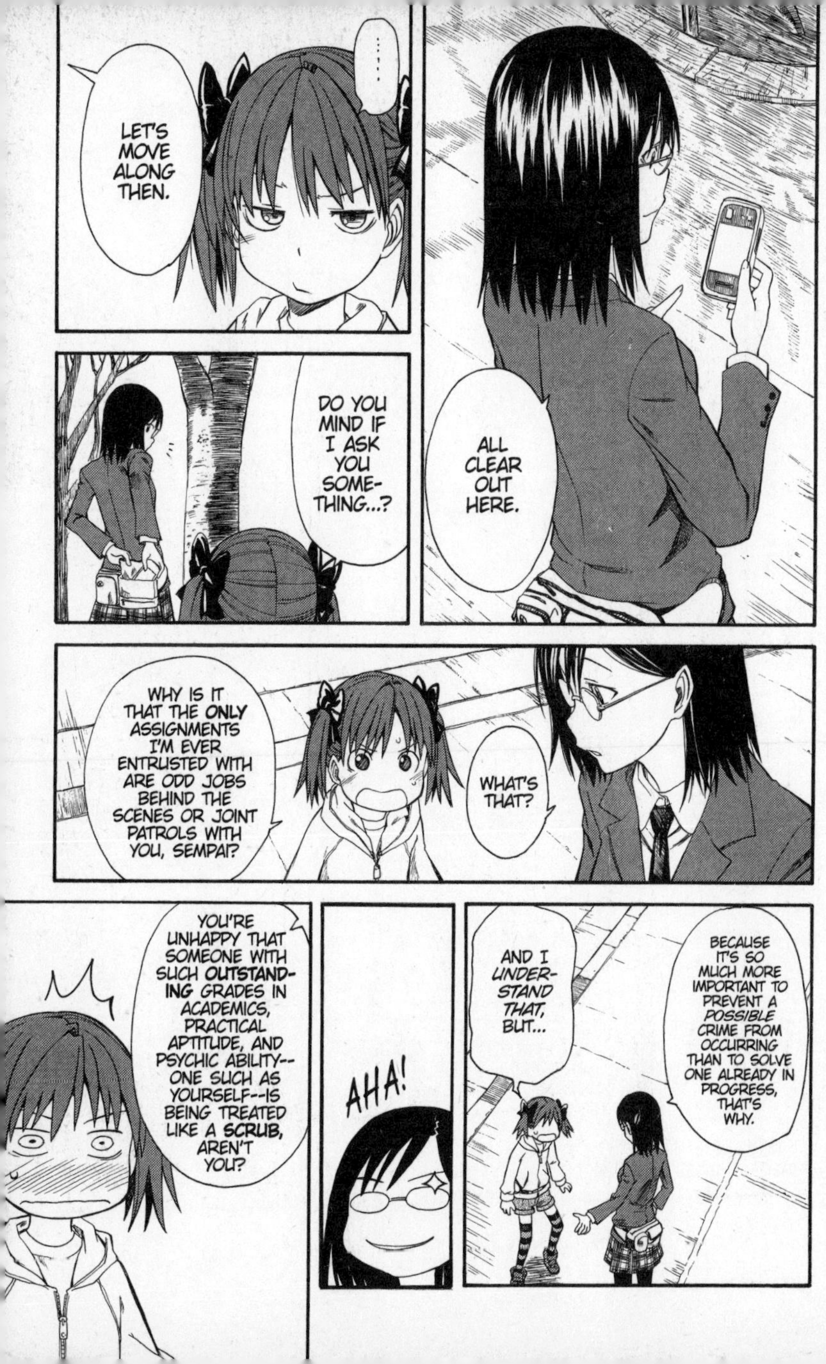
ALL CLEAR OUT HERE.
......
LET'S MOVE ALONG THEN.
DO YOU MIND IF I ASK YOU SOMETHING...?
WHAT'S THAT?
WHY IS IT THAT THE **ONLY** ASSIGNMENTS I'M EVER ENTRUSTED WITH ARE ODD JOBS BEHIND THE SCENES OR JOINT PATROLS WITH YOU, SEMPAI?
BECAUSE IT'S SO MUCH MORE IMPORTANT TO PREVENT A *POSSIBLE* CRIME FROM OCCURRING THAN TO SOLVE ONE ALREADY IN PROGRESS, THAT'S WHY.
AND I *UNDERSTAND* THAT, BUT...
AHA!
YOU'RE UNHAPPY THAT SOMEONE WITH SUCH **OUTSTANDING** GRADES IN ACADEMICS, PRACTICAL APTITUDE, AND PSYCHIC ABILITY--ONE SUCH AS YOURSELF--IS BEING TREATED LIKE A **SCRUB**, AREN'T YOU?

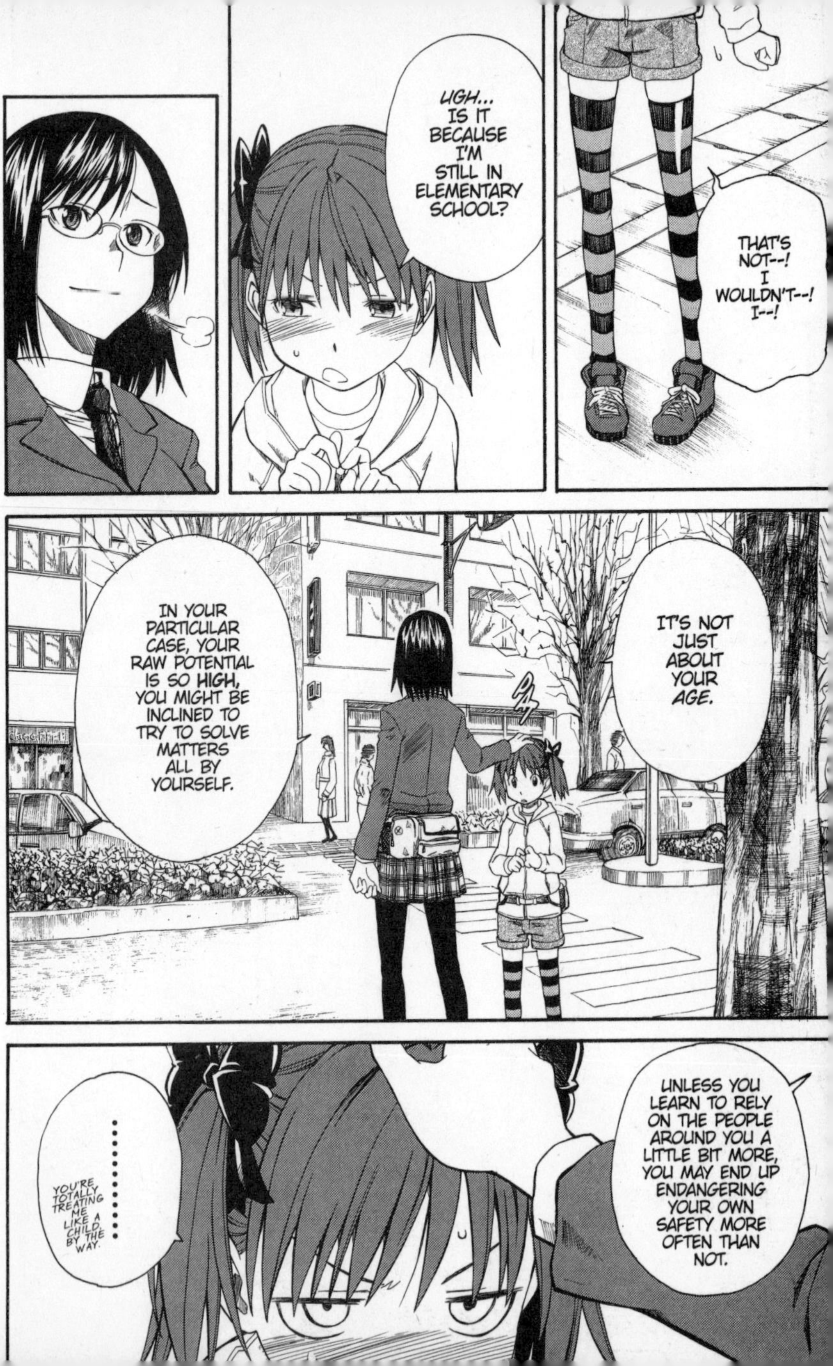
THAT'S NOT--! I WOULDN'T--! I--!
UGH... IS IT BECAUSE I'M STILL IN ELEMENTARY SCHOOL?
IT'S NOT JUST ABOUT YOUR AGE.
IN YOUR PARTICULAR CASE, YOUR RAW POTENTIAL IS SO HIGH, YOU MIGHT BE INCLINED TO TRY TO SOLVE MATTERS ALL BY YOURSELF.
UNLESS YOU LEARN TO RELY ON THE PEOPLE AROUND YOU A LITTLE BIT MORE, YOU MAY END UP ENDANGERING YOUR OWN SAFETY MORE OFTEN THAN NOT.
....
YOU'RE TOTALLY TREATING ME LIKE A CHILD, BY THE WAY.

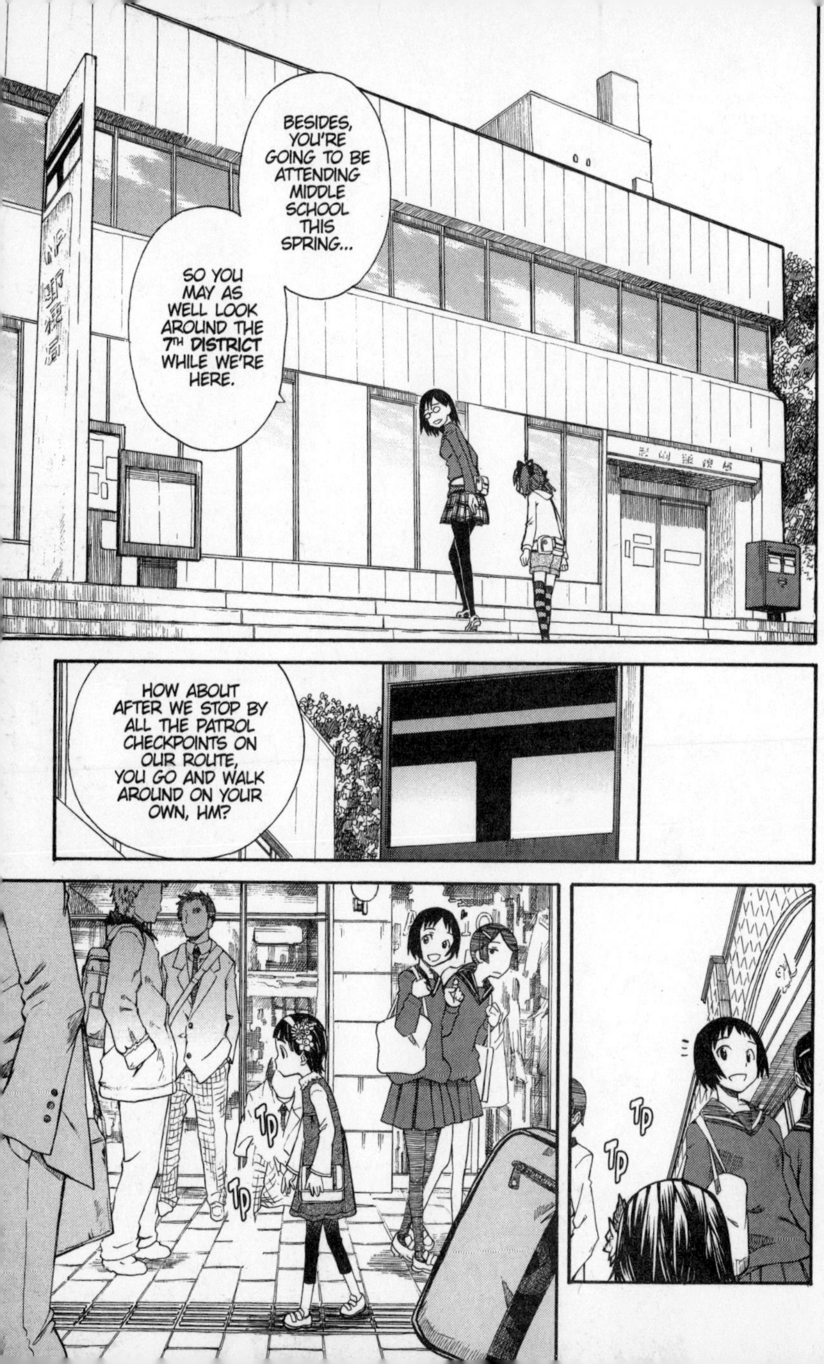
BESIDES, YOU'RE GOING TO BE ATTENDING MIDDLE SCHOOL THIS SPRING...
SO YOU MAY AS WELL LOOK AROUND THE 7TH DISTRICT WHILE WE'RE HERE.
HOW ABOUT AFTER WE STOP BY ALL THE PATROL CHECKPOINTS ON OUR ROUTE, YOU GO AND WALK AROUND ON YOUR OWN, HM?
Tp
Tp
Tp
Tp

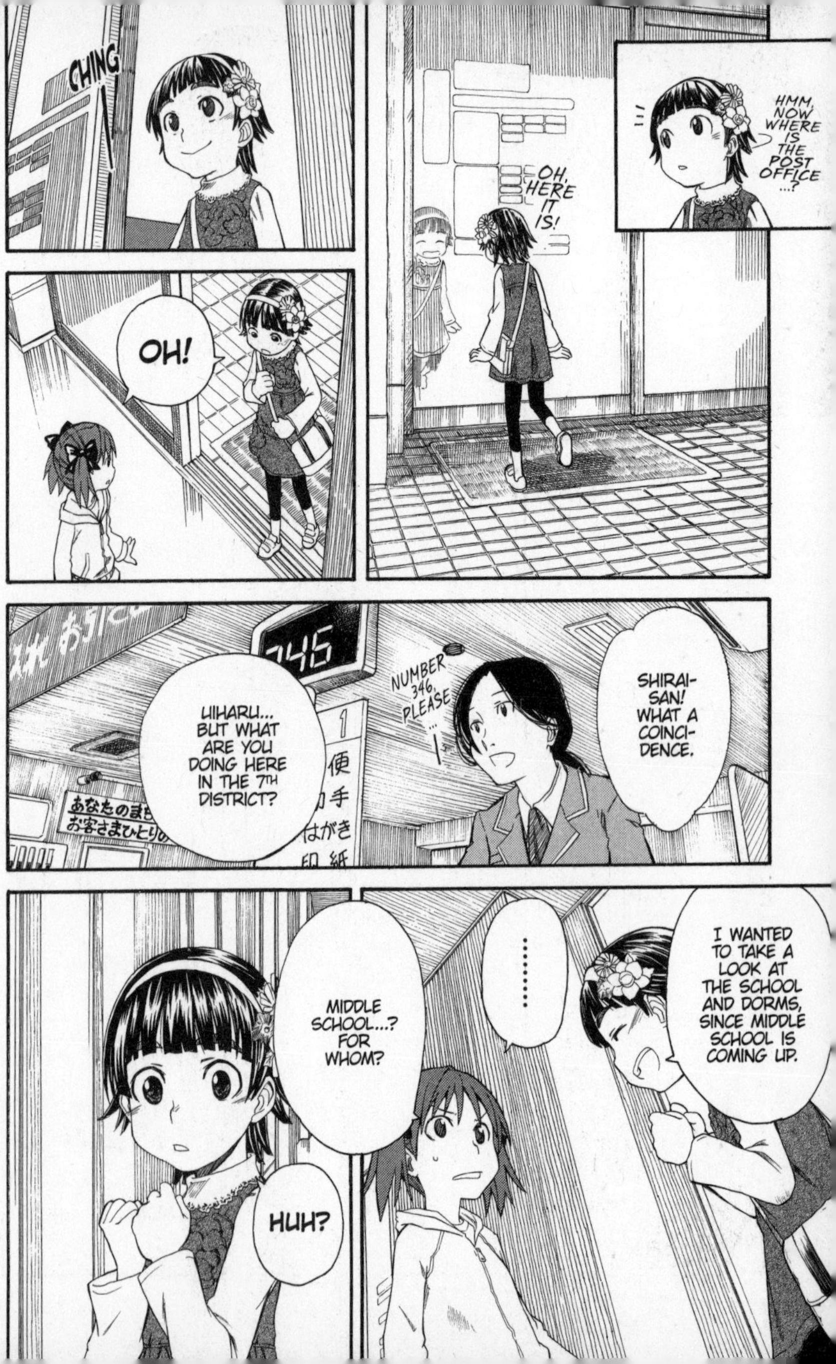
HMM, NOW WHERE IS THE POST OFFICE ...?
OH, HERE IT IS!
CHING
OH!
SHIRAI-SAN! WHAT A COINCIDENCE.
NUMBER 346, PLEASE ...
346
UIHARU... BUT WHAT ARE YOU DOING HERE IN THE 7TH DISTRICT?
はがき
I WANTED TO TAKE A LOOK AT THE SCHOOL AND DORMS, SINCE MIDDLE SCHOOL IS COMING UP.
....
MIDDLE SCHOOL...? FOR WHOM?
HUH?

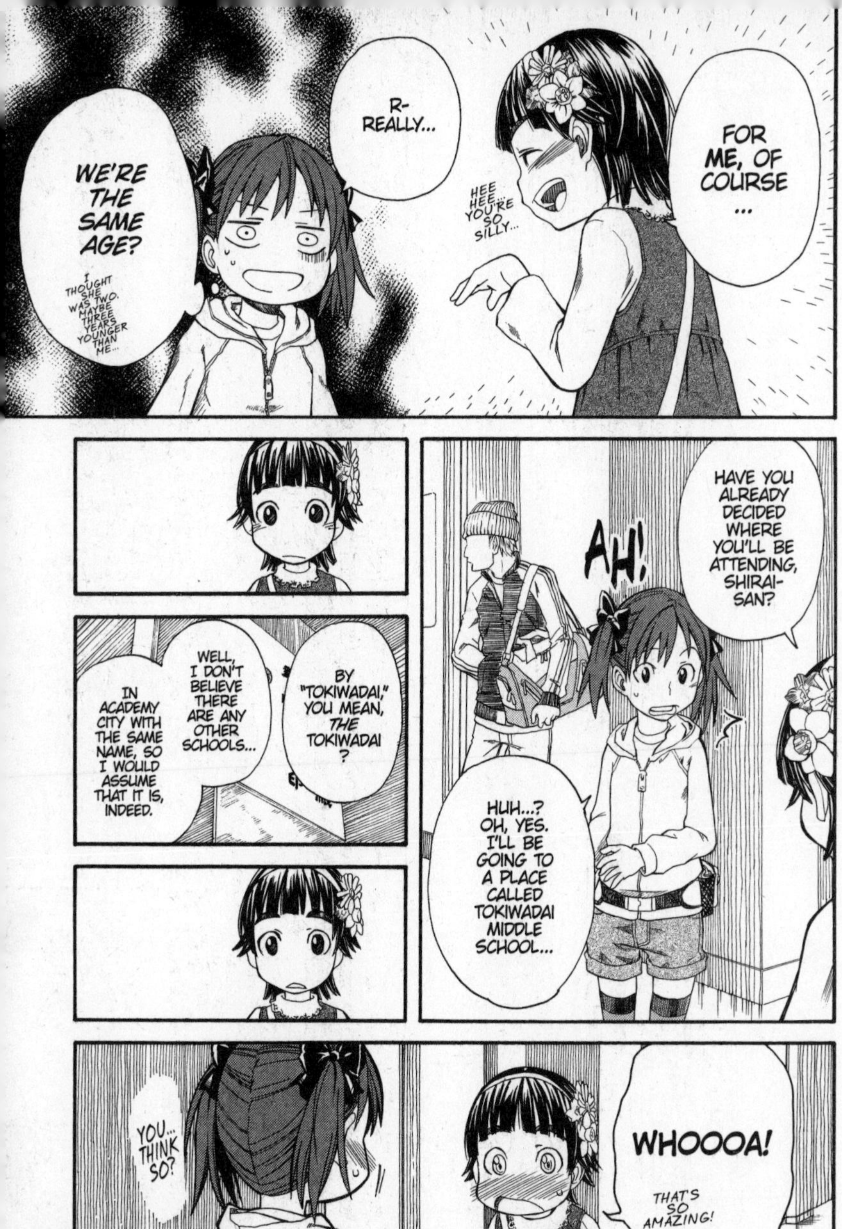
FOR ME, OF COURSE ...
HEE HEE... YOU'RE SO SILLY...
R- REALLY...
WE'RE THE SAME AGE?
I THOUGHT SHE WAS TWO, MAYBE THREE YEARS YOUNGER THAN ME...
HAVE YOU ALREADY DECIDED WHERE YOU'LL BE ATTENDING, SHIRAI-SAN?
AH!
HUH...? OH, YES. I'LL BE GOING TO A PLACE CALLED TOKIWADAI MIDDLE SCHOOL...
BY "TOKIWADAI," YOU MEAN, *THE* TOKIWADAI?
WELL, I DON'T BELIEVE THERE ARE ANY OTHER SCHOOLS...
IN ACADEMY CITY WITH THE SAME NAME, SO I WOULD ASSUME THAT IT IS, INDEED.
WHOOOA!
THAT'S SO AMAZING!
YOU... THINK SO?

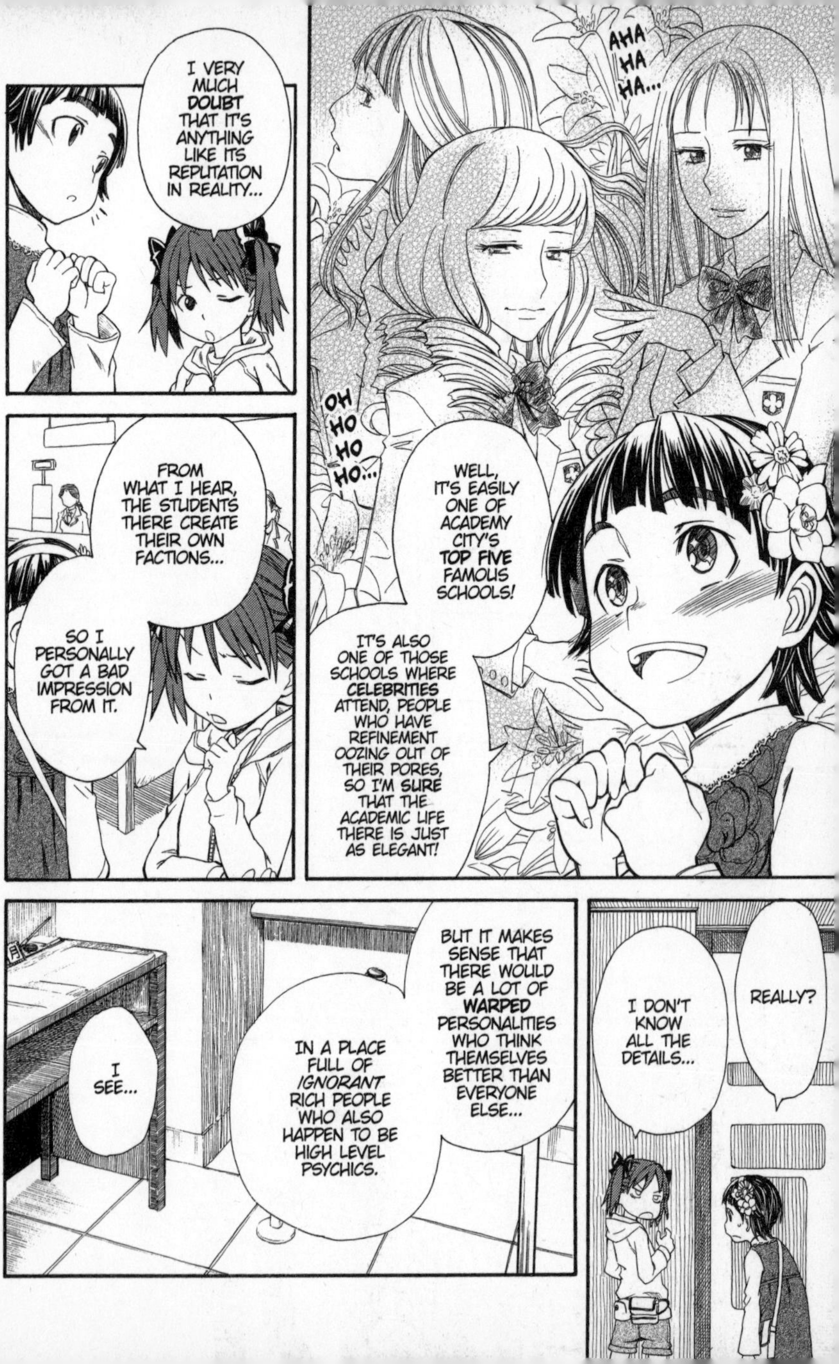
AHA HA HA...
OH HO HO HO...
WELL, IT'S EASILY ONE OF ACADEMY CITY'S **TOP FIVE** FAMOUS SCHOOLS!
IT'S ALSO ONE OF THOSE SCHOOLS WHERE **CELEBRITIES** ATTEND, PEOPLE WHO HAVE REFINEMENT OOZING OUT OF THEIR PORES, SO I'M **SURE** THAT THE ACADEMIC LIFE THERE IS JUST AS ELEGANT!
I VERY MUCH **DOUBT** THAT IT'S ANYTHING LIKE ITS REPUTATION IN REALITY...
FROM WHAT I HEAR, THE STUDENTS THERE CREATE THEIR OWN FACTIONS...
SO I PERSONALLY GOT A BAD IMPRESSION FROM IT.
REALLY?
I DON'T KNOW ALL THE DETAILS...
BUT IT MAKES SENSE THAT THERE WOULD BE A LOT OF **WARPED** PERSONALITIES WHO THINK THEMSELVES BETTER THAN EVERYONE ELSE...
IN A PLACE FULL OF *IGNORANT* RICH PEOPLE WHO ALSO HAPPEN TO BE HIGH LEVEL PSYCHICS.
I SEE...

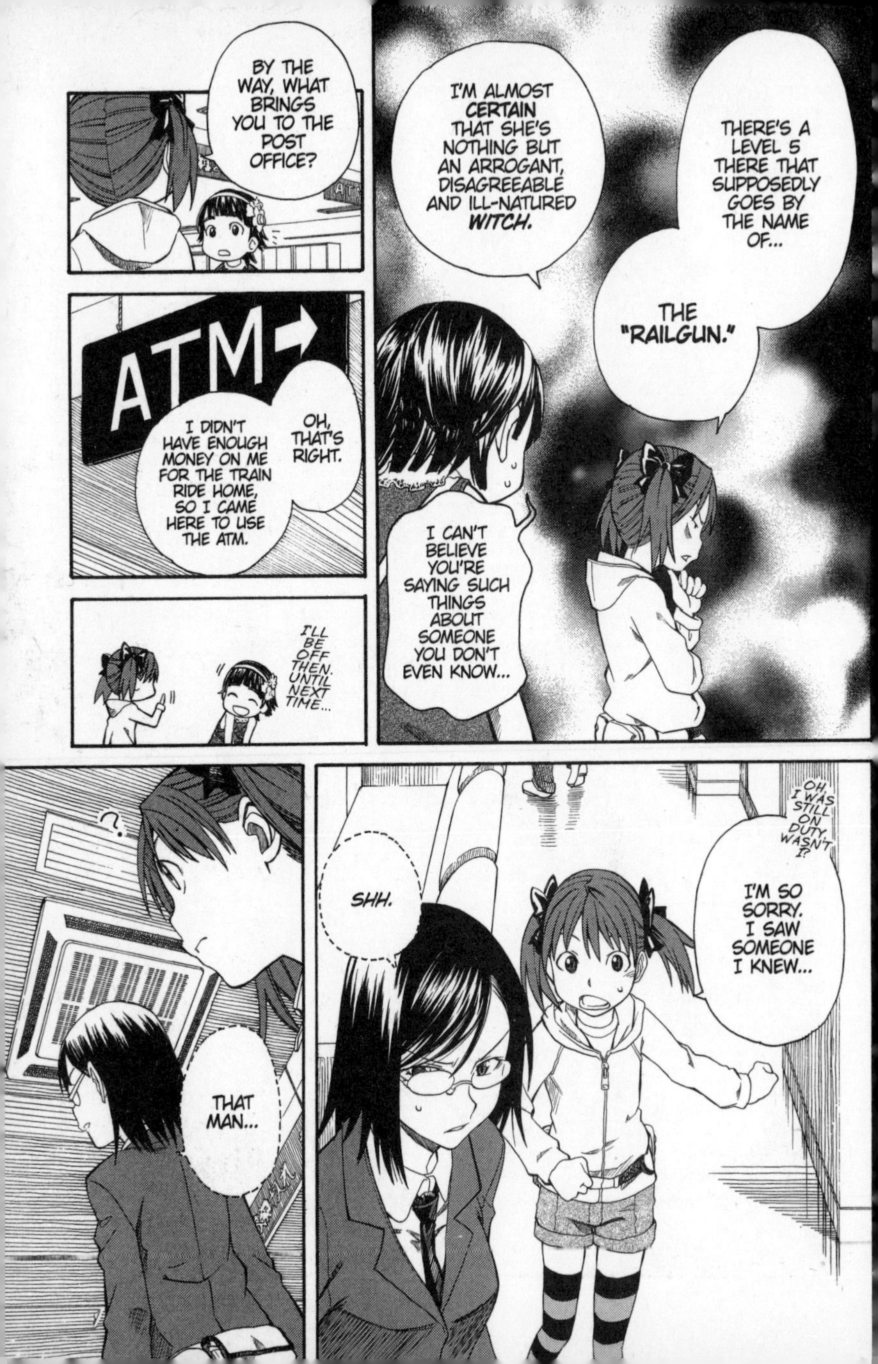
THERE'S A LEVEL 5 THERE THAT SUPPOSEDLY GOES BY THE NAME OF...
THE "RAILGUN."
I'M ALMOST CERTAIN THAT SHE'S NOTHING BUT AN ARROGANT, DISAGREEABLE AND ILL-NATURED WITCH.
I CAN'T BELIEVE YOU'RE SAYING SUCH THINGS ABOUT SOMEONE YOU DON'T EVEN KNOW...
BY THE WAY, WHAT BRINGS YOU TO THE POST OFFICE?
ATM
OH, THAT'S RIGHT.
I DIDN'T HAVE ENOUGH MONEY ON ME FOR THE TRAIN RIDE HOME, SO I CAME HERE TO USE THE ATM.
I'LL BE OFF THEN. UNTIL NEXT TIME...
OH, I WAS STILL ON DUTY, WASN'T I?
I'M SO SORRY. I SAW SOMEONE I KNEW...
SHH.
?
THAT MAN...

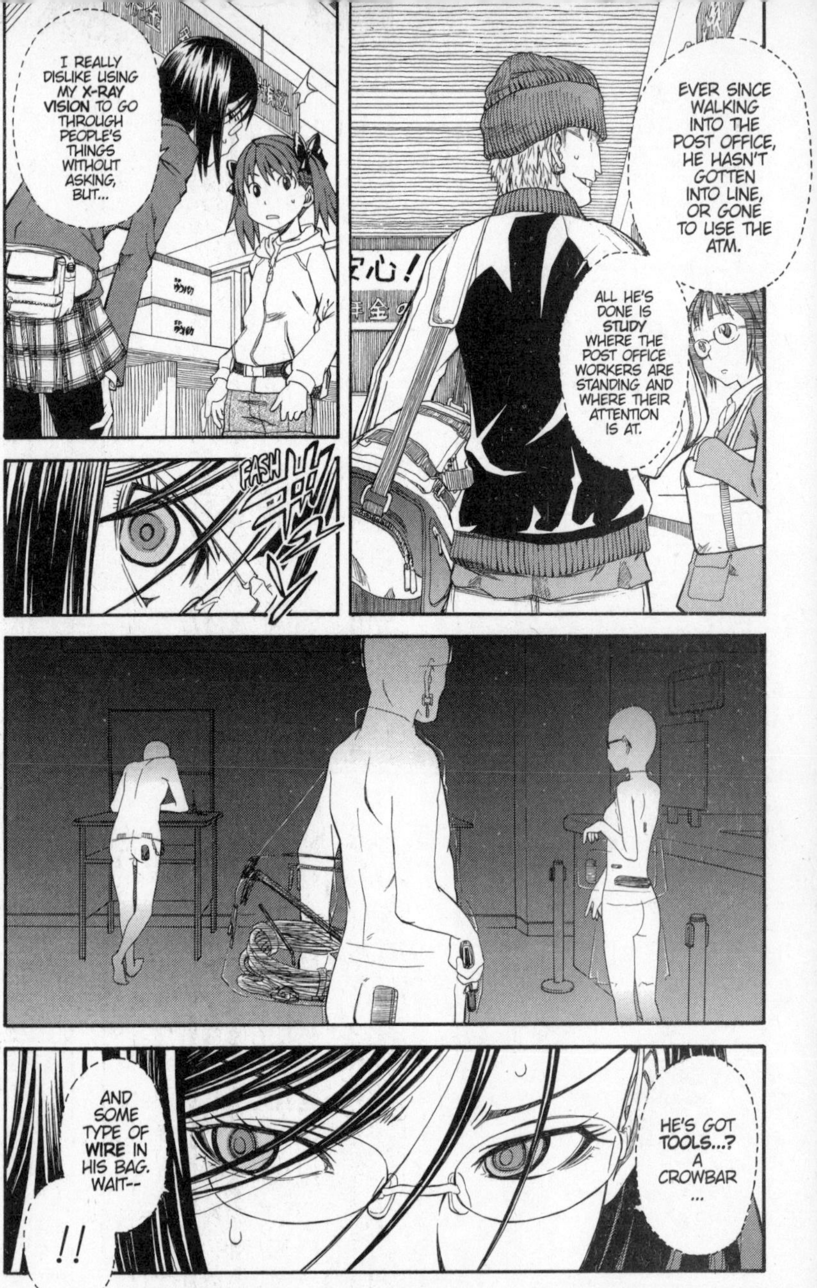
EVER SINCE WALKING INTO THE POST OFFICE, HE HASN'T GOTTEN INTO LINE, OR GONE TO USE THE ATM.
ALL HE'S DONE IS STUDY WHERE THE POST OFFICE WORKERS ARE STANDING AND WHERE THEIR ATTENTION IS AT.
安心！
I REALLY DISLIKE USING MY X-RAY VISION TO GO THROUGH PEOPLE'S THINGS WITHOUT ASKING, BUT...
FASH
HE'S GOT TOOLS...? A CROWBAR ...
AND SOME TYPE OF WIRE IN HIS BAG. WAIT--
!!

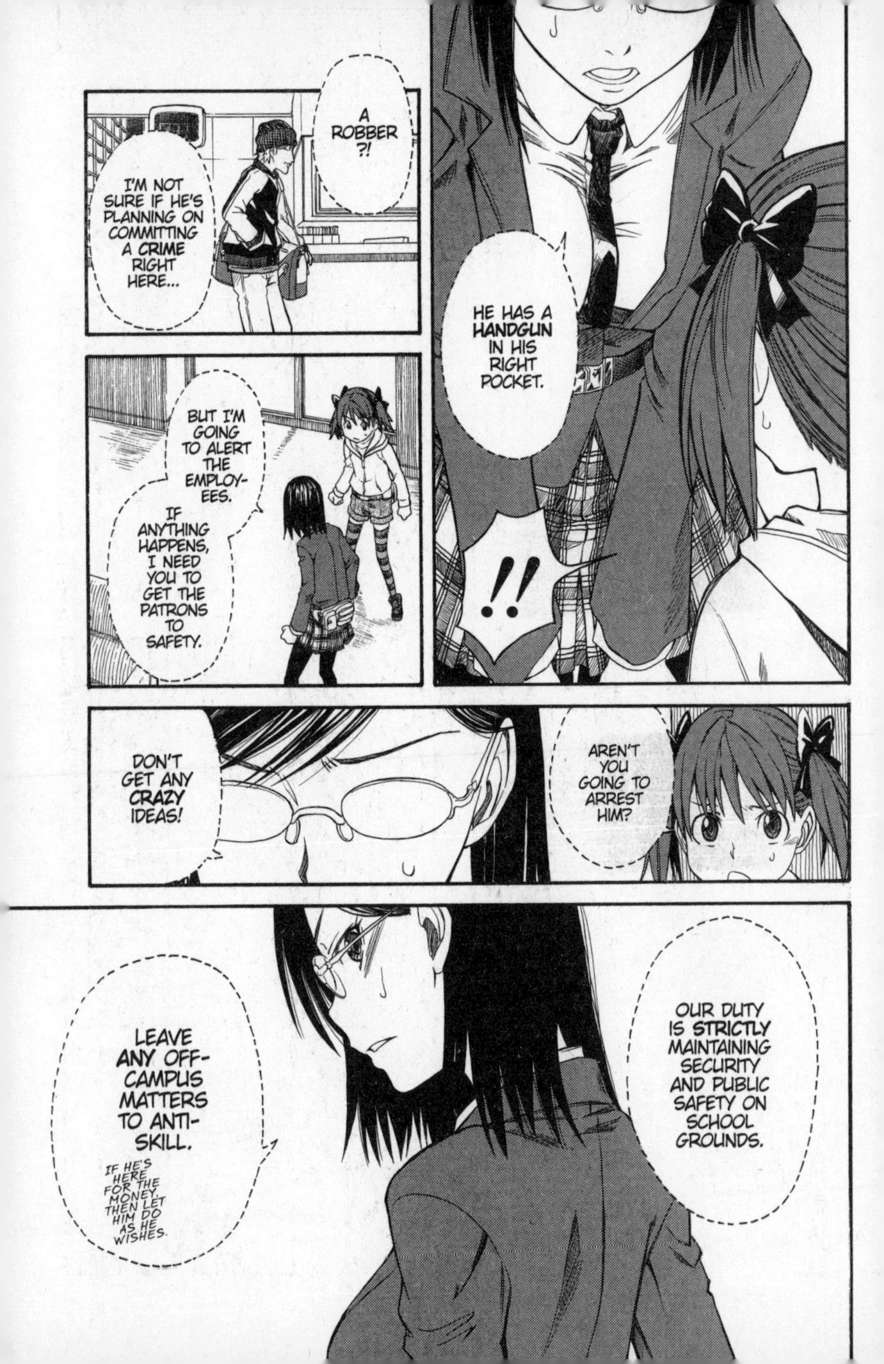
HE HAS A HANDGUN IN HIS RIGHT POCKET.
!!
A ROBBER ?!
I'M NOT SURE IF HE'S PLANNING ON COMMITTING A CRIME RIGHT HERE...
BUT I'M GOING TO ALERT THE EMPLOY-EES.
IF ANYTHING HAPPENS, I NEED YOU TO GET THE PATRONS TO SAFETY.
AREN'T YOU GOING TO ARREST HIM?
DON'T GET ANY CRAZY IDEAS!
OUR DUTY IS STRICTLY MAINTAINING SECURITY AND PUBLIC SAFETY ON SCHOOL GROUNDS.
LEAVE ANY OFF-CAMPUS MATTERS TO ANTI-SKILL.
IF HE'S HERE FOR THE MONEY, THEN LET HIM DO AS HE WISHES.

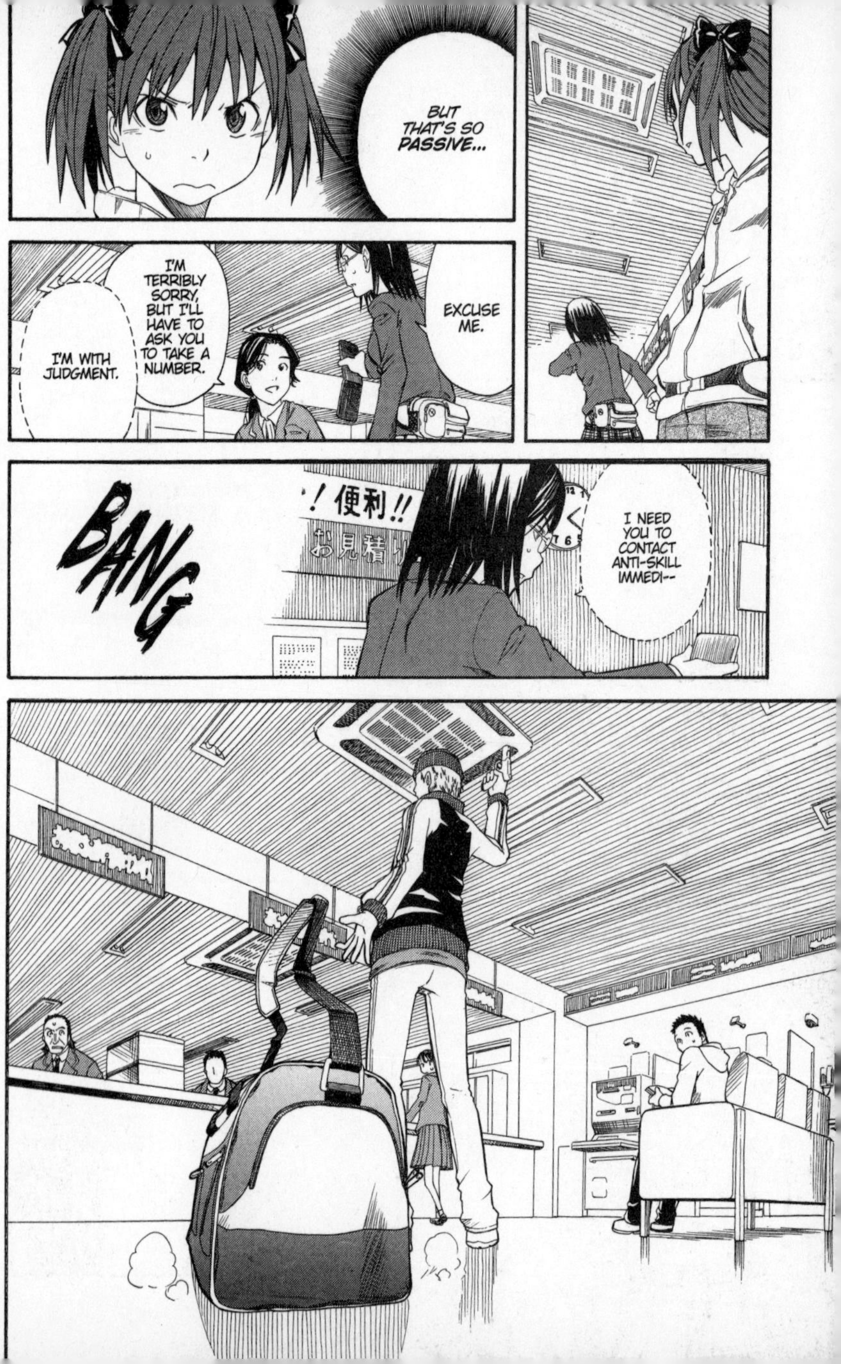
BUT THAT'S SO PASSIVE...
EXCUSE ME.
I'M TERRIBLY SORRY, BUT I'LL HAVE TO ASK YOU TO TAKE A NUMBER.
I'M WITH JUDGMENT.
I NEED YOU TO CONTACT ANTI-SKILL IMMEDI--
!便利!!
BANG

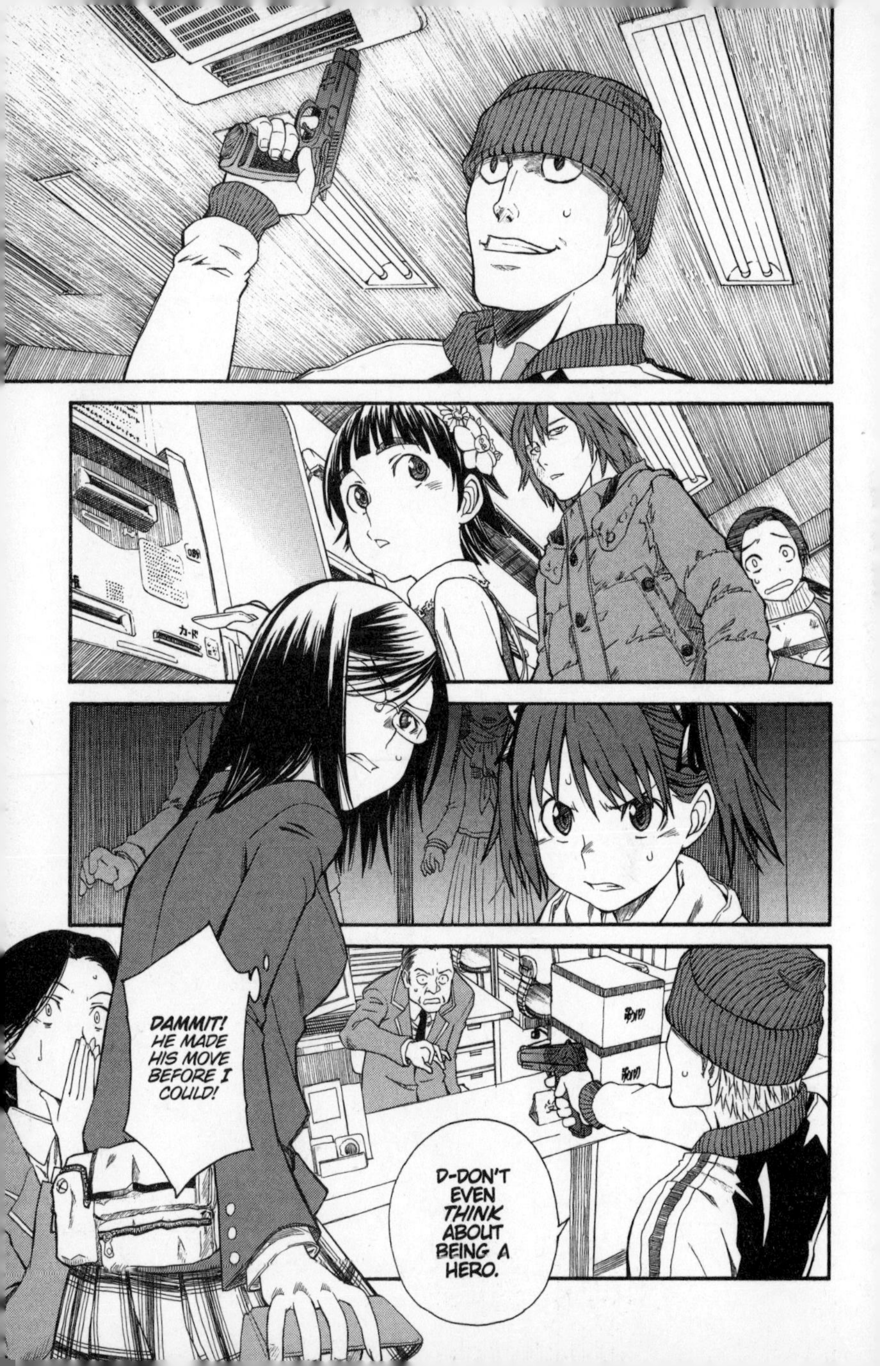
カード
D-DON'T EVEN *THINK* ABOUT BEING A HERO.
DAMMIT! HE MADE HIS MOVE BEFORE I COULD!

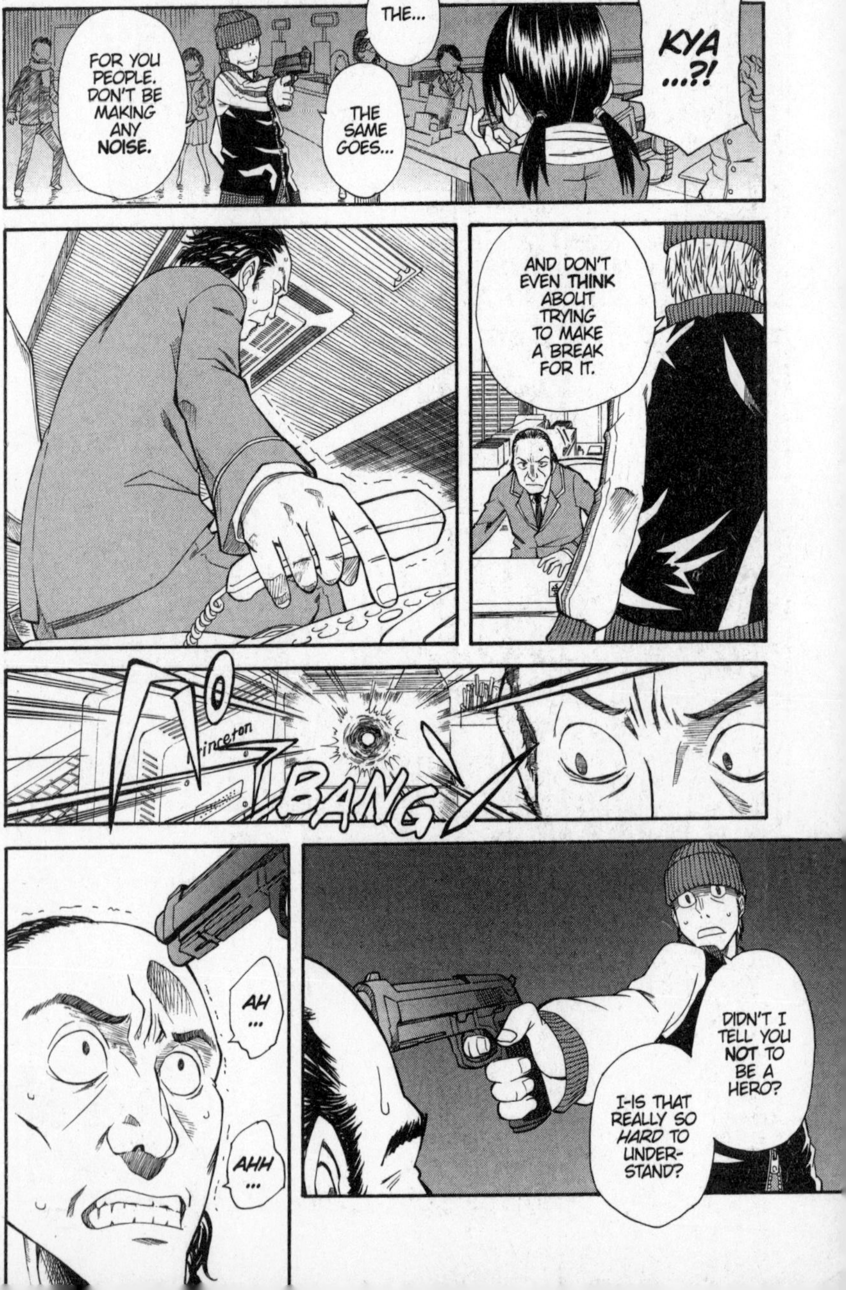
KYA ...?!
THE... THE SAME GOES...
FOR YOU PEOPLE. DON'T BE MAKING ANY NOISE.
AND DON'T EVEN THINK ABOUT TRYING TO MAKE A BREAK FOR IT.
Princeton
BANG
DIDN'T I TELL YOU NOT TO BE A HERO?
I-IS THAT REALLY SO *HARD* TO UNDER-STAND?
AH ...
AHH ...

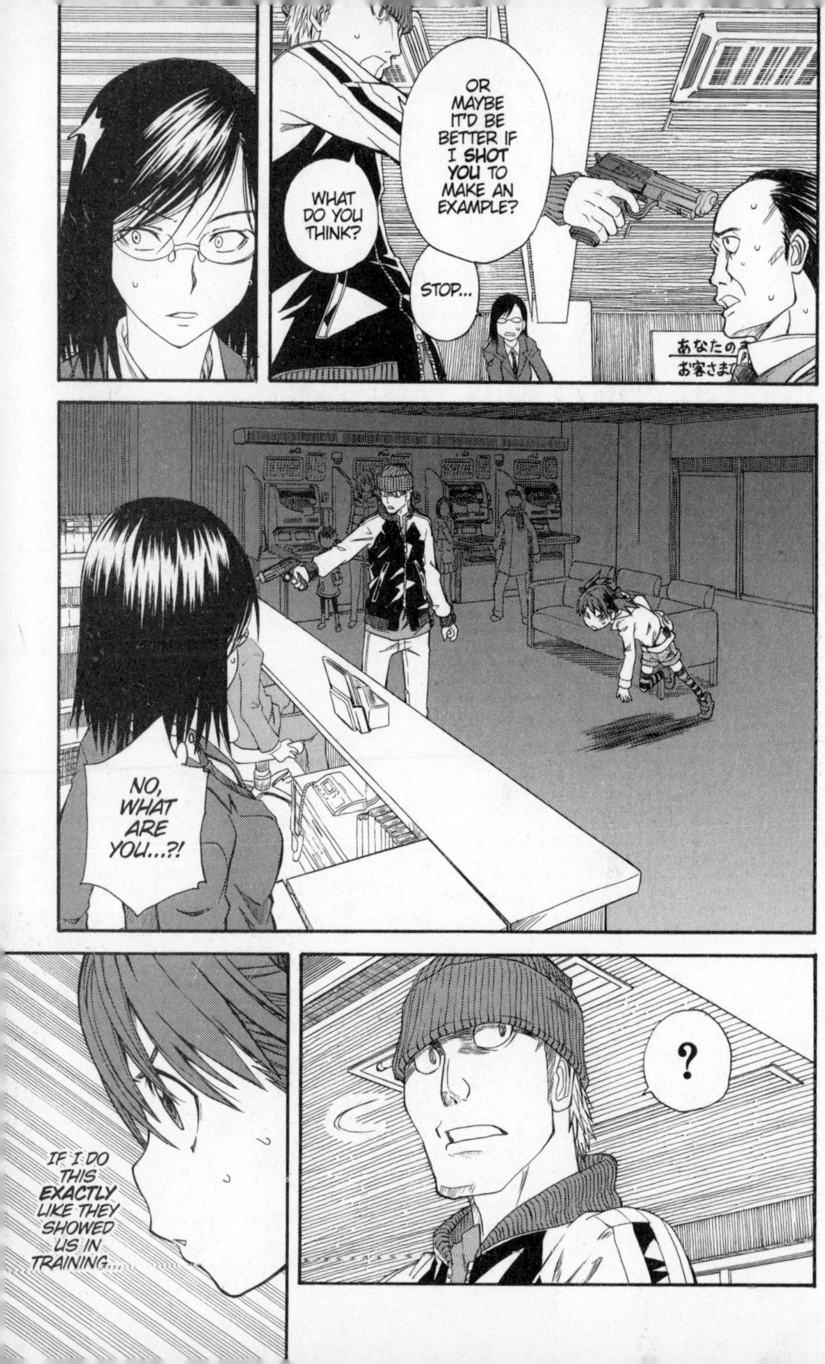
OR MAYBE IT'D BE BETTER IF I SHOT YOU TO MAKE AN EXAMPLE?
WHAT DO YOU THINK?
STOP...
NO, WHAT ARE YOU...?!
?
IF I DO THIS EXACTLY LIKE THEY SHOWED US IN TRAINING...

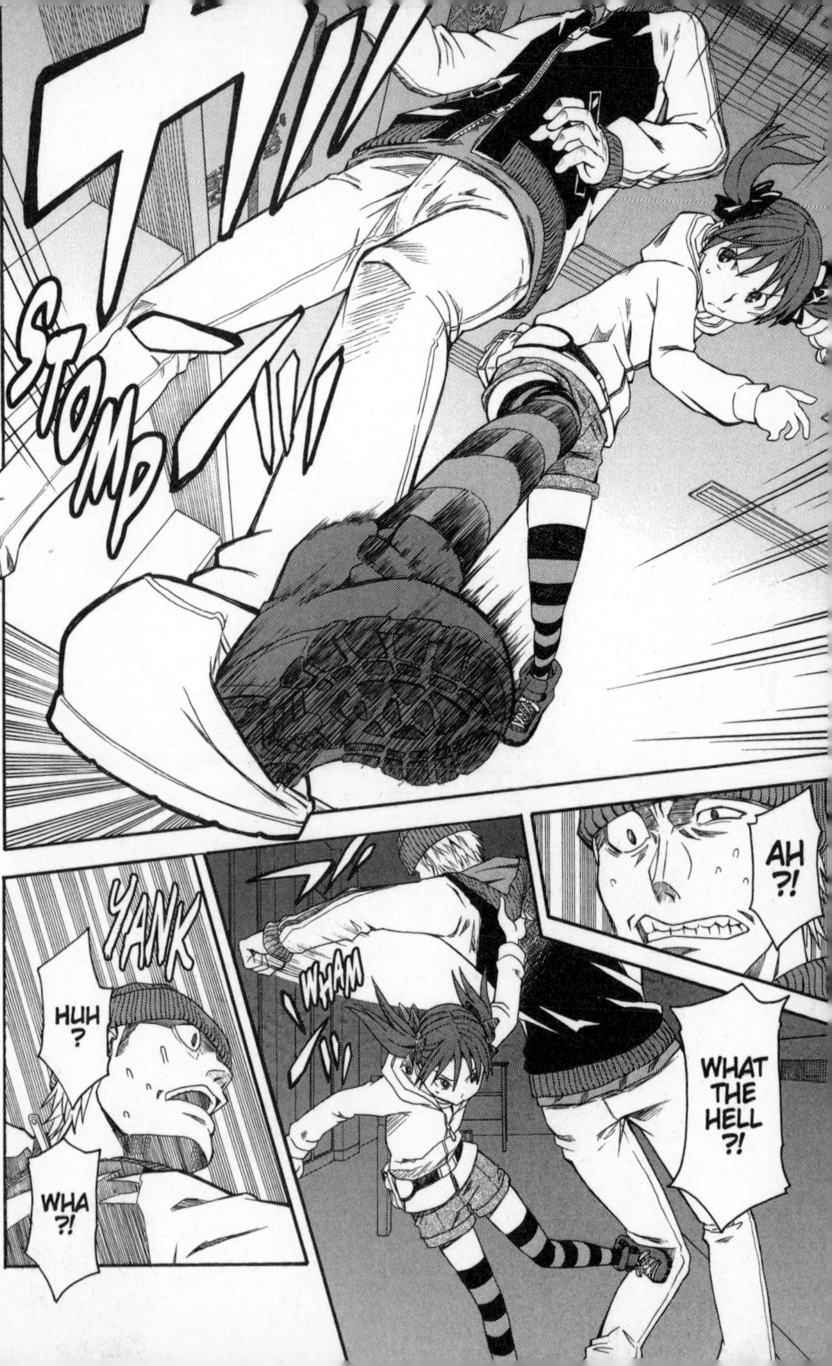
STOMP
AH ?!
WHAM
WHAT THE HELL ?!
YANK
HUH ?
WHA ?!

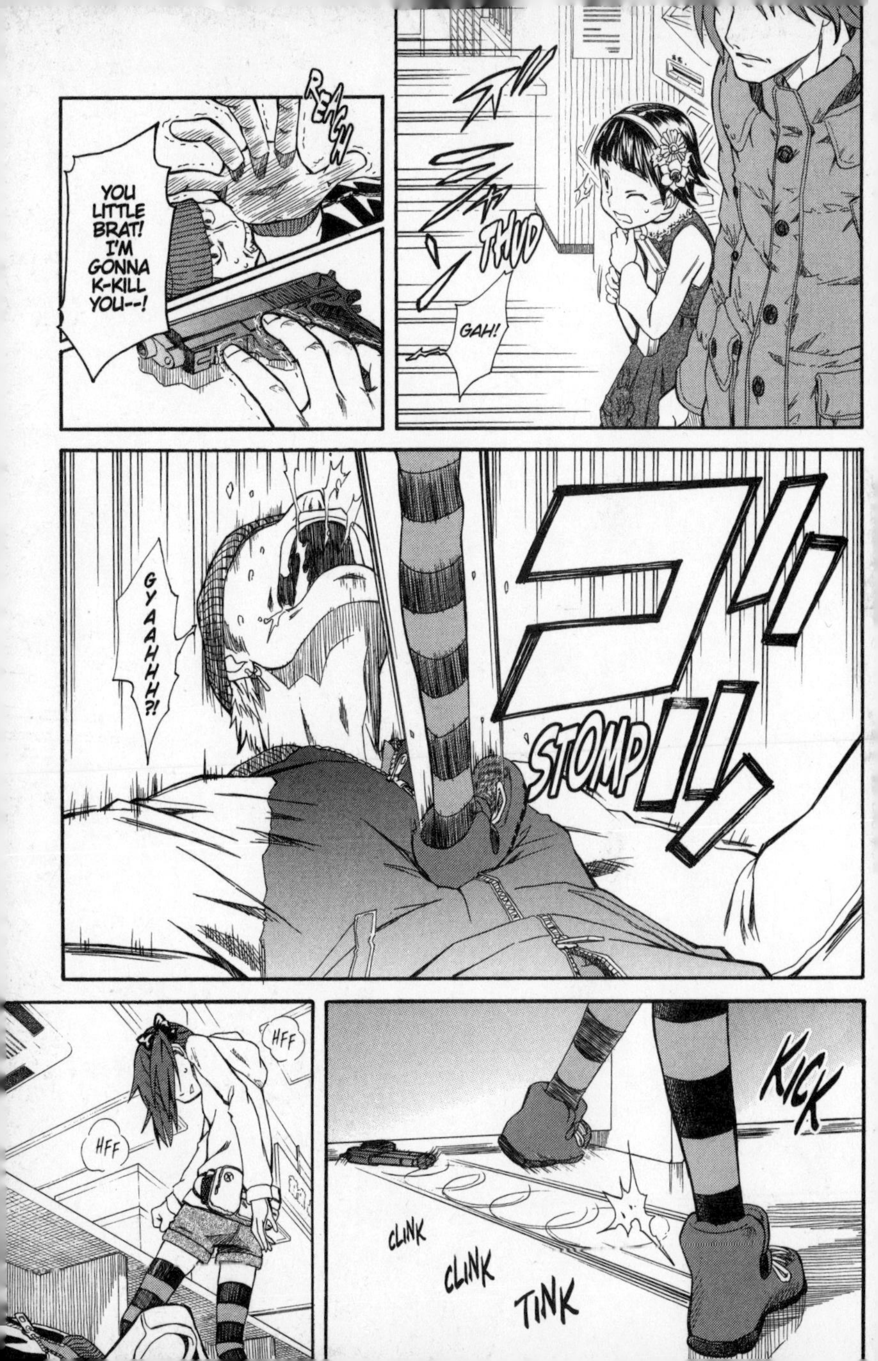
THUD
GAH!
REACH
YOU LITTLE BRAT! I'M GONNA K-KILL YOU--!
GYAAHHH?!
STOMP
KICK
CLINK
CLINK
TINK
HFF
HFF

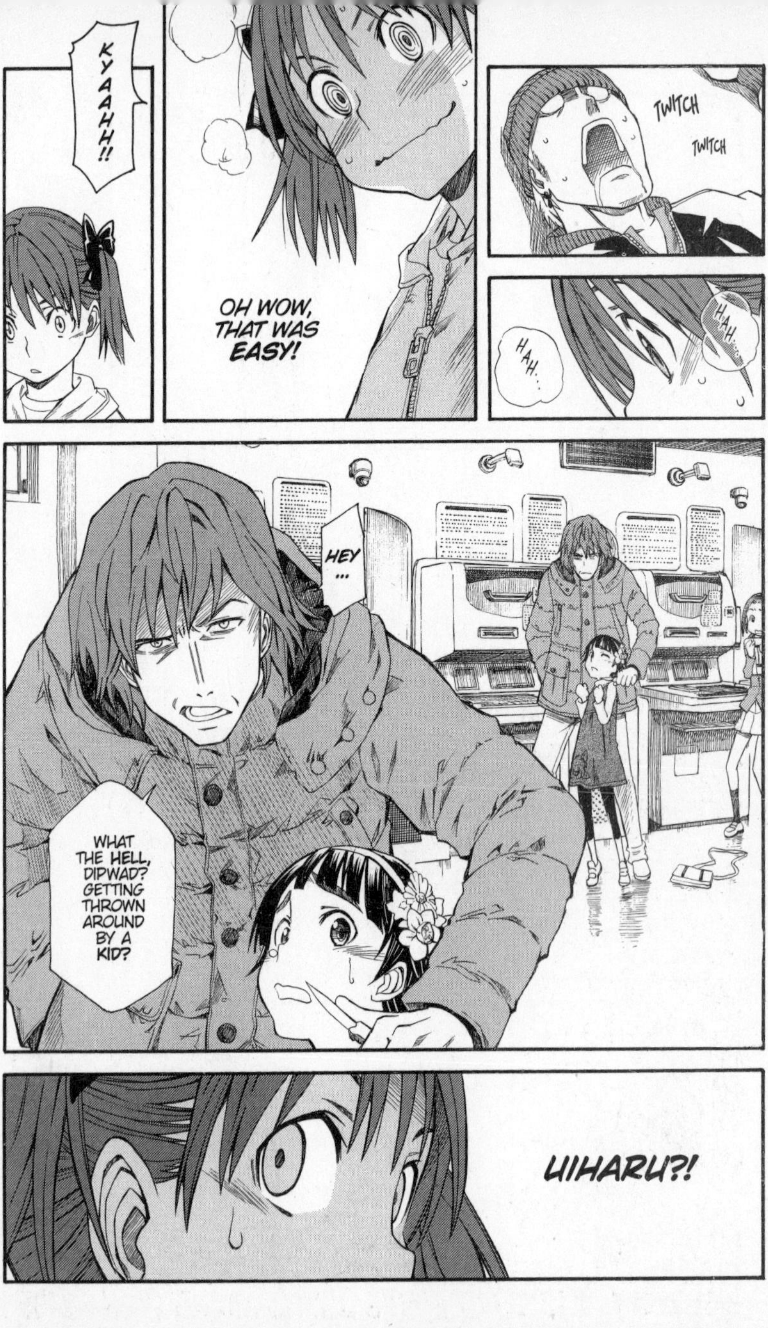
TWITCH
TWITCH
HAH...
HAH...
OH WOW, THAT WAS EASY!
KYAAAHH!!
HEY ...
WHAT THE HELL, DIPWAD? GETTING THROWN AROUND BY A KID?
UIHARU?!

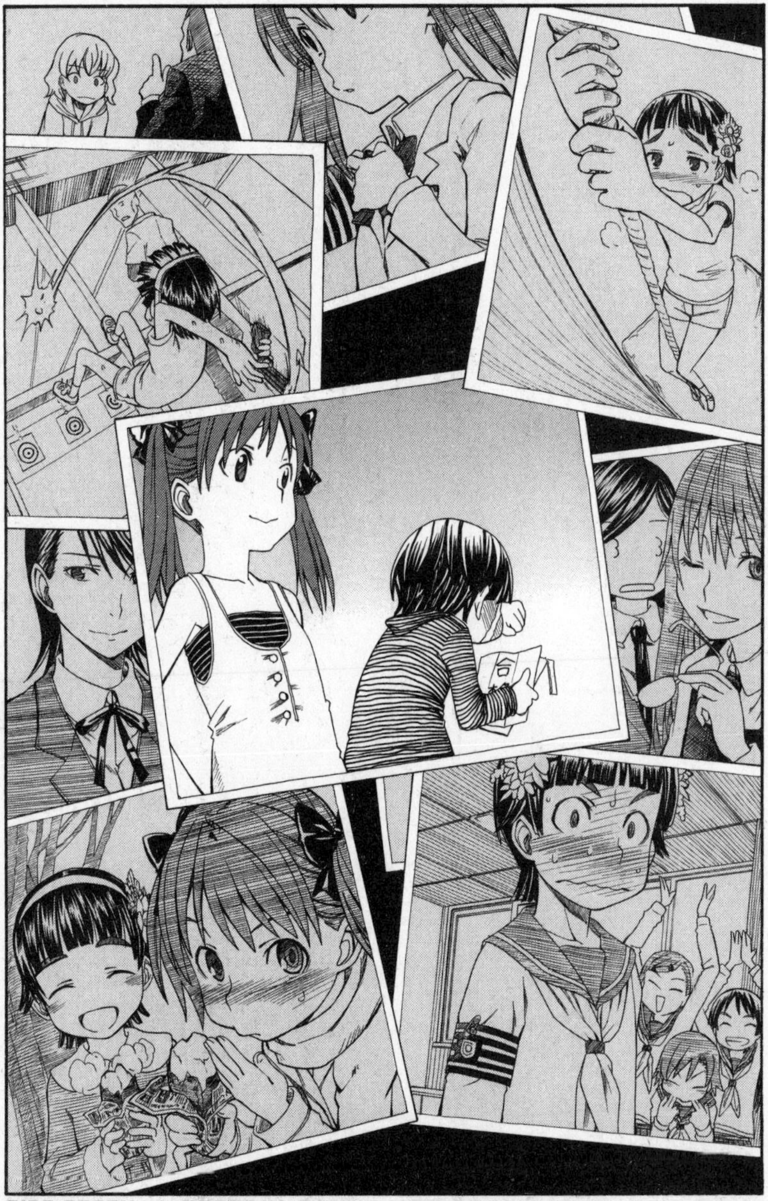

SIDE STORY: A CERTAIN PAIR'S JOB TRAINING (PART 2 OF 2)

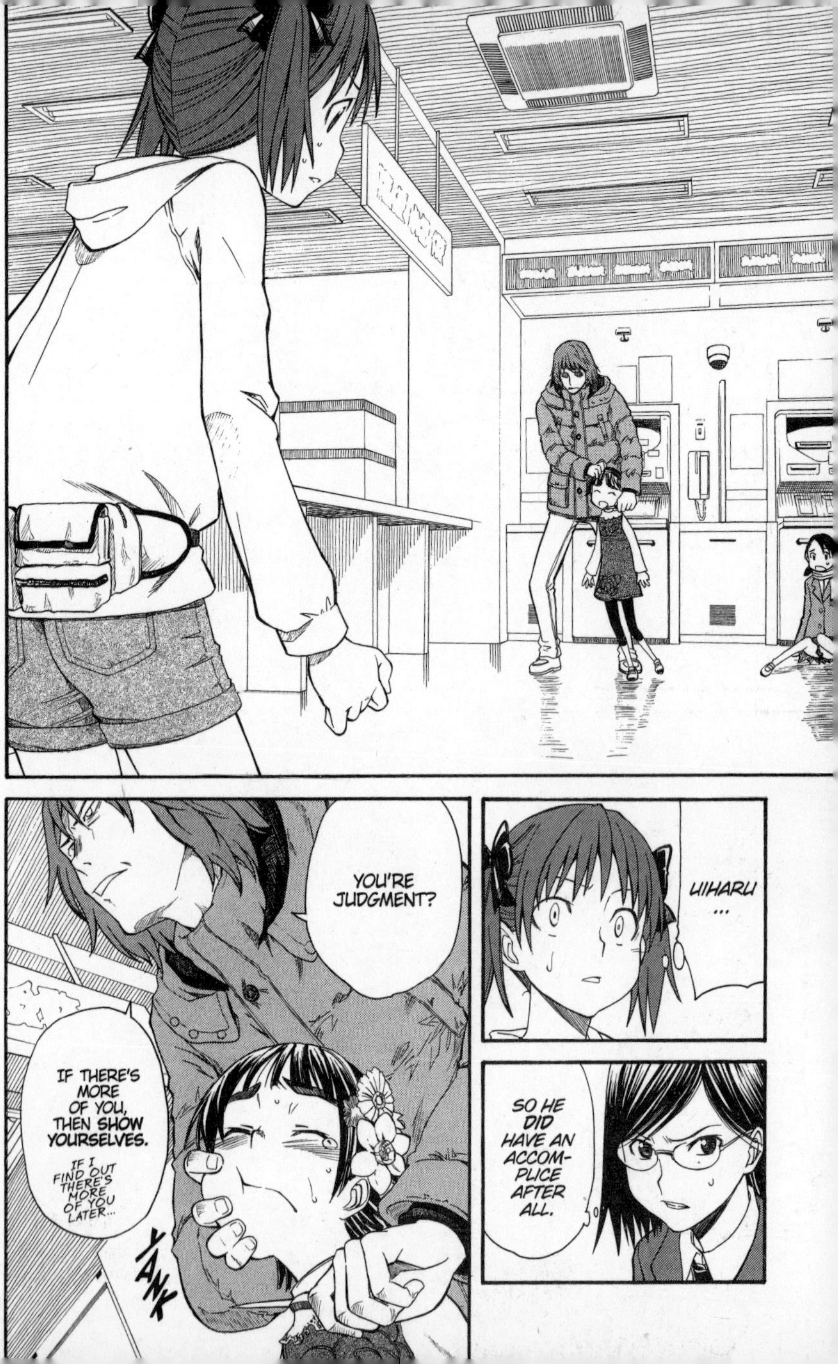
UIHARU ...
SO HE DID HAVE AN ACCOMPLICE AFTER ALL.
YOU'RE JUDGMENT?
IF THERE'S MORE OF YOU, THEN SHOW YOURSELVES.
IF I FIND OUT THERE'S MORE OF YOU LATER...
YANK

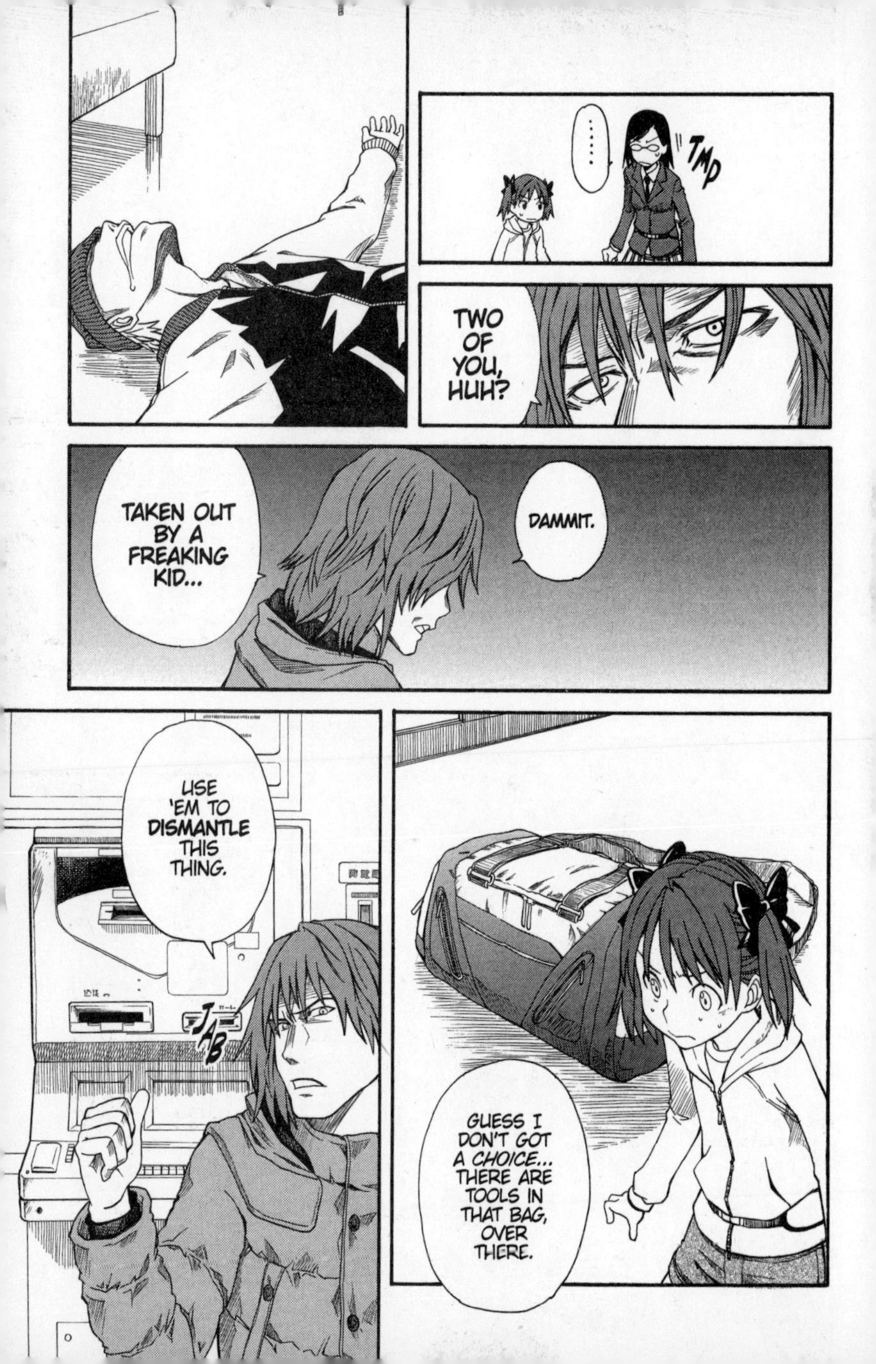
......
TMP
TWO OF YOU, HUH?
DAMMIT.
TAKEN OUT BY A FREAKING KID...
GUESS I DON'T GOT A CHOICE... THERE ARE TOOLS IN THAT BAG, OVER THERE.
USE 'EM TO DISMANTLE THIS THING.
JAB

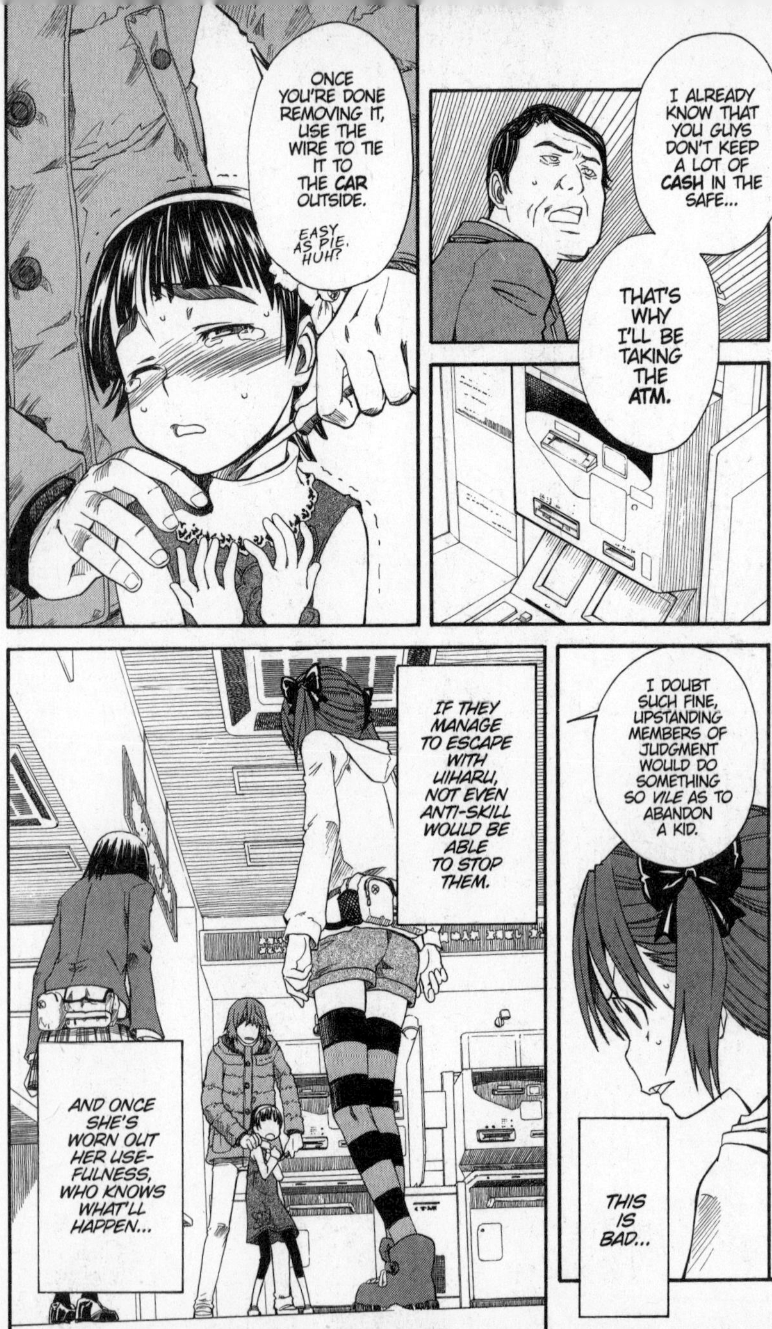
I ALREADY KNOW THAT YOU GUYS DON'T KEEP A LOT OF CASH IN THE SAFE...
THAT'S WHY I'LL BE TAKING THE ATM.
ONCE YOU'RE DONE REMOVING IT, USE THE WIRE TO TIE IT TO THE CAR OUTSIDE.
EASY AS PIE, HUH?
I DOUBT SUCH FINE, UPSTANDING MEMBERS OF JUDGMENT WOULD DO SOMETHING SO VILE AS TO ABANDON A KID.
THIS IS BAD...
IF THEY MANAGE TO ESCAPE WITH UIHARU, NOT EVEN ANTI-SKILL WOULD BE ABLE TO STOP THEM.
AND ONCE SHE'S WORN OUT HER USE-FULNESS, WHO KNOWS WHAT'LL HAPPEN...

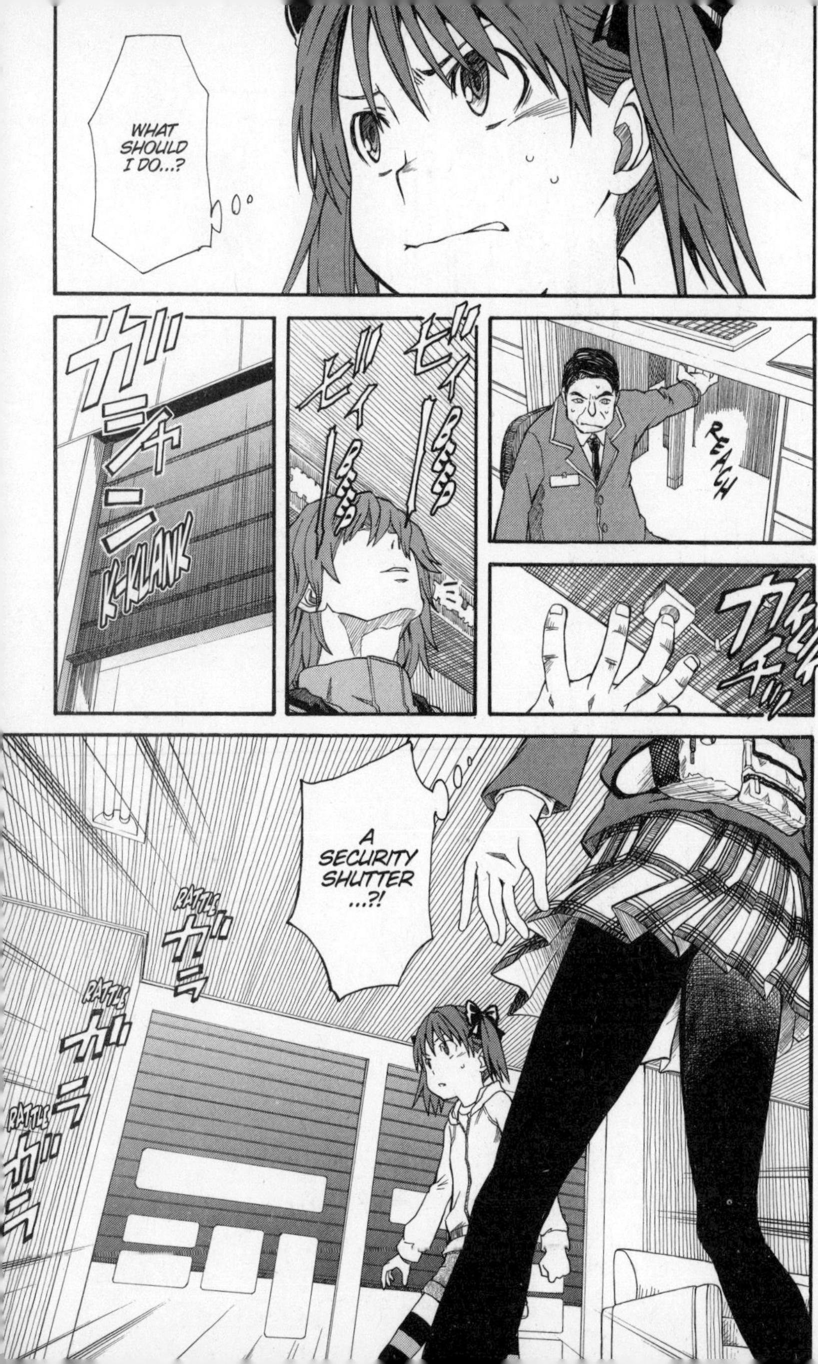
WHAT SHOULD I DO...?
REACH
KLIK
BEEP
BEEP
K-KLANK
A SECURITY SHUTTER ...?!
RATTLE
RATTLE
RATTLE

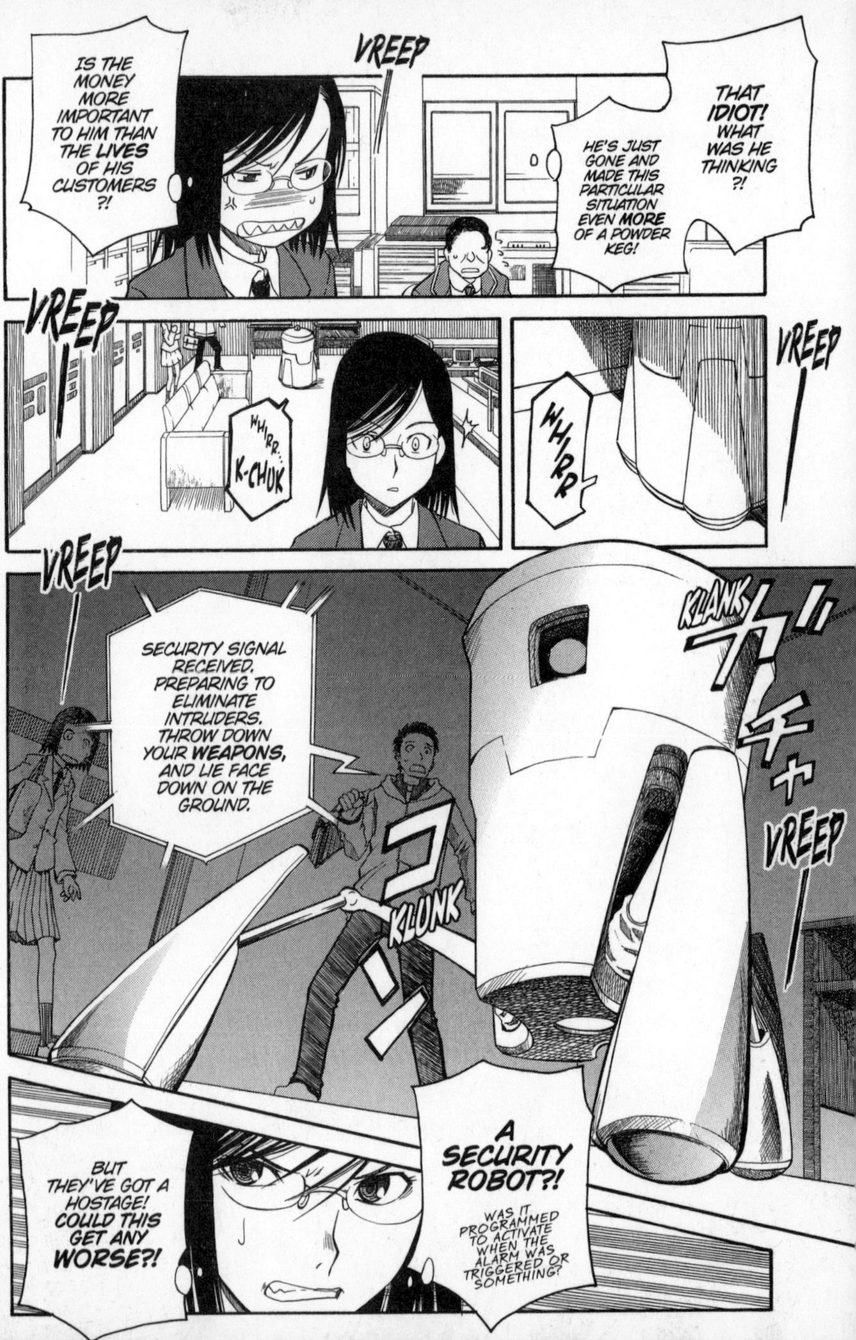
THAT IDIOT! WHAT WAS HE THINKING ?!
HE'S JUST GONE AND MADE THIS PARTICULAR SITUATION EVEN MORE OF A POWDER KEG!
VREEP
IS THE MONEY MORE IMPORTANT TO HIM THAN THE LIVES OF HIS CUSTOMERS ?!
VREEP
WHIRR
VREEP
WHIRR... K-CHUK
KLANK
ガチャ
VREEP
KLUNK
SECURITY SIGNAL RECEIVED. PREPARING TO ELIMINATE INTRUDERS. THROW DOWN YOUR WEAPONS, AND LIE FACE DOWN ON THE GROUND.
VREEP
A SECURITY ROBOT?!
WAS IT PROGRAMMED TO ACTIVATE WHEN THE ALARM WAS TRIGGERED OR SOMETHING?
BUT THEY'VE GOT A HOSTAGE! COULD THIS GET ANY WORSE?!

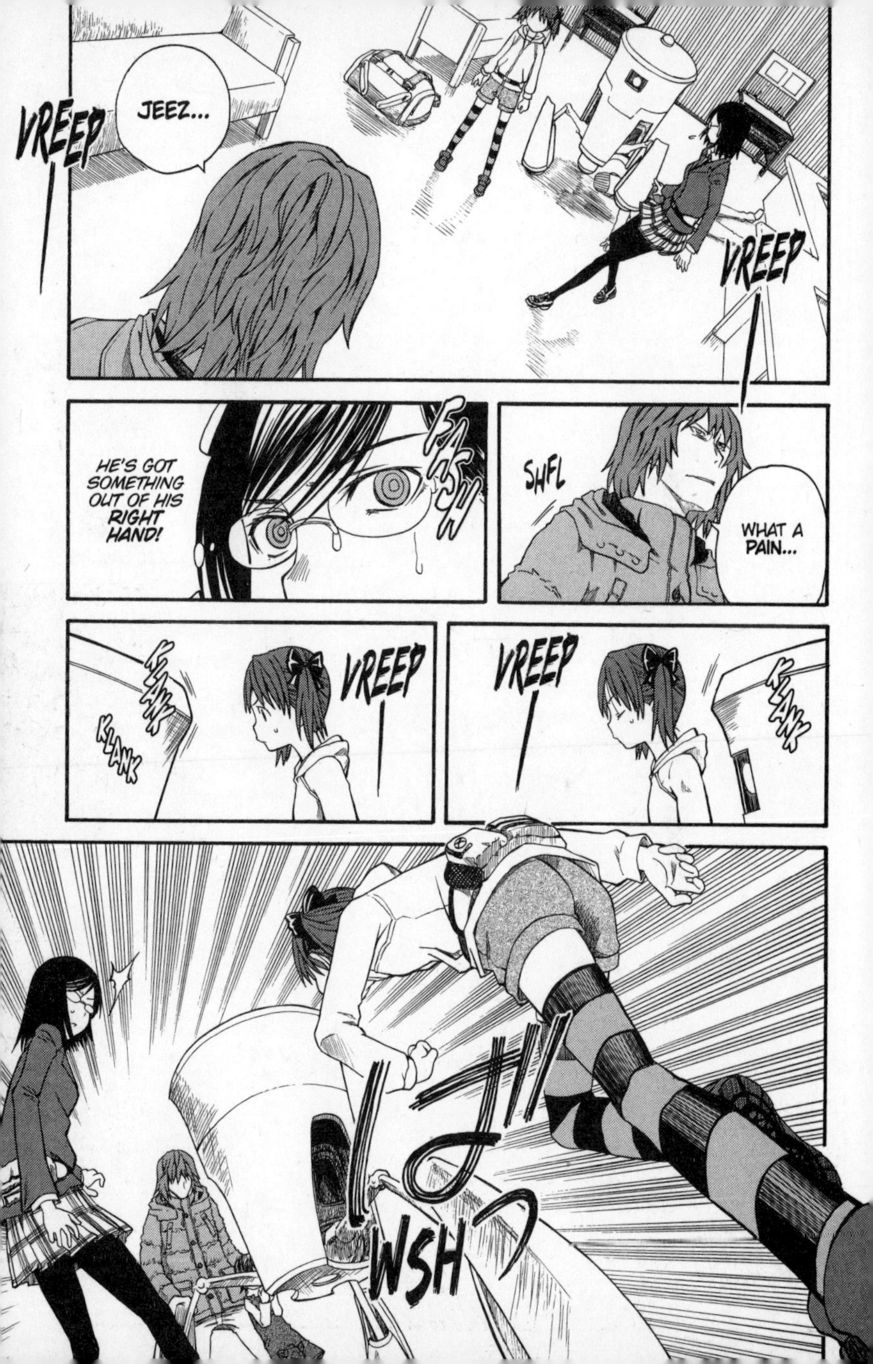
VREEP
JEEZ...
VREEP
WHAT A PAIN...
SHFL
FASH
HE'S GOT SOMETHING OUT OF HIS RIGHT HAND!
KLANK
VREEP
VREEP
KLANK
KLANK
WSH

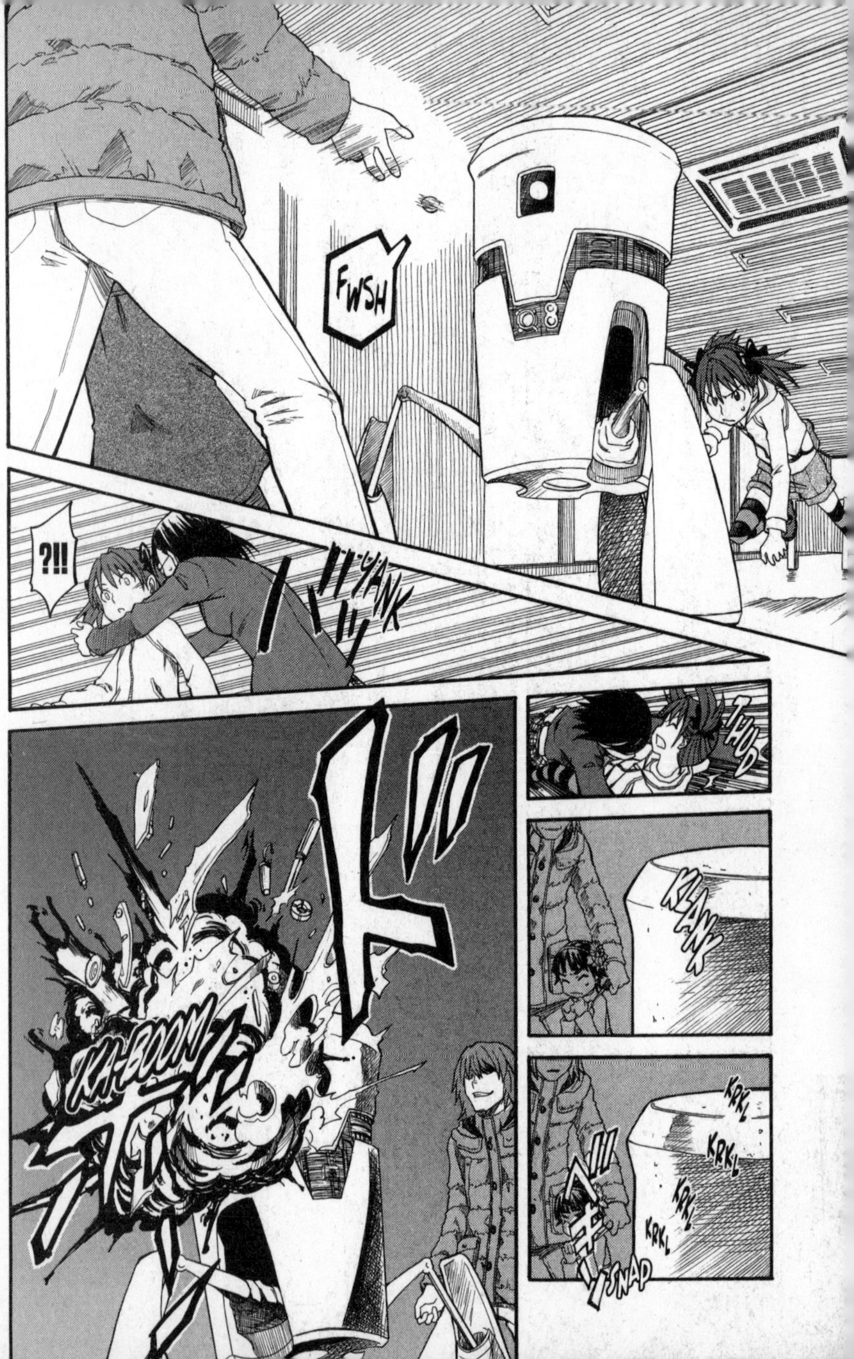
FWSH
?!!
YANK
THUD
KLANK
KRKL
KRKL
KRKL
KRKL
SNAP
KA-BOOM

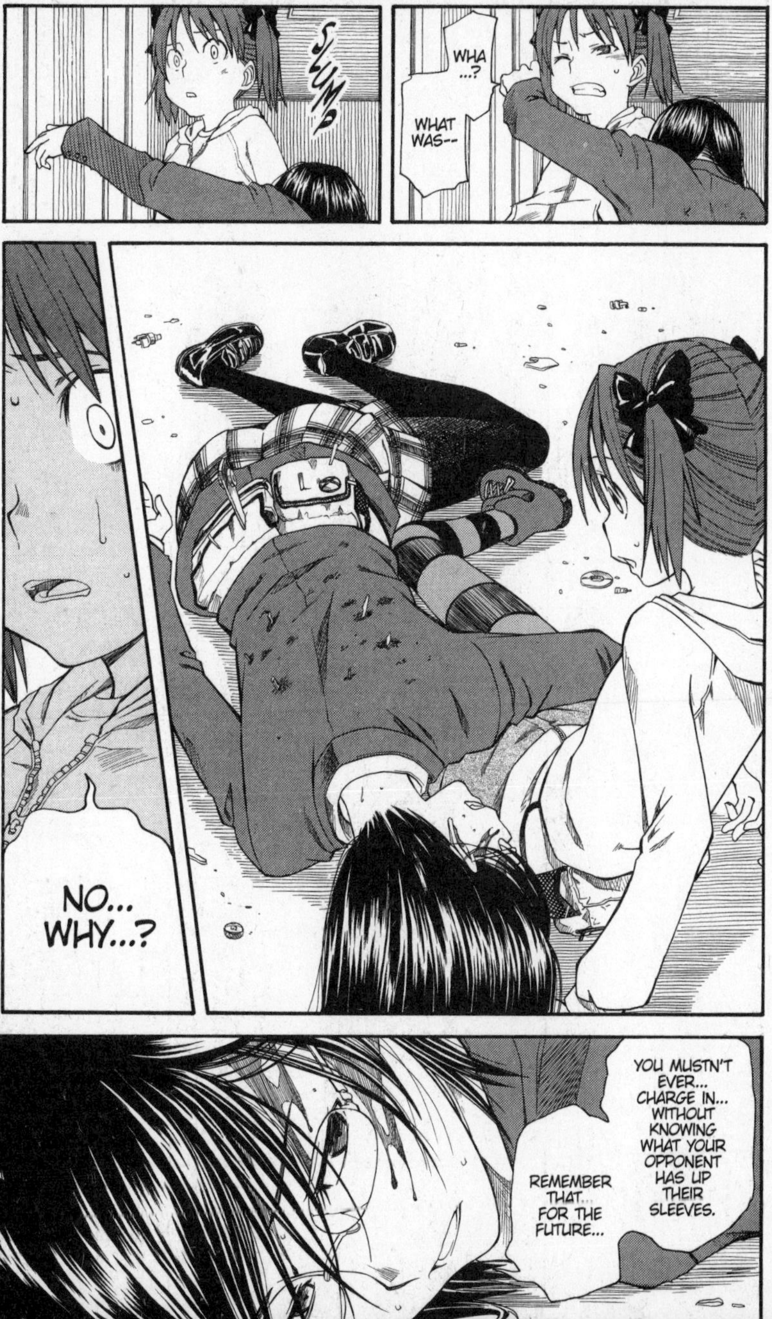
WHA ...?
WHAT WAS--
SLUMP
NO... WHY...?
YOU MUSTN'T EVER... CHARGE IN... WITHOUT KNOWING WHAT YOUR OPPONENT HAS UP THEIR SLEEVES.
REMEMBER THAT... FOR THE FUTURE...

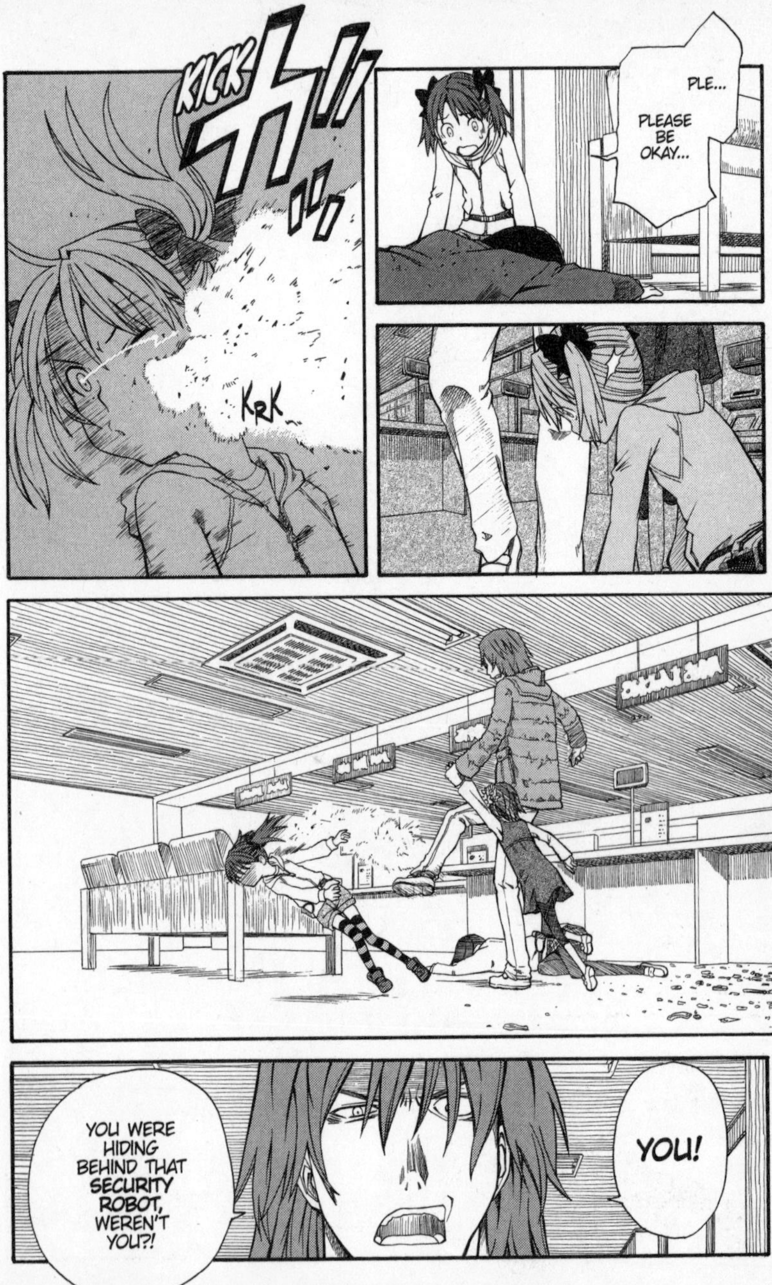
PLE...
PLEASE BE OKAY...
KICK
KRK
YOU!
YOU WERE HIDING BEHIND THAT SECURITY ROBOT, WEREN'T YOU?!

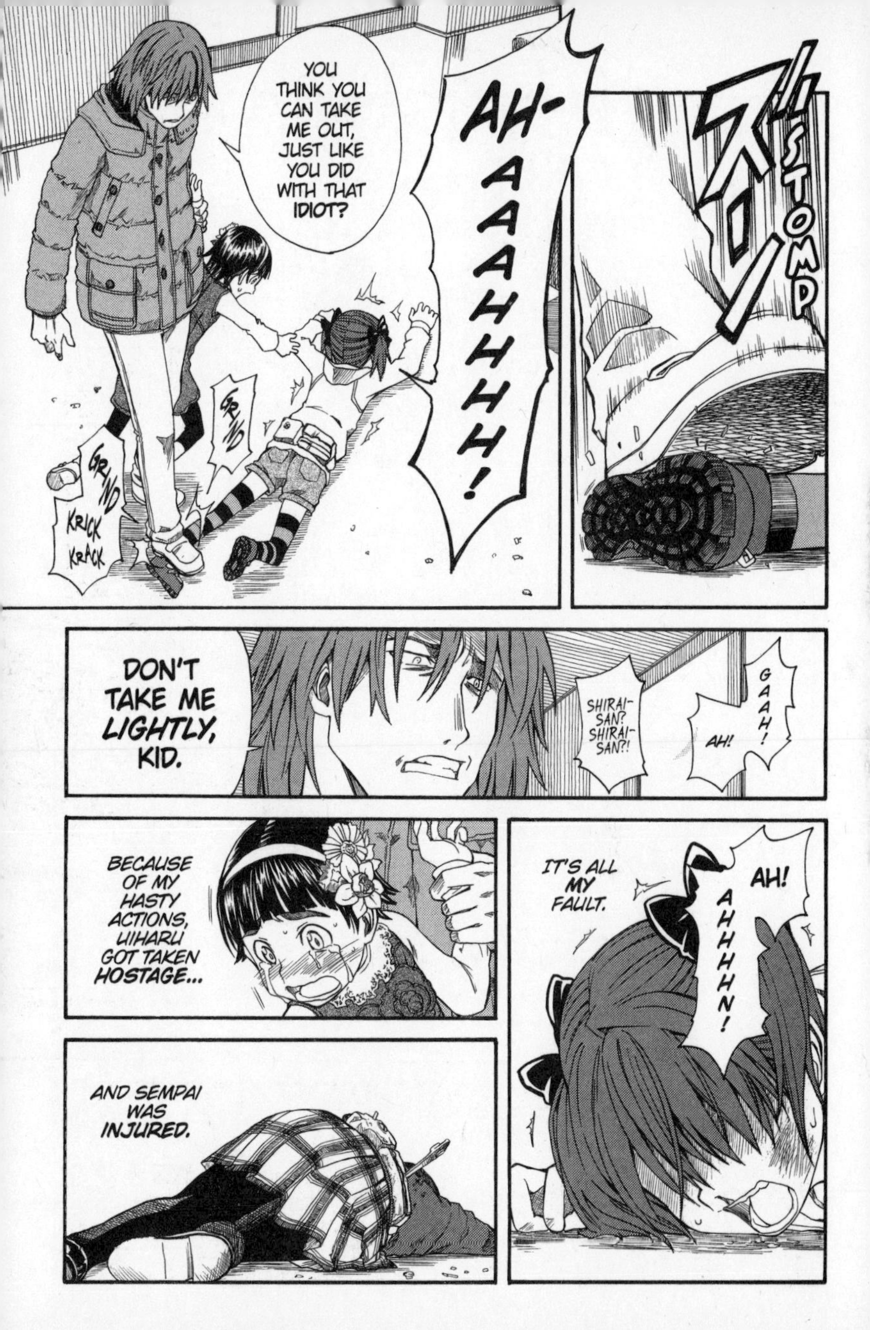
STOMP
AH-AAAAHHHHHH!
YOU THINK YOU CAN TAKE ME OUT, JUST LIKE YOU DID WITH THAT IDIOT?
GRIND
GRIND KRICK KRACK
GAAAH!
AH!
SHIRAI-SAN? SHIRAI-SAN?!
DON'T TAKE ME LIGHTLY, KID.
AH!
AHHHHN!
IT'S ALL MY FAULT.
BECAUSE OF MY HASTY ACTIONS, UIHARU GOT TAKEN HOSTAGE...
AND SEMPAI WAS INJURED.

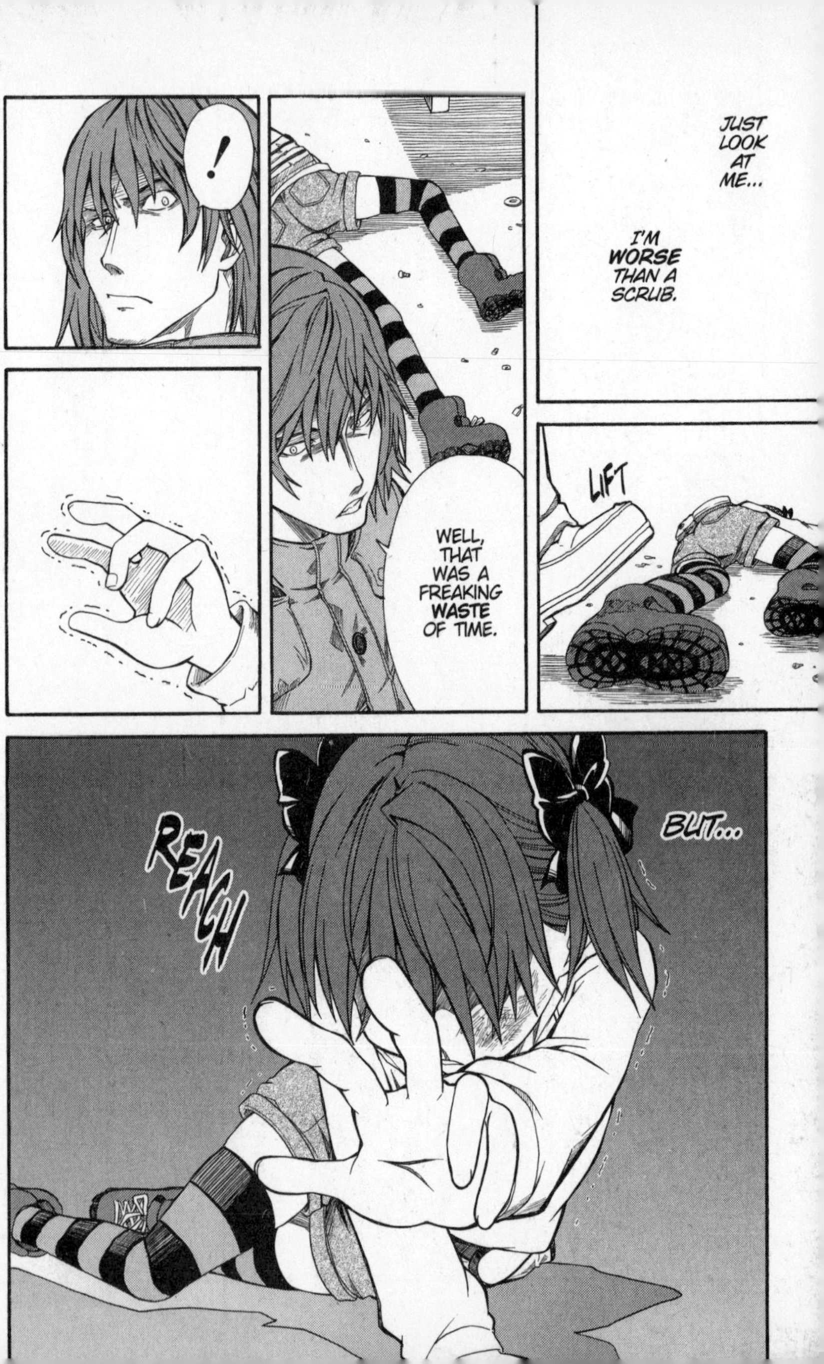
JUST LOOK AT ME...
I'M **WORSE** THAN A SCRUB.
LIFT
WELL, THAT WAS A FREAKING **WASTE** OF TIME.
!
BUT...
REACH

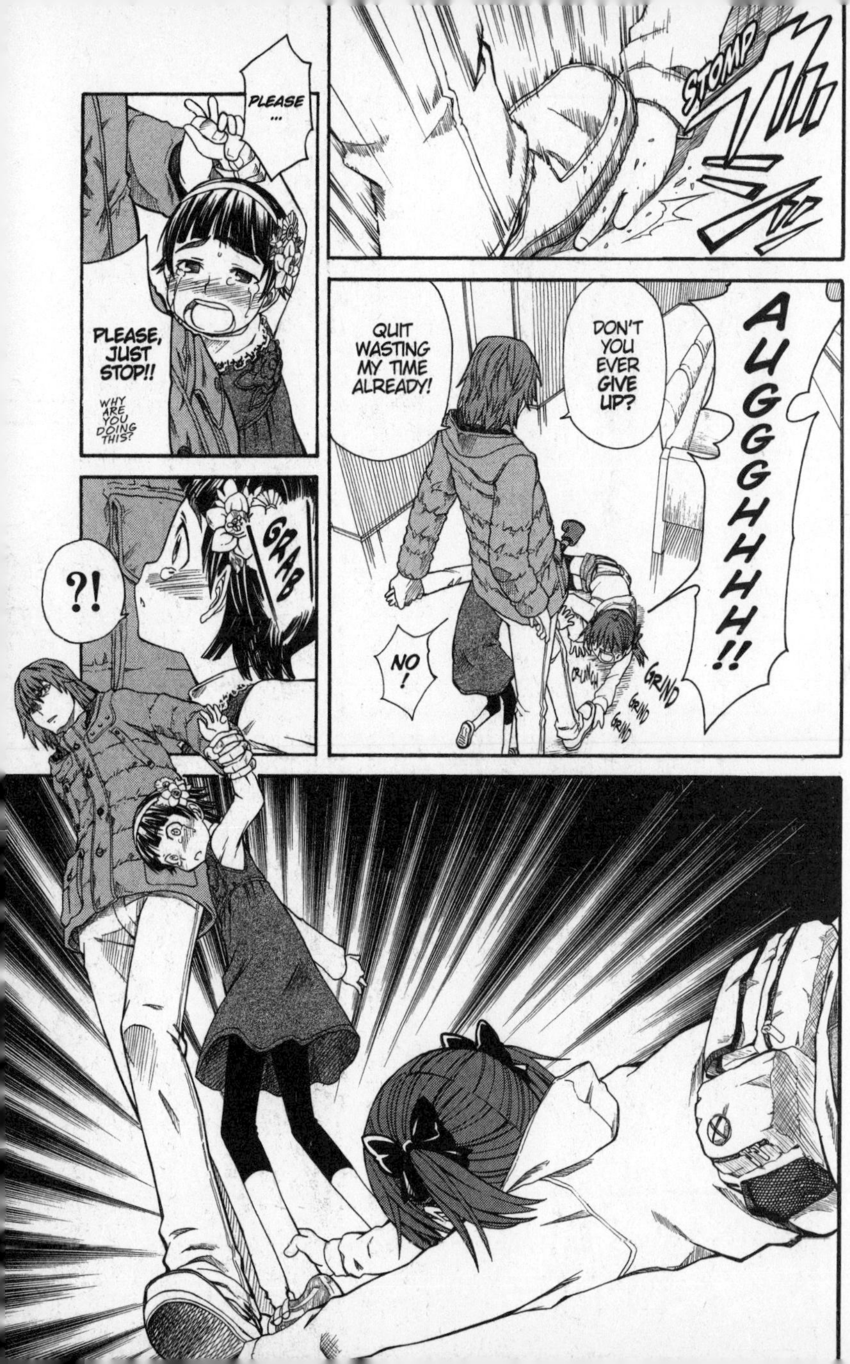
STOMP
PLEASE ...
PLEASE, JUST STOP!!
WHY ARE YOU DOING THIS?
AUGGGHHHHH!!
DON'T YOU EVER GIVE UP?
QUIT WASTING MY TIME ALREADY!
NO!
CRUNCH
GRIND GRIND GRIND
GRAB
?!

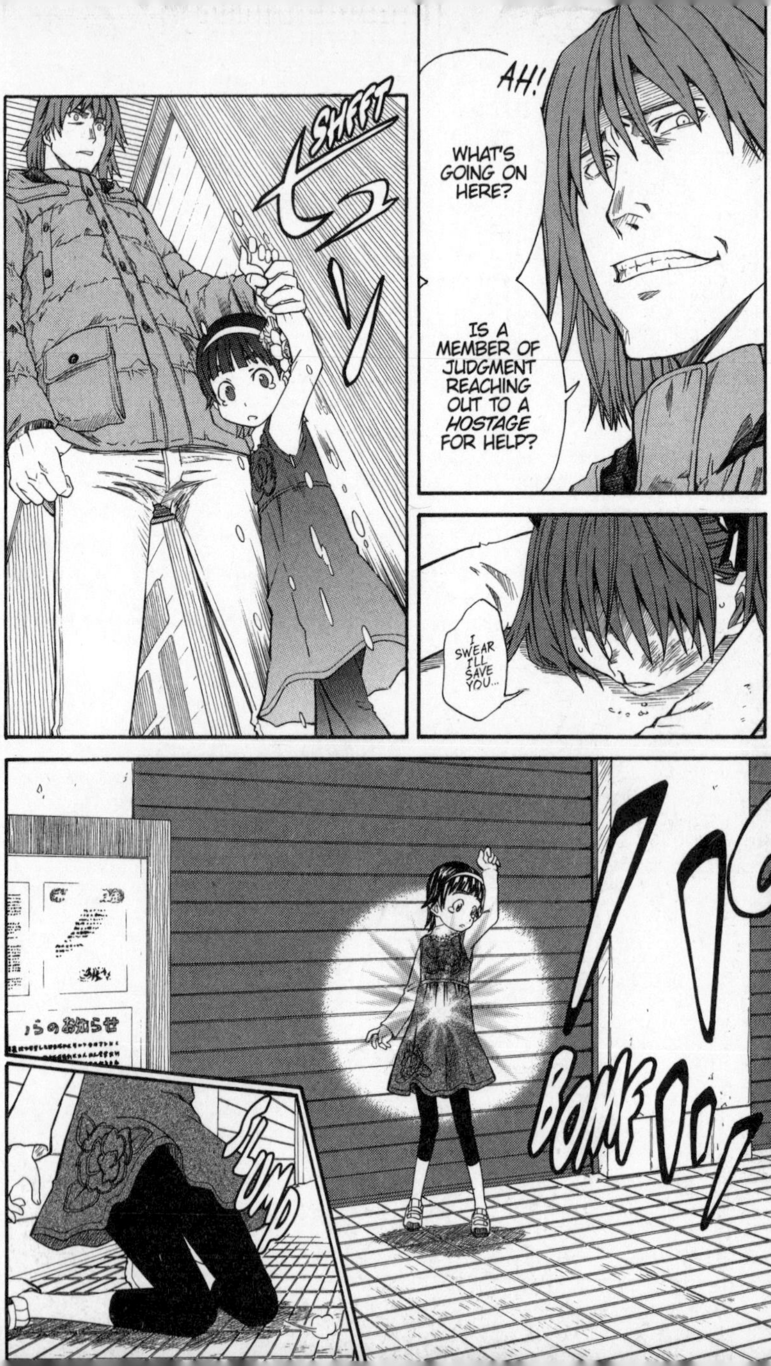
AH!
WHAT'S GOING ON HERE?
IS A MEMBER OF JUDGMENT REACHING OUT TO A *HOSTAGE* FOR HELP?
I SWEAR I'LL SAVE YOU...
SHFFT
BOMF
SLUMP
らのお知らせ

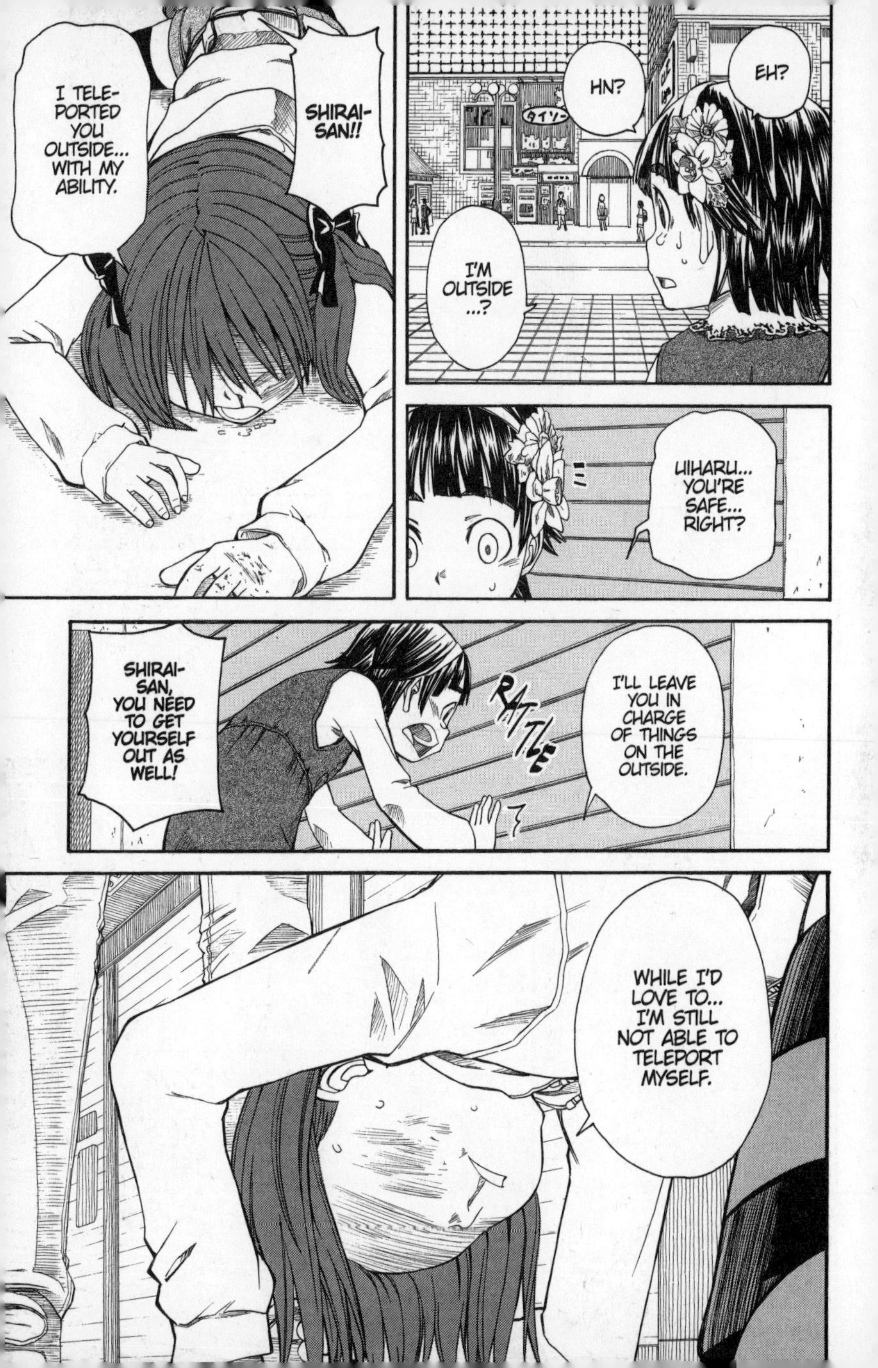
EH?
HN?
I'M OUTSIDE ...?
UIHARU... YOU'RE SAFE... RIGHT?
SHIRAI-SAN!!
I TELE-PORTED YOU OUTSIDE... WITH MY ABILITY.
I'LL LEAVE YOU IN CHARGE OF THINGS ON THE OUTSIDE.
RATTLE
SHIRAI-SAN, YOU NEED TO GET YOURSELF OUT AS WELL!
WHILE I'D LOVE TO... I'M STILL NOT ABLE TO TELEPORT MYSELF.

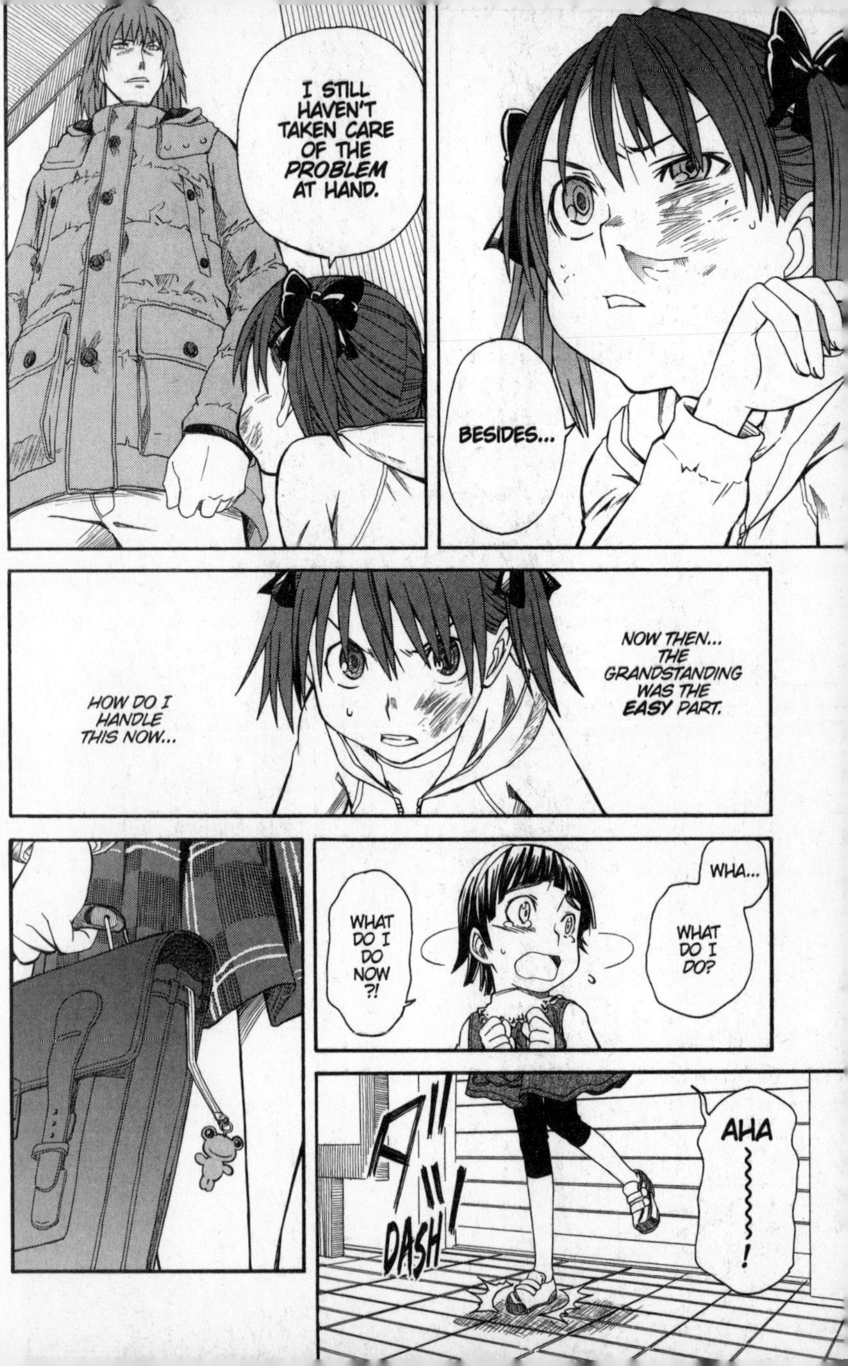
BESIDES...
I STILL HAVEN'T TAKEN CARE OF THE *PROBLEM* AT HAND.
NOW THEN... THE GRANDSTANDING WAS THE EASY PART.
HOW DO I HANDLE THIS NOW...
WHA...
WHAT DO I DO?
WHAT DO I DO NOW ?!
AHA ~~~~!
DASH

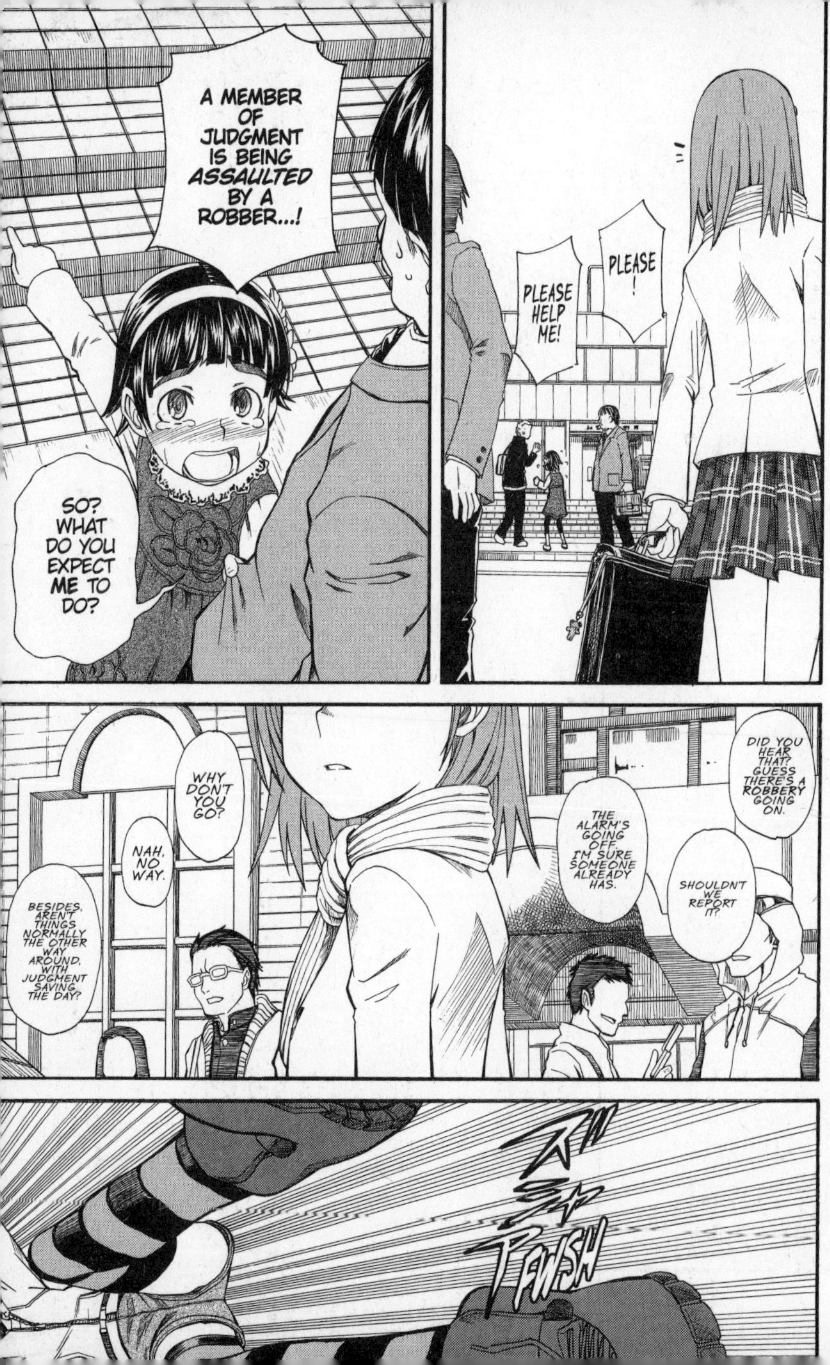
PLEASE !
PLEASE HELP ME!
A MEMBER OF JUDGMENT IS BEING ASSAULTED BY A ROBBER...!
SO? WHAT DO YOU EXPECT ME TO DO?
DID YOU HEAR THAT? GUESS THERE'S A ROBBERY GOING ON.
SHOULDN'T WE REPORT IT?
THE ALARM'S GOING OFF. I'M SURE SOMEONE ALREADY HAS.
WHY DON'T YOU GO?
NAH, NO WAY.
BESIDES, AREN'T THINGS NORMALLY THE OTHER WAY AROUND, WITH JUDGMENT SAVING THE DAY?
PFWSH

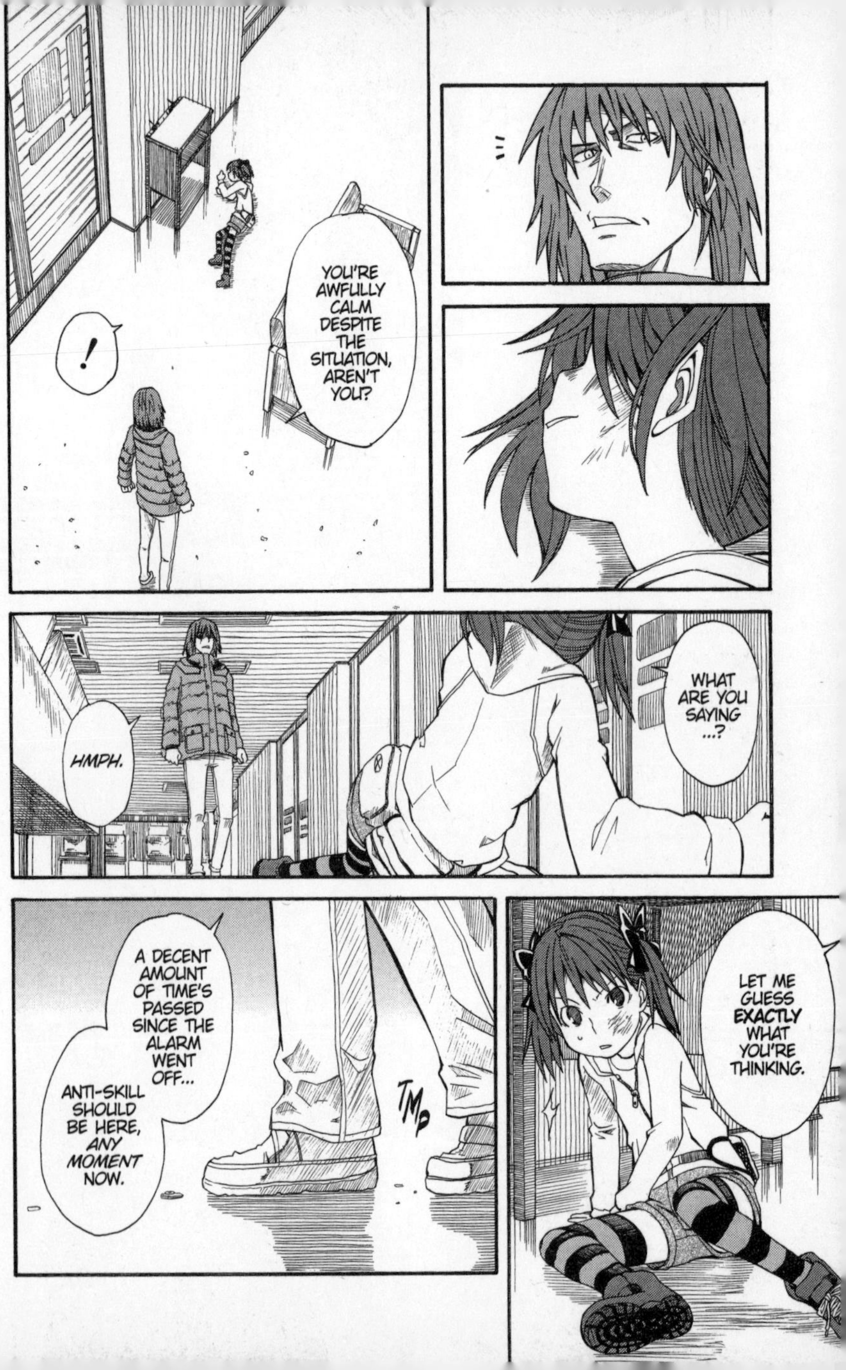
YOU'RE AWFULLY CALM DESPITE THE SITUATION, AREN'T YOU?
!
WHAT ARE YOU SAYING ...?
HMPH.
LET ME GUESS **EXACTLY** WHAT YOU'RE THINKING.
A DECENT AMOUNT OF TIME'S PASSED SINCE THE ALARM WENT OFF...
TMP
ANTI-SKILL SHOULD BE HERE, *ANY MOMENT* NOW.

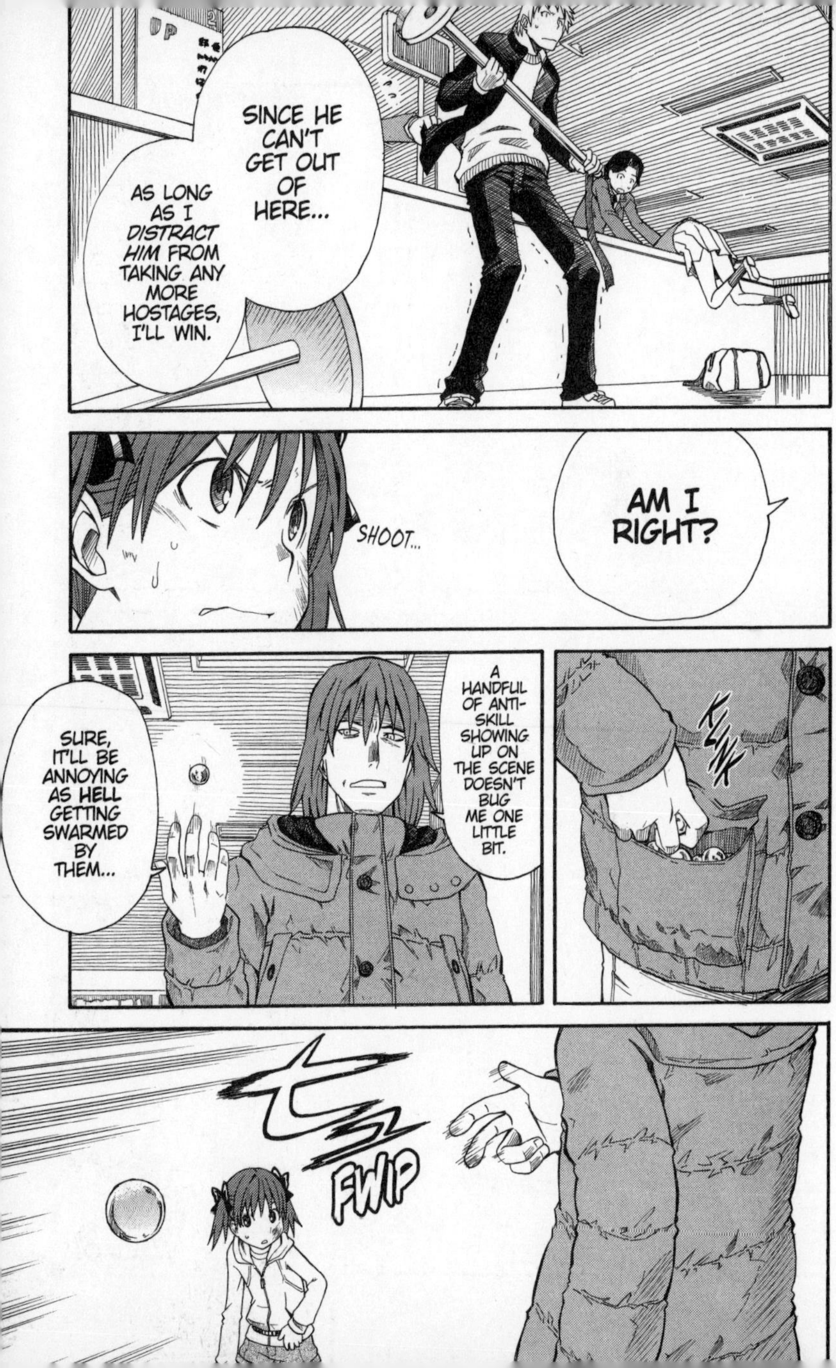
SINCE HE CAN'T GET OUT OF HERE...
AS LONG AS I *DISTRACT* HIM FROM TAKING ANY MORE HOSTAGES, I'LL WIN.
AM I RIGHT?
SHOOT...
KLINK
A HANDFUL OF ANTI-SKILL SHOWING UP ON THE SCENE DOESN'T BUG ME ONE LITTLE BIT.
SURE, IT'LL BE ANNOYING AS HELL GETTING SWARMED BY THEM...
FWIP

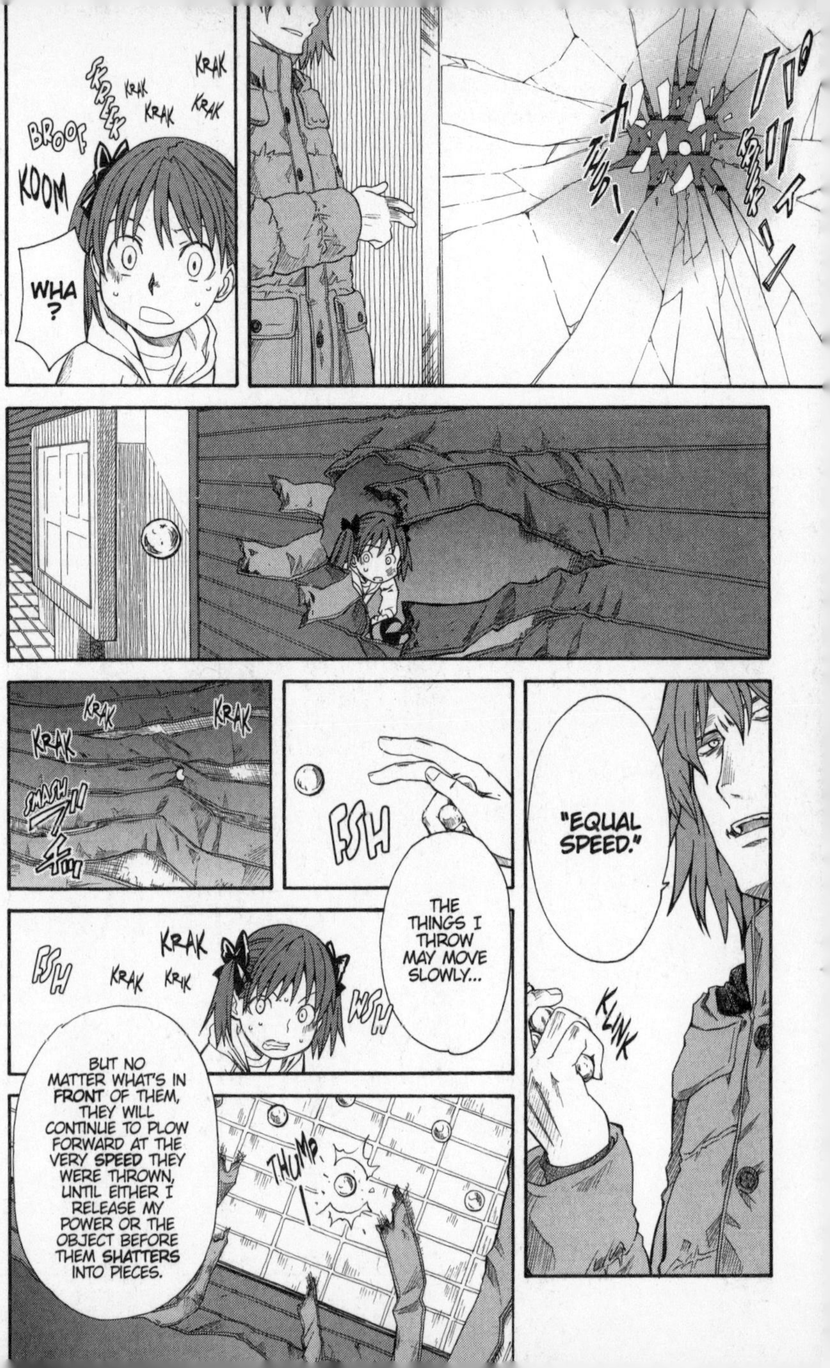
KRAKK
THUD
KRAK
SKREEK
KRAK
KRAK
KRAK
BROOF
KOOM
WHA?
"EQUAL SPEED."
KLINK
FSH
KRAK
KRAK
KRAK
SMASH
THE THINGS I THROW MAY MOVE SLOWLY...
WSH
KRAK
KRIK
KRAK
FSH
BUT NO MATTER WHAT'S IN FRONT OF THEM, THEY WILL CONTINUE TO PLOW FORWARD AT THE VERY SPEED THEY WERE THROWN, UNTIL EITHER I RELEASE MY POWER OR THE OBJECT BEFORE THEM SHATTERS INTO PIECES.
THUMP

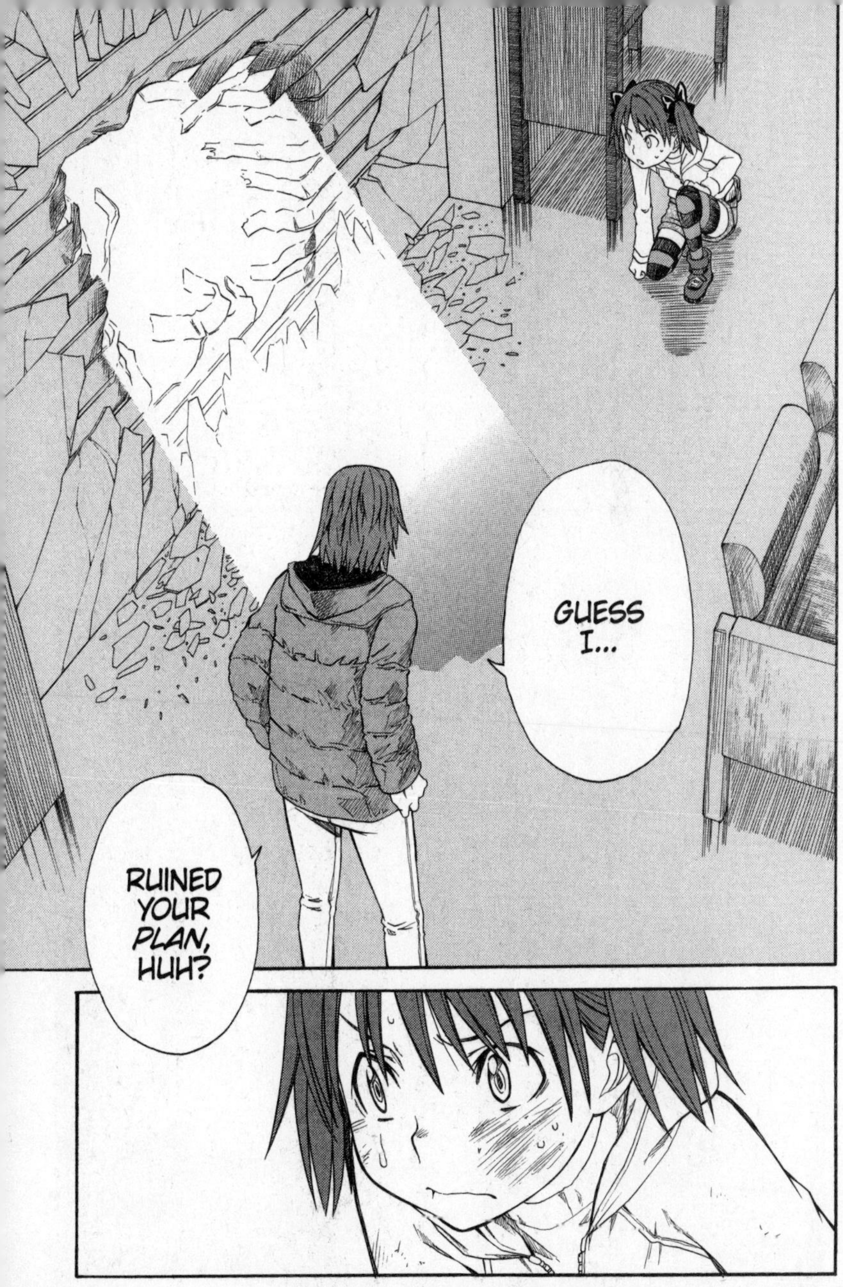
GUESS I...
RUINED YOUR PLAN, HUH?

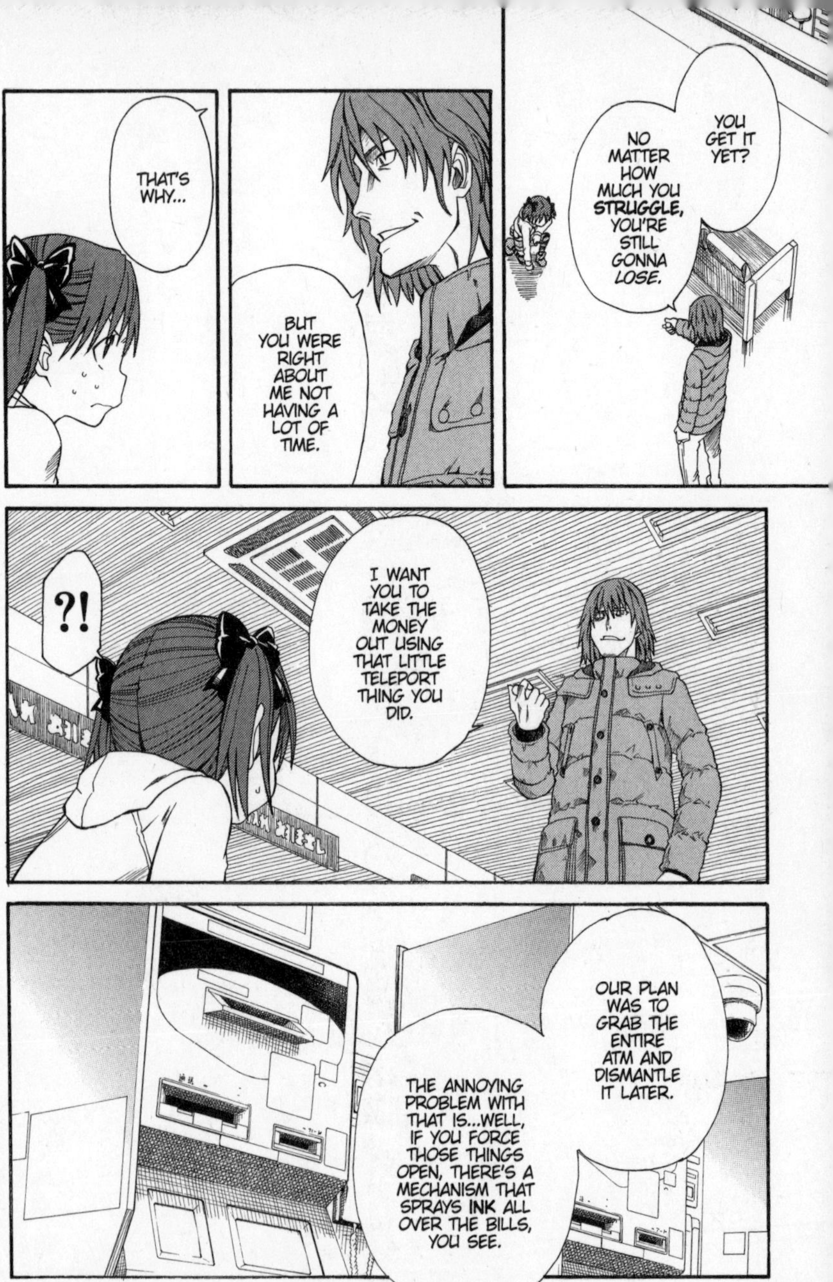
YOU GET IT YET?
NO MATTER HOW MUCH YOU STRUGGLE, YOU'RE STILL GONNA LOSE.
BUT YOU WERE RIGHT ABOUT ME NOT HAVING A LOT OF TIME.
THAT'S WHY...
I WANT YOU TO TAKE THE MONEY OUT USING THAT LITTLE TELEPORT THING YOU DID.
?!
OUR PLAN WAS TO GRAB THE ENTIRE ATM AND DISMANTLE IT LATER.
THE ANNOYING PROBLEM WITH THAT IS...WELL, IF YOU FORCE THOSE THINGS OPEN, THERE'S A MECHANISM THAT SPRAYS INK ALL OVER THE BILLS, YOU SEE.

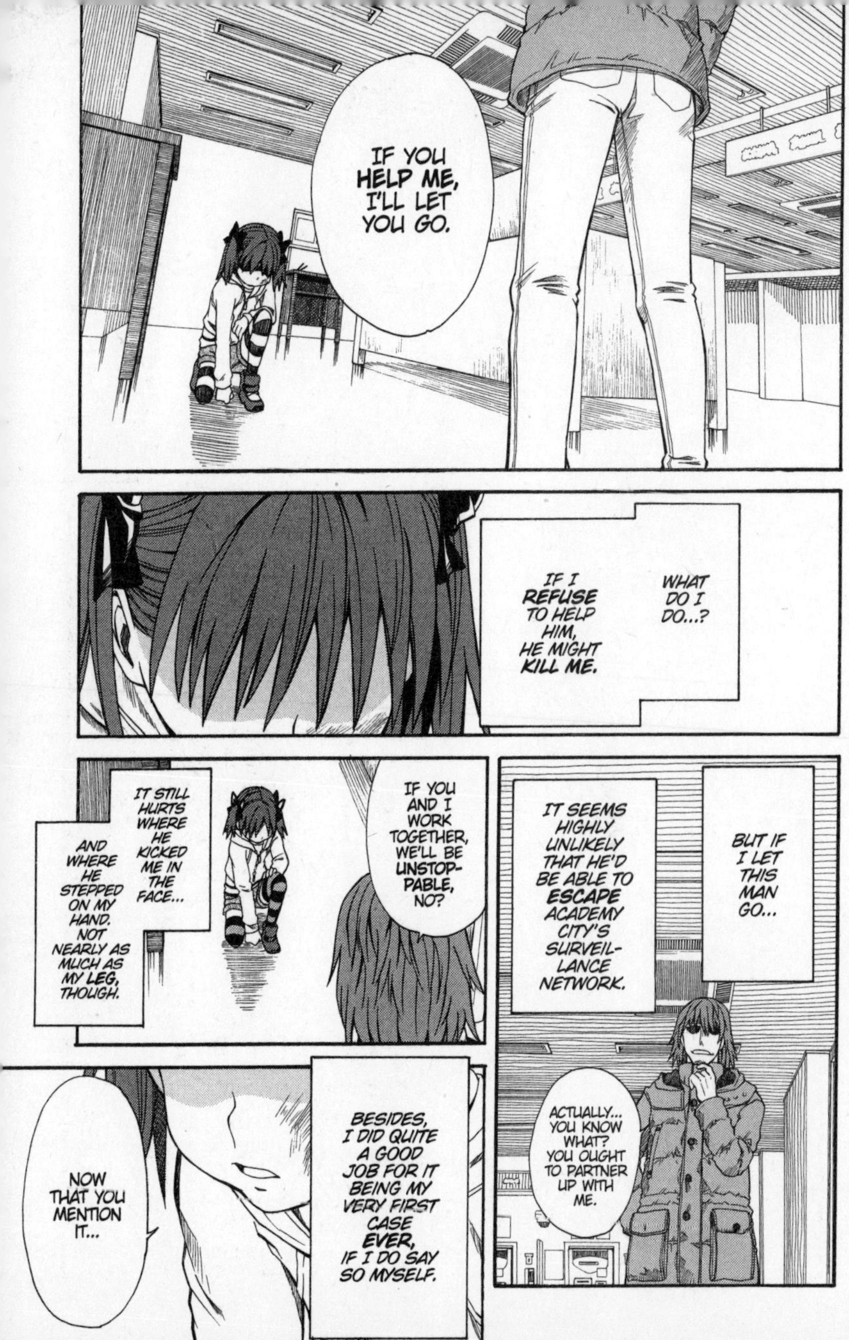
IF YOU HELP ME, I'LL LET YOU GO.
WHAT DO I DO...?
IF I REFUSE TO HELP HIM, HE MIGHT KILL ME.
BUT IF I LET THIS MAN GO...
IT SEEMS HIGHLY UNLIKELY THAT HE'D BE ABLE TO ESCAPE ACADEMY CITY'S SURVEIL-LANCE NETWORK.
ACTUALLY... YOU KNOW WHAT? YOU OUGHT TO PARTNER UP WITH ME.
IF YOU AND I WORK TOGETHER, WE'LL BE UNSTOP-PABLE, NO?
IT STILL HURTS WHERE HE KICKED ME IN THE FACE...
AND WHERE HE STEPPED ON MY HAND. NOT NEARLY AS MUCH AS MY LEG, THOUGH.
BESIDES, I DID QUITE A GOOD JOB FOR IT BEING MY VERY FIRST CASE EVER, IF I DO SAY SO MYSELF.
NOW THAT YOU MENTION IT...

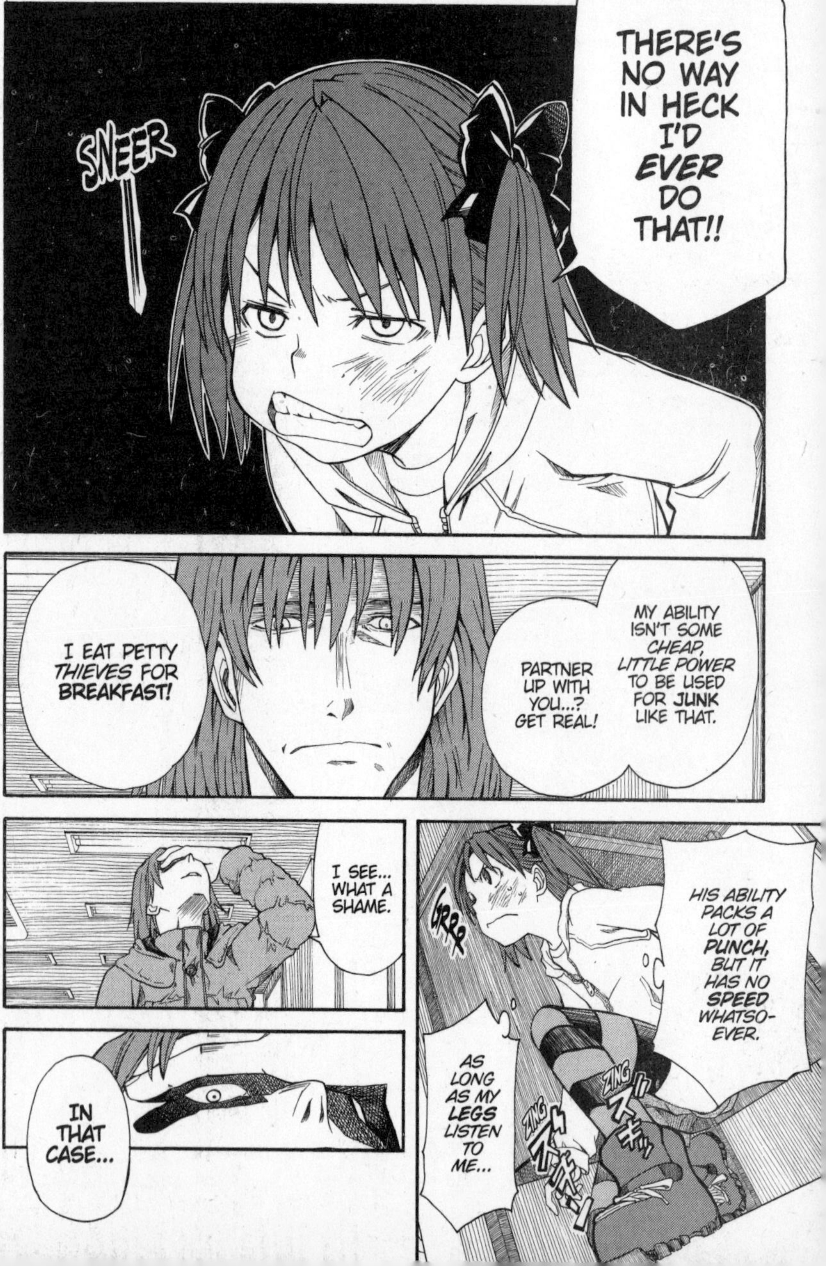
THERE'S NO WAY IN HECK I'D *EVER* DO THAT!!
SNEER
MY ABILITY ISN'T SOME *CHEAP, LITTLE POWER* TO BE USED FOR **JUNK** LIKE THAT.
PARTNER UP WITH YOU...? GET REAL!
I EAT PETTY *THIEVES* FOR **BREAKFAST!**
HIS ABILITY PACKS A LOT OF **PUNCH,** *BUT IT HAS NO* **SPEED** *WHATSO-EVER.*
GRRR
AS LONG AS MY **LEGS** LISTEN TO ME...
ZING
ZING
I SEE... WHAT A SHAME.
IN THAT CASE...

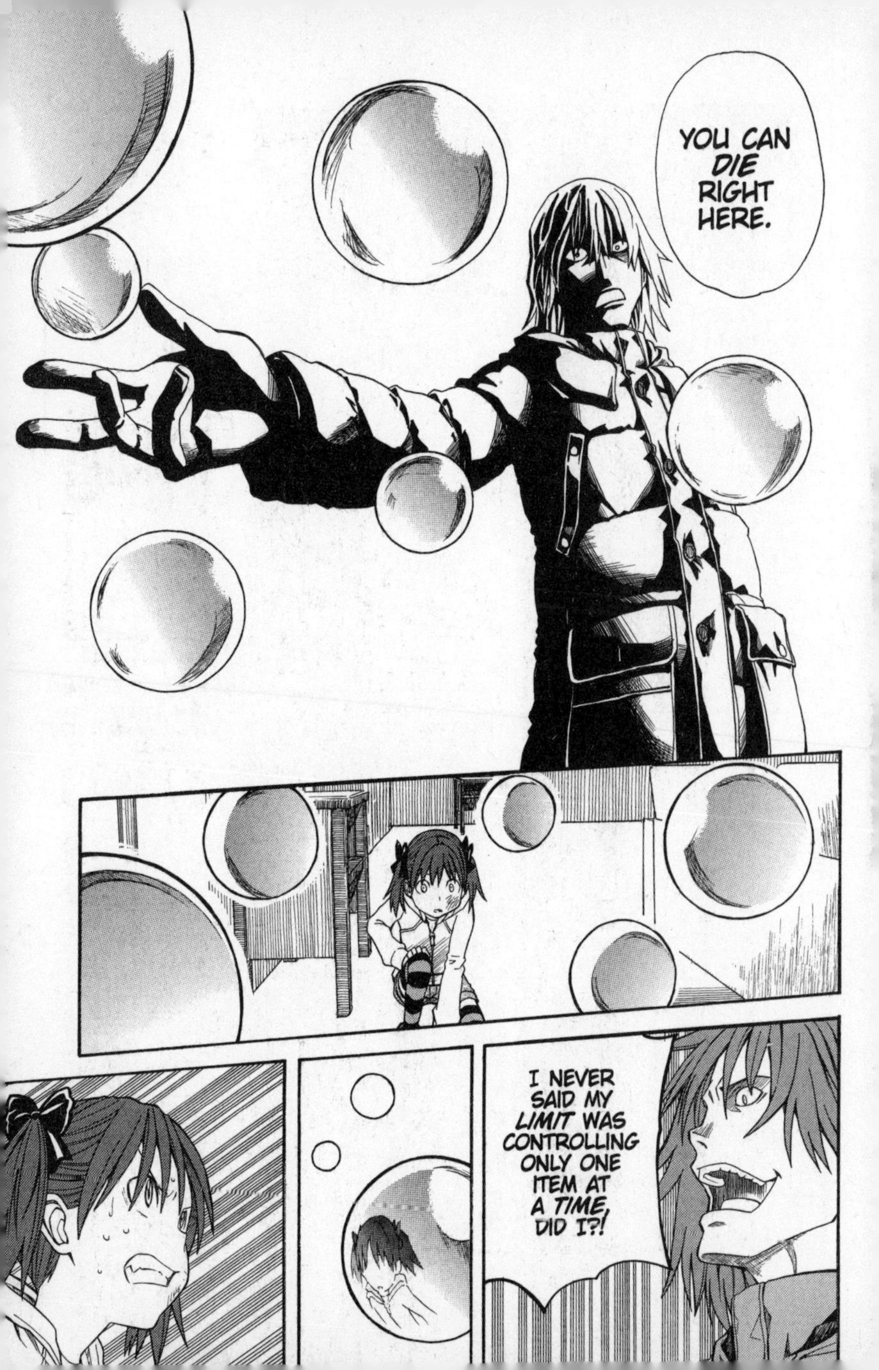
YOU CAN DIE RIGHT HERE.
I NEVER SAID MY LIMIT WAS CONTROLLING ONLY ONE ITEM AT A TIME, DID I?!

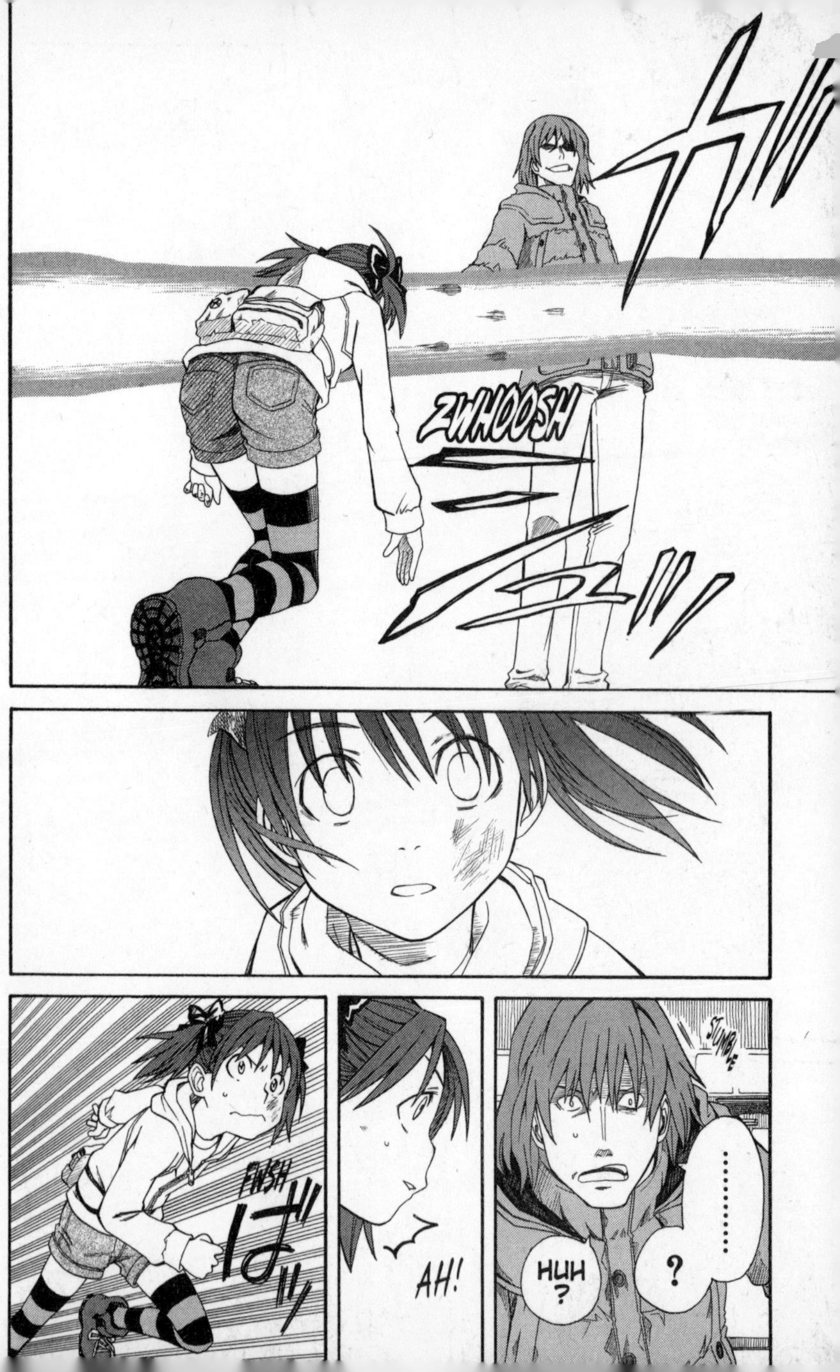
ZWHOOSH
STUMBLE
......
?
HUH?
AH!
FWSH

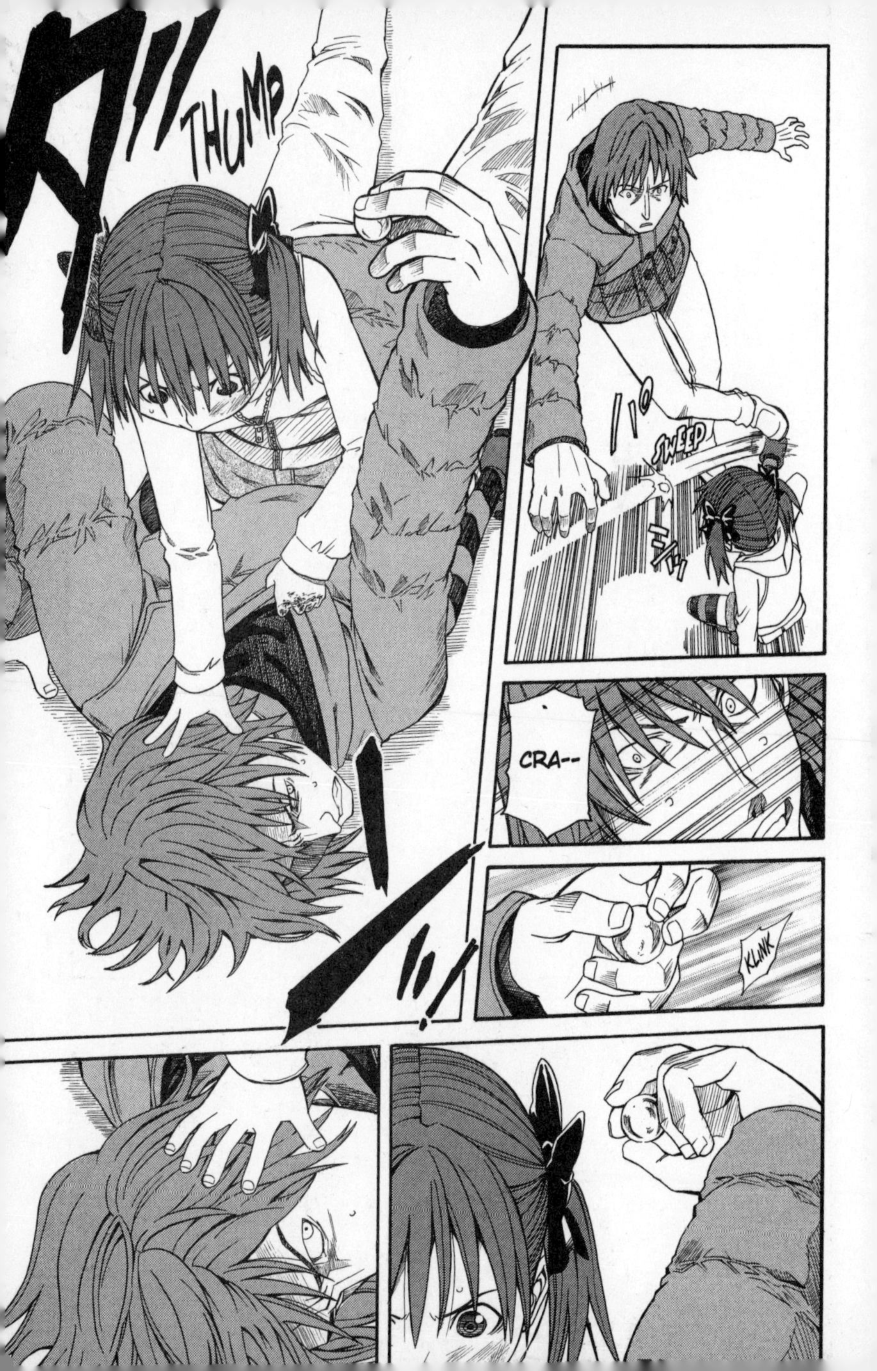
SWEEP
CRA--
KLINK
THUMP

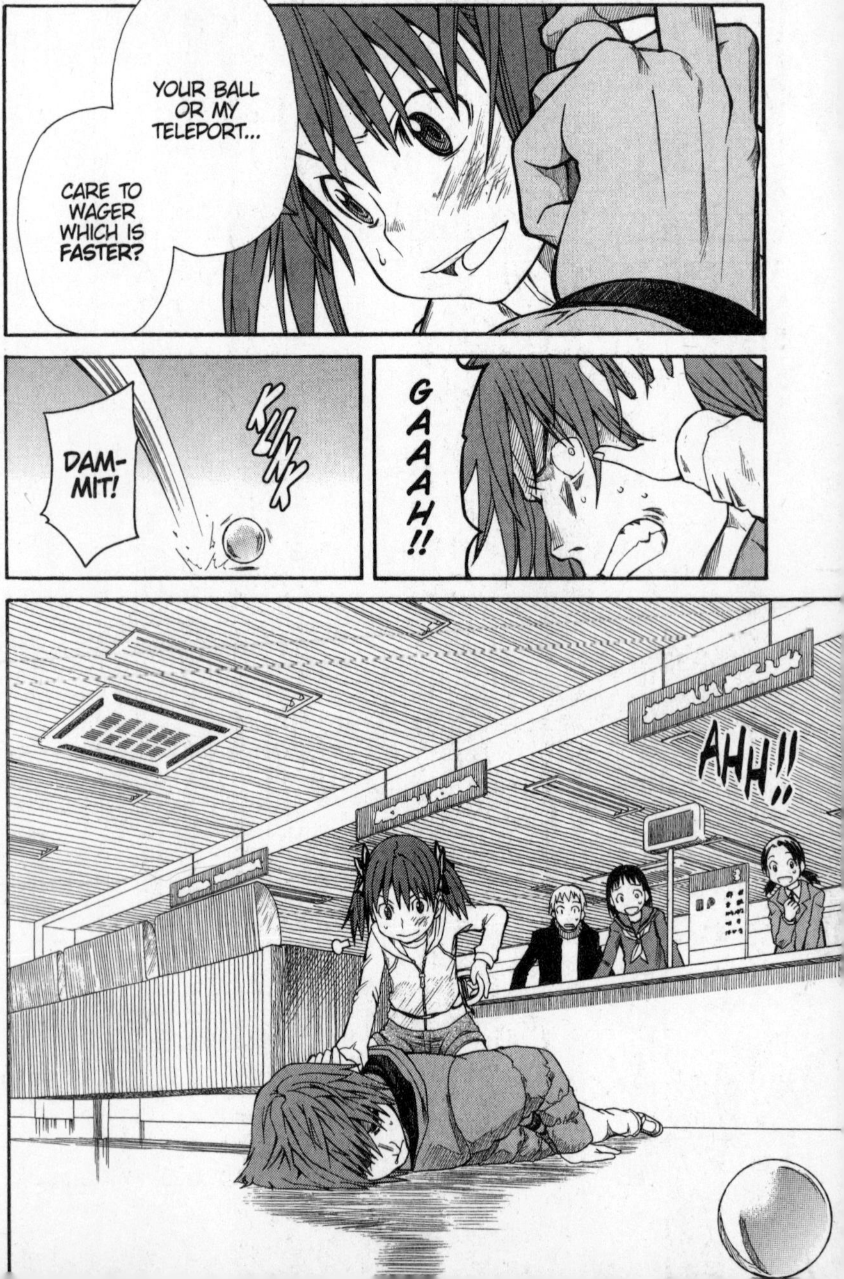
YOUR BALL OR MY TELEPORT...
CARE TO WAGER WHICH IS FASTER?
GAAAAH!!
KLINK
DAM-MIT!
AHH!!

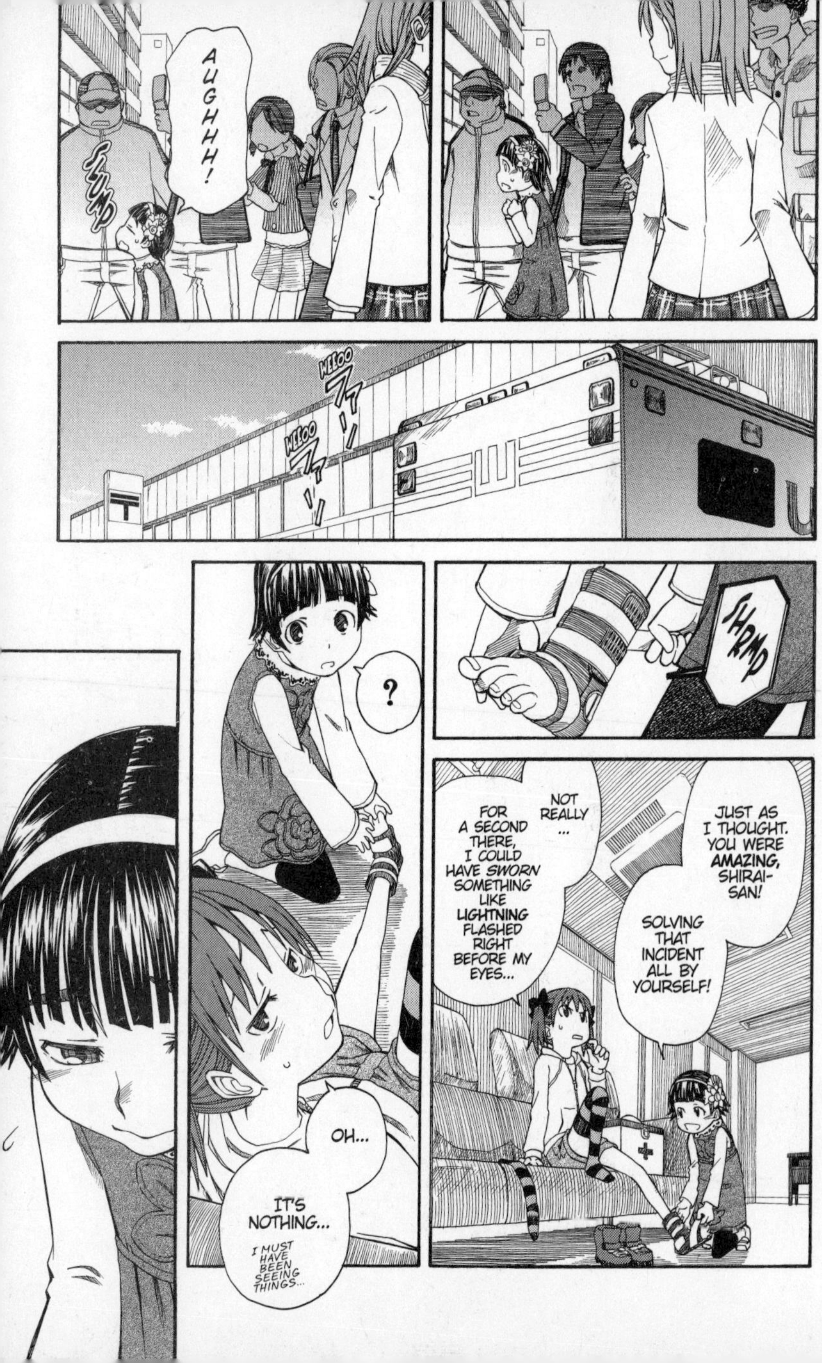
AUGHHHH!
SLUMP
WEEOO
WEEOO
SHRMP
JUST AS I THOUGHT. YOU WERE AMAZING, SHIRAI-SAN!
SOLVING THAT INCIDENT ALL BY YOURSELF!
NOT REALLY ...
FOR A SECOND THERE, I COULD HAVE SWORN SOMETHING LIKE LIGHTNING FLASHED RIGHT BEFORE MY EYES...
?
OH...
IT'S NOTHING...
I MUST HAVE BEEN SEEING THINGS...

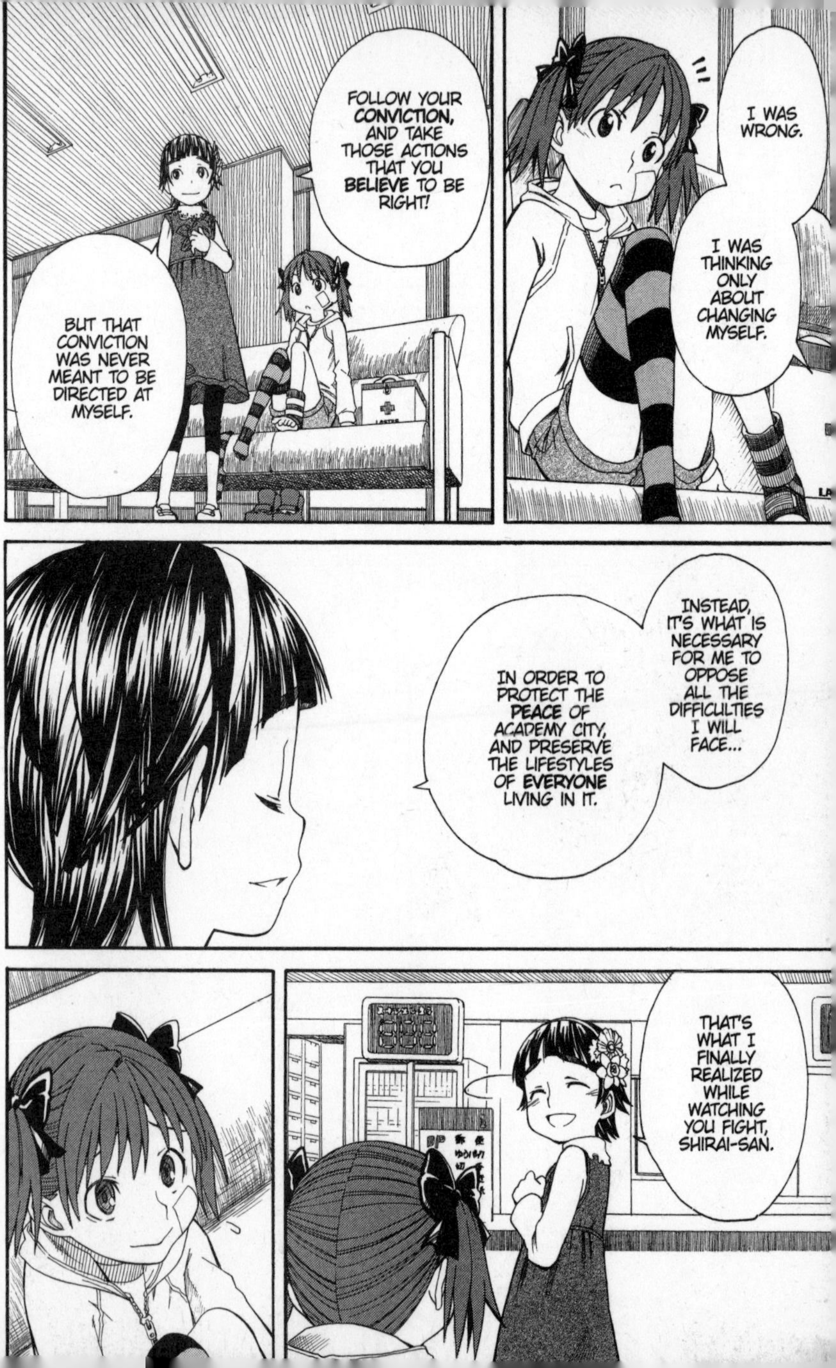
I WAS WRONG.
I WAS THINKING ONLY ABOUT CHANGING MYSELF.
FOLLOW YOUR CONVICTION, AND TAKE THOSE ACTIONS THAT YOU BELIEVE TO BE RIGHT!
BUT THAT CONVICTION WAS NEVER MEANT TO BE DIRECTED AT MYSELF.
INSTEAD, IT'S WHAT IS NECESSARY FOR ME TO OPPOSE ALL THE DIFFICULTIES I WILL FACE...
IN ORDER TO PROTECT THE PEACE OF ACADEMY CITY, AND PRESERVE THE LIFESTYLES OF EVERYONE LIVING IN IT.
THAT'S WHAT I FINALLY REALIZED WHILE WATCHING YOU FIGHT, SHIRAI-SAN.

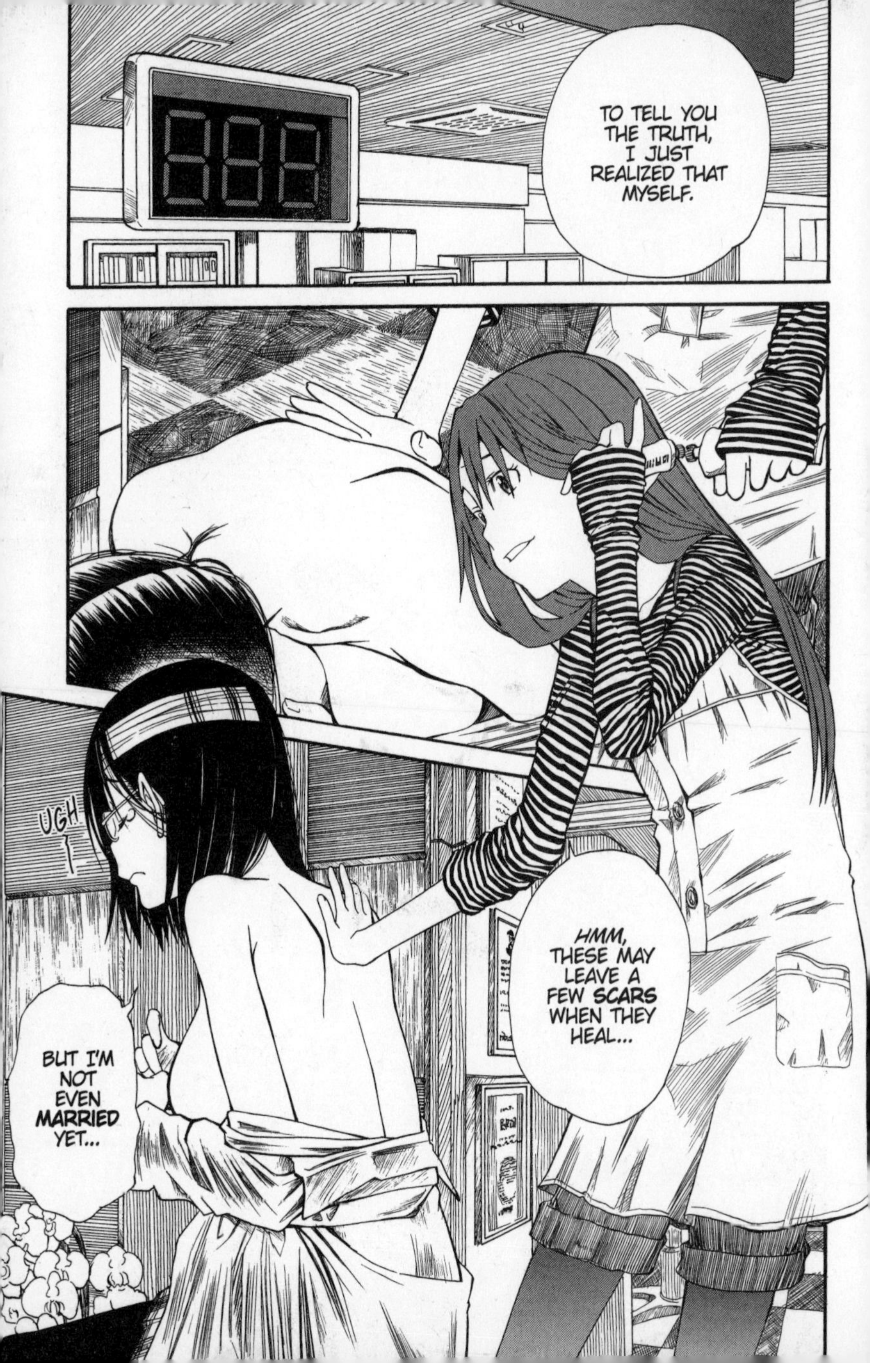
TO TELL YOU THE TRUTH, I JUST REALIZED THAT MYSELF.
HMM, THESE MAY LEAVE A FEW SCARS WHEN THEY HEAL...
UGH
BUT I'M NOT EVEN MARRIED YET...

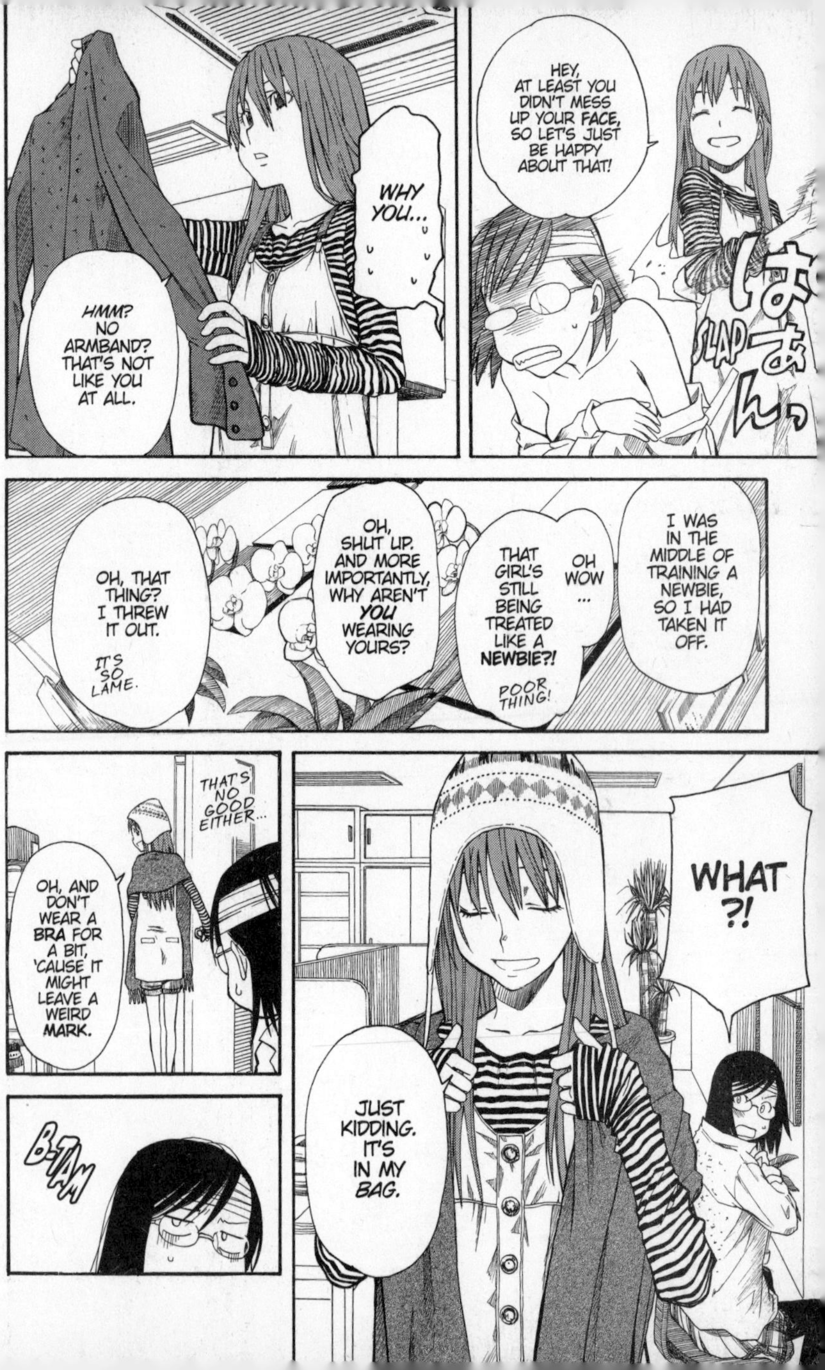
HEY, AT LEAST YOU DIDN'T MESS UP YOUR FACE, SO LET'S JUST BE HAPPY ABOUT THAT!
ぱぁんっ
SLAP
WHY YOU...
HMM? NO ARMBAND? THAT'S NOT LIKE YOU AT ALL.
I WAS IN THE MIDDLE OF TRAINING A NEWBIE, SO I HAD TAKEN IT OFF.
OH WOW ...
THAT GIRL'S STILL BEING TREATED LIKE A NEWBIE?!
POOR THING!
OH, SHUT UP. AND MORE IMPORTANTLY, WHY AREN'T YOU WEARING YOURS?
OH, THAT THING? I THREW IT OUT.
IT'S SO LAME.
WHAT?!
JUST KIDDING. IT'S IN MY BAG.
THAT'S NO GOOD EITHER...
OH, AND DON'T WEAR A BRA FOR A BIT, 'CAUSE IT MIGHT LEAVE A WEIRD MARK.
B-TAM

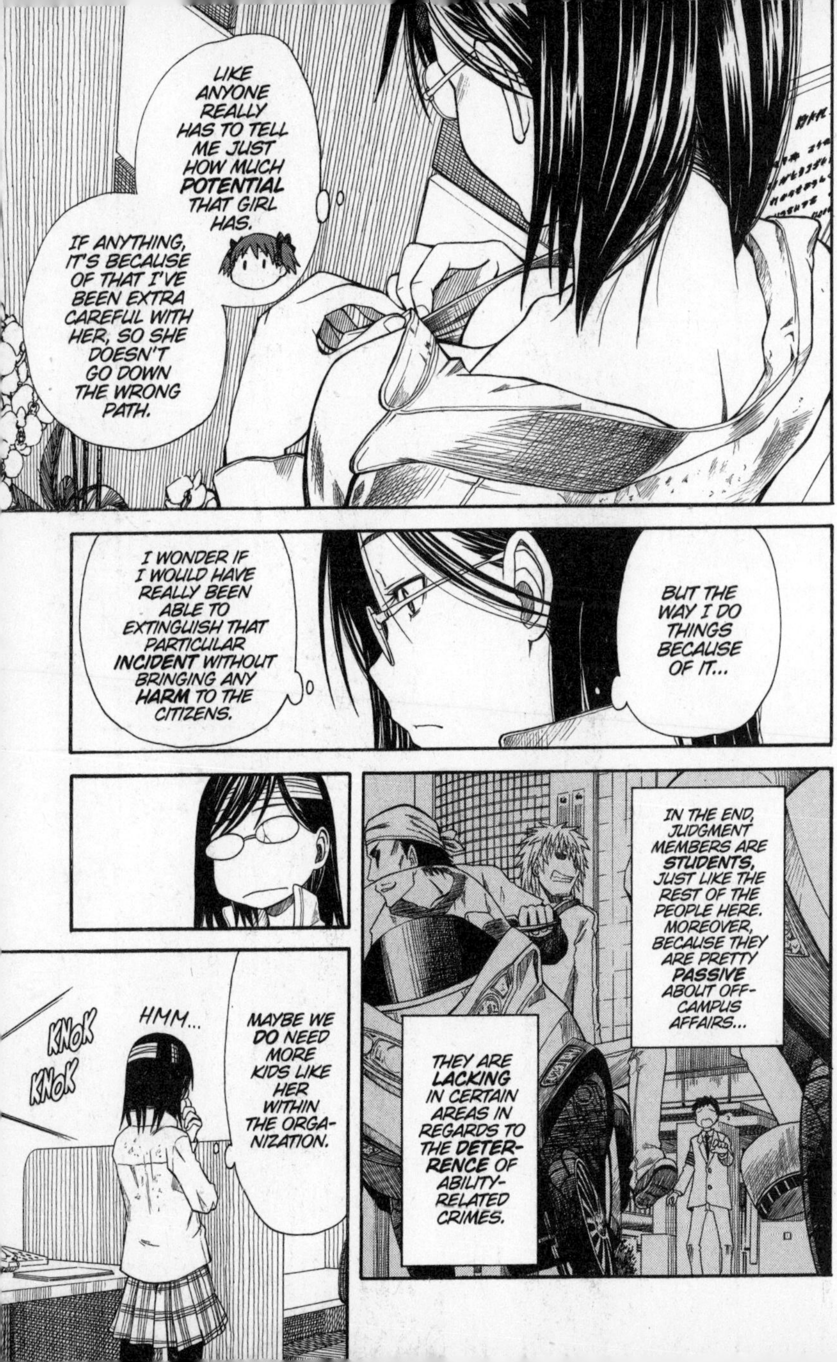
LIKE ANYONE REALLY HAS TO TELL ME JUST HOW MUCH POTENTIAL THAT GIRL HAS.
IF ANYTHING, IT'S BECAUSE OF THAT I'VE BEEN EXTRA CAREFUL WITH HER, SO SHE DOESN'T GO DOWN THE WRONG PATH.
BUT THE WAY I DO THINGS BECAUSE OF IT...
I WONDER IF I WOULD HAVE REALLY BEEN ABLE TO EXTINGUISH THAT PARTICULAR INCIDENT WITHOUT BRINGING ANY HARM TO THE CITIZENS.
IN THE END, JUDGMENT MEMBERS ARE STUDENTS, JUST LIKE THE REST OF THE PEOPLE HERE. MOREOVER, BECAUSE THEY ARE PRETTY PASSIVE ABOUT OFF-CAMPUS AFFAIRS...
THEY ARE LACKING IN CERTAIN AREAS IN REGARDS TO THE DETERRENCE OF ABILITY-RELATED CRIMES.
MAYBE WE DO NEED MORE KIDS LIKE HER WITHIN THE ORGANIZATION.
HMM...
KNOK
KNOK

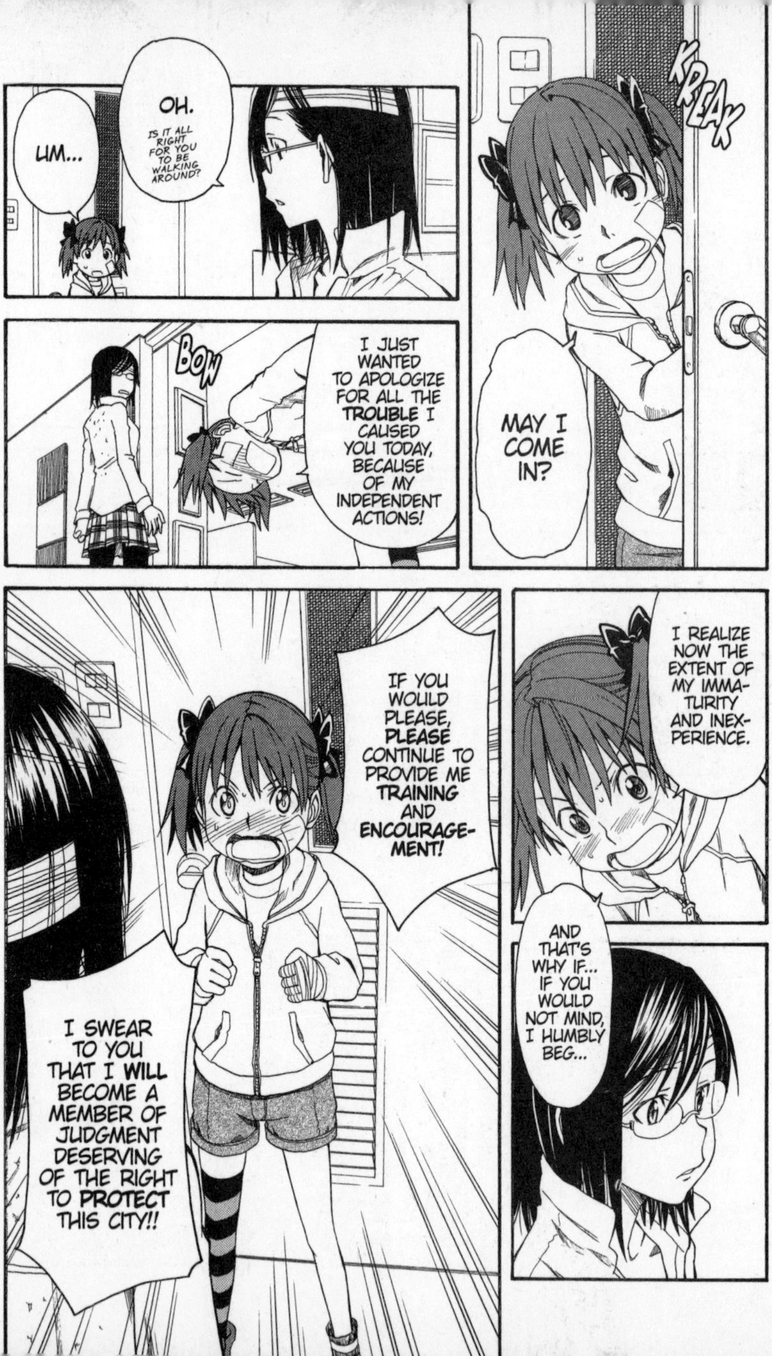
KREAK
MAY I COME IN?
OH.
IS IT ALL RIGHT FOR YOU TO BE WALKING AROUND?
UM...
BOW
I JUST WANTED TO APOLOGIZE FOR ALL THE **TROUBLE** I CAUSED YOU TODAY, BECAUSE OF MY INDEPENDENT ACTIONS!
I REALIZE NOW THE EXTENT OF MY IMMATURITY AND INEXPERIENCE.
AND THAT'S WHY IF... IF YOU WOULD NOT MIND, I HUMBLY BEG...
IF YOU WOULD PLEASE, **PLEASE** CONTINUE TO PROVIDE ME **TRAINING** AND **ENCOURAGEMENT!**
I SWEAR TO YOU THAT I **WILL** BECOME A MEMBER OF JUDGMENT DESERVING OF THE RIGHT TO **PROTECT** THIS CITY!!

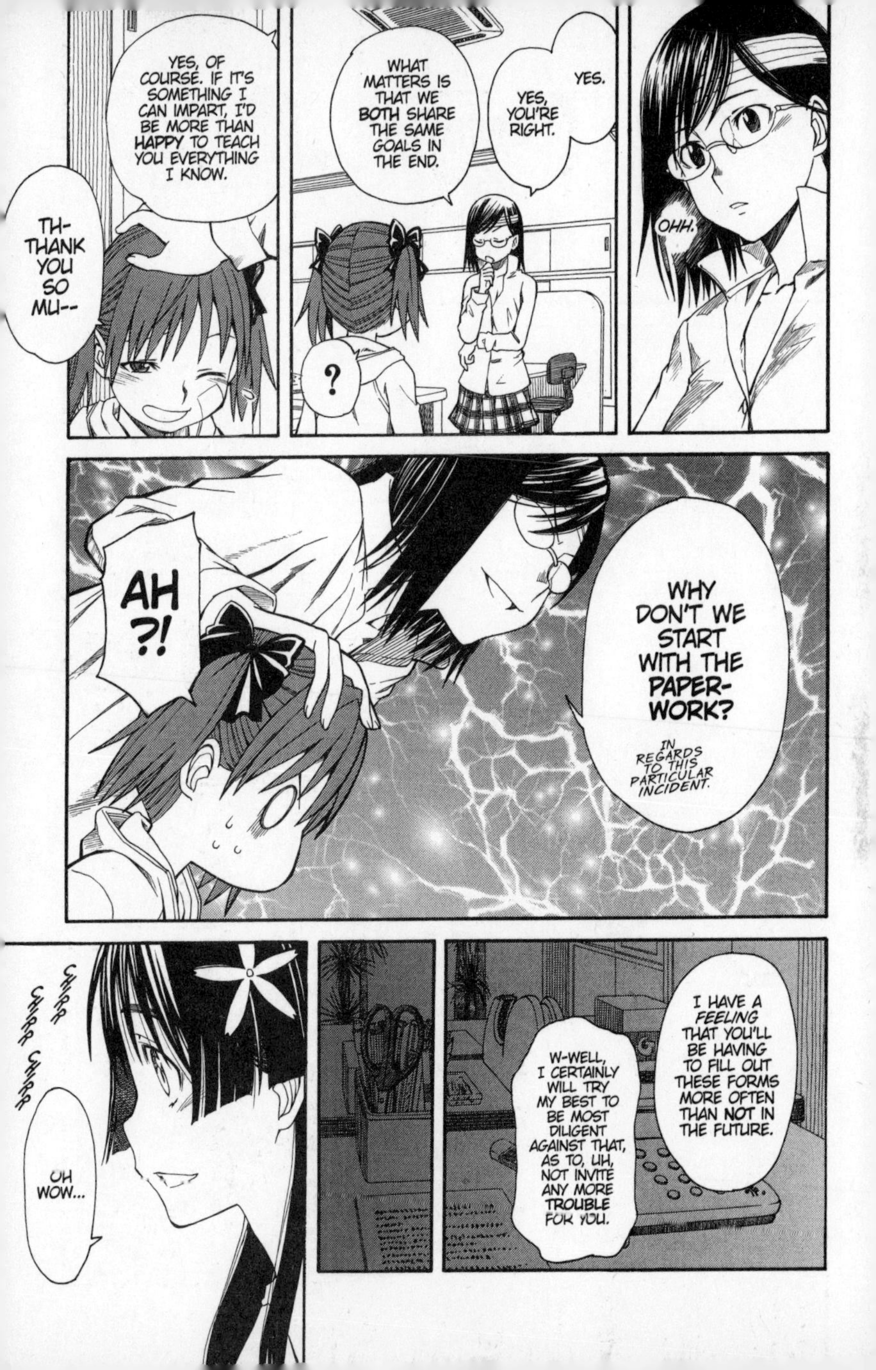
OHH.
YES.
YES, YOU'RE RIGHT.
WHAT MATTERS IS THAT WE BOTH SHARE THE SAME GOALS IN THE END.
?
YES, OF COURSE. IF IT'S SOMETHING I CAN IMPART, I'D BE MORE THAN HAPPY TO TEACH YOU EVERYTHING I KNOW.
TH-THANK YOU SO MU--
WHY DON'T WE START WITH THE PAPER-WORK?
IN REGARDS TO THIS PARTICULAR INCIDENT.
AH?!
I HAVE A FEELING THAT YOU'LL BE HAVING TO FILL OUT THESE FORMS MORE OFTEN THAN NOT IN THE FUTURE.
W-WELL, I CERTAINLY WILL TRY MY BEST TO BE MOST DILIGENT AGAINST THAT, AS TO, UH, NOT INVITE ANY MORE TROUBLE FOR YOU.
CHIRR CHIRR CHIRR CHIRR
OH WOW...

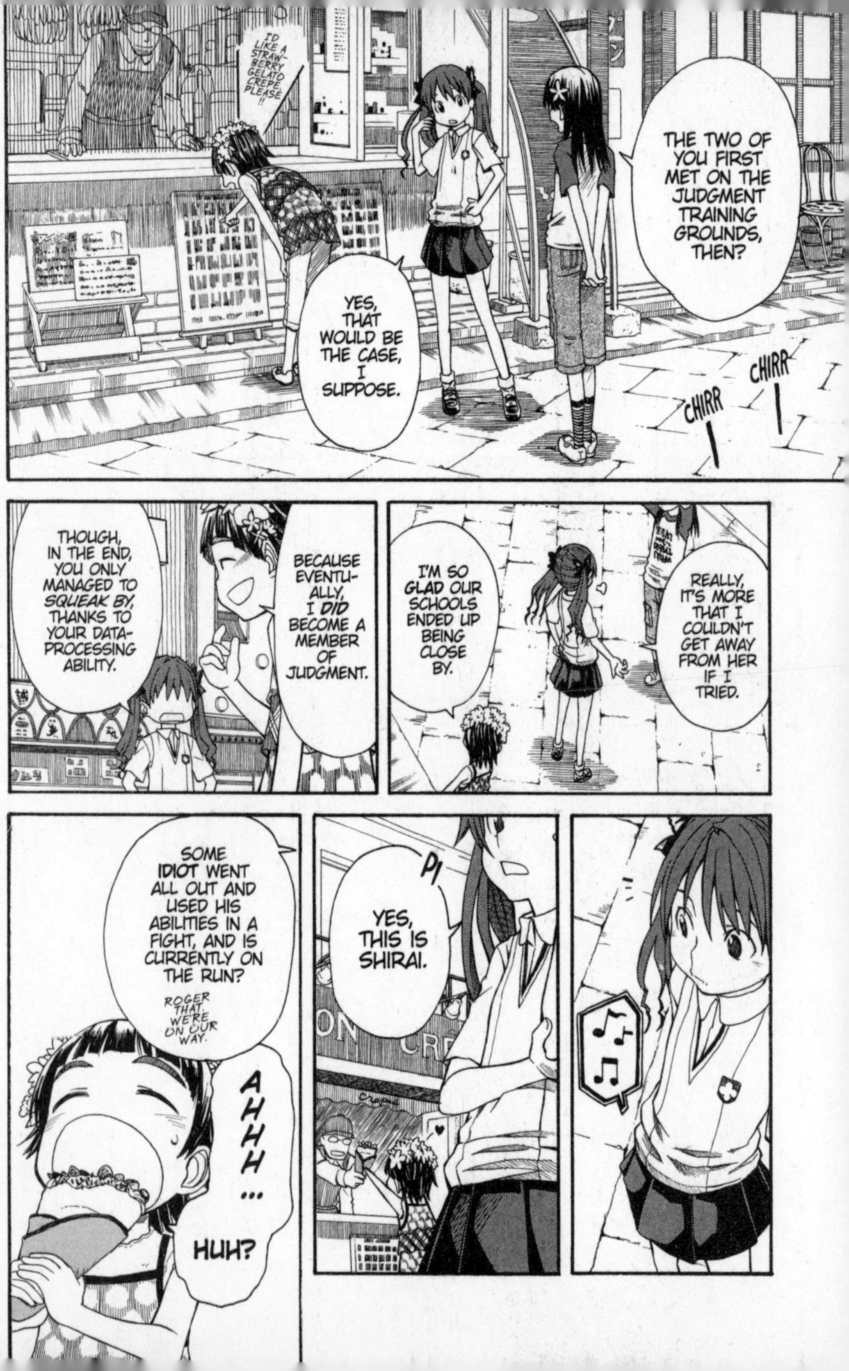
THE TWO OF YOU FIRST MET ON THE JUDGMENT TRAINING GROUNDS, THEN?
CHIRR
CHIRR
YES, THAT WOULD BE THE CASE, I SUPPOSE.
I'D LIKE A STRAWBERRY GELATO CREPE, PLEASE!!
REALLY, IT'S MORE THAT I COULDN'T GET AWAY FROM HER IF I TRIED.
I'M SO GLAD OUR SCHOOLS ENDED UP BEING CLOSE BY.
BECAUSE EVENTUALLY, I DID BECOME A MEMBER OF JUDGMENT.
THOUGH, IN THE END, YOU ONLY MANAGED TO SQUEAK BY, THANKS TO YOUR DATA-PROCESSING ABILITY.
PI
YES, THIS IS SHIRAI.
SOME IDIOT WENT ALL OUT AND USED HIS ABILITIES IN A FIGHT, AND IS CURRENTLY ON THE RUN?
ROGER THAT. WE'RE ON OUR WAY.
AHHH...
HUH?

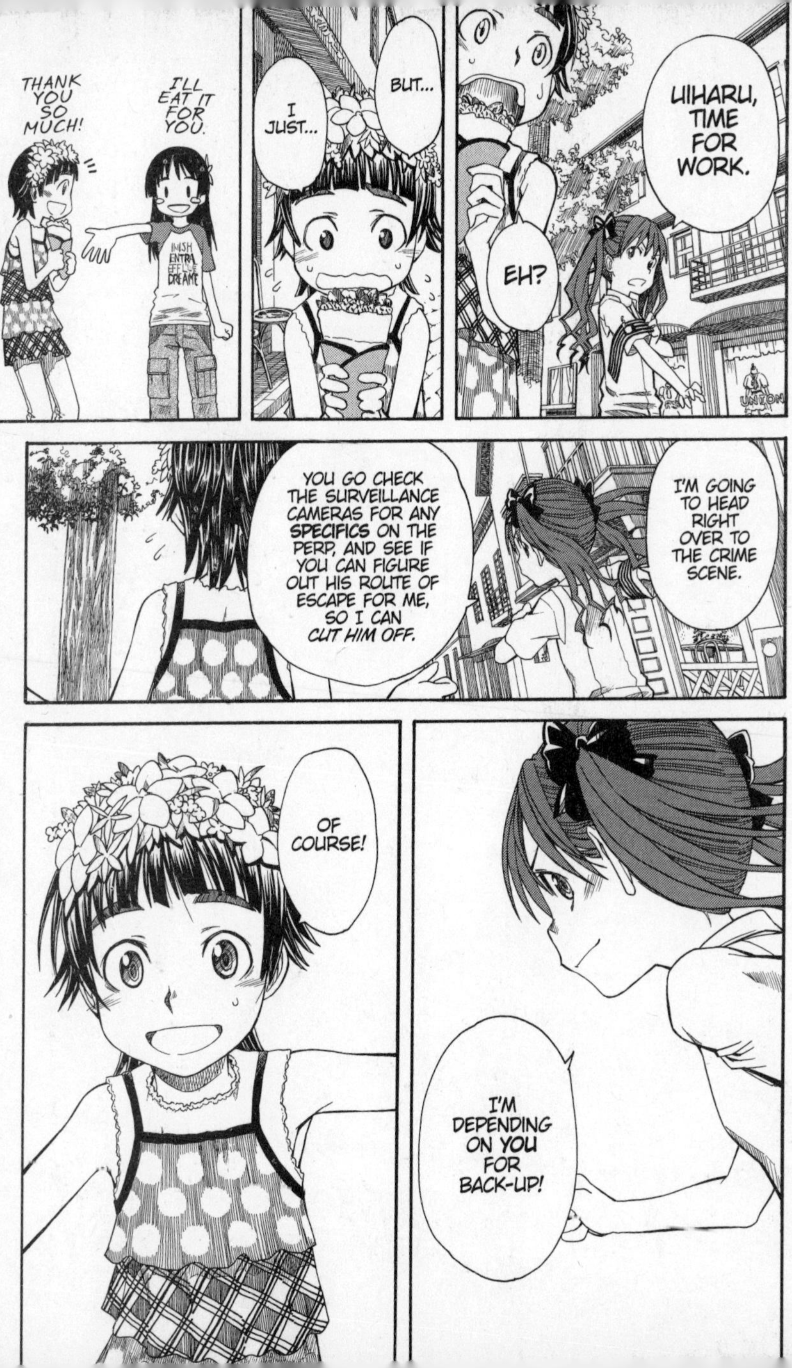
UIHARU, TIME FOR WORK.
EH?
UNION
BUT...
I JUST...
I'LL EAT IT FOR YOU.
THANK YOU SO MUCH!
I'M GOING TO HEAD RIGHT OVER TO THE CRIME SCENE.
YOU GO CHECK THE SURVEILLANCE CAMERAS FOR ANY SPECIFICS ON THE PERP, AND SEE IF YOU CAN FIGURE OUT HIS ROUTE OF ESCAPE FOR ME, SO I CAN CUT HIM OFF.
I'M DEPENDING ON YOU FOR BACK-UP!
OF COURSE!

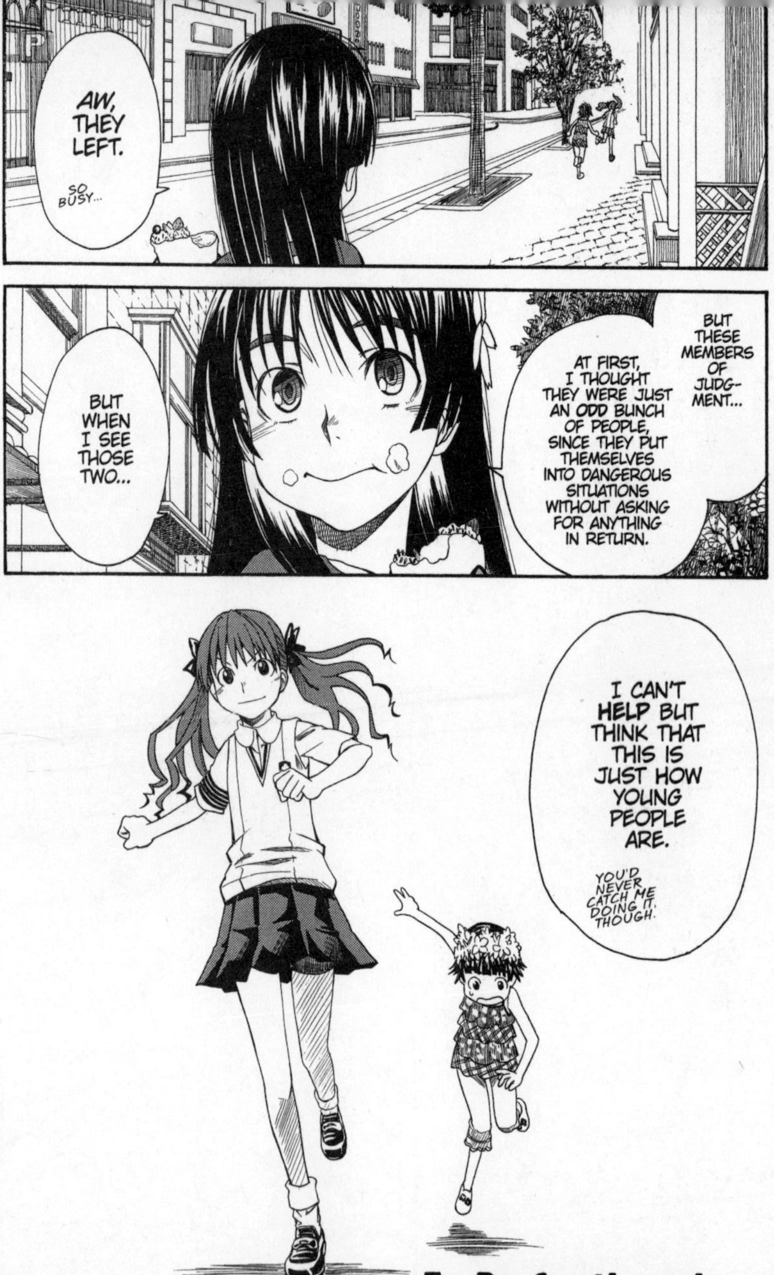
AW, THEY LEFT.
SO BUSY...
BUT THESE MEMBERS OF JUDG-MENT...
AT FIRST, I THOUGHT THEY WERE JUST AN ODD BUNCH OF PEOPLE, SINCE THEY PUT THEMSELVES INTO DANGEROUS SITUATIONS WITHOUT ASKING FOR ANYTHING IN RETURN.
BUT WHEN I SEE THOSE TWO...
I CAN'T HELP BUT THINK THAT THIS IS JUST HOW YOUNG PEOPLE ARE.
YOU'D NEVER CATCH ME DOING IT, THOUGH.

To Be Continued...

A Certain SCIENTIFIC Railgun
Haimura Kiyotaka Art Works 3

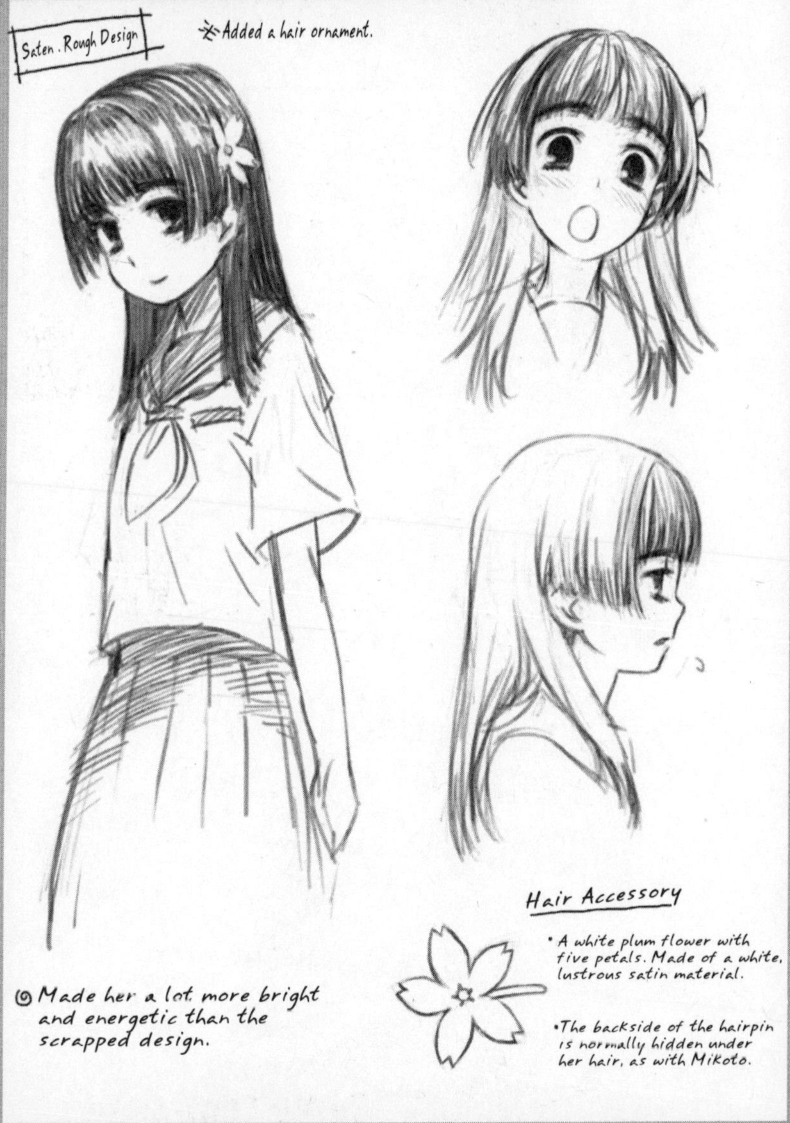
Saten . Rough Design
※Added a hair ornament.
Hair Accessory
• A white plum flower with five petals. Made of a white, lustrous satin material.
•The backside of the hairpin is normally hidden under her hair, as with Mikoto.
◎Made her a lot more bright and energetic than the scrapped design.

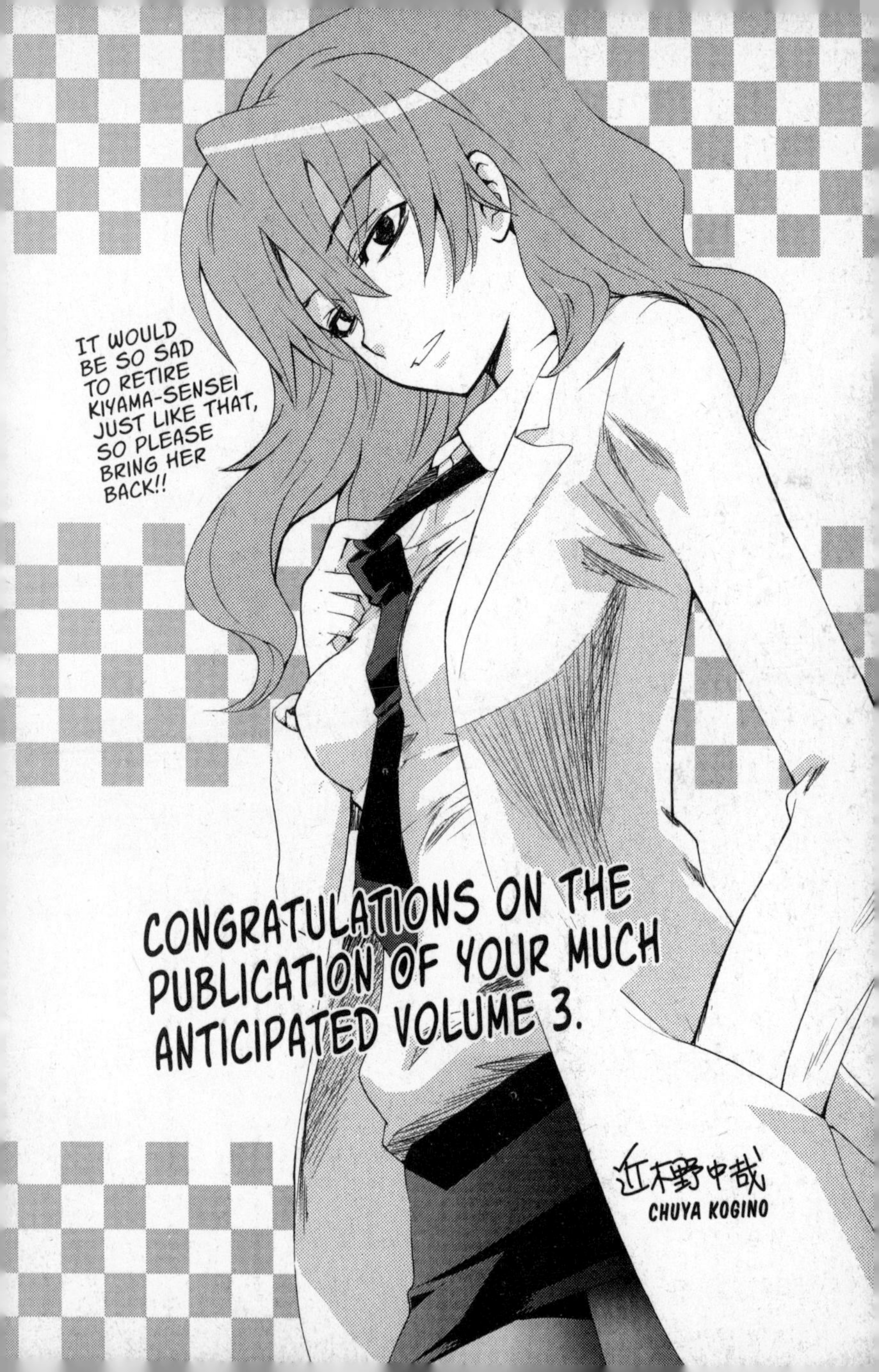
IT WOULD BE SO SAD TO RETIRE KIYAMA-SENSEI JUST LIKE THAT, SO PLEASE BRING HER BACK!!
CONGRATULATIONS ON THE PUBLICATION OF YOUR MUCH ANTICIPATED VOLUME 3.
近木野中哉
CHUYA KOGINO

Cheers from the Original Side 原作者よりお祝いメッセージ

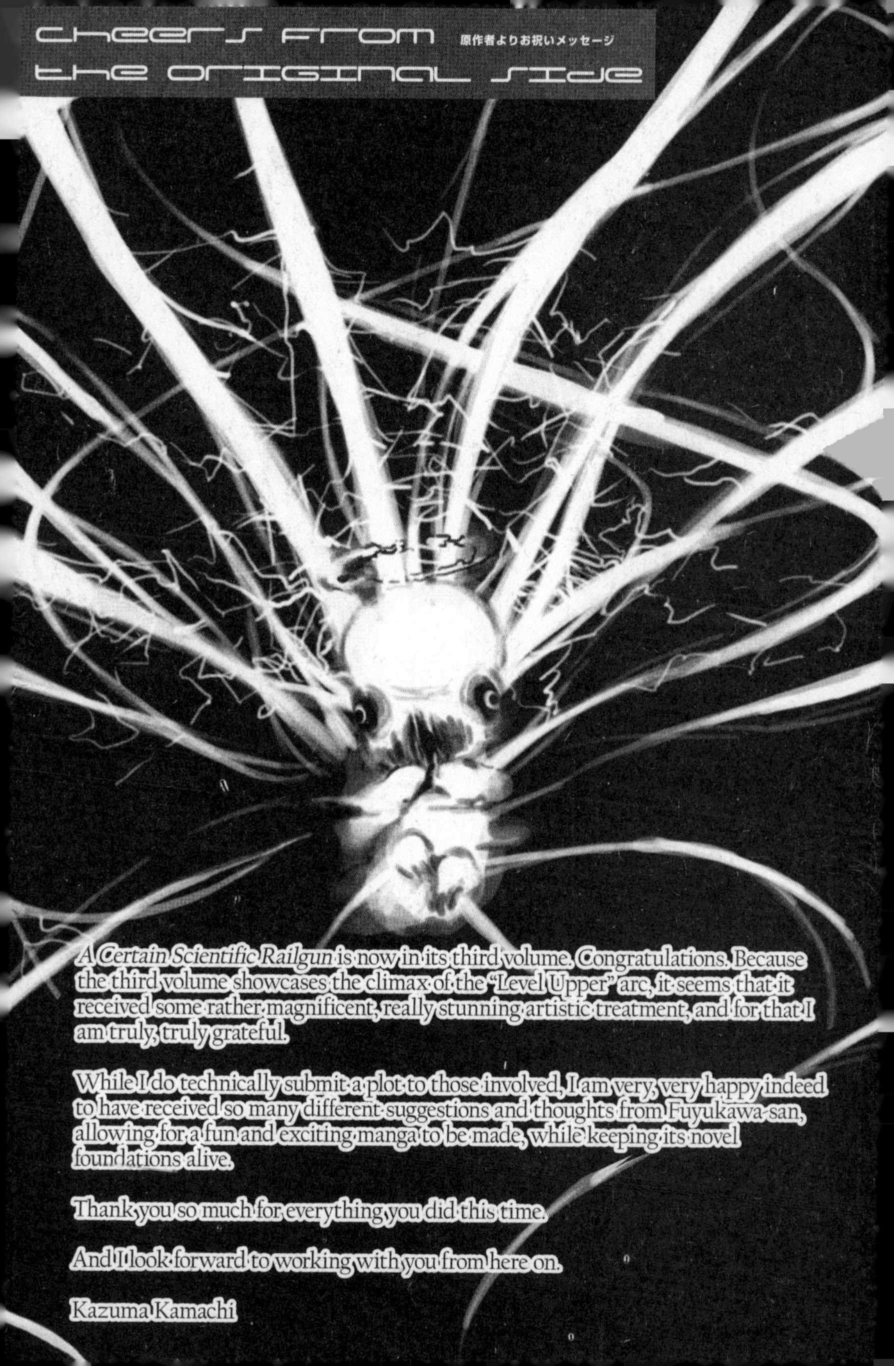

A Certain Scientific Railgun is now in its third volume. Congratulations. Because the third volume showcases the climax of the "Level Upper" arc, it seems that it received some rather magnificent, really stunning artistic treatment, and for that I am truly, truly grateful.

While I do technically submit a plot to those involved, I am very, very happy indeed to have received so many different suggestions and thoughts from Fuyukawa-san, allowing for a fun and exciting manga to be made, while keeping its novel foundations alive.

Thank you so much for everything you did this time.

And I look forward to working with you from here on.

Kazuma Kamachi

○ Month ✕ Day

......I had no idea at all of how terrifying a place like the Tokiwadai dormitories could be. And though they might have been just 1st year students, who on earth was that Dorm Supervisor who managed to take out three Level 4s in one fell swoop?! As much as it pains me to do so, I guess I have no choice but to just grin and bear my punishment in the matter.

○ Month △ Day

Today was the school entrance ceremony.
It was not at all as brutal as I thought it would be, but I quickly received some invitations from some rather astute factions. Slowly but surely, I began to feel e difference between this place and a rmal school. Since I do not like to work groups, however, I politely declined.

○ Month ◇ Day

Today, I saw the oft-rumored "Railgun" with my own eyes for the very first time. Despite her notoriety, she did not seem to be affiliated with any of the major factions, nor did it seem she was trying to establish her own.
~~I found her to be completely different from the image I~~ had put together of her from everything I had heard previously. But then again, I've seen more than enough people in my time whose inner selves do not match their outer shells at all, so I must remain cautious.
~~Then again, it may simply be that her popularity is~~ rock bottom after all. Heh heh heh.

○ Month ☆ Day

In the short time that I hadn't seen her, the flowers on top of Uiharu's head seem to have increased exponentially. If it was just in her head, that would be one thing, but it's like a flower garden on the outside as well... what on earth is that girl thinking?
It was getting on my nerves so much that ecided to teleport the flowers away from her, en watched her run after them, crying.

◎ Month ▲ Day

I happened to stumble upon two students glaring one another down, and from what I was advised by the crowd gathered around them, it seemed to be related to some inter-faction poaching incident... I was amazed that people would fight over something so utterly mundane.
But then that "Railgun" showed up, chided the involved students for their behavior, and helped to subdue the scene. Just the way that she stood up to them was so brave, so gallant... Right, not that I thought anything of it really, but...
The manner in which she handled things, with such consideration for the two parties involved, not wanting to wound anyone's pride... Her gaze was so very kind... Right, not that it means anything, but...
However, before we all knew it, the prickly atmosphere around us had dissipated, and I thought, what a wondrous person she is... Right, so...

◎Month✕Day

When I see that person in the hall or the courtyard, my gaze cannot help but to follow her.

When I see that person and another laughing together, I get the saddest feeling in my heart.

I've been acting so strangely lately, I wonder what's gotten into me...

◎Month◆Day

When I come to my senses, I find myself always thinking of her face.

Could it be that I...

No, it simply couldn't be... but...

◎Month♥Day

This is............

~~LOVE~~?!

◎Month☆Day

oneesamaoneesamaoneesamaoneesamaoneesamaoneesamaoneesamaoneesama
oneesamaoneesamaoneesamaoneesamaoneesamaoneesamaoneesamaoneesama
oneesamaoneesamaoneesamaoneesamaoneesamaoneesamaoneesamaoneesama
oneesamaoneesamaoneesamaoneesamaoneesamaoneesamaoneesamaoneesama
oneesamaoneesamaoneesamaoneesamaoneesamaoneesamaoneesamaoneesama
oneesamaoneesamaoneesamaoneesamaoneesamaoneesamaoneesamaoneesama
oneesamaoneesamaoneesamaoneesamaoneesamaoneesamaoneesamaoneesama
oneesamaoneesamaoneesamaoneesamaoneesamaoneesamaoneesamaoneesama
oneesamaoneesamaoneesamaoneesamaoneesamaoneesamaoneesamaoneesama
oneesamaoneesamaoneesamaoneesamaoneesamaoneesamaoneesamaoneesama
oneesamaoneesamaoneesamaoneesamaoneesamaoneesamaoneesamaoneesama
oneesamaoneesamaoneesamaoneesamaoneesamaoneesamaoneesamaoneesama
oneesamaoneesamaoneesamaoneesamaoneesamaoneesamaoneesamaoneesama

AHHHHHHH, Oneesama who belongs to me, and ME alone!!!...

A Certain SCIENTIFIC Railgun

Kuroko's Diary Entries

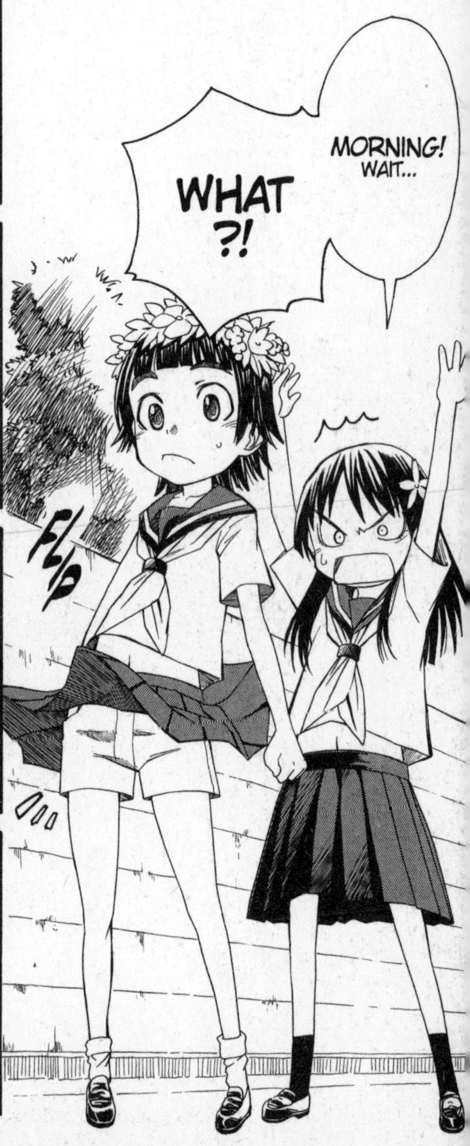
MORNING! WAIT...
WHAT ?!
FLIP

OVERKILL

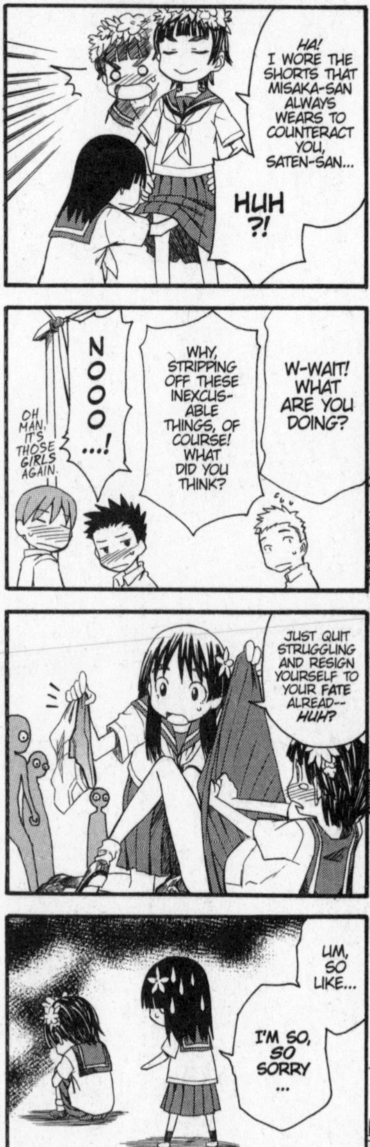
HA! I WORE THE SHORTS THAT MISAKA-SAN ALWAYS WEARS TO COUNTERACT YOU, SATEN-SAN...
HUH ?!
W-WAIT! WHAT ARE YOU DOING?
WHY, STRIPPING OFF THESE INEXCUS-ABLE THINGS, OF COURSE! WHAT DID YOU THINK?
NOOOO...!
OH MAN, IT'S THOSE GIRLS AGAIN.
JUST QUIT STRUGGLING AND RESIGN YOURSELF TO YOUR FATE ALREAD-- HUH?
UM, SO LIKE...
I'M SO, SO SORRY ...

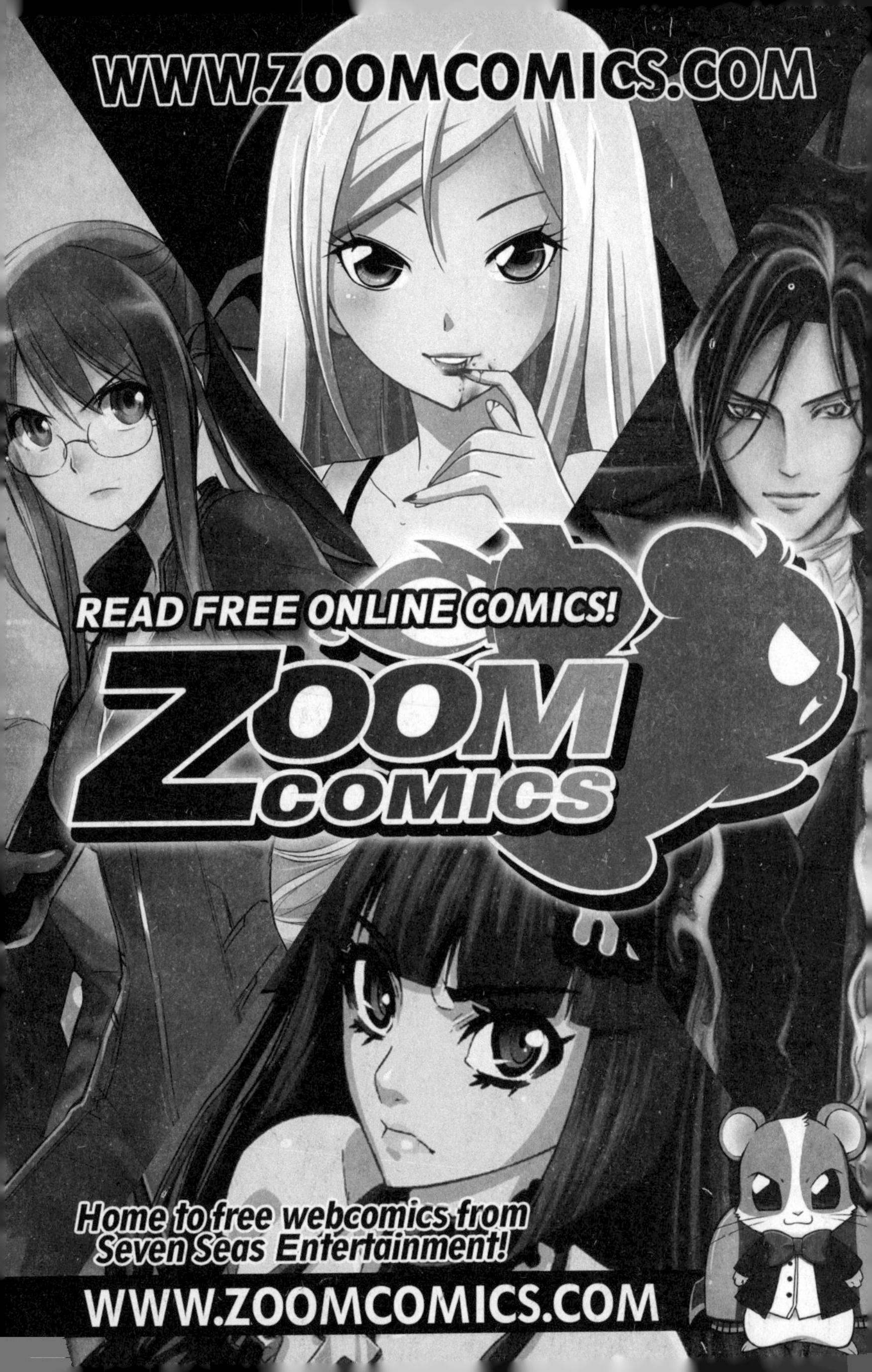

WWW.ZOOMCOMICS.COM
READ FREE ONLINE COMICS!
ZOOM COMICS
Home to free webcomics from Seven Seas Entertainment!
WWW.ZOOMCOMICS.COM

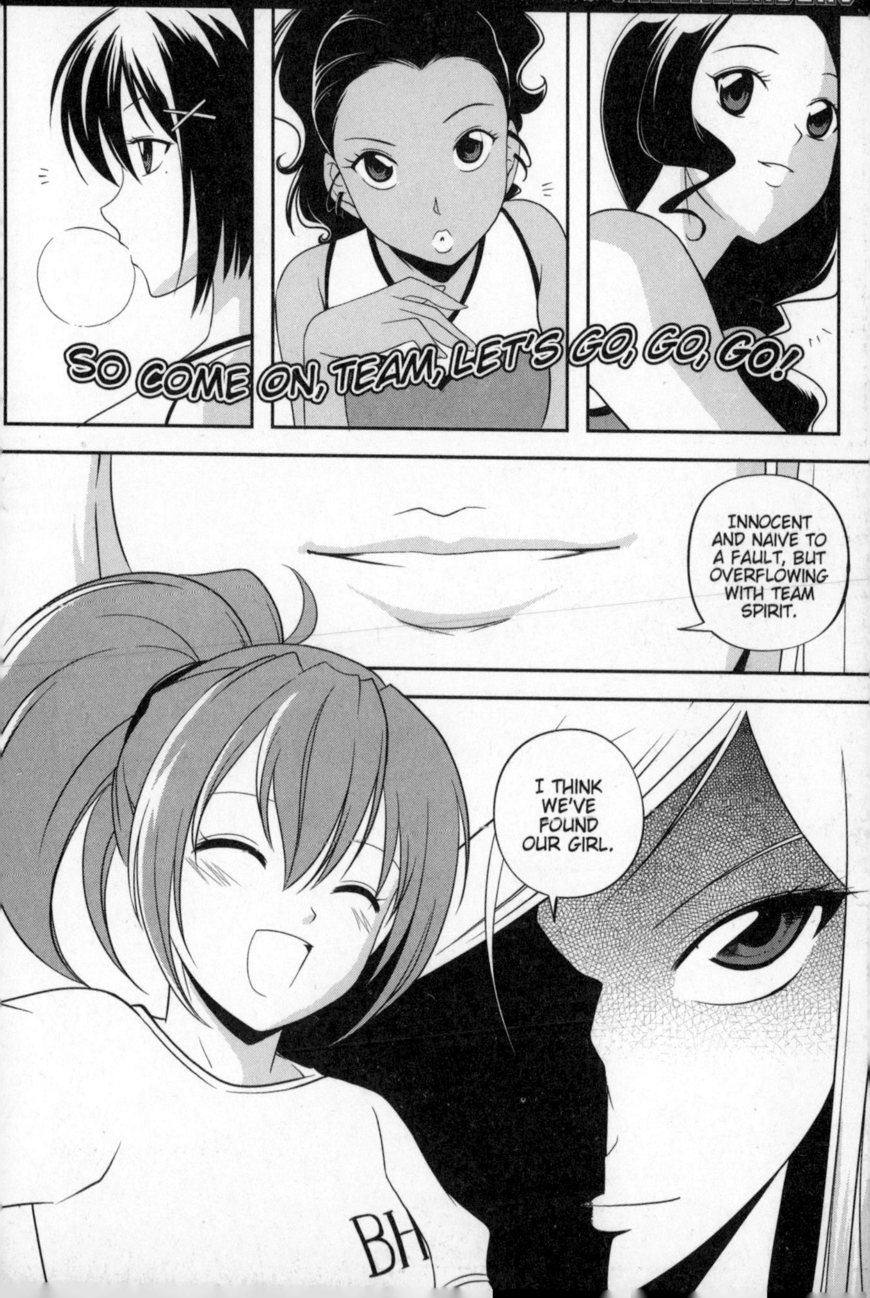
SO COME ON, TEAM, LET'S GO, GO, GO!
INNOCENT AND NAIVE TO A FAULT, BUT OVERFLOWING WITH TEAM SPIRIT.
I THINK WE'VE FOUND OUR GIRL.
BH

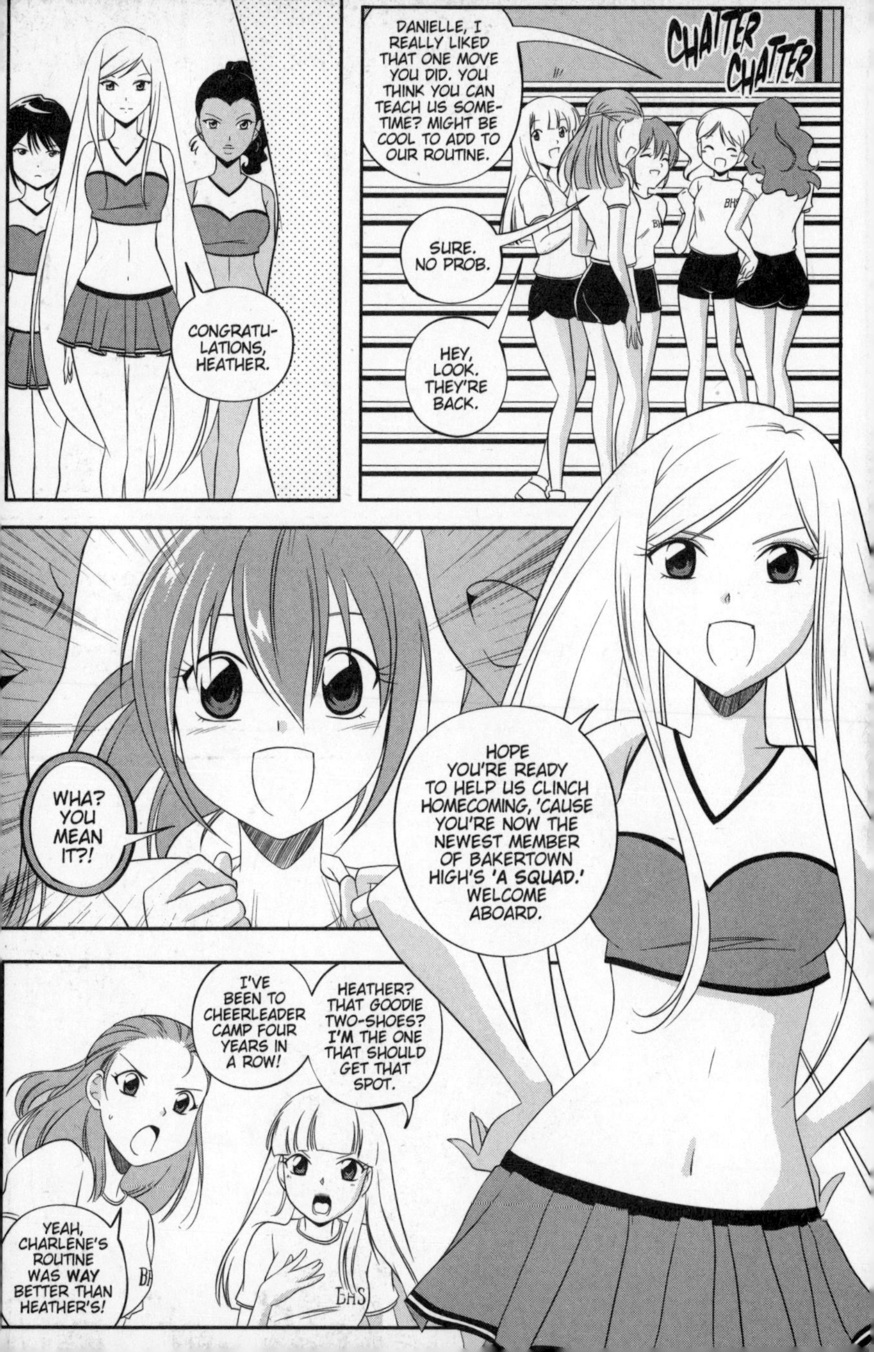
CHATTER CHATTER
DANIELLE, I REALLY LIKED THAT ONE MOVE YOU DID. YOU THINK YOU CAN TEACH US SOME-TIME? MIGHT BE COOL TO ADD TO OUR ROUTINE.
SURE. NO PROB.
HEY, LOOK. THEY'RE BACK.
CONGRATU-LATIONS, HEATHER.
HOPE YOU'RE READY TO HELP US CLINCH HOMECOMING, 'CAUSE YOU'RE NOW THE NEWEST MEMBER OF BAKERTOWN HIGH'S 'A SQUAD.' WELCOME ABOARD.
WHA? YOU MEAN IT?!
HEATHER? THAT GOODIE TWO-SHOES? I'M THE ONE THAT SHOULD GET THAT SPOT.
I'VE BEEN TO CHEERLEADER CAMP FOUR YEARS IN A ROW!
YEAH, CHARLENE'S ROUTINE WAS WAY BETTER THAN HEATHER'S!

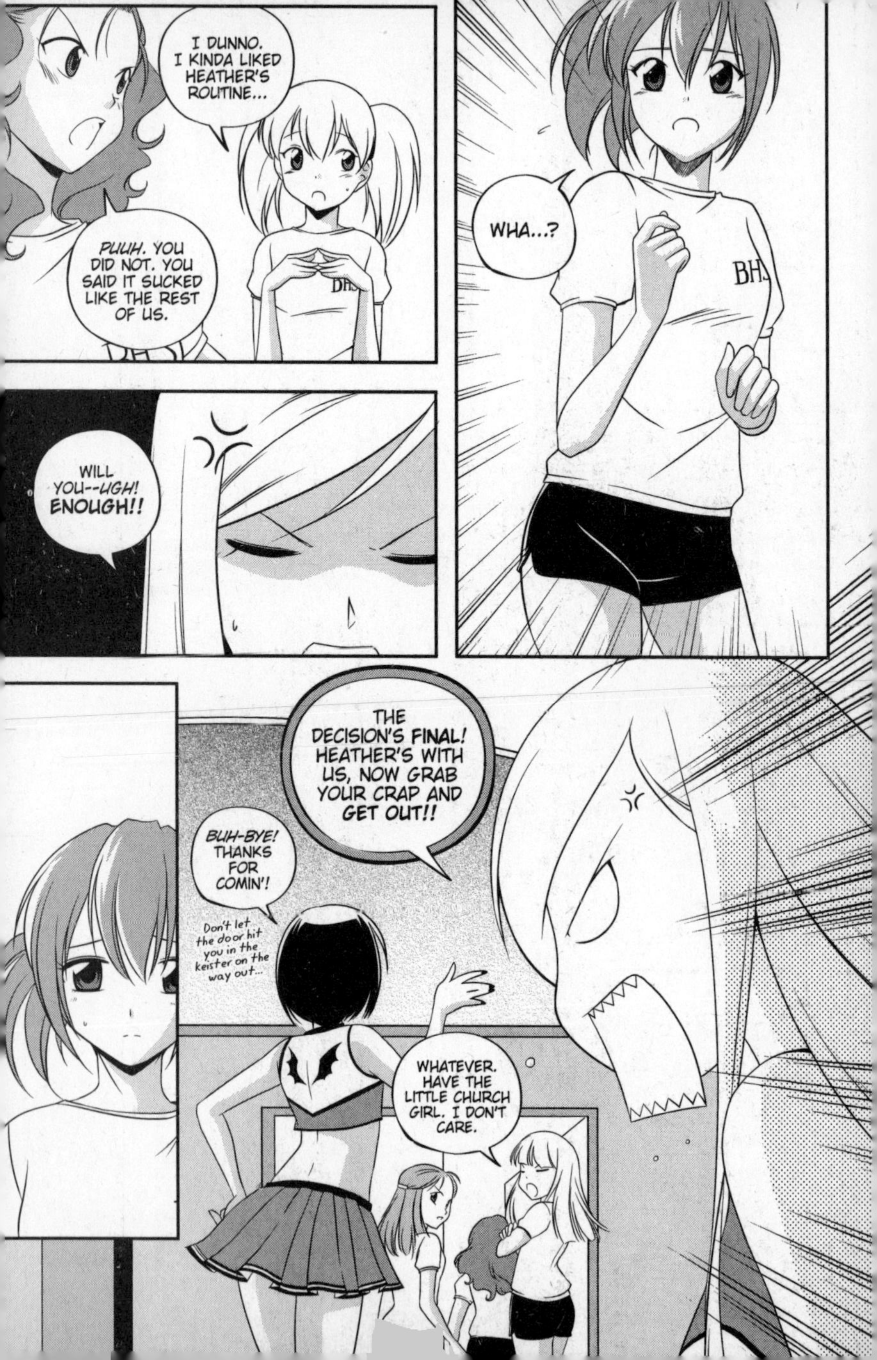
WHA...?
I DUNNO. I KINDA LIKED HEATHER'S ROUTINE...
PUUH. YOU DID NOT. YOU SAID IT SUCKED LIKE THE REST OF US.
WILL YOU--*UGH*! **ENOUGH!!**
THE DECISION'S **FINAL!** HEATHER'S WITH US, NOW GRAB YOUR CRAP AND **GET OUT!!**
BUH-BYE! THANKS FOR COMIN'!
Don't let the door hit you in the keister on the way out...
WHATEVER. HAVE THE LITTLE CHURCH GIRL. I DON'T CARE.

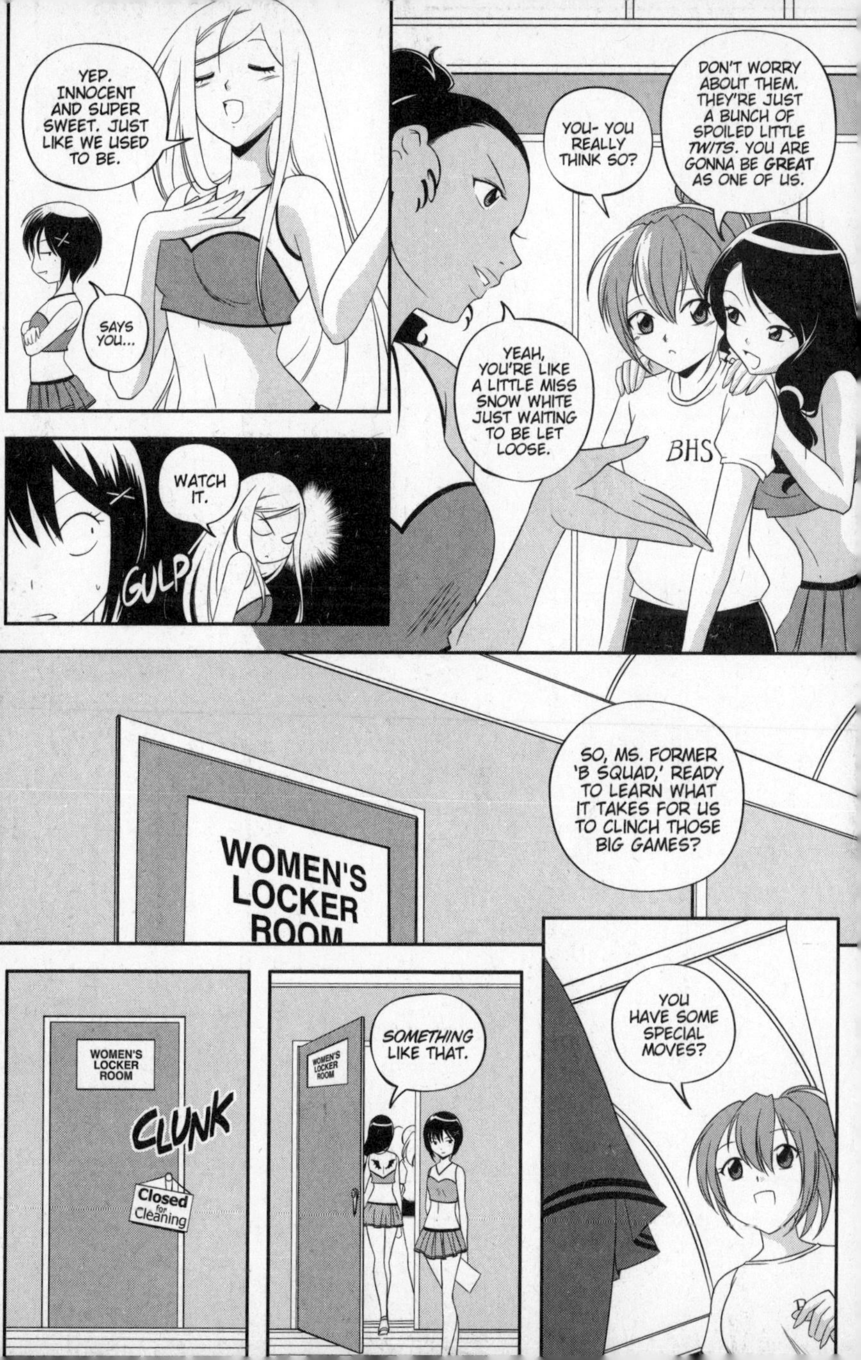
DON'T WORRY ABOUT THEM. THEY'RE JUST A BUNCH OF SPOILED LITTLE *TWITS*. YOU ARE GONNA BE **GREAT** AS ONE OF US.
YOU- YOU REALLY THINK SO?
YEAH, YOU'RE LIKE A LITTLE MISS SNOW WHITE JUST WAITING TO BE LET LOOSE.
YEP. INNOCENT AND SUPER SWEET. JUST LIKE WE USED TO BE.
SAYS YOU...
WATCH IT.
GULP
SO, MS. FORMER 'B SQUAD,' READY TO LEARN WHAT IT TAKES FOR US TO CLINCH THOSE BIG GAMES?
WOMEN'S LOCKER ROOM
YOU HAVE SOME SPECIAL MOVES?
SOMETHING LIKE THAT.
WOMEN'S LOCKER ROOM
WOMEN'S LOCKER ROOM
CLUNK
Closed for Cleaning

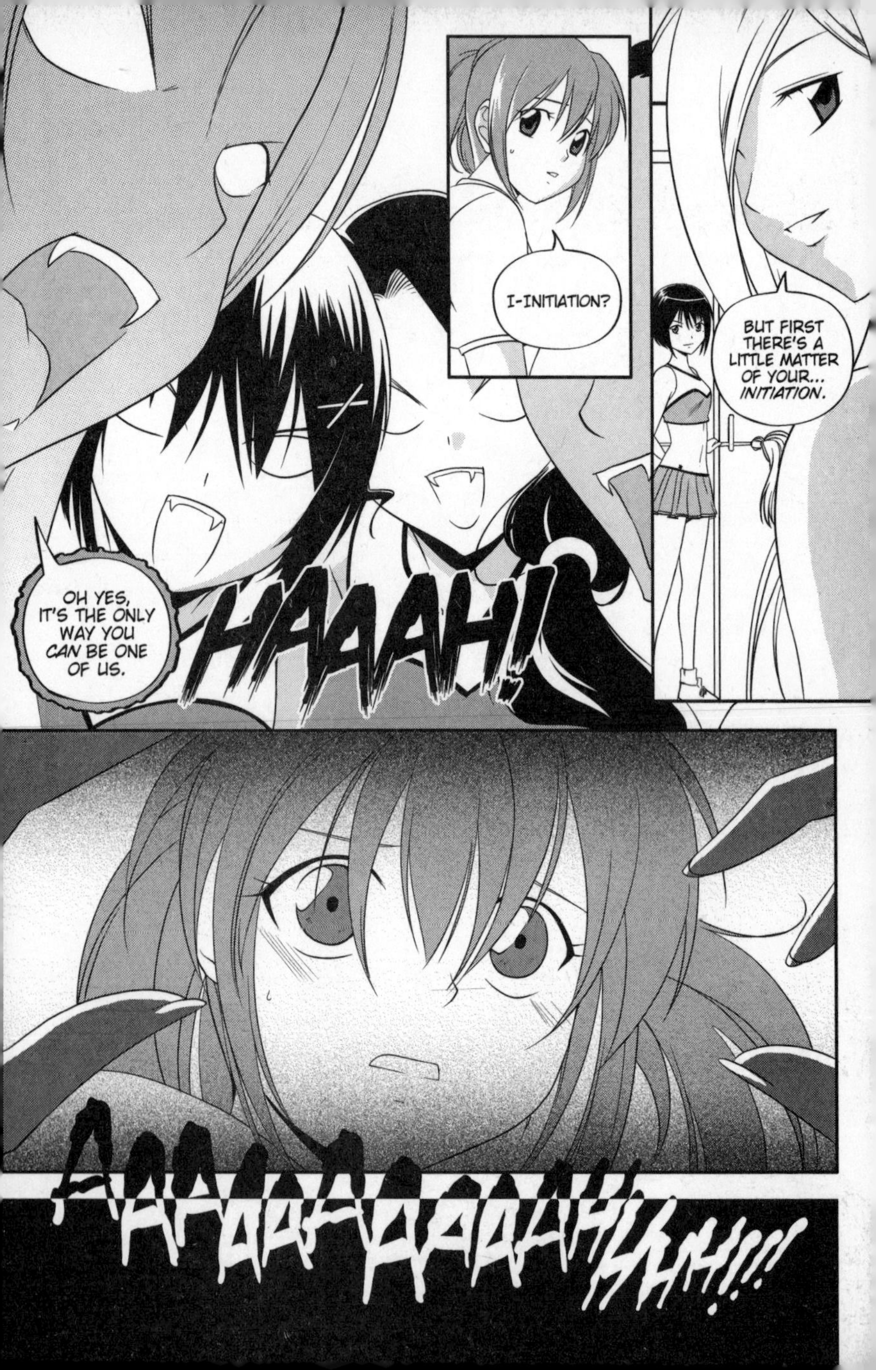
BUT FIRST THERE'S A LITTLE MATTER OF YOUR... *INITIATION*.
I-INITIATION?
HAAAH!
OH YES, IT'S THE ONLY WAY YOU *CAN* BE ONE OF US.
AAAAA-AAAAAHHHH!!!

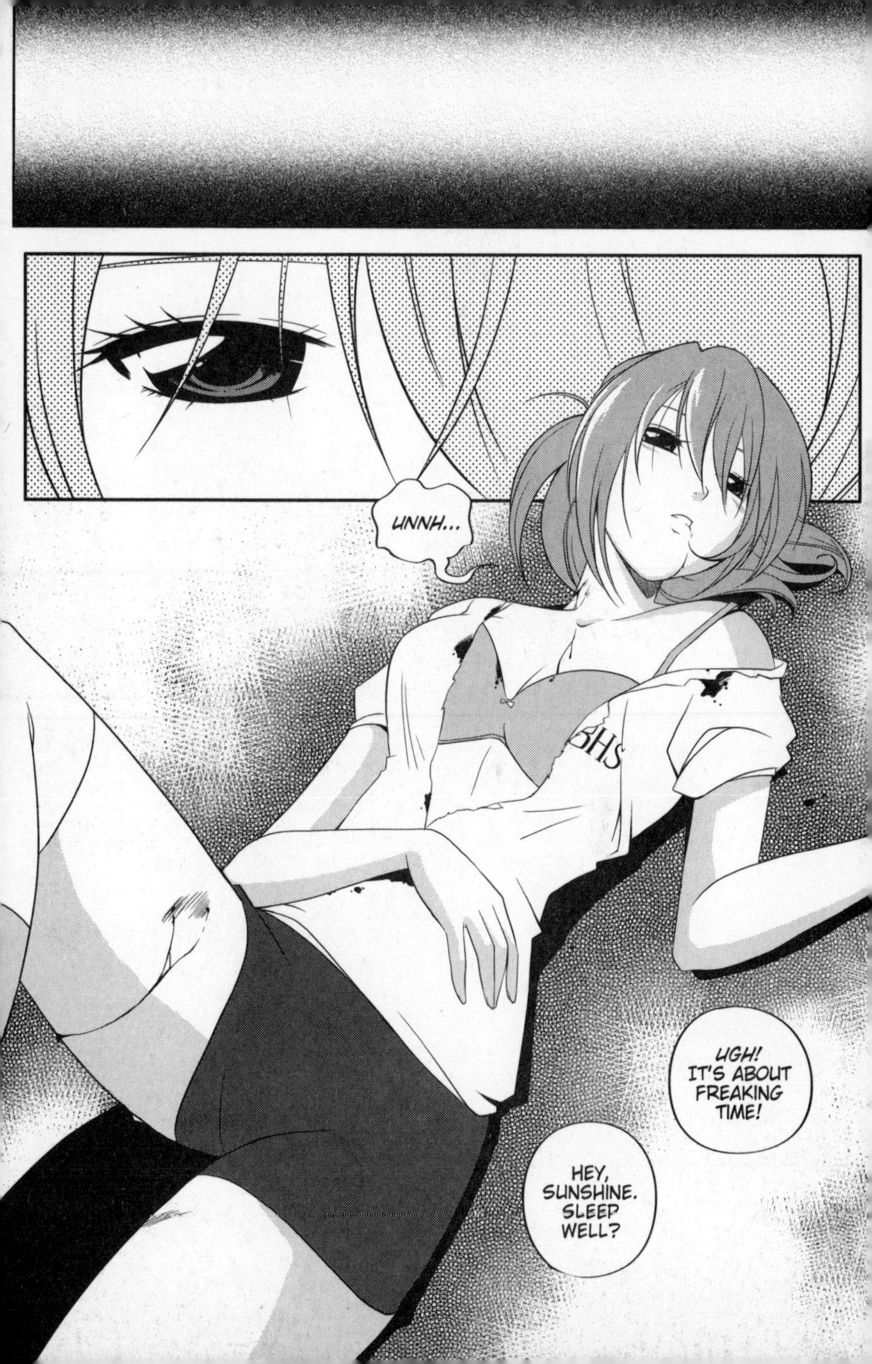
UNNH...
UGH! IT'S ABOUT FREAKING TIME!
HEY, SUNSHINE. SLEEP WELL?

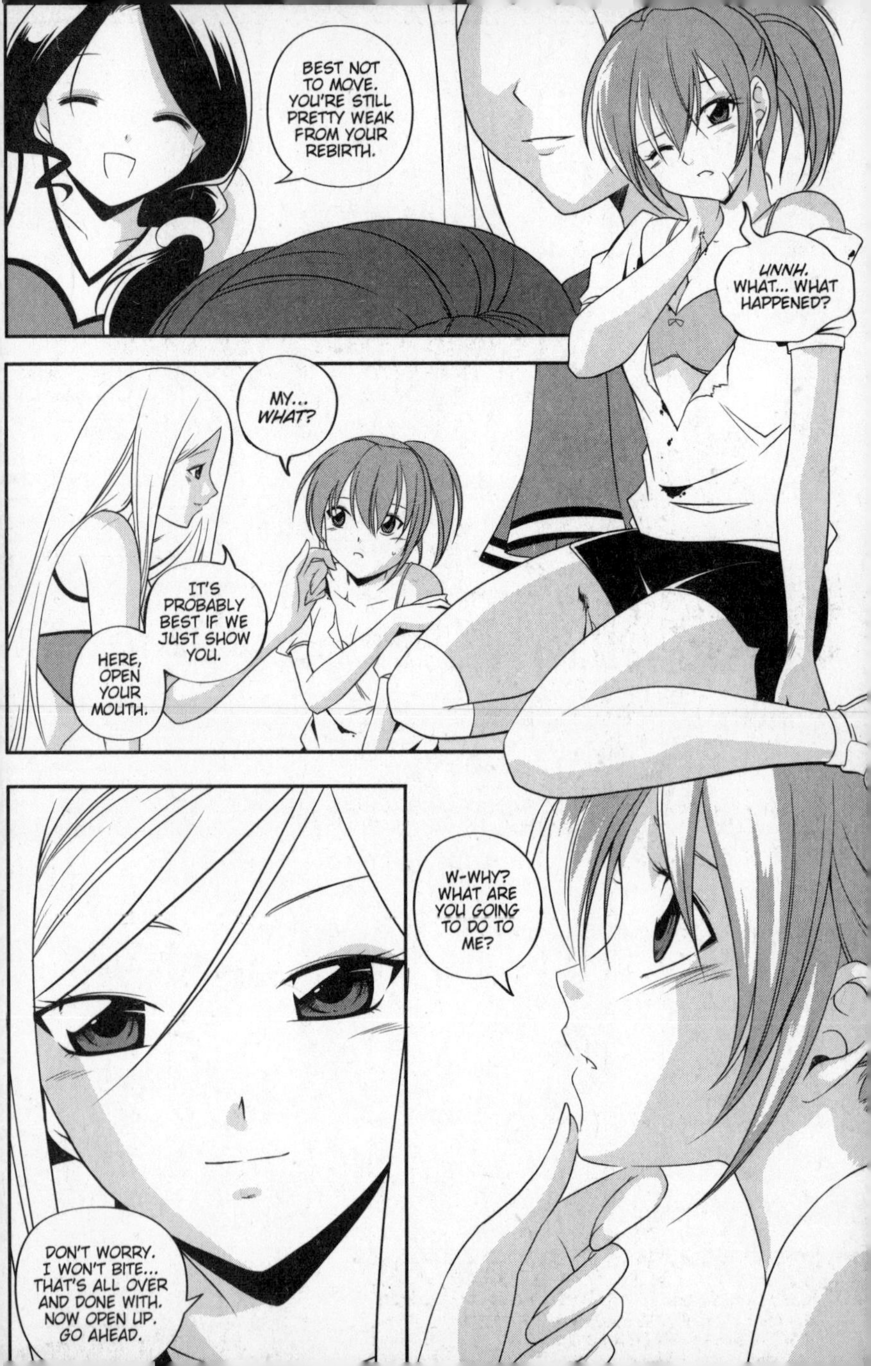
UNNH. WHAT... WHAT HAPPENED?
BEST NOT TO MOVE. YOU'RE STILL PRETTY WEAK FROM YOUR REBIRTH.
MY... WHAT?
IT'S PROBABLY BEST IF WE JUST SHOW YOU.
HERE, OPEN YOUR MOUTH.
W-WHY? WHAT ARE YOU GOING TO DO TO ME?
DON'T WORRY. I WON'T BITE... THAT'S ALL OVER AND DONE WITH. NOW OPEN UP. GO AHEAD.

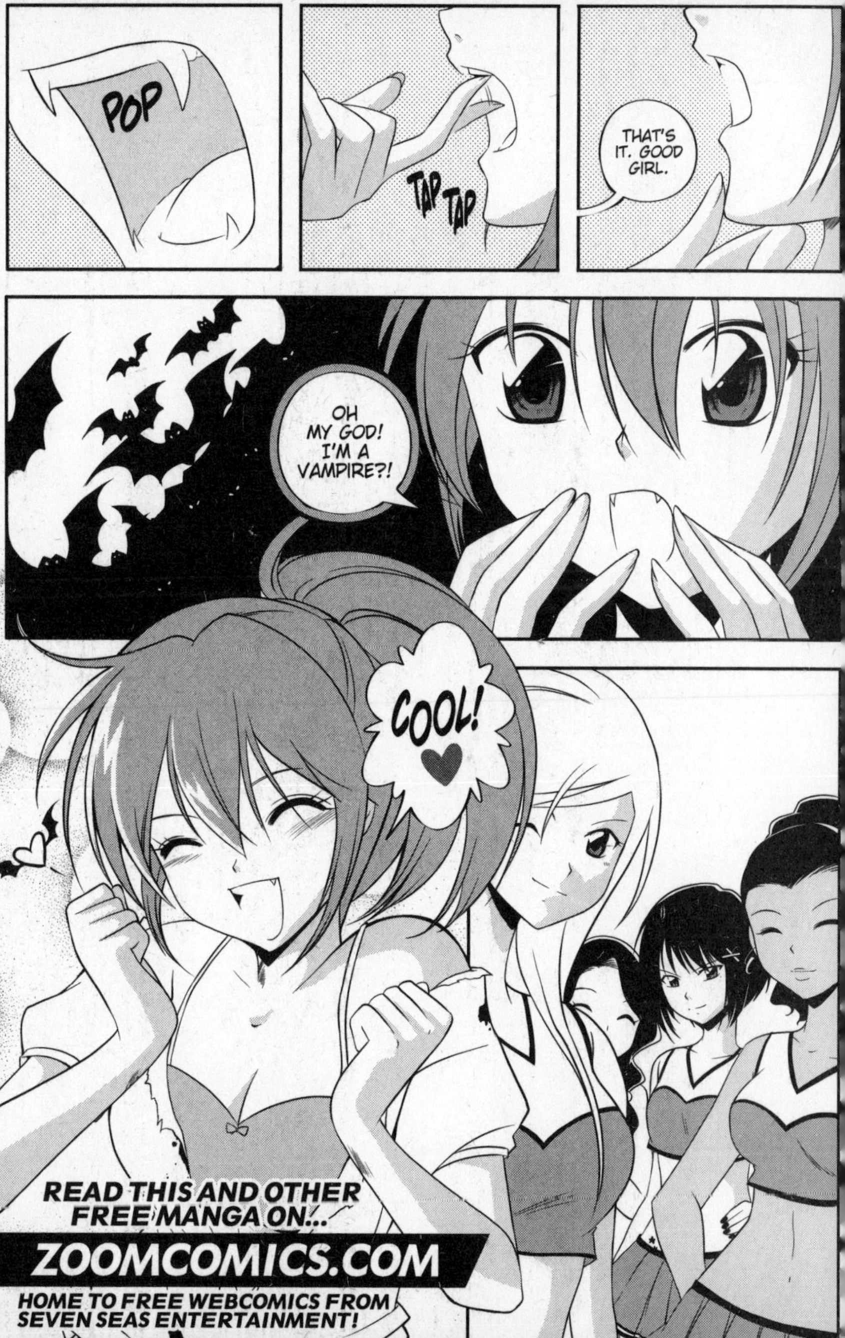
THAT'S IT. GOOD GIRL.
TAP TAP
POP
OH MY GOD! I'M A VAMPIRE?!
COOL!
READ THIS AND OTHER FREE MANGA ON...
ZOOMCOMICS.COM
HOME TO FREE WEBCOMICS FROM SEVEN SEAS ENTERTAINMENT!